CAPITAL CLAIMS: POWER AND GLOBAL FINANCE

Capital Claims: Power and Global Finance analyses how global financialized capitalism operates and reproduces itself, exploring the remarkable ability of the financial sector to maintain its dominance through even the most severe economic crises.

The book defines international financialization as a process by which the number and value, the tradability, and the enforceability of cross-border financial claims increase and are successfully defended against competing social or political agendas. By focusing on financial claims, the volume develops a conceptual toolkit for the study of the political economy of global finance and the inequalities it sustains. The book brings together leading researchers whose work is geared towards opening the black box of cross-border finance. The authors suggest shifting the analytical focus from capital flows to capital claims – credit–debt relations between identifiable actors, embedded in social and political institutions, and infused with power and hierarchy. They show how financial actors wield leverage power, infrastructural power, and enforcement power, both vis-à-vis other private actors and vis-à-vis the state.

This book will be of great interest to students, teachers, and researchers of international political economy, critical political economy, and international relations, as well as those in the fields of finance, capitalism studies, activism, policymaking, and advocacy.

An Online Appendix for Chapter 11 is available at:
www.routledge.com/9781032111193

Benjamin Braun is a senior researcher at the Max Planck Institute for the Study of Societies in Cologne, Germany. His research focuses on the political economy of financial and monetary systems.

Kai Koddenbrock leads a research group on "Monetary and Economic Sovereignty in West Africa" at the "Africa Multiple" Cluster of Excellence at Bayreuth University, Germany. His research focuses on global hierarchies, financial dependencies, and questions of self-determination.

Ripe series in global political economy

Series Editors: Susanne Soederberg (*Queen's University, Canada*),
Adrienne Roberts (*The University of Manchester, UK*),
Samuel Knafo (*University of Sussex, UK*) and
Naná de Graaff (*Vrije Universiteit Amsterdam, the Netherlands*).

For almost two decades now, the *RIPE Series in Global Political Economy* published by Routledge has been an essential forum for cutting-edge scholarship in International Political Economy, which we understand to be a broadly defined area of research that may cut across other disciplines. The series brings together new and established scholars working in critical, cultural and constructivist political economy. Books in the *RIPE Series* typically combine an innovative contribution to theoretical debates with rigorous empirical analysis.

The *RIPE Series* seeks to cultivate:

- Field-defining theoretical advances in International Political Economy.
- Novel treatments of key issue areas, such as global finance, trade, and production, both historical and contemporary.
- Analyses that explore the political economic dimensions of relatively neglected topics, such as the environment, gender, race, and colonialism from both Western and non-Western perspectives.
- Accessible work that will inspire advanced undergraduates and graduate students in International Political Economy.

Neil Dooley

Covid-19 and the Global Political Economy
Crises in the 21st Century
Edited by Tim Di Muzio and Matt Dow

Capital Claims: Power and Global Finance
Edited by Benjamin Braun and Kai Koddenbrock

For more information about this series, please visit: www.routledge.com/RIPE-Series-in-Global-Political-Economy/book-series/RIPE

CAPITAL CLAIMS: POWER AND GLOBAL FINANCE

Edited by Benjamin Braun and Kai Koddenbrock

Routledge
Taylor & Francis Group
LONDON AND NEW YORK

Cover image: © Getty Images

First published 2023
by Routledge
4 Park Square, Milton Park, Abingdon, Oxon OX14 4RN

and by Routledge
605 Third Avenue, New York, NY 10158

Routledge is an imprint of the Taylor & Francis Group, an informa business

British Library Cataloguing-in-Publication Data
A catalogue record for this book is available from the British Library

Library of Congress Cataloging-in-Publication Data
Names: Braun, Benjamin (Political scientist), editor. | Koddenbrock, Kai, editor.
Title: Capital claims : power and global finance / edited by Benjamin Braun and Kai Koddenbrock.
Description: Abingdon, Oxon ; New York, NY : Routledge, 2023. | Series: RIPE series in global political economy | Includes bibliographical references and index.
Identifiers: LCCN 2022028285 (print) | LCCN 2022028286 (ebook) | ISBN 9781032111131 (hardback) | ISBN 9781032111193 (paperback) | ISBN 9781003218487 (ebook)
Subjects: LCSH: International finance.
Classification: LCC HG3881 .C286 2023 (print) | LCC HG3881 (ebook) | DDC 332/.042—dc23/eng/20220923
LC record available at https://lccn.loc.gov/2022028285
LC ebook record available at https://lccn.loc.gov/2022028286

ISBN: 978-1-032-11113-1 (hbk)
ISBN: 978-1-032-11119-3 (pbk)
ISBN: 978-1-003-21848-7 (ebk)

DOI: 10.4324/9781003218487

Typeset in Bembo
by Apex CoVantage, LLC

Visit the online resources: www.routledge.com/9781032111193

CONTENTS

ACKNOWLEDGEMENTS

This book is the result of a series of workshops and exchanges in the "Politics of money" network, funded generously and flexibly by the German Research Council (DFG) since 2017. The administration of the network was mostly done at the University of Duisburg-Essen before moving to Bayreuth. A big thanks to Julia Nachtigall for her organizational support and to Felix Birkner and Marie Hillebrand for their research assistance. This has been a research network in the best sense of the term – a group of scholars connecting over years and engaging in deep and wide-ranging debates. This volume is very much the product of our sustained collaboration. For the time and energy they have put into hosting workshops in Brighton, Hamburg, and Amsterdam, we thank Samuel Knafo, Aaron Sahr, Jan Fichtner, and their respective administrative supporters. The work presented in this volume has benefitted from the feedback of many colleagues from within the network and beyond. Special thanks to those who have kindly agreed to serve as discussants on individual chapters. Finally, we are grateful for the feedback Marieke de Goede gave on an early version of the introduction to this book.

NOTES ON CONTRIBUTORS

Mareike Beck is an early career Leverhulme fellow at King's College London, UK. Her research focuses on the political economy of global finance, including transformations in global banking, asset-based inequalities, and financial inclusion.

Andrea Binder is a Freigeist research group leader at Freie Universität Berlin, Germany. Her research focuses on offshore finance and its implications for state power and geopolitics.

Benjamin Braun is a senior researcher at the Max Planck Institute for the Study of Societies in Cologne, Germany. His research focuses on the political economy of financial and monetary systems.

Florence Dafe is a political economist at the Chair of European and Global Governance of the Hochschule für Politik/Technical University of Munich (TUM), Germany. Her research interests revolve around finance and development, especially the political constraints that developing countries face in governing their financial sectors.

Sahil Jai Dutta is a lecturer in international political economy at City, University of London, UK. His research focuses on financialization and neoliberalism in the UK.

Jan Fichtner is a senior research fellow in the Corpnet Project at the University of Amsterdam, the Netherlands. His research focuses on the political economy of global finance, including questions of authority, power, and sustainability.

Javier Garcia-Bernardo is an assistant professor at Utrecht University, the Netherlands. His research focuses on developing methods to understand and estimate corporate tax avoidance and corporate power.

Eelke Heemskerk is an associate professor at the University of Amsterdam, the Netherlands, where he directs the Computational Social Science programme and the POPNET research group. He uses theoretical and methodological insights from network science to study socio-economic power structures.

Samuel Knafo is a reader in international political economy at the University of Sussex, UK. His current research focuses on the social history of financialization and the politics of neoliberalism.

Kai Koddenbrock leads a research group on "Monetary and Economic Sovereignty in West Africa" at the "Africa Multiple" Cluster of Excellence at Bayreuth University, Germany. His research focuses on global hierarchies, financial dependencies, and questions of self-determination.

Benjamin Lemoine is a researcher in political sociology at the National Center for Scientific Research (CNRS), France, and at Paris Dauphine University, Paris Sciences et Lettres (PSL), France. His research focuses on sovereignty, law and finance entanglements, foreign private investment, and public debt markets.

Daniel Mertens is Professor of International Political Economy at Osnabrück University, Germany. His research includes work on the politics of financialization, growth regimes, and development banking.

Caroline Metz is a senior policy officer at ShareAction in Brussels, Belgium. Her past research focused on EU capital markets and banking policies, and in her current role she advocates for stricter financial regulation at the EU level, pushing for a more sustainable financial sector.

Andreas Nölke is Professor of Political Science at Goethe University Frankfurt, Germany. His current research focuses on the intersection of comparative and international political economy, with a special focus on large emerging economies.

Johannes Petry is a postdoctoral researcher and principal investigator of the StateCapFinance Project at Goethe University Frankfurt, Germany. His research focuses on China's financial opening, the politics of financial infrastructures, and the post-crisis shifts in the global financial system.

Zoe Phillips Williams is an associate at the International Institute for Sustainable Development and the editor of *Investment Treaty News*. Her research focuses on the domestic politics of investor-state disputes.

Marie Piganiol is an associate professor at Paris Dauphine University, France. Her research focuses on the commodification of state-owned goods.

Katharina Pistor is the Edwin B. Parker Professor of Comparative Law at Columbia Law School, USA, and Director of the Law School's Center on Global Legal Transformation. Her work spans comparative law and corporate governance, law and finance, and law and development.

Arjan Reurink is a junior lecturer in the PPLE College at the University of Amsterdam, the Netherlands. His research looks into the evolving dynamics of interaction between transnational corporations and states. He is also a research fellow at the Wiardi Beckman Foundation, a think tank for social democracy in the Netherlands.

Aaron Sahr is a research group leader at the Hamburg Institute for Social Research, Germany. His research focuses on the performance of monetary theories, operational modes of monetary policy, and structural changes in capitalism.

Stefano Sgambati is a senior lecturer in international political economy at City, University of London, UK. His research calls into question theories, practices, and politics of money and finance, with a focus on issues of power, conflict, and class in contemporary capitalism.

Matthias Thiemann is Associate Professor of European Public Policy at Sciences Po's Centre des Etudes Européennes et Politiques Comparés, France. His research centers on the evolution of financial regulation post-crisis, in particular the regulation of shadow banking in the EU and the United States.

1

THE THREE PHASES OF FINANCIAL POWER

Leverage, infrastructure, and enforcement

Benjamin Braun and Kai Koddenbrock

Introduction

The process of financialization has transformed societies across the world. Financial instruments – priced and traded claims on future value creation – extend into all spheres of social and economic life. Yet large gaps remain in our understanding of how global capitalism – a highly unstable system that creates vast inequalities – continues to reproduce itself. How can we explain that the size and profitability of the financial sector recovered so quickly after the global financial crisis? Why has concentration in the financial sector continued unabated, expanding the realm of too-big-to-fail institutions from banking to asset management and financial infrastructure providers? What role do states play as regulators of, and participants in, financial markets?

The crises ravaging the world today reinforce the urgency of these questions. Following the onset of the Covid-19 pandemic, central banks again stepped into the breach (Tooze, 2021). In doing so, they both stabilized the global economy and backstopped the global shadow banking system, thus strengthening the ability of financial firms to leverage their balance sheets to acquire assets across the world. At the same time, countries from Argentina to Zambia once again had to negotiate debt moratoria with the International Monetary Fund (IMF) and private creditors. In the intensifying climate emergency, the financial sector has sought to position itself not only as part of the solution but as *the* solution to the conundrum of how to plan and finance the transformation and decarbonization of the global economy (Dafermos et al., 2021). Most recently, the sanctions the West imposed on Russia in response to its invasion of Ukraine have demonstrated the enormous power that comes with control over the legal and technological infrastructure that underpins the global financial system.

An important account of the causes of financial globalization was titled "Capital rules" (Abdelal, 2007). It focused on deregulation and the breaking down of

DOI: 10.4324/9781003218487-1

borders to international capital flows. "Capital claims" plays on the same verb–noun ambiguity but shifts the focus from the making of rules to the financial relationships those rules have engendered. Thus, this volume studies the power of financial actors to create and trade financial claims, to keep them alive, and to enforce them vis-à-vis debtors. Broadly speaking, the literature on the power of finance is divided into a Marxist strand that emphasizes the importance of money and finance for the reproduction of capitalism at the macro level and a sociological strand that studies financial actors, instruments, and practices at the micro level, often in a more descriptive way. The ambition of this volume is to straddle this divide through a focus on the financial claim relations that connect wealthy households, financial institutions, and non-financial debtors, and on the processes through which financial actors profit from their central position in those claim relations.

Financial claims exist as financial instruments, held on financial institutions' balance sheets endowed with varying degrees of power and coded in law in ways that fortify and protect the position of claim holders vis-à-vis both the debtor and the rest of the world (Pistor, 2019). The actors and mechanisms of financial power vary across types of financial claims and across their life cycle, which we conceptualize as defined by creation, circulation, and enforcement. At each of these stages, creditors (and, sometimes, debtors) exercise power. The majority of the political economy literature has studied the capacity of financial actors to influence governments via instrumental, structural, or infrastructural power.[1] In addition to this finance–government nexus at which private and public actors enter a "deal" (Koddenbrock, 2019), the contributions to this volume focus on the power relations *among* the holders of financial claims, their debtors, and their financial and legal intermediaries. Specifically, we discuss three forms of power associated with financial claims over their life cycle. The ability to issue debt or equity liabilities constitutes *leverage power*. We deliberately emphasize the power of debtors, since many actors in the financial system, notably banks, are highly leveraged and skilled at instrumentalizing their indebtedness for political or economic gain. Actors who do not hold financial claims themselves but provide the services that facilitate their creation and circulation exercise *infrastructural power*. Finally, when it comes to repayment, creditors and their lawyers exercise *enforcement power*.

Our approach locates the politics of money and finance not (only) in the governance and regulation of financial transactions but in the hierarchical, power-laden relationships financial claims establish between specific actors. Hierarchy is a central feature of international relations more broadly (Zarakol, 2017) and is an organizing principle of the global monetary and financial system (Mehrling, 2013, 2015; Pistor, 2013; Bruneau, 2021). By emphasizing hierarchy and power, the contributions to this volume consistently highlight the distributional implications of cross-border claims. Another contribution, which could be described as methodological, is that this volume renders financial actors and relations transparent by often referring to the language of balance sheets – "the *locus delicti* for leverage power" (Pistor, this volume) – thus emphasizing the claim relationships that connect creditors and debtors, assets and liabilities.

Case studies range from banking to government finance, from index providers to central counterparties, and from mortgage finance to investor-state arbitration. The selection of topics reflects the expertise of the research network from which this volume emerged.[2] Unavoidably, this leaves many areas unaddressed. Most notably, the geographical scope is uneven and tilted toward the Global North, and the climate–finance nexus is not covered. The remainder of this introductory chapter proceeds as follows: The first section will give a brief overview of the research landscape in comparative and international political economy, as well as in the emerging, interdisciplinary field of finance studies. The second is a primer on financial claims – what are the most important categories of financial claims, who issues them, and who holds them. On that basis, the third section presents the three types of power that are explored in the individual chapters and that are at the core of our collective contribution – leverage power, infrastructural power, and enforcement power.

Finance in comparative and international political economy, and beyond

The contributions to this volume study financial claims as instruments through which creditors exercise power over debtors – and, sometimes, vice versa. The contributors to this volume come from, and speak to, comparative and international political economy. They are also, however, engaged in a broader conversation with the emerging, interdisciplinary field of finance studies.

Comparative political economy (CPE) constituted itself as a discipline following the post-war decades marked by high growth rates, rising real wages, and low-income and wealth inequality in Europe and the United States. Traditionally focused on the "real economy" – industrial relations, production and, more recently, consumption – CPE has primarily been concerned with the financing of firms through either banks or capital markets. Building on Zysman's (1983) classic distinction between bank-based and market-based financial systems, CPE fell into the habit of conceptualizing the financial system as a provider of more or less patient capital (Culpepper, 2005; Hall and Soskice, 2001). Despite receiving important updates on banking (Hardie et al., 2013) and institutional investors (Deeg and Hardie, 2016), the core CPE framework continued to operate on a highly abstracted model of the financial system. More recently, the financial and debt crisis of the Euro area has sparked new interest in cross-border financial flows (Schelkle, 2017; Jones, 2021) and in mortgage finance (Kohl, 2018; Fuller et al., 2019; Schwartz, 2020), and the growth model literature has incorporated mortgage and consumption finance into its core framework (Baccaro and Pontusson, 2016). CPE scholars have also increasingly asked how the growth models and regulatory regimes of open economies are shaped by their position within, and interaction with, the European or global financial system, thus bridging the gap with international political economy (Nölke and Vliegenthart, 2009; Regan and Brazys, 2018; Ban and Bohle, 2021; Piroska et al., 2021).

In International political economy (IPE), the main focus of the literature on finance has been on US (dollar) hegemony and on the *governance* of finance. IPE has conventionally assigned the politics of money to a separate sphere of interstate monetary relations, studying money as a governmental instrument to pursue strategic foreign policy objectives (Walter, 1993; Andrews, 2006; Cohen, 2017). The literature on finance, by contrast, has focused on the (de-)regulation of financial markets and the liberalization of capital controls (Helleiner, 1994; Abdelal, 2007; Walter, 2008). At the intersection of these two literatures, the lending policies of the World Bank (Weaver, 2008) and the IMF (Kentikelenis et al., 2016; Nelson, 2017; Kentikelenis and Babb, 2019) have featured prominently. Although an IPE tradition exists that has studied finance directly (Strange, 1988), it was only after the global financial crisis that more IPE scholars began to study issues such as the political economy of banking (Copelovitch and Singer, 2020), foreign direct investment (FDI) (Danzman, 2019), financial asset ownership (Chwieroth and Walter, 2019; Pagliari et al., 2020), investor-state arbitration (John, 2018; Williams and Dafe, 2021), and financial dependency (Reis and de Oliveira, 2021). Here, too, many recent contributions are located at the intersection of IPE and CPE, boding well for the future rapprochement of the two subdisciplines.

Mainstream CPE and IPE have thus rarely sought to conceptualize national varieties of financial systems as parts of one and the same global financial system, and the power of finance remained under-theorized. Here, the Marxist tradition has clearly been unduly neglected, especially finance-driven theories of imperialism (Patnaik and Patnaik, 2021; Lenin, 1999 [1907]; Hobson, 2011 [1902]; Luxemburg, 2015 [1913]) and dependency and world systems scholarship (Amin, 1974; Arrighi, 1994). Recently, however, IPE scholars have increasingly drawn on this tradition to theorize the power of finance in the Global South (Alami, 2019; Bernards, 2019; Dafe, 2019; Kvangraven, 2021; de Goede, 2020; Koddenbrock et al., 2022; Tilley, 2020; Alami et al., 2022).[3]

Finance was eventually brought back into the political economy literature via the concept of financialization (Krippner, 2005; Perry and Nölke, 2006; van der Zwan, 2014). Although these contributions inspired a fruitful research program on the political causes and consequences of financial liberalization and expansion, often this interest did not extend to the power of financial actors and practices themselves.[4] The global financial crisis fundamentally changed this. The site of this change cannot easily be assigned to either CPE or IPE. Indeed, it would be more appropriate to speak of an emerging field concerned with the political economy of finance, in which scholars routinely read and cite each other across disciplinary boundaries. In addition to CPE and IPE, this interdisciplinary field comprises economics (Jordà et al., 2019; Bezemer et al., 2020), economic history (Monnet, 2018; Sissoko, 2019), history (Tooze, 2018; Ogle, 2020), economic sociology (Arjaliès et al., 2017; Quinn, 2019), legal studies (Desan, 2014; Pistor, 2019, 2020), and economic geography (Fernandez and Aalbers, 2016; Ouma, 2020).

From this interdisciplinary literature emerge three foundational insights that underpin our analysis of the political economy of financial claims. First, around

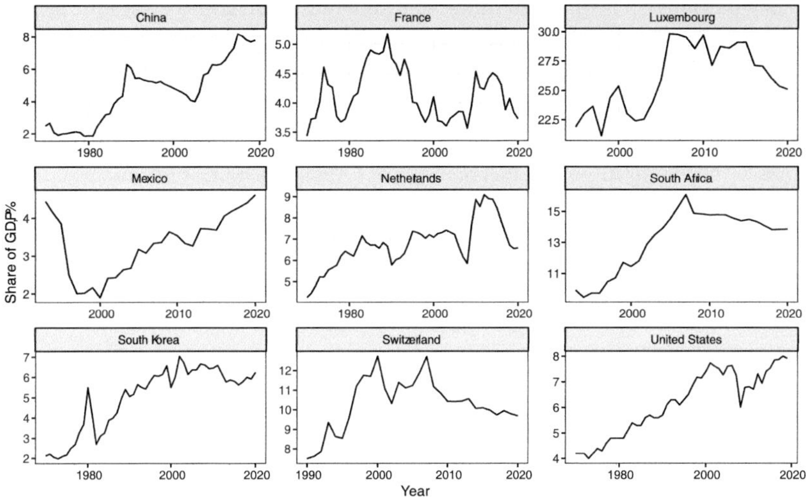

FIGURE 1.1 Value-added share of finance and insurance as a share of GDP, selected countries

Source: Data: OECD.

the world, the size of the financial sector has massively increased over the past half century (Oatley and Petrova, 2020). Figure 1.1 shows the value-added share of the financial sector as a share of a country's total gross domestic product (GDP). While value added is a dubious measure of value creation at best in the case of finance (Christophers, 2011; Assa, 2016), it nevertheless provides a way of comparing the relative size of finance across time and across countries. Figure 1.1 shows that the familiar US pattern – where the relative size of finance doubled between 1970 and 2020, from 4 percent to 8 percent of GDP – is not an outlier. Over the same period, South Korea's financial sector tripled, while China's quadrupled in size (see also Petry et al., 2021). While countries such as France or Germany have not seen the same upward trend, their neighboring "offshore" financial centers Switzerland and Luxembourg have grown very large financial sectors over the same period.

Second, whereas the conventional economic perspective emphasizes the generative role of finance by channeling past savings toward new productive projects, we conceptualize financial claims as "forward-looking claim[s] on future resources" (Naidu, 2017: 108). This perspective means to abandon the conceptualization of finance "as a system for the allocation of resources" in favor of a conceptualization of finance as "a form of authority – a weapon by which the claims of wealth holders are asserted against the rest of society" (Jayadev et al., 2018: 360; see also Durand, 2017). Financial claims acquire their weapon-like qualities also through legal coding, which bestows on capital the qualities of "priority, durability, universality and convertibility" (into state money) (Pistor, 2019: 3). Thus, unlike suggested by the "capital flow" metaphor, financial capital exists in the form of solid, enduring claims on future value and their underlying social and economic relations of (re-)production.

The main contribution of this volume is to offer a perspective on the political economy of financial claims that is holistic – in that the various chapters cover the whole life cycle of financial claims – yet also opens the black box of financial claims by zooming in on the mechanisms of leverage power, infrastructural power, and enforcement power, which underpin the continued profitability of financial investment and financial intermediation. We discuss these three forms of financial power in detail here. To prepare the ground for this discussion, however, a primer on financial claims is in order.

Capital claims crash course: what are they, who issues them, and who holds them?

This section offers a very short, textbook-style introduction on cross-border financial claims, combined with a selective review of the relevant literature in IPE and in adjacent fields. The focus is on introducing the actors, instruments, and relationships that constitute the analytical scaffolding of this volume. It should be noted at the outset that most financial assets are held by rich households and that returns from financial investment, as well as profits made in the financial sector, have been major contributors toward the rise in wealth and income inequality over recent decades.

What are financial claims?

In the pre-industrial past, the asset portfolios of the wealthy were dominated by land (Piketty, 2014). Markets for securities issued by governments and, increasingly, corporations deepened and broadened in the aftermath of the Napoleonic Wars in the early nineteenth century and, in the context of accelerating industrialization and advances in communication technology, reached an "unprecedented degree of sophistication, coverage, and intensity" toward the end of that century (Michie, 2006: 117). The rise of securities markets was intimately linked to imperialism, since securities made it possible for metropolitan wealth elites to invest in, and derive returns from, colonial expansion (Hudson, 2017; Wennerlind, 2011). Today, while housing reigns supreme in the middle-class "asset economy" (Ansell, 2019; Adkins et al., 2020), financial claims dominate in the portfolios of the very wealthy and of institutional capital pools (Pfeffer and Waitkus, 2021; see Figure 1.4).

Although the landscape of financial instruments can seem dauntingly complex, the basic distinction between debt and equity goes a long way toward clarifying the picture. Debt claims tend to be temporary and entitle *creditors* to regular interest payments and to the eventual repayment of the principal – that is, the sum of money lent initially. By contrast, equity claims tend to be permanent and give *shareholders* certain ownership or control rights, which translate into dividend payments. These ownership or control rights compensate holders of equity claims for

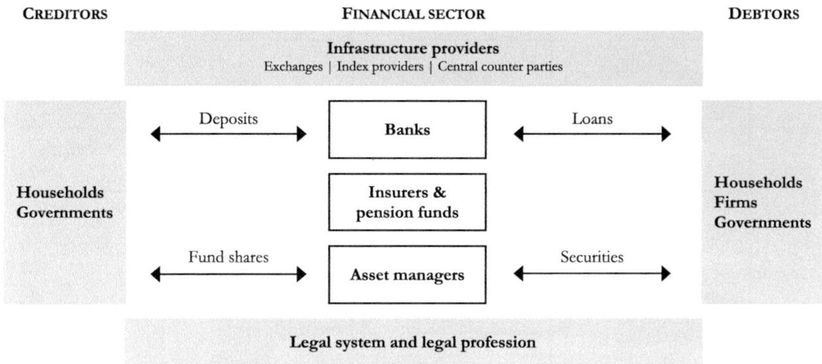

FIGURE 1.2 Actors and claim relationships

Source: The authors.

their subordinate position in the creditor hierarchy, and thus for the higher risk. In the following we will, for ease of exposition, use the term "creditor" to refer to holders of both debt and equity claims.

The main actors and relationships that populate this volume are depicted in Figure 1.2. A claim relationship generally connects non-financial investors (colloquially: "savers") in search of financial investment opportunities to debtors who, for one reason or another, seek to – or are forced to – borrow. While all institutional sectors – households, firms, and governments – appear as debtors on the right-hand side of Figure 1.2, only households or states can be ultimate beneficiaries (since firms, too, are owned by either households or the state). Note that since holdings of financial assets by households are extremely unequally distributed, the household category on the left-hand side overwhelmingly represents wealthy and very wealthy households. Financial investment chains vary in length and composition, depending on the asset class (Arjaliès et al., 2017).[5] Generally speaking, however, it is safe to say that the relationship between investors and debtors runs via financial institutions, depicted in the center column. Thus, non-financial creditors on the left-hand side hold financial claims (notably bank deposits and various types of fund shares) against financial intermediaries at the center, who, in turn, hold financial claims against non-financial debtors.

Today, non-financial assets (housing, land, buildings, machinery and equipment, and intangible capital) account for just over one-third of total investable assets, whereas the remainder consists of financial assets (Jordà et al., 2019: 1233). Here, the largest category is corporate equity, followed by deposits, other financial assets (corporate bonds and asset-backed securities), and government bonds. Seen over the long run, the volume of financial claims relative to GDP shows a hockey-stick pattern (Kuvshinov and Zimmermann, 2021). This same pattern can be observed for the subset of financial claims that is the focus of this volume, namely cross-border claims. As shown in Figure 1.3, which plots balance of payments data, the

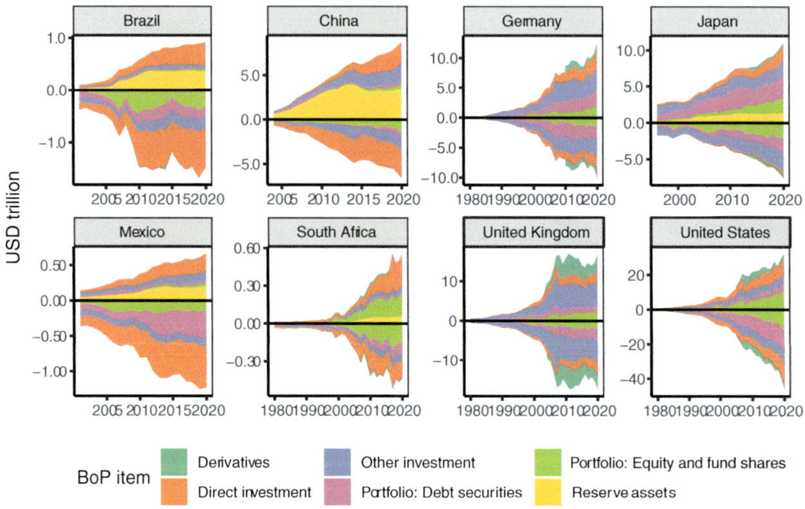

FIGURE 1.3 Foreign assets and liabilities in US dollars, 1980–2020

Source: Data: IMF, balance of payments data.

foreign assets and liabilities of countries have skyrocketed since 1980. The figure disaggregates the international investment position into its main components. We can see that the foreign assets of even very large economies such as China and Japan are dominated by official reserve assets, whereas countries at the core of the global monetary and financial system, notably the United States and Germany (as a member of the Euro area), barely hold any reserves – a simple measure of a country's degree of monetary sovereignty, which is discussed in the chapter by Aaron Sahr. Cross-border bank leverage – the topic of the chapter by Mareike Beck, Samuel Knafo, and Stefano Sgambati – is subsumed in the category "other investments," which consists primarily of deposits with foreign banks (besides "other loans" and "other equity"). Derivatives are concentrated in the UK, the world leader in derivatives clearing, which is the topic of the chapter by Matthias Thiemann. Portfolio assets, especially fund shares – that is, the kind of investment that is guided by index providers studied in the chapter by Jan Fichtner, Eelke Heemskerk, and Johannes Petry and that features prominently in Daniel Mertens and Caroline Metz's study of institutional investment in European mortgage debt – are highest in those countries that have large institutional capital pools, especially pension funds. FDI – discussed in the chapter by Arjan Reurink and Javier Garcia-Bernardo – is a major component of the international investment position of most countries.

Issuers of financial claims

Who are the issuers of debt and equity liabilities? The System of National Accounts (SNA), initially devised in 1947 at the League of Nations, structures the universe

TABLE 1.1 Types of liabilities issued by the four institutional sectors

Public	*Private*		
Government	*Financial corporations*	*Non-financial corporations*	*Households*
Government bonds			Mortgage debt
Non-tradable government debt	*Banks*	Shares	Consumer debt
	Deposits	Bonds	Student debt
Central bank	Bonds		Micro credit
Money: cash	*Investment funds*		
Money: central bank reserves	Fund shares		
	Insurance		
State-owned banks and enterprises	Insurance policies		
	Pension funds		
Bonds	Pension liabilities		

of issuers by institutional sectors: government, financial corporations, non-financial corporations, and households.[6] Although financial instruments evolve over time, in general terms the liabilities these sectors issue are easily listed (see Table 1.1).

Among public issuers, the *government* is usually the largest. Sovereign debt issued by governments in the Global North has assumed a pivotal role in the global financial system, providing the "safe assets" without which collateralized shadow banking could not operate on the scale it has achieved (Boy, 2015; Gabor and Ban, 2016; Gabor and Vestergaard, 2018; Thiemann, 2018; Vermeiren, 2019). The political economy of sovereign debt plays out differently in the Global South (Deforge and Lemoine, 2021). Whereas many lower- and middle-income countries used to borrow directly from foreign banks, today, they mostly borrow by issuing tradable bonds (Hardie, 2012; Kvangraven et al., 2021). In search of lower interest rates and deeper pools of investment capital, governments have, since the 1980s, actively marketized and internationalized their debt issuance (Lagna, 2016; Lemoine, 2016; Fastenrath et al., 2017; Dutta, 2019). The result has been an increase in the exposure of sovereign debtors to the fluctuations in international capital markets and to the pressures exerted by private foreign creditors, especially in the Global South (Akyüz, 2017; Bortz and Kaltenbrunner, 2018; Alami, 2019; Binder, 2019; Koddenbrock and Sylla, 2019; Naqvi, 2019; Bonizzi et al., 2020). These pressures are exacerbated by the continued importance of foreign-currency borrowing, which, despite some improvements to the global financial safety net, frequently forces debtor countries to turn to the IMF when private capital inflows reverse (Roos, 2019; Stubbs et al., 2021).

The second major liability issued by the public sector are central bank liabilities (commonly called "money"), which take the form of cash and, more importantly for our purposes, reserves held by banks in reserve accounts with their respective central banks. At the top of the global monetary hierarchy, central banks whose currencies are used beyond their own jurisdiction – in the offshore, or Eurocurrency, system – act as international lenders of last resort. The global liquidity facilities provided by the US Fed both in late 2008 and in early 2020 provide the most dramatic illustration of the systemic importance of this role of central banks (McDowell, 2017; Tooze, 2018; Sahasrabuddhe, 2019). In addition to governments and central banks, states issue financial liabilities via various "off-balance sheet entities" (Murau et al., 2021), notably public development banks that finance their lending by issuing quasi-sovereign bonds (Mertens et al., 2020).

Among *financial corporations*, banks occupy a privileged position.[7] Only they may issue deposits, that is, bank money. However, in what was arguably the most important development in global banking over the past half century, banks also developed ways of funding themselves via short-term borrowing (Hardie et al., 2013; Knafo, 2022). By borrowing against collateral in the short-term money market, banks could increase the size of their balance sheets far above what was possible with only traditional deposit funding (Fernandez and Wigger, 2016; Gabor, 2016; Sgambati, 2019, Beck, 2021). The remainder of this category includes all non-bank financial institutions, notably asset owners such as pension funds and insurers, as well as the various types of asset managers (providers of mutual and exchange-traded funds, hedge funds, private equity funds, and venture capital funds).

Non-financial corporations generally only issue two types of liabilities, equity and debt. Corporate debt may take the form of loans or, especially for large firms, corporate bonds. From a global perspective, three trends are noteworthy. First, in many advanced economies – and most dramatically in the United States – the number of publicly listed corporations has declined since the crash of the dotcom bubble (Doidge et al., 2017). Second, corporate debt has dramatically increased, in both advanced and emerging market economies (Abraham et al., 2020). Third, FDI has exploded.[8] There are two – largely complementary – explanations of this growth. On one hand, the global rise of FDI since the 1990s reflects the globalization of production, which implies geographically dispersed value chains with varying degrees of vertical integration (Milberg, 2008). On the other hand, FDI flows reflect the attempts to optimize corporate structures to optimize tax "efficiency" (see Reurink and Garcia-Bernardo, 2022, this volume). FDI has been an important conduit for capital exports from the Global South, both during and since colonial times (Koddenbrock et al., 2022; Ogle, 2020).

Finally, the financial liabilities of *households* comprise a growing variety of debts, including credit card debt and student debt, but mortgage debt remains the most important category by far (Montgomerie, 2009; Sparkes and Wood, 2020; Wiedemann, 2021). In the Global South, various forms of financial innovation such as microfinance and digital financial services have brought tens of millions of households into the financial system as bearers of financial liabilities (Soederberg, 2014; Mader, 2015; Gabor and Brooks, 2017).

Holders of financial claims

Financial actors and the assets they control tend to concentrate in financial centers. Empires invariably relied on a metropolitan center to finance colonial expansion and trade, be it from Amsterdam, Paris, or London (Inikori, 2002; Wennerlind, 2011; Cain and Hopkins, 2016). Since the heyday of British imperialism, London has been joined by New York, Tokyo, and Hong Kong. Clustered around these are offshore financial centers (Hong Kong itself arguably falls into that category), which often specialize in attracting particular types of financial actors: hedge funds in the Cayman Islands, European investment funds in Luxembourg, and so on (Palan, 1998; Fernandez and Hendrikse, 2020; Ogle, 2017). The fact that financial assets are often registered in offshore financial centers has serious distorting effects on other countries' international investment positions as measured in balance of payments data, which should therefore be read and used with caution (Coppola et al., 2021).

In addition to geographic concentration, market concentration is also an important characteristic of most of the financial segments discussed here. For instance, the world's five largest investment banks by revenue – all on the US East Coast – jointly account for 35 percent of global investment banking revenue, giving them vast power over securities issuance and mergers and acquisitions globally. Even more dramatic is the concentration in the asset management sector, where BlackRock and Vanguard – both on the US East Coast – controlled USD 18.5 trillion by early 2022. The two firms today are among the largest holders of most states' sovereign debt and the largest shareholders in most publicly listed corporations, certainly in the United States but also in the United Kingdom and in many other advanced-economy stock markets (Fichtner et al., 2017; Braun, 2021).

The holders of financial claims are the same aforementioned four institutional sectors. In Table 1.2, they are listed with some minor modifications, in order to highlight the sub-sectors most relevant as holders of financial claims. Although all sectors appear as holders of financial claims, it is important to understand that from the bird's eye perspective of the System of National Accounts, the investment chain always leads to either the state or, for the vast majority of claims, private households. This is because firms, whether financial and non-financial, have shareholders, which are either households or the state.

The most important thing to know about *household* holdings of financial claims is that their distribution is extremely unequal (Pfeffer and Waitkus, 2021). To

TABLE 1.2 Holders of financial claims

Public	*Private*		
Central banks Public pension funds Sovereign wealth funds	*Households* Includes non-profit institutions serving households, such as foundations and family offices of the ultra-rich	*Financial corporations* Banks Insurers Investment funds Private pension funds	*Non-financial corporations* Firms holding FDI claims Firms holding portfolio assets

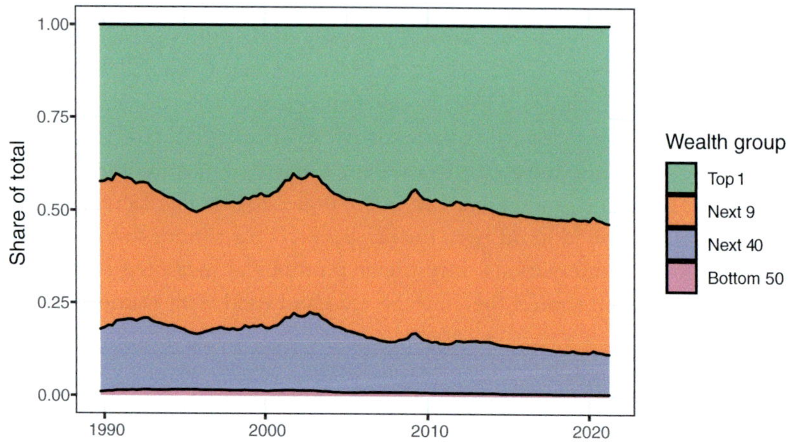

FIGURE 1.4 US household holdings of equities and mutual fund shares by wealth group, 1989–2021

Source: Data: Federal Reserve, Enhanced Financial Accounts.

illustrate this, Figure 1.4 presents data on the distribution of financial assets in the United States. This focus makes sense because US households hold 30 percent of the world's wealth (Credit Suisse, 2021). The share for financial assets would almost certainly be higher still. As shown in Figure 1.4, the richest 1 percent of US households own more than half of the USD 40 trillion of corporate equities and mutual fund shares that are held directly by households. The top 10 percent own almost 90 percent, whereas the bottom 50 percent of households own virtually no such securities.[9]

The unequal distribution of financial asset holdings increases income and wealth inequality because households derive income from financial assets. This income comes in the form of cash payments (interest and dividends) as well as capital gains. When an Oxfam headline announces that the "ten richest men double their fortunes in pandemic," what made these men twice as rich was a doubling of the market value of their assets, the overwhelming majority of which consists of corporate equity (Oxfam, 2022). Only for the richest households does income from interest, dividends, and, especially, capital gains outweigh income from salary and wages.

In the *public sector*, three types of institutions dominate financial claim holdings. Historically, central banks have always been important holders of public debt, either of the bonds issued by their own governments or, for the purpose of foreign reserve accumulation, of the sovereign debt (and other safe assets) issued by issuers nearer the top of the international monetary hierarchy. With the rise of quantitative easing, central banks have become giant institutional investors in their own right (Ronkainen and Sorsa, 2018; van 't Klooster and Fontan, 2019; Walter and Wansleben, 2020; Wullweber, 2021). Since public pension funds and sovereign wealth funds have long been major investors across the globe, it is clear that public actors are a force to be reckoned with in global capital markets (Babic et al., 2020; Dixon, 2020).

In the *financial corporations sector*, banks fall into two main categories, commercial banks and investment banks. Commercial banks tend to hold the majority of the loans they extend on their own balance sheets, although the securitization model – the bundling and selling of mortgage loans in particular – has survived the global financial crisis. The most significant development in bank lending over the past half century has been the shift, across most advanced and some emerging economies, from corporate lending to mortgage lending (Jordà et al., 2016; Bezemer et al., 2020). Investment banks, in addition to also being lenders, specialize in supporting other actors in the creation of financial claims, be it as underwriters of private security listings or as primary dealers for government bonds.

The remainder of the universe of financial corporations is made up of non-bank financial institutions, notably insurers, pension funds, and investment funds. These are institutional capital pools that, rather than creating money via loans, invest "other people's money." Investment funds, whose business model is to invest other people's money for a fee, can be subdivided into three broad groups. By far the largest pools of assets are mutual fund and exchange-traded fund companies, notably the "Big Three" – Blackrock, Vanguard, and State Street Global Advisors (Fichtner et al., 2017). These firms invest predominantly in listed equities and in public and private bonds. The second group comprises hedge, private equity, and venture capital funds, which are subject to far fewer regulations and whose business models generally involve high fees, high risks, and – or so they promise – high returns. Private equity in particular has emerged as a powerful driver of financialization across virtually all asset classes (Eaton, 2020; Morgan and Nasir, 2020; Benquet and Bourgeron, 2021; Christophers, 2021). The growth of institutional capital pools relative to the traditional banking sector is one of the most important developments in the global financial system over the past 15 years. Although already underway before, this divergence accelerated in the wake of the global financial crisis of 2008, as depicted in Figure 1.5.

Power and the creation, trading, and enforcement of financial claims

The central premise of this volume is that in order to study the various ways in which financial sector actors exercise power in the economy and society at large we need to focus on the claim relationship. From this premise follow two implications. First, the carriers and mechanisms of financial power differ across the *different types* of financial claims discussed in the previous section. For instance, bondholders lack the control rights enjoyed by shareholders, but when it comes to enforcing repayment, insolvency law puts bondholders at the top of the creditor hierarchy. Second, the carriers and mechanisms of financial power differ along the *life cycle* of financial claims. This is a cycle because the creation of claims has to start afresh once it has

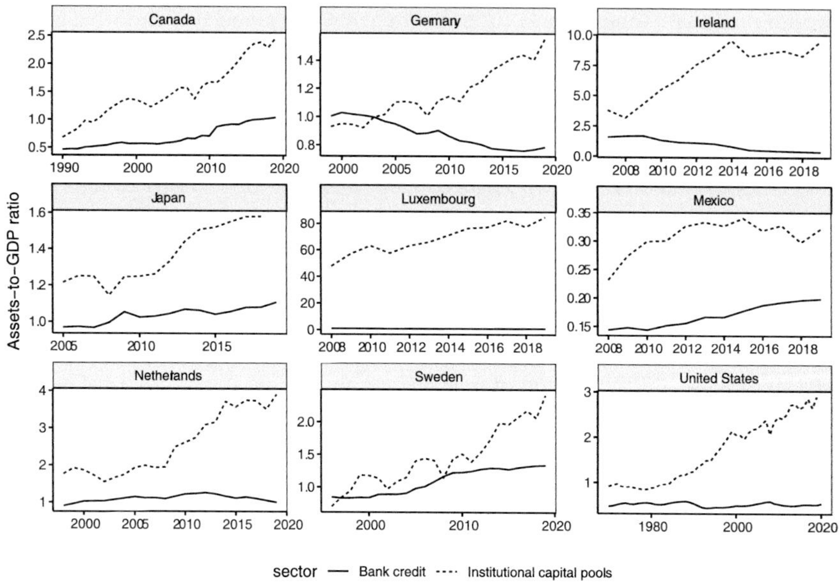

FIGURE 1.5 The growth of institutional capital pools relative to the banking sector

Source: Data: BIS, World Bank.

temporarily come to a halt in repayment because of the capitalist compulsion to turn money into more money by having it move through commodity production.

This life cycle consists of three distinct stages – creation, trading, and enforcement. There are two main variants of claim creation. A financial claim is created when a bank issues a loan, which enters the bank's balance sheet both on the liability side (formally as a liability in the form of a newly credited customer deposit) and on the asset side (as a loan, which is a claim on the borrower). Alternatively, non-financial actors create financial claims when – usually with the help of investment banks – they issue debt or equity securities. Once they exist, financial claims are frequently *traded*. Traditional bank loans used to remain on the originating bank's balance sheet, but securitization has transformed loans into marketable instruments. Bonds and the shares of listed corporations tend to be highly liquid instruments that are frequently traded. This requires exchanges, actors that buy and sell securities, as well as payment and settlement infrastructures. Finally, financial claims must be *enforced*. Here, the central role of law is particularly visible, notably when creditors enforce their claims against non-compliant debtors via the court system and, eventually, the state's monopoly on coercion. Unlike domestic financial claims, cross-border claims exist in the shadow of national sovereignty and in the absence of a global judiciary. While never guaranteed, enforceability is therefore particularly fragile in the case of cross-border claims. The boundaries between these stages are blurry. For instance, trading is linked to enforcement in that it can help to "keep

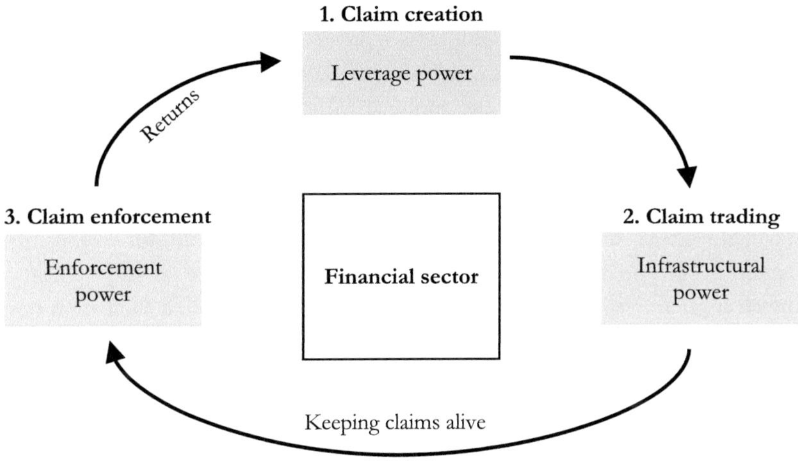

FIGURE 1.6 Three forms of financial power, mapped onto the claim life cycle

Source: The authors

claims alive" – claims that one investor has written off as unenforceable may be sold to a different investor, as is the case in the market for non-performing loans (Mertens and Metz, 2022, this volume). At each of these stages, creditors (and, sometimes, debtors) exercise power – leverage power, infrastructural power, and enforcement power (Figure 1.6).

Creating claims: leverage power

The contributions to this volume study claim creation through the conceptual lens of leverage power. Other approaches focus on "capitalization" or "assetization" and operate at a higher level of abstraction (Nitzan and Bichler, 2009) or through a micro-practical focus on how things are turned into assets (Birch and Muniesa, 2020; Langley, 2020). Our approach zeroes in on one specific financial practice – leverage. When banks create a deposit or borrow in the wholesale money market, they exercise leverage power. While banks are the masters of the "art of leverage" (Sgambati, 2019, 2022), other actors, too, have leverage power. Hedge funds and private equity funds – so-called levered investors – rely heavily on debt to boost returns for their equity investors, while minimizing the latter's downside risks (Appelbaum and Batt, 2014). For multinational corporations, too, debt is a powerful instrument, while for some governments and central banks the capacity to issue liabilities is virtually unlimited. Traditional notions of "creditor power" tend to obscure that for financial actors, leverage is a resource more than a constraint. Therefore, we emphasize the crucial importance of "leverage power" for the study of the political economy of global finance. Simply put, actors enjoy leverage power when they are able to increase their balance sheets by borrowing cheaply in order to acquire profitable assets.

The financial system tends to revolve around the actors wielding the greatest leverage power. At the top of the monetary-financial hierarchy, leverage power is exercised by the issuer of the safe asset. The largest states and central banks are able to expand their balance sheets at will. Aaron Sahr's chapter explores the state's leverage power through the lens of Modern Monetary Theory (MMT). According to Sahr (2022, this volume), this power has been neglected due to the rule of a "technical imaginary" of monetary order. In this imaginary, money appeared as a universal, hence apolitical, tool. Many governments disarmed their own power to create money through unrestricted access to their own central bank's balance sheet. Today, this regime is challenged on a theoretical and political level, most prominently by MMT.

The ability of states and central banks to wield leverage power is highly unevenly distributed. The United States, as the issuer of the dominant global funding and reserve currency, continues to enjoy an "exorbitant privilege." Other large currency areas at the core of the international monetary system, such as the Euro area, Japan, and China, face relatively few constraints, especially if, as is the case with Japan and China, they have accumulated large foreign currency reserves. The situation is very different for most countries in the Global South, who still often borrow in foreign currency, and are exposed to the ebb and flow of a global financial cycle that is beyond their control (Rey, 2015; Naqvi, 2019; Ben Gadha et al., 2021). Nevertheless, as Andrea Binder argues in her chapter, states are not without leverage power, especially when borrowing in the Eurodollar market. Her comparative analysis of the experience of Brazil and Mexico shows that by navigating "the bifurcation of nationality, currency and jurisdiction," Brazil in particular managed to retain substantial autonomy vis-à-vis its foreign creditors. Binder's central messages are that creditors' power is not unidirectional but requires a relational understanding, and that leverage power exists also in the Global South.

The origins of large-scale sovereign borrowing from private international banks are closely intertwined with those same banks, as early as the 1960s, discovering the technique of liability management. This story is told in the chapter by Mareike Beck, Samuel Knafo, and Stefano Sgambati (2022, this volume), who show how liability management paved the way for a massive shift of leverage power toward the largest and most internationally active banks. The Eurodollar lending spree during the 1970s oil price crisis and the shadow banking system that collapsed in 2008 can both be traced back to the liability management techniques studied by Beck et al. (see also Wansleben, 2020; Braun et al., 2021). Beck et al. make a strong argument that the business model of (shadow) banking – "sourcing and constructing dollar-denominated assets that were at once liquid, safe and offered a high yield" – amounts to an "impossible task." European banks turned out to be particularly vulnerable to the pitfalls of this model.

Banks are not, however, the only actors playing the leverage game. As argued by Sahil Jai Dutta, far from being victims of financialization, states and non-financial corporations have, in many cases, seen their leverage power greatly increase as a result of the liberalization of financial markets. As issuers of the "safe assets" that form the backbone of repo markets and, by implication, of the wider financial system, governments of large, advanced economies have been able to increase their power to govern the economy (Dutta, 2019). Similarly, corporate managers, rather than falling victim to aggressive outside shareholders, learned to wield leverage power as early as the 1960s (Knafo and Dutta, 2020). As a result, corporations have acquired the "capacity to source and capture funds and assets from others, which then form the basis for further borrowing in a recursive cycle" (Dutta, 2022, this volume). From a normative perspective, it follows that advocates of definancialization, rather than focusing on the redistribution of financial wealth, need to pay more attention to the redistribution of leverage power.

Trading claims: infrastructural power

Large parts of the financial system consist of actors who do not create, hold, or trade financial claims themselves but provide the services that allow these other activities to be performed. These are the providers of financial infrastructures such as exchanges, indices, payment services, or central counterparties (Quaglia, 2009; Petry, 2020; Westermeier, 2020). These infrastructure providers are profit-oriented actors with fee-based business models. Their power vis-à-vis those whose business model depends on creating or trading financial claims, and those who wish to issue debt or equity claims, is captured by the concept of infrastructural power. Specific financial actors exercise infrastructural power vis-à-vis state actors that depend on specific financial markets for governance purposes (Braun, 2020). More broadly, the infrastructural power of finance underpins the rise of private authority in financial standard settings, regulation, and the imposition of financial sanctions (Büthe and Mattli, 2011; Farrell and Newman, 2019). Infrastructure providers also exercise power vis-à-vis other financial actors whose business models depend on them.

The chapter by Jan Fichtner, Eelke Heemskerk, and Johannes Petry (2022) studies how index providers such as S&P and MSCI, without buying or selling securities themselves, act as "gatekeepers of financial claims." Index providers have become vastly more powerful as more and more investors have moved their money into index funds. Private index providers exercise infrastructural power by defining the criteria based on which firms or countries are included in or excluded from their indices. In one striking display of the infrastructural power of private index providers, the finance minister of Peru, together with other high-ranking officials, flew to New York to prevent the ejection of Peru from MSCI's emerging markets index. As highlighted by the authors, the conditionalities imposed by index providers during such bilateral negotiations bear a striking resemblance with the conditionalities imposed by the IMF or the World Bank.

The most fundamental financial infrastructure of all is the global payments system, examined in the chapter by Andreas Nölke (2022). Without payments, there can be no financial transactions, which is why the power to shut countries out of the global payments system is one of the most severe forms of economic sanctioning. The private-sector actors who run SWIFT, as well as the states in which they are domiciled, wield infrastructural power at a geopolitical scale – they can "weaponize" the network by opening or closing it to individual firms or entire countries (Farrell and Newman, 2019). This is powerfully illustrated by the experience of Iran, whose exclusion from the SWIFT network from 2012 to 2015 had a devastating economic impact on the country. Nölke focuses on countries' attempts to establish alternatives to the dominant SWIFT network, notably Russia's System for Transfer of Financial Messages (SPFS) and the China International Payments System (CIPS). His analysis shows that financial infrastructures, while often semi-invisible, can, under certain circumstances, become highly politicized.

The profitability of a private financial infrastructure is often a function of the absence or availability of alternative, public options. Matthias Thiemann's (2022) chapter on the rise of central counterparties as a solution to the derivatives clearing conundrum provides a powerful case study. Central counterparties are clearing houses that stand at the opposite side of derivative deals and serve to enforce cross-border claims of financial market participants even if their initial counterparty has declared bankruptcy (Lockwood, 2018). It shows that the web of financial claims and liabilities in a liberalized financial system creates systemic risks that are impossible to insure without some form of public backstop (Özgöde, 2021). Thiemann shows that the extraordinary profitability of central counterparties is the flipside of the incapacity, or unwillingness, of the state to directly assume the role of systemic risk manager and the decision to delegate that function, along with certain regulatory privileges, to private companies. In doing so, he renders visible the enormous, but usually hidden, political stakes involved in the institutional setup of financial infrastructures.

Enforcing claims: enforcement power

Different kinds of cross-border financial claims come with different practices and strategies of keeping them alive and, eventually, of enforcement. Whereas under imperialism, such enforcement routinely involved military coercion, today, creditors have access to an impressive variety of tools to enforce their claims through the legal system (Pistor, 2019). What is more, creditors can often count on the support of international institutions such as the IMF, whose evolution into an enforcer of foreign financial claims is well documented. The rise and spread of financial claims since the early 1970s took place in parallel to the IMF's developing of more intrusive conditionality policies that served to make the Global South "safe" for international bank lending and corporate investment (Kentikelenis and Babb, 2019: 1740). In his analysis of the relative absence of sovereign non-default in recent history, Jerome Roos (2019: 79) shows how the creditor cartels of the syndicated-loan era morphed into the underwriting cartels of today's bond era of sovereign lending, and how banking-sector concentration therefore remains decisive for sovereign debtors in the Global South. This is evident, for example, in those West African countries – Senegal, Ivory Coast, Ghana, and Nigeria – that have begun to issue Eurobonds in the wake of the global financial crisis, and in doing so have been dealing with the same six to eight major international banks.

Claim enforcement requires that a financial claim is still alive when creditors seek repayment. Daniel Mertens and Caroline Metz make a powerful case in favor of the view that the expiry date of financial claims is ultimately a political question. Their chapter provides a comparative analysis of "how zombie debt claims are kept (profitably) alive – often to the detriment of debtors." Focusing on the Risk Mitigation Act in Germany in the early 2000s and of the EU's attempts at creating a market for non-performing loans after the global financial crisis, Mertens and Metz (2022) argue that these policies should be understood as attempts to keep creditors' claims alive by making them (more) tradable, thus delaying the moment of default indefinitely. Their detailed empirical analysis of the broader moral economy of debt reveals that under certain conditions – in the German case but not in the EU case – debtor resistance can thwart creditors' enforcement power.

Strategies to keep financial claims alive are not limited to households. The emergent infrastructure of investor-state arbitration has begun to offer services to creditors seeking to enforce their claims on foreign governments (John, 2018).[10] The chapter by Florence Dafe and Zoe Phillips Williams examines how international investment agreements and their adjudication have fostered a new investment strategy in the form of third-party funding for investor-state dispute settlement. This transformation of "the decisions of international arbitrators into a new asset class" (Dafe and Williams, 2022, this volume) constitutes a striking illustration of the "financialization of international law" (Kalyanpur and Newman, 2021). What is more, creditors seeking such third-party funding effectively "re-leverage" in order to keep financial claims alive well past their expiry date, namely the moment when a creditor without access to third-party funding would have decided that securing repayment through costly legal action was not profitable. This newly devised technique to extend the lifespan of financial claims constitutes a substantial increase in cross-border investors' enforcement power.

Whereas Dafe and Williams' investors actively seek payment from governments, the corporate actors in the story told by Arjan Reurink and Javier Garcia-Bernardo (2022) are masters of shielding their assets against government claims. They examine the power of multinational corporations to optimize their own corporate structure via cross-border FDI claims and liabilities. From this perspective, the global rise of FDI represents a "great fragmentation of the firm" that responds primarily to tax and regulatory incentives, as opposed to production or labor cost considerations. Transnational corporations (TNCs) adopt a range of legal-financial strategies to undermine the enforcement of these competing tax claims on the future value generated by their global subsidiaries. Crucially, these strategies revolve around the use of holding companies located in jurisdictions whose legal and tax frameworks confer on FDI investors certain privileges that have the effect of increasing the "firmness" of their claims vis-à-vis those of the tax authorities of the countries in which their productive activities are located. Effectively, then, TNCs use holding companies as vehicles for exercising financial *enforcement power*.

Enforcement power is rarely absolute, however, as debtors may resist repayment or enforcement. The source of debtors' power to resist is the threat of nonpayment, or default. Benjamin Lemoine and Marie Piganiol (2022) show in their chapter how successive Greek governments navigated the power of foreign creditor institutions seeking to impose a radical privatization agenda. Based on data from interviews with key participants, they trace the politico-legal battle over the nature and activities of the Hellenic Republic Asset Development Fund. In the Greek case, a fundamental legal distinction with global relevance comes into view. Whereas domestic creditor–debtor relations are regulated by domestic insolvency law, cross-border financial claims are routinely subject to the law of the jurisdictions that underpin a particular security issuance, most frequently New York State or the City of London (Pistor, 2019). In essence, these legal regimes make it more difficult for sovereign debtors to default. Having organized claims under New York, London, or local law makes a difference. Sovereign bonds, for example, are either issued in domestic or foreign law.

Conclusion

Generating returns and making profits with the help of the financial sector is at the heart of private accumulation strategies in financial capitalism. This volume brings together a group of scholars who have been at the forefront of studying the various forms of financial power that underpin and stabilize the global network of financial claims. The most finance-specific form is leverage power, that is, the ability of financial actors, and banks in particular, to enlarge their balance sheets through ever new techniques of collateralized borrowing and liability management. States and central banks also enjoy leverage power – the question is what they decide to use it for. Infrastructural power is exercised by a myriad of institutions providing the financial, legal, and technological infrastructure for the uninterrupted circulation of claims across the globe. Offering quasi-public goods on a for-profit basis, firms such as index providers or central counterparties have come to wield enormous private authority over non-financial firms and states. When financial claims mature, enforcement power comes into play. Here, creditor public international organizations, such as the IMF, and private law are key. In addition, the financial sector has devised new ways of keeping claims alive by turning investment in investor-state arbitration lawsuits into an asset class.

Does all this amount to the financial sector exercising *autonomous* power – power that financial actors can wield in relative autonomy from the state? This is the question discussed by Katharina Pistor in her concluding chapter (2022, this volume). Pistor reflects and expands on the contributions to the volume by relating them to her own influential work on the legal theory of finance. The code of capital, she argues, has carved out spaces that are sufficiently fortified for financial actors to wield considerable autonomous power in the areas of claim creation, trading, and enforcement.

The main purpose of this volume is to showcase cutting-edge research on these forms of financial power. In our reading, the work collected in this volume points toward three promising areas for future research in international political economy. First, we believe that the speed of developments in the financial sector has outpaced IPE scholarship. In order to catch up, there is a need for research on the various types of financial firms, their business models, and their sometimes conflictive, sometimes collaborative relationships with state actors. This volume gives a sense of the complexity of today's financial landscape and offers specific cues for how to study financial logics and actors as part of a larger, global system. Second, this volume offers a conceptual framework to study power dynamics in a deeply hierarchical global financial system. Leverage power, infrastructural power, and enforcement power provide the conceptual tools to take the complexity of novel financial instruments seriously but also, in a second step, to move to a higher level of abstraction in order to understand the political economy of creditor–debtor relations across the life cycle of financial claims. Finally, the financial claims perspective allows us to ask larger questions about current and future mechanisms of economic coordination – questions that political economy scholarship urgently needs to engage with in the context of the climate crisis and exacerbating within- and between-country inequalities. One way to think about financial claims is as the predominant mechanism under financialized capitalism to plan investment and thus steer economic activity. The promise of the "green finance" discourse is that if recoded via regulatory interventions, the private creation of financial claims and liabilities is our best hope for a swift decarbonization of the global economy. This is doubtful. The question is whether, after half a century of expanding the creation, circulation, and enforcement of private financial claims, the capacity still exists to envision ways of planning and coordinating economic activity that are guided by a logic of social and environmental purpose, rather than by the logic of private profit.

Notes

1 On the instrumental, structural, and infrastructural power of finance vis-à-vis governments, see Young and Pagliari (2017), Woll (2014) and Roos (2019), and Braun (2020).
2 The Politics of Money network funded by the German Research Council: www.politicsofmoney.org/network.
3 This volume is keenly aware of the systemic imperatives that come with the capital relation. However, in the interest of foregrounding specific empirical case studies, the individual chapters speak little about the ever-evolving relationship between capital, money, and finance (often approximating "credit" (Koddenbrock, 2019). For eloquent discussions of this question, see Ingham (2004) and de Brunhoff (2015 [1976]).
4 For recent reviews of the financialization literature, see van der Zwan (2014) and Mader et al. (2020). See also Godechot (2016).
5 For a discussion of the related concept of "wealth chains," see Seabrooke and Wigan (2017).
6 See https://unstats.un.org/unsd/nationalaccount/hsna.asp, last accessed on 24 January 2022.
7 Financial corporations comprise the following sub-sectors (besides the central bank, which in the SNA is classified as a public financial corporation): deposit-taking corporations, money market funds (MMFs), non-MMF investment funds, other financial intermediaries, financial auxiliaries, captive financial institutions and money lenders, insurance corporations, and pension funds.

8 FDI is defined as cross-border equity or debt claims held by non-financial corporations that reflect "a lasting interest and control by a foreign direct investor, resident in one economy, in an enterprise resident in another economy." In the SNA, this is operationalized as a holding of 10 per cent or more of the voting power.

9 The distribution is less unequal for the roughly USD30 trillion of pension entitlements, which are mostly invested in financial assets via pension funds. However, even here, the bottom 50 percent of households are almost entirely excluded from financial asset ownership.

10 National courts may come into play only relatively rarely. A high-profile case was the hedge funds that successfully sued the Argentinian government over sovereign debts in a New York court.

References

Abdelal R (2007) *Capital Rules: The Construction of Global Finance*. Cambridge, MA: Harvard University Press.

Abraham F, Cortina JJ and Schmukler SL (2020) *Growth of Global Corporate Debt: Main Facts and Policy Challenges* (World Bank Policy Research Working Paper No. 9394). Washington, DC: World Bank.

Adkins L, Cooper M and Konings M (2020) *The Asset Economy*. Cambridge: Polity.

Akyüz Y (2017) *Playing with Fire: Deepened Financial Integration and Changing Vulnerabilities of the Global South*. Oxford: Oxford University Press.

Alami I (2019) Money Power and Financial Capital in Emerging Markets: Facing the Liquidity Tsunami. London: Routledge.

Alami I, Alvarez C, Bonizzi B, Kaltenbrunner A, Koddenbrock K, Kvangraven IH and Powell J (2022) International financial subordination: A critical research agenda. *Review of International Political Economy*, Advance Online Publication, 1–27.

Amin S (1974) *Accumulation on a World Scale: A Critique of the Theory of Underdevelopment*. New York: Monthly Review Press.

Andrews DM (2006) *International Monetary Power*. Ithaca, NY: Cornell University Press.

Ansell BW (2019) The politics of housing. *Annual Review of Political Science* 22(1): 165–185. doi:10.1146/annurev-polisci-050317-071146.

Appelbaum E and Batt R (2014) *Private Equity at Work: When Wall Street Manages Main Street*. New York: Russell Sage Foundation.

Arjaliès DL, Grant P, Hardle I, MacKenzie D and Svetlova E (2017) *Chains of Finance: How Investment Management Is Shaped*. Oxford: Oxford University Press.

Arrighi G (1994) *The Long Twentieth Century: Money, Power, and the Origins of Our Times*. London: Verso.

Assa J (2016) *The Financialization of GDP: Implications for Economic Theory and Policy*. London: Routledge.

Babic M, Garcia-Bernardo J and Heemskerk EM (2020) The rise of transnational state capital: State-led foreign investment in the 21st century. *Review of International Political Economy* 27(3): 433–475. doi:10.1080/09692290.2019.1665084.

Baccaro L and Pontusson J (2016) Rethinking comparative political economy: The growth model perspective. *Politics & Society* 44(2): 175–207. doi:10.1177/0032329216638053.

Baines J and Hager SB (2021) The great debt divergence and its implications for the covid-19 crisis: Mapping corporate leverage as power. *New Political Economy* 26(5): 885–901.

Ban C and Bohle D (2021) Definancialization, financial repression and policy continuity in East-Central Europe. *Review of International Political Economy* 28(4): 874–897. doi:10.1080/09692290.2020.1799841.

Beck M (2021) Extroverted financialization: How US finance shapes European banking. *Review of International Political Economy*. Advance Online Publication.

Beck M, Knafo S and Sgambatti S (2022) Leveraging financial claims: Transatlantic bank struggles and the power of US finance. In: Braun B and Koddenbrock K (eds) *Capital Claims: The Political Economy of Global Finance*. London: Routledge, pp. 33–49.

Ben Gadha M, Koddenbrock K, Mahmood I, Kaboub F and Sylla NS (2021) *Monetary and Economic Sovereignty in 21st Century Africa*. London: Pluto Press.

Benquet M and Bourgeron T (2021) Building a centre of capital accumulation: A study of the institutional emergence of the French private equity sector (from the early 1980s to 2017). *New Political Economy* 26(1): 52–68. doi:10.1080/13563467.2019.1708877.

Bernards N (2019) Latent' surplus populations and colonial histories of drought, groundnuts, and finance in Senegal. *Geoforum*. doi:10.1016/j.geoforum.2019.10.007.

Bezemer D, Samarina A and Zhang L (2020) Does mortgage lending impact business credit? Evidence from a new disaggregated bank credit data set. *Journal of Banking & Finance* 113. doi:10.1016/j.jbankfin.2020.105760.

Binder A (2019) All exclusive: The politics of offshore finance in Mexico. *Review of International Political Economy* 26(2): 313–336.

Binder A (2022) In good times and in bad: Offshore dollar markets and the international monetary power of borrowers. In: Braun B and Koddenbrock K (eds) *Capital Claims: The Political Economy of Global Finance*. London: Routledge, pp. 69–87.

Birch K and Muniesa F (2020) *Assetization: Turning Things into Assets in Technoscientific Capitalism*. Cambridge, MA: MIT Press.

Bonizzi B, Kaltenbrunner A and Powell J (2020) Subordinate financialization in emerging capitalist economies. In: Mader P, Mertens D and van der Zwan N (eds) *The Routledge International Handbook of Financialization*. London: Routledge, pp. 177–187.

Bortz PG and Kaltenbrunner A (2018) The international dimension of financialization in developing and emerging economies. *Development and Change* 49(2): 375–393.

Boy N (2015) Sovereign safety. *Security Dialogue* 46(6): 530–547.

Braun B (2020) Central banking and the infrastructural power of finance: The case of ECB support for repo and securitization markets. *Socio-Economic Review* 18(2): 395–418. doi:10.1093/ser/mwy008.

Braun B (2021) Asset manager capitalism as a corporate governance regime. In Hacker J, Hertel-Fernandez A, Pierson P and Thelen K (eds) *American Political Economy: Politics, Markets, and Power*. Cambridge: Cambridge University Press.

Braun B, Krampf A and Murau S (2021) Financial globalization as positive integration: Monetary technocrats and the Eurodollar market in the 1970s. *Review of International Political Economy* 28(4): 794–819. doi:10.1080/09692290.2020.1740291.

Bruneau Q (2021) In the club: How and why central bankers created a hierarchy of sovereign borrowers, c. 1988–2007. *Review of International Political Economy* 1–23.

Büthe T and Mattli W (2011) *The New Global Rulers*. Princeton, NJ: Princeton University Press.

Cain PC and Hopkins AG (2016) *British Imperialism: 1688–2015*. London: Routledge.

Christophers B (2011) Making finance productive. *Economy and Society* 40(1): 112–140.

Christophers B (2021) Mind the rent gap: Blackstone, housing investment and the reordering of urban rent surfaces. *Urban Studies*. Advance Online Publication.

Chwieroth JM and Walter A (2019) *The Wealth Effect: How the Great Expectations of the Middle Class Have Changed the Politics of Banking Crises*. Cambridge: Cambridge University Press.

Cohen BJ (2017) The IPE of money revisited. *Review of International Political Economy* 24(4): 657–680. doi:10.1080/09692290.2016.1259119.

Copelovitch MS and Singer DA (2020) *Banks on the Brink: Global Capital, Securities Markets, and the Political Roots of Financial Crises*. Cambridge: Cambridge University Press.

Coppola A, Maggiori M, Neiman B and Schreger J (2021) Redrawing the map of global capital flows: The role of cross-border financing and tax havens. *The Quarterly Journal of Economics* 136(3): 1499–1556.

Credit Suisse (2021) Global wealth report 2021. *Credit Suisse*. Available at: www.credit-suisse.com/about-us/en/reports-research/global-wealth-report.html (accessed 10 January 2022).

Culpepper PD (2005) Institutional change in contemporary capitalism: Coordinated financial systems since 1990. *World Politics* 57: 173–199. doi:10.1353/wp.2005.0016.

Dafe F (2019) Fuelled power: Oil, financiers and central bank policy in Nigeria. *New Political Economy* 24(5): 641–658. doi:10.1080/13563467.2018.1501353.

Dafe F and Phillips Williams Z (2022) The financialization of investor-state dispute settlement. In: Braun B and Koddenbrock K (eds) *Capital Claims: The Political Economy of Global Finance*. London: Routledge, pp. 189–204.

Dafermos Y, Gabor D and Michell J (2021) The Wall Street consensus in pandemic times: What does it mean for climate-aligned development? *Canadian Journal of Development Studies/Revue canadienne d'études du développement* 42(1–2): 238–251.

Danzman SB (2019) *Merging Interests: When Domestic Firms Shape FDI Policy*. Cambridge: Cambridge University Press.

de Brunhoff S (2015 [1976]) *Marx on Money*. London: Verso Books.

Deeg R and Hardie I (2016). What is patient capital and who supplies it? *Socio-Economic Review*, *14*(4), 627–645.

Deforge Q and Lemoine B (2021) The global south debt revolution that wasn't. In: Pénet P and Flores Zendejas J (eds) *Sovereign Debt Diplomacies: Rethinking Sovereign Debt from Colonial Empires to Hegemony*. Oxford: Oxford University Press, pp. 232–256.

de Goede M (2020) Finance/security infrastructures. *Review of International Political Economy* 1–18. doi:10.1080/09692290.2020.1830832.

Desan C (2014) *Making Money: Coin, Currency, and the Coming of Capitalism*. Oxford: Oxford University Press.

Dixon AD (2020) The strategic logics of state investment funds in Asia: Beyond financialisation. *Journal of Contemporary Asia* 1–25. doi:10.1080/00472336.2020.1841267.

Doidge C, Karolyi AG and Stulz RM (2017) The US listing gap. *Journal of Financial Economics* 123(3): 464–487.

Durand C (2017) *Fictitious Capital: How Finance Is Appropriating Our Future*. London: Verso Books.

Dutta SJ (2019) Sovereign debt management and the transformation from Keynesian to neoliberal monetary governance in Britain. *New Political Economy* 25(4): 675–690.

Dutta SJ (2022) Countering financial claims: On the political economy of de-financialization. In: Braun B and Koddenbrock K (eds) *Capital Claims: The Political Economy of Global Finance*. London: Routledge, pp. 50–68.

Eaton C (2020) Agile predators: Private equity and the spread of shareholder value strategies to US for-profit colleges. *Socio-Economic Review* 20(2). doi:10.1093/ser/mwaa005.

Farrell H and Newman A (2019) Weaponized Interdependence: How global economic networks shape state coercion. *International Security* 44(1): 42–79.

Fastenrath F, Schwan M and Trampusch C (2017) Where states and markets meet: The financialisation of sovereign debt management. *New Political Economy* 22(3): 273–293. doi:10.1080/13563467.2017.1232708.

Fernandez R and Aalbers MB (2016) Financialization and housing: Between globalization and varieties of capitalism. *Competition & Change* 20(2): 71–88.

Fernandez R and Hendrikse R (2020) Offshore finance. In: Mader P, Mertens D and van der Zwan N (eds) *The Routledge International Handbook of Financialization*. London: Routledge, pp. 224–237.

Fernandez R and Wigger A (2016) Lehman brothers in the Dutch offshore financial centre: The role of shadow banking in increasing leverage and facilitating debt. *Economy and Society* 45(3–4): 407–430.

Fichtner J, Heemskerk EM and Garcia-Bernardo J (2017) Hidden power of the Big Three? Passive index funds, re-concentration of corporate ownership, and new financial risk. *Business and Politics* 19(2): 298–326. doi:10.1017/bap.2017.6.

Fichtner J, Heemskerk EM and Petry J (2022) The new gatekeepers of financial claims: States, passive markets, and the growing power of index providers. In: Braun B and Koddenbrock K (eds) *Capital Claims: The Political Economy of Global Finance*. London: Routledge, pp. 107–128.

Fuller GW, Johnston A and Regan A (2019) Housing prices and wealth inequality in Western Europe. *West European Politics* 1–24. doi:10.1080/01402382.2018.1561054.

Gabor D (2016) The (impossible) repo trinity: The political economy of repo markets. *Review of International Political Economy* 23(6): 967–1000.

Gabor D and Ban C (2016) Banking on bonds: The new links between states and markets. *Journal of Common Market Studies* 54(3): 617–635.

Gabor D and Brooks S (2017) The digital revolution in financial inclusion: International development in the fintech era. *New Political Economy* 22(4): 423–436.

Gabor D and Sylla NS (2020) Planting budgetary timebombs. Available at: https://geopolitique.eu/en/2020/12/23/planting-budgetary-time-bombs-in-africa-the-macron-doctrine-en-marche/ (accessed 10 January 2022).

Gabor D and Vestergaard J (2018) Chasing unicorns: The European single safe asset project. *Competition & Change* 22(2): 139–164.

Godechot O (2016) Financialization is marketization! A study of the respective impacts of various dimensions of financialization on the increase in global inequality. *Sociological Science* 3: 495–519.

Hall PA and Soskice D (2001) An introduction to varieties of capitalism. In: Hall PA and Soskice D (eds) *Varieties of Capitalism. The Institutional Foundations of Comparative Advantage*. Oxford: Oxford University Press, pp. 1–68.

Hardie I (2012) *Financialization and Government Borrowing Capacity in Emerging Markets*. Basingstoke: Palgrave Macmillan.

Hardie I, HowArth D, Maxfield A and Verdun A (2013) Banks and the false dichotomy in the comparative political economy of finance. *World Politics* 65(4): 691–728.

Helleiner E (1994) *States and the Reemergence of Global Finance: From Bretton Woods to the 1990s*. Ithaca, NY: Cornell University Press.

Hobson J (2011 [1902]) *Imperialism: A Study*. Cambridge: Cambridge University Press.

Hudson PJ (2017) *Bankers of Empire: How Wall Street Colonized the Caribbean*. Chicago, IL: Chicago University Press.

Ingham G (2004) *The Nature of Money*. Cambridge: Polity.

Inikori JE (2002) *Africans and the Industrial Revolution in England: A Study in International Trade and Economic Development*. Cambridge: Cambridge University Press.

Jayadev A, Mason JW and Schröder E (2018) The political economy of financialization in the United States, Europe and India. *Development and Change* 49(2): 353–374. doi:10.1111/dech.12382.

Jones E (2021) The financial consequences of export-led growth in Germany and Italy. *German Politics* 30(3): 422–440.
Jordà Ò, Knoll K, Kuvshinov D, Schularick M and Taylor AM (2019) The rate of return on everything, 1870–2015. *Quarterly Journal of Economics* 134(3): 1225–1298.
Jordà Ò, Schularick M and Taylor AM (2016) The great mortgaging: Housing finance, crises and business cycles. *Economic Policy* 31(85): 107–152. doi:10.1093/epolic/eiv017.
Kalyanpur N and Newman AL (2021) The financialization of international law. *Perspectives on Politics* 19(3): 773–790.
Kentikelenis AE and Babb S (2019) The making of neoliberal globalization: Norm substitution and the politics of Clandestine institutional change. *American Journal of Sociology* 124(6): 1720–1762.
Kentikelenis AE, Stubbs TH and King LP (2016) IMF conditionality and development policy space, 1985–2014. *Review of International Political Economy* 23(4): 543–582. doi:10.1080/09692290.2016.1174953.
Knafo S (2022) The power of finance in the age of market based banking. *New Political Economy* 27(1): 33–46.
Knafo S and Dutta SJ (2020) The myth of the shareholder revolution and the financialization of the firm. *Review of International Political Economy* 27(3): 476–499. doi:10.1080/09692290.2019.1649293.
Koddenbrock K (2019) Money and moneyness: Thoughts on the nature and distributional power of the 'backbone' of capitalist political economy. *Journal of Cultural Economy* 12(2): 101–118.
Koddenbrock K (2020) Hierarchical multiplicity in the international monetary system: From the slave trade to the Franc CFA in West Africa. *Globalizations* 17(3): 516–531.
Koddenbrock K, Kvangraven IH and Sylla NS (2022) Beyond financialisation: The need for a Longue Durée understanding of finance in imperialism. *Cambridge Journal of Economics*, Advance Online Publication.
Koddenbrock K and Sylla NS (2019) Towards a political economy of monetary dependency: The case of the CFA franc in West Africa. *MaxPo Discussion Paper* 19(2).
Kohl S (2018) More mortgages, more homes? The effect of housing financialization on homeownership in historical perspective. *Politics & Society* 46(2): 177–203. doi:10.1177/0032329218755750.
Krippner GR (2005) The financialization of the American economy. *Socio-Economic Review* 3(2): 173–208.
Kuvshinov D and Zimmermann K (2021) The big bang: Stock market capitalization in the long run. *Journal of Financial Economics* 145(2): 527–552.
Kvangraven IH (2021) Beyond the stereotype: Restating the relevance of the dependency research programme. *Development and Change* 52: 76–112. doi:10.1111/dech.12593.
Kvangraven IH, Koddenbrock J and Sylla NS (2021) Financial subordination and uneven financialization in 21st century Africa. *Community Development Journal* 56(1): 119–140.
Lagna A (2016) Derivatives and the financialisation of the Italian state. *New Political Economy* 21(2): 167–186.
Langley P (2020) Assets and assetization in financialized capitalism. *Review of International Political Economy*. Available at: www.tandfonline.com/doi/abs/10.1080/09692290.2020.1830828 (accessed 24 March 2021).
Lemoine B (2016) *L'ordre de la dette: Enquête sur les infortunes de l'État et la prospérité du marché*. Paris: La Découverte.
Lemoine B and Piganiol M (2022) Claiming the wealth of a nation: Creditor-enforced privatization in Greece. In: Braun B and Koddenbrock K (eds) *Capital Claims: The Political Economy of Global Finance*. London: Routledge, pp. 232–247.

Lenin V (1999 [1907]) *Imperialism: The Highest Stage of Capitalism*. Sydney: Resistance Books.
Lockwood E (2018) The politics and practices of central Clearing in OTC derivatives markets. In: Helleiner E, Pagliari S and Spagna I (eds) *Governing the World's Biggest Market: The Politics of Derivatives Regulation After the 2008*. Oxford: Oxford University Press.
Luxemburg R (2015 [1913]) *The Accumulation of Capital*. London: Routledge.
Mader P (2015) *The Political Economy of Microfinance: Financializing Poverty*. London: Palgrave Macmillan.
Mader P, Mertens D and van der Zwan N (2020) *The Routledge International Handbook of Financialization*. London: Routledge.
McDowell D (2017) *Brother, Can You Spare a Billion? The United States, the IMF, and the International Lender of Last Resort*. Oxford: Oxford University Press.
Mehrling P (2013) Essential hybridity: A money view of FX. *Journal of Comparative Economics* 41(2): 355–363.
Mehrling P (2015) Elasticity and discipline in the global swap network. *International Journal of Political Economy* 44(4): 311–324.
Mertens D and Metz C (2022) Night of the living debt. Non-performing loans and the politics of making an asset class in Europe. In: Braun B and Koddenbrock K (eds) *Capital Claims: The Political Economy of Global Finance*. London: Routledge, pp. 169–188.
Mertens D, Thiemann M and Volberding P (2020) *The Reinvention of Development Banking in the European Union: Industrial Policy in the Single Market and the Emergence of a Field*. Oxford: Oxford University Press.
Michie RC (2006) *The Global Securities Market: A History*. Oxford: Oxford University Press.
Milberg W (2008) Shifting sources and uses of profits: Sustaining US financialization with global value chains. *Economy and Society* 37(3): 420–451.
Monnet E (2018) *Controlling Credit: Central Banking and the Planned Economy in Postwar France, 1948–1973*. Cambridge: Cambridge University Press.
Montgomerie J (2009) The pursuit of (past) happiness? Middle-class indebtedness and American financialisation. *New Political Economy* 14(1): 1–24.
Morgan J and Nasir AM (2020) Financialised private equity finance and the debt gamble: The case of toys R us. *New Political Economy* 1–17. doi:10.1080/13563467.2020.1782366.
Murau S, Pape F and Pforr T (2021) *The Hierarchy of the Offshore US-Dollar System. On Swap Lines, the FIMA Repo Facility and Special Drawing Rights. GEGI Study*. Boston: Boston University, Global Development Policy Center.
Naidu S (2017) A political economy take on W/Y. In: Boushey H, Bradford J and Steinbaum M (eds) *After Piketty: The Agenda for Economics and Inequality*. Cambridge, MA: Harvard University Press, pp. 99–125.
Naqvi N (2019) Manias, panics and crashes in emerging markets: An empirical investigation of the post-2008 crisis period. *New Political Economy* 24(6): 759–779. doi:10.1080/13563467.2018.1526263.
Nelson S (2017) *The Currency of Confidence: How Economic Beliefs Shape the IMF's Relationship with Its Borrowers*. Ithaca, NY: Cornell University Press.
Nitzan J and Bichler S (2009) *Capital as Power: A Study of Order and Creorder*. London: Routledge.
Nölke A (2022) Geoeconomic infrastructures: Building Chinese-Russian alternatives to SWIFT. In: Braun B and Koddenbrock K (eds) *Capital Claims: The Political Economy of Global Finance*. London: Routledge, pp. 147–166.
Nölke A and Vliegenthart A (2009) Enlarging the varieties of capitalism: The emergence of dependent market economies in East Central Europe. *World Politics* 61(4): 670–702.
Oatley T and Petrova B (2020) The global deregulation hypothesis. *Socio-Economic Review* 20(2): 611–633. doi:10.1093/ser/mwaa028.

Ogle V (2017) Archipelago capitalism: Tax havens, offshore money, and the state, 1950s – 1970s. *The American Historical Review* 122(5): 1431–1458. doi:10.1093/ahr/122.5.1431.
Ogle V (2020) Funk money': The end of empires, The expansion of tax havens, and decolonization as an economic and financial event. *Past & Present* 249(1): 213–249. doi:10.1093/pastj/gtaa001.
Ouma S (2020) *Farming as Financial Asset: Global Finance and the Making of Institutional Landscapes*. Newcastle upon Tyne: Agenda Publishing.
Oxfam (2022) Ten richest men double their fortunes in pandemic while incomes of 99 percent of humanity fall. Available at: www.oxfam.org/en/press-releases/ten-richest-men-double-their-fortunes-pandemic-while-incomes-99-percent-humanity (accessed 20 January 2022).
Özgöde O (2021) The emergence of systemic risk: The federal reserve, bailouts, and monetary government at the limits. *Socio-Economic Review*. Advance Online Publication.
Pagliari S, Phillips LM and Young KL (2020) The financialization of policy preferences: Financial asset ownership, regulation and crisis management. *Socio-Economic Review* 18(3): 655–680. doi:10.1093/ser/mwy027.
Palan R (1998) Trying to have your cake and eating it: How and why the state system has created offshore. *International Studies Quarterly* 42(4): 625–643.
Patnaik P and Patnaik U (2021) *Capital and Imperialism: Theory, History and the Present*. New York: Monthly Review Press.
Perry J and Nölke A (2006) The political economy of international accounting standards. *Review of International Political Economy* 13(4): 559–586.
Petry J (2020) From national marketplaces to global providers of financial infrastructures: Exchanges, infrastructures and structural power in global finance. *New Political Economy* 1–24. doi:10.1080/13563467.2020.1782368.
Petry J, Koddenbrock K and Nölke A (2021) State capitalism and capital markets: Comparing securities exchanges in emerging markets. *Environment and Planning A: Economy & Space*. Advance Online Publication.
Pfeffer FT and Waitkus N (2021) The wealth inequality of nations. *American Sociological Review* 86(4): 567–602.
Piketty T (2014) *Capital in the 21st Century*. Cambridge, MA: Harvard University Press.
Piroska D, Gorelkina Y and Johnson J (2021) Macroprudential policy on an uneven playing field: Supranational regulation and domestic politics in the EU's dependent market economies. *JCMS: Journal of Common Market Studies* 59(3): 497–517.
Pistor K (2013) A legal theory of finance. *Journal of Comparative Economics* 41(2): 315–330.
Pistor K (2019) *The Code of Capital: How the Law Creates Wealth and Inequality*. Princeton, NJ: Princeton University Press.
Pistor K (2020) The value of law. *Theory and Society* 49(2): 165–186. doi:10.1007/s11186-020-09388-z.
Quaglia L (2009) Political science and the 'Cinderellas' of economic and monetary union: Payment services and clearing and settlement. *Journal of European Public Policy* 16(4): 623–639. doi:10.1080/13501760902872759.
Quinn SL (2019) *American Bonds: How Credit Markets Shaped a Nation* (vol 164). Princeton, NJ: Princeton University Press.
Regan A and Brazys S (2018) Celtic phoenix or leprechaun economics? The politics of an FDI-led growth model in Europe. *New Political Economy* 23(2): 223–238.
Reis N and de Oliveira F A (2021). Peripheral financialization and the transformation of dependency: A view from Latin America. *Review of International Political Economy*, Advance Online Publication: 1–24.

Reurink A and Garcia-Bernardo J (2022) Firm claims: Reinterpreting the global race for foreign direct investment. In: Braun B and Koddenbrock K (eds) *Capital Claims: The Political Economy of Global Finance*. London: Routledge, pp. 205–231.

Rey H (2015) *Dilemma Not Trilemma: The Global Financial Cycle and Monetary Policy Independence* (NBER Working Paper no. 21162). Cambrige, MA: National Bureau of Economic Research.

Ronkainen A and Sorsa VP (2018) Quantitative easing forever? Financialisation and the institutional legitimacy of the Federal Reserve's Unconventional Monetary Policy. *New Political Economy* 23(6): 711–727.

Roos J (2019) *Why Not Default? The Political Economy of Sovereign Debt*. Princeton, NJ: Princeton University Press.

Sahasrabuddhe A (2019) Drawing the line: The politics of federal currency swaps in the global financial crisis. *Review of International Political Economy* 26(3): 461–489. doi:10.1080/09692290.2019.1572639.

Sahr A (2022) Claims to sovereignty. MMT as a challenge to money's technical imaginary. In: Braun B and Koddenbrock K (eds) *Capital Claims: The Political Economy of Global Finance*. London: Routledge, pp. 88–103.

Schelkle W (2017) *The Political Economy of Monetary Solidarity: Understanding the Euro Experiment*. Oxford: Oxford University Press.

Schwartz HM (2020) Covering the private parts: The (re-)nationalisation of housing finance. *West European Politics* 43(2): 485–508.

Seabrooke L and Wigan D (2017) The governance of global wealth chains. *Review of International Political Economy* 24(1): 1–29.

Sgambati S (2019) The art of leverage: A study of bank power, money-making and debt finance. *Review of International Political Economy* 26(2): 287–312.

Sgambati S (2022) Who owes? Class struggle, inequality and the political economy of leverage in the 21st century. *Finance and Society* 8(1): 1–21.

Sissoko C (2019) Repurchase agreements and the (de) construction of financial markets. *Economy and Society* 48(3): 315–341.

Soederberg S (2014) *Debtfare States and the Poverty Industry: Money, Discipline and the Surplus Population*. London: Routledge.

Sparkes M and Wood JDG (2020) The political economy of household debt & the Keynesian policy paradigm. *New Political Economy* 26(4): 598–615.

St John T (2018) *The Rise of Investor-State Arbitration: Politics, Law, and Unintended Consequences*. Oxford: Oxford University Press.

Strange S (1988) *States and Markets*. London: Continuum.

Stubbs T, Kring W, Laskaridis C, Kentikelenis A and Gallagher K (2021) Whatever it takes? The global financial safety net, covid-19, and developing countries. *World Development* 137: 105–171.

Thiemann M (2018) *The Growth of Shadow Banking: A Comparative Institutional Analysis*. Cambridge: Cambridge University Press.

Thiemann M (2022) The benefits of network centrality: Central counterparties, the enforceability of claims and the securing of extra-profits. In: Braun B and Koddenbrock K (eds) *Capital Claims: The Political Economy of Global Finance*. London: Routledge, pp. 129–146.

Tilley L (2020) Extractive investibility in historical colonial perspective: The emerging market and its antecedents in Indonesia. *Review of International Political Economy* 1–20. doi:10.1080/09692290.2020.1763423.

Tooze A (2018) *Crashed: How a Decade of Financial Crises Changed the World*. London: Penguin.

Tooze A (2021) *Shutdown: How Covid Shook the World's Economy*. London: Penguin.

van der Zwan N (2014) Making sense of financialization. *Socio-Economic Review* 12(1): 99–129. doi:10.1093/ser/mwt020.

van 't Klooster J and Fontan C (2019) The myth of market neutrality: A comparative study of the European Central Bank's and the Swiss National Bank's Corporate security purchases. *New Political Economy* 25(6): 865–879.

Vermeiren M (2019) Meeting the world's demand for safe assets? Macroeconomic policy and the international status of the Euro after the crisis. *European Journal of International Relations* 25(1): 30–60.

Walter A (1993) *World Power and World Money: The Role of Hegemony and International Monetary Order*. New York: Harvester Wheatsheaf.

Walter S (2008) A new approach for determining exchange-rate level preferences. *International Organization* 62(3): 405–438.

Walter T and Wansleben L (2020) How central bankers learned to love financialization: The Fed, the Bank, and the enlisting of unfettered markets in the conduct of monetary policy. *Socio-Economic Review* 18(3): 625–653. doi:10.1093/ser/mwz011.

Wansleben L (2020) Formal institution building in financialized capitalism: The case of repo markets. *Theory and Society* 49(2): 187–213.

Weaver C (2008) *Hypocrisy Trap: The World Bank and the Poverty of Reform*. Princeton, NJ: Princeton University Press.

Wennerlind C (2011) *Casualties of Credit*. Cambridge, MA: Harvard University Press.

Westermeier C (2020) Money is data – the platformization of financial transactions. *Information, Communication & Society* 23(14): 2047–2063.

Wiedemann A (2021) *Indebted Societies: Credit and Welfare in Rich Democracies*. Cambridge: Cambridge University Press.

Williams Z and Dafe F (2021) Banking on courts: Financialization and the rise of third-party funding in investment arbitration. *Review of International Political Economy* 28(5): 1362–1384.

Woll C (2014) *The Power of Inaction: Bank Bailouts in Comparison*. Ithaca, NY: Cornell University Press.

Wullweber J (2021) The politics of shadow money: Security structures, money creation and unconventional central banking. *New Political Economy* 26(1): 69–85.

Young K and Pagliari S (2017) Capital united? Business unity in regulatory politics and the special place of finance. *Regulation & Governance* 11(1): 3–23.

Zarakol A (2017) *Hierarchies in World Politics* (Vol. 144). Cambridge: Cambridge University Press.

Zysman J (1983) *Governments, Markets, and Growth: Financial Systems and the Politics of Industrial Change*. Ithaca, NY: Cornell University Press.

PART I

Leverage power

2

LEVERAGING FINANCIAL CLAIMS

Transatlantic bank struggles and the power of US finance

Mareike Beck, Samuel Knafo, and Stefano Sgambati

Introduction: banking on financial markets

The 2007–2008 Great Financial Crisis (GFC) cast in harsh light the profound transformation of banking in contemporary times. Over the past few decades, banking has become fully engrossed in financial market activities. Today banks no longer simply make loans and accept deposits. Instead, they make investments in the capital market and fund their portfolios of financial assets in the money market. Banks have effectively become broker-dealers as their business is now based on leveraging their positions in financial markets through trading and the active management of both bank assets and liabilities. This chapter reflects upon this transformation and draws out its implications for the power of banks and the struggles they face as they make these markets.

Research on the growing involvement of banks on financial markets has put into question the traditional view of banks as functional intermediaries tasked with recycling unused savings. To make sense of the hybridisation of banking and financial markets, scholars in the field of international and comparative political economy have coined the concept of "market-based banking" (see Hardie et al., 2013). The latter signals a secular trend in advanced economies away from traditional banking and towards more speculative practices involving financial market trading, securitisation, and shadow banking. Under traditional settings, bank assets and liabilities were "locked in" and mostly fixed. By contrast, the balance sheets of today's banks are "opened up": a considerable proportion of their assets and liabilities consists of capital market instruments (securities, derivatives) and money market instruments (repos, certificates of deposits). Through securitisation and shadow banking, banks' loan-making and deposit-taking activities are today no longer analytically separable from (proprietary) trading.

Framing these developments as part of a marketisation of banking has often underscored the new vulnerabilities of banks and the volatility of their new financial

DOI: 10.4324/9781003218487-3

arrangements. In particular, the literature on market-based banking highlights how banks are increasingly subjected to "market forces" – pressures coming from institutional investors, money managers, and wealth holders to search for yield – and have to adopt a short-term, risk-seeking approach. This problem is often said to have been particularly salient for European banks in the lead up to GFC, as they exploited a lack of regulation to expand further their balance sheets and take on greater risks.

In this chapter, we reflect on the recent debates about these transformations and examine how the crisis became the catalyst for a profound rethinking of the role of banks in the global economy. We agree that the recent literature on macro-finance has made important contributions challenging old conceptions about how banks operate and generate resources for their operations. In doing so, these approaches have brought heterodox understandings of money and banking into the mainstream. Yet after more than two centuries of conceiving banks as intermediaries, it remains difficult to grasp the full significance of what was revealed by the crisis and its implications for critical macro-financial and political economy approaches. As we show, key elements of the "intermediation view" continue to hold sway in mainstream economists' account of the global economy and more generally in their understanding of the production of financial claims. This vitiates today's macroeconomic and macro-financial understanding of what contemporary global banks do and why they do it and, consequently, what we perceive to be the problem within contemporary banking.

Partly to blame is the ongoing "economic" framing based on the idea of the market which downplays the political dimensions of these developments connected to the power struggles among banks and more generally financial actors. The result is a tendency to reify and depoliticise banking, namely to present banks as powerless actors that mostly react to changes in the environment with a view to accommodating greater market forces.

By contrast, we point to the need for a political economy of banking that is not prey to old-fashioned conceptions of banks as functional and seemingly neutral intermediaries. Instead of casting banks as passive agents governed by market forces (a process usually read as a fragilisation of finance tout court), we look at the processes through which banks empower themselves. In the process we examine leveraging as a distinct form of financial power (Braun and Koddenbrock, 2022, this volume). For this purpose, we highlight the significance of (money market) funding and the practices of (capital market) leveraging through which banks build up their balance sheets (Sgambati, 2019) and show how they became central to the competitive struggles among banks and the imperatives that now govern their business models.

In particular, we make two interrelated claims: first, the shift towards what some refer to as market-based banking is located in the rise of liability management from the 1960s onwards, when US banks started to pioneer new ways to manage and expand their balance sheets. As a result, US banks started to invert their business models – from *borrowing-funds-to-invest* to *sourcing-assets-to-borrow* (Knafo, 2022).

Second, this shift started to affect European banks via the Eurodollar markets. Since then, European banks have attempted to emulate the construction of US-style assets with mixed results. We describe this process as an "extroverted financialisation" (Beck, 2021) because European banks had to negotiate foreign financial practices. We also argue in this connection that the excessive leveraging of European banks prior to the crisis was driven by a broadly unsuccessful attempt to catch up and compete with US banks on the tilted playing field of USD-denominated financial markets.

To make our argument, we structure the chapter as follows. In the first section, we outline the mainstream economic view of banking as intermediation and highlight its problematic assumptions. In the second, we discuss how these assumptions inform mainstream explanations of the GFC of 2007–2008. In particular, we revisit two prevalent accounts of the GFC: the Asian saving glut and the European banking glut arguments to highlight the ongoing legacy of the loanable fund theory in our thinking of banking. In the third section, we outline a different theoretical framework which emphasises the centrality of funding and its relationship to leverage power. In the fourth section, we provide an account of the European banks' response to the marketisation of US banking and the unique problems they have faced in constructing their own US-style assets in Europe.

Intermediating other people's money: a nonsense view of contemporary banking

Debates since the global financial crisis have helped challenge an old conception of the role of banks and the production of financial claims in the economy. This traditional understanding presented banks as intermediaries of other people's money or, more specifically, of other people's "loanable funds." In this conception, the role of banks was a functional one which consisted in recycling unused savings by redirecting them through loans to entrepreneurs or other economic agents who might make more efficient use of these funds. According to this intermediation view, banks cannot create money out of nowhere. Instead, they can only increase the availability and circulation of money in the process of matching the supply of already existing savings (loanable funds) with the demand for loans and investments. In other words, banking consists in transforming short-term liabilities (deposits) into longer-term assets (loans): a process known as "maturity transformation." This view anchors two key premises of classical political economy and neoclassical economics: that (a) capital is a fund of saving, or else the outcome of thrift, and that (b) money's price (or rate of interest) represents a reward for saving.

Loanable fund theory initially took shape in the late eighteenth century and early nineteenth century when the regulation of banking became a hotly debated and much politicised issue. Since these debates were shaped by bankers who were keen to minimise the responsibility of banks, or the risks that their operation posed to society, they came to depict the role of banks as a passive transmission belt in the process of money creation. It was a conception that further consolidated its foothold in the first half of the twentieth century when it became the consensus position in mainstream economics. This consensus, however, broke down after the GFC of 2007–2008, when a number of mainstream economists from major monetary authorities worldwide (including the Bank for International Settlement (BIS), the IMF, and the Bank of England) embraced the long-standing heterodox notion that banks do not intermediate already existing savings but create money out of thin air when they make loans (e.g. McLeay et al., 2014; Jakab and Kumhof, 2015). A new consensus then formed around the notion that "loans make deposits," not the other way around – an idea that is also widely accepted in social science circles (e.g. Mellor, 2010; Sgambati, 2016; Koddenbrock, 2019).

Despite this institutional opening to economic heterodoxy, we argue that the old intermediation view continues to shape the mainstream economic imaginary, with problematic outcomes for today's macro-economic and macro-financial modelling of what contemporary global banks do and why they do it. In particular, scholarship on banking continues to downplay the agency of banks. The not-so-subtle subtext in traditional mainstream accounts of finance is that banking is in principle beneficial – indeed a stabilising factor – for the economy. The underlying logic is simple: as intermediaries, banks borrow cheap and lend dear so that they can earn the spread between lower interest-yielding deposits and higher interest-earning loans. In the process of arbitraging between supply and demand for money, banks enable the clearing of accounts between savers (creditors) and borrowers (debtors) and facilitate the price discovery of money. In so doing, they contribute to promoting market efficiency. The corollary is that "market failures" and "financial instabilities" ought to stem from factors that are exogenous to banking itself.

Mainstream economists, it is true, often concede that banking has become far more speculative and reckless than it used to be and drifted away from what people took to be its main function. However, this is often presented as a product of exogenous shocks caused by economic globalisation and financial liberalisation that have forced banks to innovate, take on greater risk, and compete with other financial institutions in the growingly complex environment of global finance. Similarly, they explain the roots of the GFC by invoking exogenous factors which destabilised finance such as the exacerbation of global trade imbalances in the 2000s, the monetary mismanagement by central banks, the faulty or lax regulation by financial authorities, or the fiscal irresponsibility by governments and their people. All these factors are said to have contributed to creating a "culture of risk" and "moral hazard" among banks, a breeding ground for speculation, shadow banking, and other "dysfunctional" financial practices that have led to the 2008 crash. While it is undeniable that non-financial factors should be accounted for, it is striking how explanations for what was essentially a *financial sector* crisis are found in factors beyond banks' control and, indeed, outside of the financial sector itself. As it were, for mainstream economists, finance can only "accelerate" dysfunctionalities generated elsewhere.

In the next section, we highlight two major ways in which recent literature on macro-finance frames banks as agency-less actors that merely react to changes in their environment – in particular to their *regulatory* environment. We show how this often entails another problematic assumption tied to the old conception of banks as intermediaries: the tendency to emphasise the "demand side" or those who have funds to park and who are seen to generate market pressures on banks. The reconfiguration of global finance and the turn to riskier assets are commonly presented as a product of the rise of institutional funds of various sorts which are now placing growing demands on banks to increase their reward for saving, forcing them to take more risk to serve them. Altogether, these two tendencies contribute to reifying and de-historicising struggles among banks, reducing the latter to a cog in the machine of states and markets.

Macro-finance: moving beyond an economic conception of banks?

A first misdiagnosis of the causes of the GFC was offered by the "global saving glut" hypothesis first exposed by Bernanke (2005). Speaking at the Sandridge Lecture to an audience of economists back in 2005, the then governor of the Fed argued that at the roots of global financial instability was an excess supply of global savings by non-US dollar holders, mostly from China, the Organization of the Petroleum Exporting Countries (OPEC), and other Asian emerging economies. Asian excess savings were being recycled back in the United States as investments in medium- to long-term Treasury and Agency securities. This abundance of international dollar savings held down long-term interest rates in the United States. This fuelled a surge in risky mortgage credit – whence the subprime mortgage bubble.

Bernanke rested his case for the Asian saving glut on a revamped version of Say's Law, or "law of markets," a cornerstone of neo-classical economics and a key to dynamic stochastic general equilibrium (DSGE) models employed by mainstream economics. At its most general level, Say's Law states that, under general conditions of perfect competition (when no economic participant can make prices, let alone markets, but ought to take the prices generated by supply and demand forces), "supply creates its own demand" (Keynes, 1936: 18). This is consistent with the intermediation view of banking: ceteris paribus, as the banking system channels the supply of savings into loans, its overall ability to affect the price of money will be negligible. Indeed, banks' arbitrage in the aggregate will push the price of money towards an equilibrium point where supply and demand clear, thus fulfilling the "law of markets." This means that the prevailing rate of interest on loans will be determined not by the banking system but by "market forces" – a combination of savers' propensity to abstain from immediate consumption and borrowers' propensity to borrow. Of the two, the propensity to save will be the fundamental determinant of money's price: this is because, from a loanable-fund perspective, the availability of credit is inherently "supply-constrained" and interest rates will reflect *scarcity* rather than *need* – in conformity with the logic that supply creates its own demand and the neoclassical notion that capital is a fund of saving.

This said, even mainstream economists do recognise that the real-world price of money is never practically determined by supply and demand factors but is typically "distorted" by non-market factors and adverse shocks; as a result, the money market never *automatically* clears today, and clearing is systematically deferred to a tomorrow that never comes. Meanwhile, a secondary market is needed for the (primary) money market to carry on daily: this is the interbank money market. Banks ought to routinely lend to one another to meet their liabilities, and when interbank lending fails to provide a "temporal fix" to the money market (i.e. when it fails to ensure that uncleared, maturing liabilities are discounted and payments are deferred to the next day), the central bank is called upon to buy "unsold inventories" and save the day. The central bank can also choose to pre-emptively buy (sell) or sell (buy) money (securities) through open-market operations and repo agreements to target a specific interest rate. In short, while the price of money is in theory determined by market forces, it is in practice shaped by "market makers," which comprise both central banks and primary dealers (big banks) that routinely make two-way, secondary markets for both money and securities (see Hicks, 1987).

As the Fed's governor, Bernanke must have been aware of the enormous power that both big banks and the Fed exerted on the US money market. This notwithstanding, he maintained that the root cause of "frictions," "distortions," and "irrationalities" in the build-up of the GFC lied *outside* the global banking infrastructure. It was instead the consequence of an excess of supply over demand – a persistent current account imbalance originating in Transpacific trade that was moving interest rates away from their equilibrium point for too long, thus fuelling a speculative bubble in the United States. This early explanation of the GFC had to be updated once it became clear that the main losses were made in Europe, not Asia. Puzzlingly enough, Europe was not a net exporter of savings to the rest of the world. Nevertheless, its banks had managed to lever up their balance sheets in the build-up of the subprime bubble to buy substantial amounts of US private-label mortgage-backed securities (MBSs) and other structured products, such as collateralised debt obligations (CDOs). In light of this new evidence, Bernanke et al. (2011) argued that, because of their burgeoning dollar surpluses, Asian central banks and sovereign wealth funds had developed a unique appetite for US treasury and agency securities in the mid-2000s. These were sought as "safe assets," ideal for purposes of reserve accumulation and foreign exchange management. Alas, the Asian excess demand for safe assets caused a global deficit of US treasury and agency securities, "push[ing] Europeans and other advanced-economy investors, including U.S. investors, into apparently safe 'private-label' MBS. . ., putting downward pressures on interest rates on these private assets as well" (Bernanke et al., 2011: 3).

This new version of the saving glut argument raised more questions than answers. Why would European banks be crowded out by Asian savers? After all, since Europe was not a net exporter of savings, European banks' demand for US securities could only be marginally motivated by reserve and foreign exchange requirements. In other words, European banks had no excess dollars to *save* in the first place, therefore no reason to compete with Asian investors for safe assets. Also, related to this first point, where did European banks get the dollar funding for their investment in US private-label securities? Had they learned to create dollars out of nowhere? Or did they perhaps act as intermediaries of Asian excess dollars?

Some of these questions found partial answers in a new breed of macro-financial studies published in the last decade or so. These studies – many of which carried out under the aegis of the BIS – have looked more closely at transatlantic banks' balance sheets and gross money flows, and they have found that Asian excess saving played no significant role in the GFC: the key factor was instead unrestrained leverage in the European banking sector. This new rationale for the GFC is today known as the "European banking glut" (McCauley, 2018). According to the new glut hypothesis, European banks took highly levered-up positions in US MBSs and CDOs and got the dollar funds to back their excessive exposure in US securities from US money market funds (MMFs). In the years leading to the GFC, much of the gross money flows between the two sides of the Atlantic were "round-tripping" offshore dollars borrowed by European banks from US residents via the US money market and then poured back into the US capital market to finance US residents (He and McCauley, 2012). In short, European banks had managed to position themselves at the heart of US financial markets and had practically become "bankers to the United States" (Hardie and Thompson, 2021: 781).

While it seems to provide an alternative to the Asian saving glut, the European banking glut continues to place explanatory power on factors that are exogenous to banking – this time, not Asian excess saving, but the lax European regulatory environment. According to its proponents, European banks were either permitted to over-leverage their positions in risky MBSs and CDOs to chase higher yield (Shin, 2011) or "were blithely ignored by European governments" (Hardie and Thompson, 2021: 783). In the process, European banks were able to take on the role of intermediary previously fulfilled by US banks, because of their "regulatory freedom" (Bayoumi, 2017). As a result, European banks drew "wholesale funding from the United States and then lend it back to US residents" (Shin, 2011: 3; see also Klein and Pettis, 2020: 63). In fact, things went the other way around. European banks had to *first* leverage their position in the US capital market to source the MBSs and CDOs that they *then* used as collateral security for their money market funding. This is in line with the heterodox notion that loan-making (in this case, capital market leverage) creates the conditions for deposit-taking (in this case, money market funding).[1]

Notably, the bank imperative of balancing capital market leverage with money market funding is not a form of "maturity transformation" by a pure intermediary (as described in the first section) but the opposite: it is the process of transforming longer-term assets (capital market instruments) into shorter-term liabilities (money market instruments) – a process termed "liquidity transformation" (Sgambati, 2019). Far from simply intermediating funds, through their capital market leverage (which involves proprietary trading as well as lending to other financial firms, such as hedge and private equity funds), banks generate the conditions for their money market funding: in the process, they make two-way (secondary) markets for the securities that they source in the capital market and then collateralise in the money market. The key here is that market-making has today become a major mechanism by which banks systematically expand their balance sheets and generate new purchasing power that inflates financial markets and keeps them liquid in the first place.

Liquidity transformation is a fairly simple process when the objects of market-making are public debt securities that are already safe and readily tradable. It is more complicated when the assets sourced in the capital market by banks are not that safe and liquid – for instance, MBSs. In the pre-GFC period, banks and shadow banks had to first slice, dice, and repackage MBSs as higher-yield, more appealing CDOs to give them the appearance of safe assets. Banks and hedge funds eagerly levered up their positions in CDOs and contributed to fuelling a bubble. European banks, in particular, developed a strong appetite for CDOs. Since the latter provided a means to easily engineer attractive assets, they were used to generate US funding and further expand their balance sheet. Yet, as we will show in the fourth section, the excessive risk-taking by European banks was the symptom of a congenital weakness rather than a sign of their strength. Indeed, they levered up their investment in CDOs partly to match their higher funding costs vis-à-vis US banks rather than simply to exploit their lax regulatory framework to generate extra profits.

As we explain in in the fourth section, even though CDOs are no longer eligible collateral for money market instruments, global finance after the GFC continues to operate on the basis of this inverted logic of banking whereby saving in the money market (bank funding) is a consequence, rather than a cause, of investment (bank leverage) in the capital market. This does not mean that bank funding is an *automatic* outcome of bank leverage or that bank loans and investments in the capital market naturally generate bank deposits in the money market. Conditions for bank funding via the money market must be created in the first place. As we argue in the next section, these conditions were initially created through practices of liability management (LM), first developed by US banks in the 1960s, which made the sourcing of assets a central strategy for channelling funds to US money markets and at once promoted the internationalisation of US banking. In turn, we explain in the fourth section that the marketisation of European banks is best understood as an extroverted process of financialisation whereby European banks have attempted to catch up with US banks by sourcing synthetic CDOs externally in US capital markets prior to the GFC.

Liability management and the financialisation of US banking

In bringing to the fore the problem of bank funding in relation to leverage, we note how the macro-financial literature that has emerged in the wake of the GFC has mostly reduced the issue of funding to a matter of market liquidity. From this perspective, banks can generate their funds or the assets they need as long as the claims they produce in this process remain liquid – that is, as long as the market continues to have confidence in these claims. This is clearly true. However, turning the problem of funding into one of liquidity largely downplays the significance of this issue – for it narrowly turns it into a matter of concern only during times of crises, when collective action problems on markets lead to a deterioration in the liquidity of these claims (Knafo, 2020). By contrast, we wish to suggest that there is more to the question of funding and more generally to the process by which banks generate and collect assets to fund their operations.

From our perspective, the issue of funding has always been central to the development of banking (Knafo, 2013), and it was innovations in the way banks fund their operations that would mark them out historically (Sgambati, 2016). In particular, the rise of banknote-issuing and later modern deposit banking profoundly lessened the pressure on banks to make final payments. Yet the fact that banks have gained great flexibility does not take away the issue of funding. In fact, it is precisely because they can in principle expand their balance sheets and take *net* positions in other people's debts as they leverage their investments in securities and derivatives markets that banks ought to devise new ways to match their books, reduce their asset–liability mismatches, and fill their *funding gaps*.

In this respect, our main theoretical argument is that the era of financialisation is mainly characterised by a revolution in funding which has transformed and indeed nourished the ways in which banks leverage their operations (Beck and Knafo, 2020; Dutta, 2020; Knafo, 2022). This came with the rise of liability management which dramatically transformed not only the way banks fund themselves but the very nature of their business models. Liability management essentially introduced a new approach to fund bank activities by relying mainly on money markets or more specifically by raising money from other financial agents. This explains why so many of the innovations that have characterised financialisation revolved around money market funding.

The key turning point in this shift were a series of innovations by US commercial banks in the late 1950s and 1960s that came in response to numerous corporate clients taking their deposits out of these banks to reinvest the funds themselves. In response, US commercial banks sought to address the resulting funding gap by raising short-terms funds on money markets. The most iconic development was the creation of negotiable certificate of deposits (CDs), deposit-like debt instruments – akin to the more familiar time deposits but sold as money market instruments. US banks quickly realised that CDs, initially developed as part of a defensive liability management strategy, could be used more aggressively to pry away deposits from other institutions. By offering better terms on money markets than what firms and individuals could get on deposits, money flew into money markets consolidating the systematic reliance of banks on the new forms of funding. In the process they began to manage the liability side of the balance sheet much more actively. This practice would eventually allow US banks to increase their flexibility to generate funding, a flexibility that would put them way ahead of most other global banks operating on the Eurodollar markets.

However, by the 1970s, surging inflation and climbing interest rates increased the banks' cost of funding, crashing their profit margins and impacting their borrowers' ability to service their debts (Knafo, 2022: 10). This pushed banks to rethink the nature of their business and embrace a new and riskier business model based on active asset and liability management, as a way to generate the conditions for what scholars today call "the money market funding of capital market lending" (Mehrling et al., 2013). By the 1980s, a defensive liability management strategy, first developed by US commercial banks in the late 1950s and 1960s, had become a trader's activity. Part of this transformation was tied to the growing involvement of US investment banks. Banks such as Merrill Lynch began to offer cash management accounts that looked like deposits, except they were balanced by investments in higher-return capital market securities. In this evolution, the ability to source higher-return assets became all the more vital to the success (and failures) of banks in the years of the Great Moderation, as yields became further depressed by monetary policy. For many US banks, seeking high yield in the capital market to meet liabilities in the money market became an imperative.

This sourcing of asset to secure funding was itself increasingly predicated on the ability to transform assets. In the search for higher-yielding assets, banks were usually forced to turn to riskier ones (Sanford, 1996). But such assets, while attractive, had to be transformed to make them palatable for various investors, notably institutional funds constrained by fiduciary commitments and regulatory constraints. The search for yield thus fuelled the dynamics of securitisation through which banks found ways to manipulate yields, essentially by downplaying the risk of their assets. Those with the greater chances of beating the competition and securing "funding liquidity" became the ones more able to generate the largest shares of "market liquidity" in secondary financial markets with their trading – including proprietary trading.[2]

It would be wrong to read this as a product of the demand for yield as if investors were the main drivers in this story. After all, investors always want better yields. What is more interesting is the fact that banks have been very effective at driving funds onto the money markets through their various innovations, which expanded their capacity to generate more funding and, at once, their ability to ensure greater returns in spite of the fact that so much money was going around, thus effectively depressing yield. In this context, most of the innovations that have allowed financiers to generate more attractive claims mostly came from banking innovations and the various offshoots of banking activities running from the MMFs, to the private equity funds or the monolines[3] – all created by ex-bankers that took their "in house" business outside of banks where they were initially created. The fact that more and more banks and other financial agents have followed on the path pioneered by the developers of liability management illustrates that it was the edge provided by these strategies to innovators that forced the hand of others.

What this short history highlights is that competition between banks became increasingly driven by concerns for funding and innovations to channel funds on money markets, a process that became supported by the ability of banks to source assets from capital markets in order to provide greater yields that would further enhance their strategies of leveraging. As Beck (2021) argues, it was precisely this dynamic which shaped the internationalisation of banking, as European banks were forced to radically overhaul their practices in an attempt to meet the challenge posed by the new practices of US banks. This shift would create new imperatives for European banks as they struggled to gain agency and meet the conditions required for them to become big players in this financialised context.

The extroverted financialisation of European banking

The shift to LM initiated by American banks in the 1960s forced the European banks to leave their home markets in Europe to play a game of global banking that ultimately rested on the platform of US capital and money markets, which to date remain at the heart of markets for dollar-denominated claims. As European banks slowly developed new capacities for trading in US securities and capturing wholesale dollar funds, they nurtured these dollar-denominated markets with their broker-dealing, proprietary trading, or securitisation on and off balance sheet. In the process, they went "big," but they also became more and more dependent on US financial markets. More importantly, they never led the way but always followed on the footsteps of US banks as they had to adapt to foreign practices and markets that were institutionalised in the United States. In short, the financialisation of European banks was from the start an "extroverted" process (Beck, 2021) – that is, an uneven process in which European banks learned to source assets and leverage financial claims in an attempt to catch up with US banks, with mixed results at best.

The European reliance on the platform of US financial markets came with various costs. To begin with, European banks have had limited access to traditional dollar deposits, which forced them to rely more prominently on money market funding, a strategy that was originally ill-suited for their banking models and which were often more costly.[4] While the importance of deposits for funding has declined, European banks must still go an extra step to acquire USD (Beck, 2021). Recently, for example, European banks have had to rely on expensive FX swaps to convert euro funding into dollar funding, because their need for dollar funding is not met by a complementary need by US banks for European currencies. This naturally raises the cost of raising dollars vis-à-vis other (European) currencies in wholesale markets (Baba et al., 2009: 66). As dollar funding has become central to acquiring a competitive edge over other financial actors, this has created a major disadvantage for European banks (Beck, 2021), for they have been forced to rely on greater capital market leverage with a view to sourcing dollar-denominated assets that could be collateralised for dollar funding purposes. In practice, this has generated a competitive imperative for European banks to get involved in US capital markets.

When analysing this struggle, scholars often misunderstand the significance of regulation by turning a blind eye to a widely accepted conceptual point: markets are shaped by institutions, not by their absence. Contrary to the prevailing tendency to read this development as a marketisation of finance, one which usually places the emphasis on the evasion of regulation by banks, we argued that this transformation was based on a specific institutionalisation of US finance and the power relations that these institutions buttressed. The new banking practices that came to define financialisation were partly tied to a response to a more regulated environment, not simply because banks tried to evade these regulations through technical innovations, but more importantly because these regulations would be key for the possibilities they opened up to create new claims. The rising importance of credit rating agencies, the accounting pressures of market-to-market or the tight restrictions on institutional funds are all examples of a specific regulatory environment that provided the foundations for some US banks to raise funds, bolster their balance sheet and position themselves at the centre of US financial markets (Knafo, 2022; Konings, 2011). It is no surprise then if European banks struggled to generate similar assets to source on a wide scale, they did not have the same institutional context to work with. This would represent an ongoing competitive advantage for US financial markets and US banks where innovations in LM and securitisation were tailor-made for the environment where they were first conceived.

Indeed, the sourcing of assets for money market funding has been more difficult for European banks because capital and money markets in Europe have been more fragmented and less deep than their US counterparts. The corporate bond markets, securitisation of mortgages, or SME loans have all been less suited to sourcing and constructing high-return assets on a large scale. While the European banks' attempts to follow US banks in establishing the conditions for market-based banking were successful to an extent (e.g. the large-scale project Finanzplatz Deutschland in Germany, large securitisation projects in the Netherlands), securitisation markets in Europe only took hold in the late 1990s. Securitisation grew from about EUR150 billion in 2001 to just over 800 billion in 2008 (European Commission, 2015, figure 2). However, despite this concentrated effort to ramp up securitisation markets, these are only a fraction of securitisation issued in the United States in the lead up to the crisis of 2007–2008[5] (Fligstein and Habinek, 2014).

The relative weakness of European banks in keeping up with US banks was an important factor of their excessive leverage in the lead up to the GFC. In effect, the European involvement in US MBSs and CDOs can only be described as an "Icarus' flight" – an ill-conceived attempt to accomplish the impossible task of sourcing and constructing dollar-denominated assets that were at once liquid, safe, and offered a high yield to US MMFs. European banks and other global investors entered the market in any significant way only in 2003 (Fligstein and Habinek, 2014). While a few large banks such as ABN Amro, Deutsche Bank, and BNP Paribas were among the top ten banks in 2001 and managed to compete with Morgan Stanley and JP Morgan in arranging CDOs (Hart, 2002), from an estimated USD 11 trillion ABS and USD 3 trillion CDOs outstanding in mid-2007, only 17 per cent were originated by European banks (Lysandrou and Shabani, 2018: 542). And while ABN Amro was one of the leading European banks in underwriting both funded and synthetic CDOs, "the bank still [hadn't] run the books on any U.S. CDOs in almost five years, according to Asset-Backed Alert's ABS Database" (Anonymous, 2004). The origination of CDOs, the flexibility to source assets in a way that is most profitable for the originator, stayed in the hands of US banks.

The European CDO market on the other hand was largely synthetic. This means that the collateral underlying the CDOs was not "cash-based" – or had no underlying loans – but instead was made up of derivatives and indices. In 2004, EUR 160 billion worth of CDOs were issued, of which 140 billion were synthetic (ECB, 2005: 141).[6] This reliance on synthetic assets stemmed from the limited availability of European raw materials that could be used for cash-funded CDOs. With synthetic CDOs, there was no such limit because the notional value can be much larger than the underlying assets. As a Deutsche Banker said for one of its largest synthetic CDO issue, "It's not your classic arbitrage cash flow deal where they have to go out and source $2.5 billion of ABS collateral; the larger structured product deals are the main event right now" (Global Capital, 2003). ABN Amro pioneered constant proportion debt obligations (CPDOs), for example, highly leveraged bets on the main investment-grade US and European credit derivatives indices, the CDX IG and iTraxx Europe (Davies and O'Connor, 2008). Put simply, the raw materials were lacking in Europe due to the fragmentation and smaller size of its capital markets, and so European banks had to resort to sourcing synthetic assets in order to play the game of US finance.

The banking glut argument conceptualises European banks' excessive leverage as the consequence of a regulatory failure which allowed European banks to take advantage of high-risk, high-return investments. In other words, it assumes a positive association between leverage and risk, as it contends that higher-leverage European banks invested in high-risk assets, while lower-leverage US banks were less inclined to pursue high-risk assets. If so, European banks should have enjoyed instead higher return on assets (ROA) as their investments were skewed towards higher-risk, higher-return assets compared to US banks over the 2002–2006 period (i.e. before risky investments turned into toxic assets). In turn, since European banks' leverage ratios were higher, we should also find that European banks enjoyed a much higher return on equity (ROE) compared to US banks.[7]

However, this was not what happened. Data from the IMF confirm that it was not a simple opportunity for arbitrage in which European banks would have outsmarted their US counterparts. In fact, the opposite seems to be the case. Over the 2002–2006 period, ROA for European banks was on average much lower compared to their American counterparts: 0.4, 0.5, 0.5, 0.5, and 0.6 per cent for the 50 largest European banks (IMF, 2008: 154) compared to 1.3, 1.4, 1.3, 1.3, and 1.3 per cent respectively for US banks (IMF, 2008: 189). At the same time, ROE on average did not diverge substantially over those years with 13.14 per cent for European banks compared to 13.46 for US banks (IMF, 2008: 154, 192).

We argue that in many ways, European banks attempted to compensate for their lack of financial power by investing into assets that were riskier and more obscure, not simply to generate higher profits per se, but to produce suitable assets that were attractive to US MMFs so as to gain dollar funding. While the precise reasons for individual investments into MBS and CDOs are diverse and complex, it is no surprise that European banks predominantly invested into synthetic CDOs, rather than cash CDOs, packed into conduits refinanced by ABCP (Goda and Lysandrou,

2014; Merritt et al., 2000). Apart from a few large European banks, most foreign banks did not themselves have the financial capacity to originate and hold the asset-backed securities needed to construct complex CDOs and feed them with ABS.

The contribution of the European banks in the phenomenal rise of the debt bubble in the 2000s is therefore an outcome of the position of weakness of European banks in negotiating the shift to LM. While the MBS–ABCP market does not exist anymore in its pre-crisis form, and therefore ceased to be the primary source of leverage for European banks, its dynamics represent the struggles that European banks have had with sourcing the types of assets needed in the game of money-making: Because the sourcing of high-yielding assets as raw material for funding has been limited, European banks found a way to compete in highly leveraged bets to compensate for their disadvantaged position. In that sense, European banks were central actors in the construction of the big financial crash, but it is US banks that determined the rules of the game. And if the raw materials in the global banking system continue to be tied to US money markets, leverage for European banks might be a sign of their desperate attempts to respond to the game of money-making from a peripheral position, rather than proof of how much they are driving global financial markets.

Conclusion

This chapter has reflected on the profound transformation of banking in recent decades. We have shown that the problems of funding have received crucial attention in the recent literature on macro-finance and the causes of the 2008 financial crisis. However, paradoxically, most accounts miss the significance of the rise of funding as a key imperative in financial markets and, therefore, its implication for the power of banks and their ability to make financial claims. The literature has therefore largely sidestepped the issue of funding as an integral part of what banks do – and the complications this causes – and continues to read the problems of banking in terms of external "market" or "regulatory failures," which fails to appreciate the integral problems of contemporary financialised banking. Instead, we redirected the focus on what banks do to demonstrate that the problems of levered-up banks are not part of misdirected savings of greedy investors and only partly a problem of lax regulation. Instead, the problems are the financialised banks themselves.

We point to a political economy of finance that foregrounds banks not as passive intermediaries of other people's money but as active agents that make money predominantly to empower themselves. By leveraging their positions in capital markets to source assets as bases for funding in money markets, banks have dramatically expanded their balance sheets. In other words, going beyond what a loanable funds theory would deem possible, banks create the means of leverage by constructing suitable (capital market) assets to fund their claims on money markets. The practices of leverage – or at least the attempts thereof – could be generalised across most large global banks. However, by putting the emphasis on the issue of funding, we highlight that the possibilities for leveraging are not the same for all banks. As the raw materials of global finance are centred on US capital and money markets, the power of leverage lies in the capacity to create claims suitable for US money markets. From the perspective of this form of extroverted financialisation, European banks' excessive leverage in the run-up to the 2008 financial crisis – the CDO bubble – appears as a sign of weakness, rather than as a sign of power for European banks – for the construction of most CDOs, and the bulk of its profits, remained firmly in the hands of US banks, while European banks have struggled to source similar US-style assets since.

Notes

1 To recall, traditional understandings of banking assume (wrongly) that banks receive savings (deposits) which they then pass on as loans (assets) to firms that could invest these funds.
2 Market liquidity refers to the ease with which financial market participants can trade, whereas funding liquidity corresponds to the ease with which they can obtain funding in the money market (see Brunnermeier and Pedersen, 2009).
3 A monoline is a company that invests in or insures one type of product only. Monoline insurance companies were heavily involved in the GFC as they insured (too) many MBSs that defaulted.
4 As is now common financial knowledge in mainstream policy circles, as a BIS study demonstrates, "given the cost and challenges associated with building a retail deposit base, some non-US banks – particularly European banks – chose to meet their US dollar funding needs during the pre-GFC period by issuing US dollar-denominated wholesale debt" (Davies and Kent, 2020: 61).
5 Ironically, in 2008 and 2009 when overall securitisation plummeted, European securitisation was a larger share of US securitisation that in US markets, it in fact grew in 2008 and only declined in 2009 (European Commission, 2015, figure 1).
6 This is more than double from just over 70 trillion in 2003 of which just under 60 were synthetic.
7 More precisely, leverage ratios of banks in the Euro area were just over 30 per cent, in the United States it was about 20 per cent (Noeth and Sengupta, 2012: 470), 40 per cent for UK banks in 2006, while the return on assets fluctuated at a mere 0.5 per cent and 1.5 per cent for the Europeans (Bell and Hindmoor, 2015: 9).

References

Anonymous (2004) ABN overhauls CDO leadership. *Asset – Backed Alert* 3. Available at: www.proquest.com/docview/216584685/abstract/A730419855BA49F3PQ/7 (accessed 23 February 2022).

Baba N, McCauley R and Ramaswamy S (2009) US dollar money market funds and non-US banks. *BIS Quarterly Review*: 47–63.

Bayoumi T (2017) *Unfinished Business: The Unexplored Causes of the Financial Crisis and the Lessons Yet to be Learned*. London: Yale University Press.

Beck M (2021) Extroverted financialization: How US finance shapes European banking. *Review of International Political Economy*. Epub ahead of print 09 July 2021.

Beck M and Knafo S (2020) Financialisation and the uses of history. In: Mertens D, Mader P and van der Zwan N (eds) *Handbook of Financialisation*. London: Routledge, pp. 136–146.

Bell S and Hindmoor A (2015) Masters of the universe but slaves of the market: Bankers and the great financial meltdown. *The British Journal of Politics and International Relations* 17(1): 1–22.

Bernanke B (2005) The global saving glut and the US current account deficit. Sandridge Lecture, Virginia Association of Economists, 14 April, Richmond.

Bernanke B, Bertaut C, DeMarco LP and Kamin S (2011) International capital flows and the returns to safe assets in the United States, 2003–2007. Board of Governors of the Federal Reserve System, International Finance Discussion Papers Number 1014, February.

Braun B and Koddenbrock K (2022) Introduction. In: Braun B and Koddenbrock K (eds) *The Three Phases of Financial Power: Leverage, Infrastructure, and Enforcement*. London: Routledge, pp. 1–30.

Brunnermeier MK and Pedersen LH (2009) Market liquidity and funding liquidity. *The Review of Financial Studies* 22(6): 2201–2238.

Davies PJ and O'Connor S (2008) Default protection puts CPDOs at risk. *Financial Times*, 19 February, p. 27.

Davies SM and Kent C (2020) *US Dollar Funding an International Perspective* (CGFS Papers 65). Switzerland: Bank for International Settlements.

Dutta SJ (2020) Sovereign debt management and the transformation from Keynesian to neoliberal monetary governance in Britain. *New Political Economy* 25(4): 1–16.

ECB (2005) Has the European collateralised debt obligations market matured? *Financial Stability Review* 7.

European Commission (2015) A European framework for simple and transparent securitisation. Fact Sheet, MEMO/15/5733, September.

Fligstein N and Habinek J (2014) Sucker punched by the invisible hand: The world financial markets and the globalization of the US mortgage crisis. *Socio-Economic Review* 12(4): 637–665.

Global Capital (2003) Deutsche bank shops largest-ever ABS CDO, 23 June. Available at: www.globalcapital.com/article/k6cm95478vtc/deutsche-bank-shops-largest-ever-abs-cdo (accessed 16 April 2021).

Goda T and Lysandrou P (2014) The contribution of wealth concentration to the subprime crisis: A quantitative estimation. *Cambridge Journal of Economics* 38: 301–327.

Hardie I, Howarth D, Maxfield S and Verdun A (2013) Banks and the false dichotomy in the comparative political economy of finance. *World Politics* 65(4): 691–728.

Hardie I and Thompson H (2021) Taking Europe seriously: European financialization and US monetary power. *Review of International Political Economy* 28(4): 775–793.

Hart J (2002) 'Toxic' synthetic CDOs balloon to pounds 92 billion: [C Edition]. *Evening Standard, West End Final Ed*, 31 January, p. 41. Available at: www.proquest.com/docview/329546471/abstract/A730419855BA49F3PQ/5

He D and McCauley RN (2012) Eurodollar banking and currency internationalisation. *BIS Quarterly Review* 17(2): 33–46.

Hicks J (1987) *A Market Theory of Money*. Oxford: Oxford University Press.

IMF (2008) *Global Financial Stability Report: Containing Systemic Risks and Restoring Financial Soundness*. Washington: IMF.

Jakab Z and Kumhof M (2015) *Banks Are Not Intermediaries of Loanable Funds, and Why This Matters* (Working Paper No. 529). London: Bank of England.

Keynes J (1936 [1978]) The General Theory of Employment, Interest and Money (*in The Collected Writings of John Maynard Keynes*). London: Royal Economic Society.

Klein M and Pettis M (2020) *Trade Wars Are Class Wars*. New Haven, CT and London: Yale University Press.

Knafo S (2013) *The Making of Modern Finance: Liberal Governance and the Gold Standard*. London: Routledge.

Knafo S (2020) Macro-finance and the financialisation of economic policy. *Finance and Society* 6(1): 87–94.

Knafo S (2022) The power of finance in the age of market based banking. *New Political Economy* 27(1): 33–46.
Koddenbrock K (2019) Money and moneyness: Thoughts on the nature and distributional power of the 'backbone' of capitalist political economy. *Journal of Cultural Economy* 12(2): 101–118.
Konings M (2011) *The Development of American Finance*. Cambridge: Cambridge University Press.
Lysandrou P and Shabani M (2018) The explosive growth of the ABCP market between 2004 and 2007: A "search for yield" story. *Journal of Post Keynesian Economics* 41(4): 526–546.
McCauley R (2018) The 2008 crisis: Transpacific or transatlantic? *BIS Quarterly Review* 39–58.
McLeay M, Radia A and Thomas R (2014) Money creation in the modern economy. *Bank of England Quarterly Bulletin* Q1: 14–27.
Mehrling P, Pozsar Z, Sweeney J and Neilson DH (2013) *Bagehot Was a Shadow Banker: Shadow Banking, Central Banking, and the Future of Global Finance*. SSRN Scholarly Paper ID 2232016.
Mellor M (2010) *The Future of Money: From Financial Crisis to Public Resource*. London: Pluto Press.
Merritt R, Gerity M, Irving A, et al. (2000) Synthetic CDOs: A growing market for credit derivatives. *Financier* 7(1–4): 78–86.
Noeth BJ and Sengupta R (2012) Global European Banks and the financial crisis. *Federal Reserve Bank of St. Louis Review* 94(6): 457–479.
Sanford C (1996) Managing the transformation of a corporate culture: Risks and rewards. In: *1996–97 Musser-Schoemaker Leadership Lecture Series*, Wharton School, University of Pennsylvania. Available at: www.terry.uga.edu/about/history/sanford/managing-transformation (accessed 23 June 2021).
Sgambati S (2016) Rethinking banking. Debt discounting and the making of modern money as liquidity. *New Political Economy* 21(3): 274–290.
Sgambati S (2019) The art of leverage: A study of bank power, money-making and debt finance. *Review of International Political Economy* 26(2): 287–312.
Shin HS (2011) Global banking glut and loan risk premium. Mundell-Fleming Lecture, *IMF Economic Review* 60(2): 155–192.

3

COUNTERING FINANCIAL CLAIMS

On the political economy of definancialisation

Sahil Jai Dutta

Introduction: discourses of definancialisation

Definancialisation is a political programme that promises to reverse what its proponents perceive as the growing dominance of finance over society (see, e.g., Sawyer, 2016). Broadly, it aims to shield the users of funds from the pressure of external financial markets and, by doing so, allow real economy investment and growth to flourish. It is founded on a rentier reading of financial power, in which financial institutions capture the value produced by others (Foroohar, 2016; Mazzucato, 2018; Lapavitsas, 2013). In this, capital market deregulation is thought to have empowered financial capitalists, as the providers of funds, to dictate terms to the users. Since financial capitalists can now use liberal financial markets to whip funds away at any moment, and threaten a crisis of financial scarcity, the users of funds must put financier interests first. The result is 'debt states' prioritise 'market volk' over citizens (Streeck, 2014: 84) and corporations maximise shareholder returns over everyone else (Lazonick and O'Sullivan, 2000). In such accounts, rentiers are the takers, not makers, of value, extracting an ever greater share of output from those into whom they invest.

To counter this rentier power, definancialisation aims to shield the users of funds from the external pressure of financial rentiers, principally by generating stable sources of 'patient' investment. Mariana Mazzucato's (2014) series in the *Financial Times* about definancialisation, for example, called for the development of 'mission-orientated finance' that provides 'long-term' investment rather than short-term speculation. In academic literature, definancialisation is defined as a programme of financial repression that reigns in the financial motives, markets, and institutions that have taken over economy and society since the 1980s (Dagdeviren and Karwowski, 2022; Sawyer, 2016). Specifically, it would involve policies like a financial transactions tax, the development of not-for-profit local and national banking institutions,

DOI: 10.4324/9781003218487-4

regulatory changes to reverse the liberalisation of financial markets (Sawyer, 2016: 60), and moves to withdraw from financial markets altogether (Ban and Bohle, 2021: 875). In these accounts, it is argued that when the users of funds are shielded from the pressures of financial markets, they will prioritise the 'real investment' that generates economic growth and benefits wider society in the process.

Through important aims, this chapter will examine the significant issues that accompany the definancialisation agenda. It will explore how the rentier reading of financial power overlooks the way that the users of funds can be empowered by their capacity to borrow. Far from being the passive recipients of the agendas of their financiers, many institutions have developed strategies to use the stable provision of funds to leverage up, capture assets from others, inflate asset prices, and collect great returns in the process. I suggest that leverage is a crucial lens through which to read the power of finance today and should feature more centrally in a definancialisation programme.

To do so, the chapter focuses specifically on the financialisation of non-financial companies (NFCs). Though indebted states and financial companies have also acquired significant power through their capacity for leverage (see Beck et al., 2022, this volume), the transformation of NFCs is considered one of the central planks of financialisation (van der Zwan, 2014: 100; Stockhammer et al., 2021: 3; Mohamed, 2020: 439) and is a primary issue definancialisation seeks to tackle. In particular, I challenge the common depiction that financial markets act as an exogenous, structural force on corporations, forcing a 'shareholder primacy' that extracts an ever-greater rentier share to the wealth holders. Instead, I show that the institutional history of the financialisation of NFCs demonstrates that leveraged strategies developed endogenously from these NFCs executives themselves. They innovated ways to leverage, capture assets, and inflate the price of their assets, instrumentalising shareholder and creditor resources for this purpose. In contrast to a parasitic extraction of value (which rentiership implies), I argue leveraged NFCs are part of an institutional process that systematically both dispossesses others and also inflates asset values. Crucial is the infrastructure of valuation that has empowered leveraged firms and relies on reinforcing the 'speculative' outlook definancialisation seeks to overcome.

The concept of leverage is a particularly useful vantage point to consider financial power and definancialisation today, because firms now operate in an environment of abundant financial resources. Many large corporations borrow vast sums very cheaply, and the threat of a sudden financial scarcity is somewhat neutered (Dutta, 2018; Braun, 2021). Yet still this has not revived 'productive investment' and 'real economic growth'. Moreover, by seeking to provide stable sources of patient funds, definancialisation reforms could risk playing into the hands of leveraged NFCs and the executives that they so greatly enrich. As Magdoff and Sweezy (1987: 149 cited in Copley, 2022: 8) have put it, 'there is no reason whatever to assume that if you could deflate the financial structure, the talent and energy now employed there would move into productive pursuits.'

As this chapter explores, the financialisation of the firm did not come from financial markets imposing terms on borrower companies but developed endogenously from NFCs themselves. As a result, definancialisation strategies must develop a politics based on countering powerful firms' sources of leverage, rather than trying to undo the rentier disruption to the supposed idyll of productive investment and economy-wide growth.

The chapter begins by examining the changing ways that critical political economy literature has tried to conceptualise financial power and how it privileges the notion of rentiership. It then provides a sympathetic critique founded in an alternative conception of leverage. It will then provide a short overview of the history of the financialisation of the firm, and outline how strategies for leverage remain central to many NFCs today. Finally, it sketches out an alternative definancialisation programme predicated less on countering rentiership and more on confronting leverage.

Rentiership or leverage? Structural power in the financialised firm

The financialisation of the firm is commonly characterised as a shift to 'shareholder primacy' in which corporate strategy was repurposed to maximise returns for rentier shareholders. By such accounts (e.g. Krier, 2005; Lazonick and O'Sullivan, 2000; Mazzucato, 2018), the collapse in corporate profitability in the 1970s, combined with the concentration of share ownership in professional institutional investors, and an ideological assault against manager-led capitalism, to produce a shareholder revolution that disciplined NFC executives. Financial capitalists were able to use their position as the gatekeepers of financial resources on capital markets to wrestle control from managers. That is, financial capitalists had a structural power, exercised indirectly through capital markets, that shaped the conditions and preferences of NFC executives. Shareholders and creditors did not need a direct line or social connection to the executives of the firms in which they invested, because the simple threat that they could use liberalised capital markets to easily take their money elsewhere was enough for NFC executives to reorient corporate governance in their favour.

Despite the ubiquity of this perspective, the actual legacy of the shareholder revolution is more ambiguous. As van der Zwan notes (2014: 109), it has been paradoxical, because the very thing supposed to limit and discipline executives, shareholder primacy, instead coincided with an explosion of executive pay and political unrest about the outsized power of corporate elites (Linsi et al., 2021). While shareholders and creditors have indeed gained from financialisation, to do so they were enrolled into a dynamic where their own returns became irrevocably entwined with the strategies and objectives of those to whom they lent and invested.

Though the literature recognises this paradoxical legacy, I argue it focuses overwhelmingly on the side of shareholders and investors – the providers of funds – rather than the users. In most accounts (Braun, 2020; Mazzucato, 2018; Palladino, 2021), the turn to financialised corporate strategies is depicted as the outcome of the growth of the power of rentier investors and lenders vis-á-vis borrower NFCs, and the acceptance of NFC executives of that external discipline.

Though rentier power is one form of financial power, there are others (see Introduction) which, when overlooked, risks a misconception of the politics of definancialisation – in particular, the extraordinary power of some NFC executives to leverage their assets and drive liquidity in their favour. Moreover, when executive remuneration depends on high share prices, this liquidity is often channelled into share buybacks, whose high value in turn provides a basis for further leveraging in a recursive process. The way this empowers the users of financial funds is too easily occluded by a focus on rentiership and overlooked in programmes of definancialisation as a result. My central claim, therefore, is that our understanding of financial power may be advanced by paying more attention to the institutional basis and technical underpinning of the production of leverage, rather than an abstracted focus on the potential power of exogenous rentiers.

The relative inattention to the institutions and practices that underpin the power of leverage in the financialised firm is evident in the way key authors have depicted the history of the financialisation of NFCs. Lazonick and O'Sullivan (2000), Fligstein (2002), and Mazzucato (2018), for example, all focus on the 1980s and the wave of corporate takeovers as the key moment of transformation. Though many mention earlier developments in the 1960s, their focus on the exogenous force of financial markets means they centre the 'shareholder revolution' of the 1980s and the role played by corporate raiders and hostile takeovers. These, alongside the attendant ideological charge led by Milton Friedman (1970) and then Fama and Jensen's (1983) development of Agency Theory, are all thought to have established an active 'market for corporate control' that empowered exogenous rentiers to use capital markets to impose terms on the firms they financed. Lazonick and O'Sullivan (2000) see shareholder power emerging through the concentration of equity ownership within institutional investors, while Mazzucato (2018), among others, focuses on regulatory and ideological shifts that made trading equity and launching takeovers more possible, which thereby shaped the external conditions within which firms operated and the choices executives faced. In these accounts, the rise of rentier domination in corporate governance is depicted as a process of disembedding finance markets from institutional, regulatory, and ideological constraints. With such obstacles removed through the 1980s, rentiers were able to assert their dominance over corporate executives, and shareholder primacy was the result.

Yet on conceptual and empirical grounds, this perspective is questionable. Conceptually, it is a view that risks overplaying the capacity of financial rentiers to share a common interest, understand this interest, and clearly articulate and achieve what is in their interests.

More importantly, empirically, it also underplays how corporate insiders – the executives thought to bear the brunt of the shareholder revolution and rentier power – became key protagonists in the financialisation of the firm. As I will demonstrate in the next section, the history of the financialisation of the firm is characterised by NFC executives instrumentalising shareholder and creditor resources for their own leveraged strategies, greatly enriching themselves in the process. Rather than seeing this as a development imposed by financial markets from 'the outside in', we should see how it developed by NFCs from 'the inside out' (see Konings, 2007).

This is especially true today when 'scarcity' of financial capital does not always appear to be a decisive threat, especially for large corporations. While in the 1980s interest rates were high and financial capital harder to come by, now financial resources (for some) appear almost limitless. The world economy is still characterised by historically low interest rates and a great abundance of funds searching for yield. The result is that corporate debt has increased greatly in the last few decades, and large firms now borrow very cheaply (Abraham et al., 2020). Moreover, firms tend to finance investment from retained earnings rather than borrowing anyway (Auvray et al., 2021: 4). All of this means the threat of a sudden scarcity of financial resources, which is the supposed basis of shareholder empowerment, appears neutered (Braun, 2021). In sum, by treating the financialisation of the firm as a consequence of exogenous financiers imposing their will, these accounts cannot make clear sense of the way these providers of funds have in fact been instrumentalised more than empowered under financialisation.

These issues have led an alternative, new strand of literature to emerge in response. It argues that to understand financial power today we need to update the conception of rentier power in recognition that the era of shareholder capitalism has given way to what they describe as 'asset manager capitalism' (Braun, 2020, 2021; Braun and Buller, 2021). In this, financial power derives not from the capacity to withdraw funds and create a scarcity crisis but from the ubiquity of asset managers as universal owners. These specialist intermediary firms, like BlackRock, form a kind of 'shareholder superpower' that deploy vast quantities of 'other people's money' to become near universal owners, controlling major stakes in every firm, asset class, industry, and geography of the global economy (Braun and Buller, 2021). With diverse portfolios, asset management firms passively track stock market indexes, rather than actively 'picking' stocks they favour, and are empowered by their status both as financial intermediaries into whom people invest and as shareholder owners. Generally, it is the latter that the literature focuses on. Asset managers are less interested in extracting higher returns from any one particular company, and more in a generalised extraction of resources in aggregate, and creating a generalised inflation of asset prices in total (ibid).

This perspective is better attuned to the ambiguous legacy of shareholder primacy because it demonstrates how NFC executives, asset managers, and everyday investors are all bound up with a shared material interest in rising asset prices. Nonetheless, when it comes to depicting the significance of the shift to asset manager capitalism, and the politics of this new financial power, the analytical focus again lies on rentier ownership. This literature depicts asset managers as financial capitalists who use capital markets to exert an external force on corporate executives, driving corporate strategy towards the maximisation of equity and asset prices. The focus is less on the capacity of asset managers to instrumentalise other people's financial resources, and an examination of how they source funds, and more on how their ownership status gives them a privileged position to extract gains and direct capitalism 'in general' to their own ends (see Christophers, 2019). Asset managers are depicted as representative of the unified general interest of rentiers who, as pecuniary *owners* of wealth, enforce the general escalation of asset prices.

In that sense, finance capitalists are still exercising a structural power that influences the conditions in which NFC executives make decisions, but do so less by the threat of scarcity and more by their ubiquitous presence as owners. This is thought to explain why asset manager fees, shareholder pay-outs, and executive pay are as high as they have ever been. The focus on the pecuniary power of rentier ownership is shared with the more traditional accounts of financialisation, but draws more deeply on the German tradition of financial power analysis characterised by Rudolph Hilferding (Hilferding, 2019 [1919]). For Hilferding, it was the direct presence of bankers on corporate boards that empowered 'financial capital', whereas today asset managers try to secure their fee incomed by ensuring asset prices remain high, and corporate strategy gets skewed to that end as a result.

As such, the literature on asset manager capitalism still depicts the financialisation of the firm as a transformation led exogenously by financial institutions using financial markets to impose their interests on NFCs, rather than the other way round. For that reason, this literature does not provide a concrete answer to the question of why asset managers have so rarely used their ownership stakes, and their elevated status as voting shareholders, to exercise their strong 'voice' in corporate governance in a way that counters existing NFC strategies, and why they have been so easily enrolled into the financialised projects these managers have undertaken.

To specify how financial power works today, it is instead worth examining how some economic actors, especially some NFCs, establish themselves as central to the development of what became the era of financialisation. From this perspective, creditors, shareholders, and financialised NFCs themselves have helped constitute new avenues for accumulation based on the issuance, enforcement, and inflation of forward looking claims on value. The escalating volume and prices of financial assets, from which asset managers profit, was itself a consequence of the growing ability of corporations to sell their debt, and this has a basis in qualitatively new financial techniques, valuation practices, and investor relations, all of which any programme of definancialisation must confront.

Rethinking financialisation of the firm through the power of leverage

In rentier accounts of financial structural power, it is sometimes difficult to articulate clearly how some corporate executives have been empowered through financialisation. There is often no clear account of the *internal* connections between capital markets and the changing way NFCs, as users of funds, organise and develop their strategies. It is not that literature fails to take into account the mutual interaction between NFCs and financial markets, but rather that many accounts do not sufficiently emphasize the constitutive, transformative impact of some NFCs on the very nature and operation of those capital markets. Thus, I draw on emerging work about the power of leverage to conceptualise how shareholders and creditors get used under financialisation. This literature on the 'power of leverage' does not juxtapose creditors against debtors but instead looks at the power relation between different classes of debtors (see Introduction; Sgambati, 2022; Konings, 2018; Knafo, 2020; Baines and Hager, 2021). Sgambati (2019), whose analysis of leverage in banking has done much to develop the concept, has a useful schema for understanding differences between classes of debtors. There is conventional debt – borrowing to make basic payments – and there is leverage – which entails borrowing to acquire assets with the aim of future profits. Within this, financial power does not stem from straightforward ownership claims and rentiership but entails a more expansive notion of binding others to your own financial success, and in doing so, sourcing funds in a way that actively shapes market outcomes. This applies as much to some NFCs and states as it does to banks and other financial firms.

Examining the power of leverage entails analysing how some borrowers construct, gear, and game financial markets for their own gain. In contrast to rentier accounts of financial power which analyse from the outside-in how externalised financial markets impinge and impose terms on borrower firms, this chapter suggests that a more institution-based 'inside-out' analysis can help conceptualise how the leveraged firm and the dynamics and strategies generated within it have shaped financialisation in the first place.

This establishes a basis for fundamentally rethinking the political project of definancialisation. The rentier conception of financial power puts the focus onto financial market liberalisation as the fundamental shift of the basic structure of the economy to favour the financial sector (Oatley and Petrova, 2020). The definancialisation programme that follows is about regulatory change and ownership reform to take assets outside the sphere of influence of financial markets so as to free the users of funds from the pressure those markets impose and revive the basis for productive investment.

By contrast, an analysis that begins from the power of leverage depicts the politics of definancialisation differently. Those borrowers able to source finance and pull liquidity in their favour have significant power, while it is those locked out of leverage and unable to 'bind the fate of others into their own financial fortunes' that need political support (Konings, 2018). It might be that political projects that *support* leverage for some and demand significant *deleveraging* for others is preferable to a project of definancialisation that is predicated on the idea that it is possible to dissolve distributional struggle by returning to real investment and growth.

To develop the insights of the literature on leverage power, the next section explores how it was central to the rise of the financialised firm in 1960s America and how leverage power remains central to financialised firms today.

The growth of leveraged corporate power

The period from the end of the Second World War to the 1980s 'shareholder revolution' is usually described as an era of Chandlerian 'managerial capitalism' that belonged to the broader postwar Golden Era of embedded liberalism and 'productive' capitalism (Chandler, 1977). The period was characterised by an inactive and dispersed market for corporate equity and, as a result, an absence of any dynamic 'market for corporate control' that could threaten corporate executives (Jensen and Ruback, 1983). According to most accounts, that changed when the generalised crisis of profitability combined with a concentration of share ownership among professional institutional investors and the rise of agency theory. The consequence was that company managers were forced to shift course, ending the managerial era of corporate capitalism and unleashing shareholder capitalism and the structural power of rentier financiers.

In recent times, as ownership has concentrated even further into asset manager companies that deal on behalf of pension and insurance funds, this dynamic has shifted once more, intensifying the looming and inescapable presence of dominant 'owners' whose ownership rights allow profits to be extracted from the companies they lend and invest into.

As I have argued in the previous section, the nature and operation of financial power can only be fully understood if we delve into aspects of the financialised firm that have received comparatively less attention, namely how companies use shareholder and creditor resources as a basis to leverage and profit. This is predicated on their capacity to source and capture funds and assets from others, which then form the basis for further borrowing in a recursive cycle. It is a financial power forged more in the capacity to borrow than it is the traditional capacity to lend. The following section will present an 'inside-out' interpretation of this financial power looking at how leveraged firms have been central to the construction of financialised conditions today.

The emergence of the financialised firm and the turn to 'shareholder primacy'

The turn to distinctly financialised forms of corporate management began with the conglomerate firms in corporate America in the 1960s. As Knafo and Dutta (2016, 2019) have described, these firms, like Litton Industries, Teledyne, and LTV, developed a business strategy predicated on leverage. They created mechanisms for turning promises about future performance – articulated in terms of rising share prices – into current capital which they could use to capture and inflate assets. The gambit was a virtuous cycle of growth financed by issuing debt securities backed by high-value assets. Their acquisitive strategy was targeted particularly on firms whose assets would be favoured on financial markets (rather than any productive synergies), as these would then form the basis for further leverage. The conglomerates were distinctive in how they took on great quantities of debt to back this strategy. Partly as a result, they then engaged in balance sheet, accounting, and tax manipulation that helped sustain the impression of good financial health and attract further lending. The 'narrative' of performing on behalf of shareholders became important during this period, with firms coming up with new valuation practices like 'Earnings per Share' (EPS) and new accounting practices like 'pooling', which would then inflate EPS by treating the costs of acquired assets at market value rather than the actual cost paid (which was often far higher) (Grieman, 1970).

For a while this was a staggeringly successful model, driving a wave of takeovers in corporate America in the late 1960s that saw smaller firms leveraging up to take on and acquire bigger firms for the first time. But the precarious practice of borrowing for acquisition and relying on the bull market to make debt payments sustainable was always vulnerable to any generalised turn in equity markets. This is precisely what happened when the bear market of the 1970s toppled many of the most leveraged conglomerate firms.

What can be seen in this is how practices that emerged in notionally *non*-financial corporations could transform how financial markets operated. The conglomerates instrumentalised creditor and shareholder resources for their own ends and helped construct an environment where equity prices especially *had* to continue an upwards escalation. Far from finance imposing terms from the outside in, this was a more complex and co-constitutive turn. The rapid rise and sudden demise of the conglomerates like Litton Industries made corporate executives especially aware of their standings on financial markets.

The leveraged strategy they pioneered was then taken up by the 1980s corporate raiders. The raiders, who occupy such a central position in much of the literature on the shareholder revolution (e.g. Dobbin and Zorn, 2005; Fourcade and Khurana, 2017), organised themselves through leverage. Indeed, the leveraged buy-out was popularised by them, tapping pension and insurance funds to finance takeovers and gain control of well-established corporations. The purpose was to then dispossess and asset strip, but crucially they were reliant on just the same dynamics of inflating equity and asset prices to make their strategy successful. In this 'shareholders' were useful functionaries, whose importance was talked up but rarely actually empowered. It was, rather, the professional leveragers – the raiders – who took control.

The rhetoric of 'shareholder primacy' and 'maximising shareholder value' was a tool in this power play. Though leveraged-up executives spoke about delivering on behalf of the true 'owners' of capital, their leveraged strategies often put shareholders resources at great risk – something that we still see today. Through this, the interests of shareholders were fused to the interests of the leveraged firm executives. There is a lot of literature that now focuses on how insider managers are aligned to shareholders through share options, as part of the paradoxical legacy of the shareholder value maximisation, but it is important to see how that happened. Share options was an old idea developed by management consultants like McKinsey in the 1950s to try and boost top-manager pay (Bhidé, 1995) and was then relaunched by the raiders like Carl Ichan and Michael Milken in the context of the supposed 'shareholder revolution'. Share options were more effectively a way to ensure the gains made through leverage and inflating equity prices could be captured by top-level managers than they were a way to discipline executives. The fact that since 1990 CEO pay has rocketed, creating what Piketty (2014: 331) has described as a new class of 'supermanagers', is testament to this. Similarly, the new metrics that emerged, like 'Economic Value Added', which are often depicted as symptomatic of the rentier power of exogenous shareholders, in fact came the other way round. Financialised executives, playing leverage, developed these tools to help better understand and tap into financial markets.

This is a necessarily potted and partial history but lays out some of the qualitative and institutional developments that propelled the shift from managerial capitalism to the supposed 'shareholder' capitalism and what came to be known as the financialisation of the firm. Accounting for this construction provides a different perspective on the power of finance, demonstrating the co-construction of large borrowing and asset price inflation. If the power of leverage is the capacity to use debt to bind others to your own financial fortunes, then a good route to understanding this power within the firm is an examination of the practices that bind shareholders, workers, and customers to the interests of leveraged-up executives.

Zombie companies and the inflation of assets

The corporate landscape that was transformed by the conglomerates, and again by the raiders, has helped drive the increase in market capitalisation since the 1960s and the vast increase in corporate debt that has marked the last few decades. Ever since the 2008 financial crisis, the value of corporate debt has only continued to climb. US investment-grade non-financial corporate bonds grew from approximately \$1.5 trillion in 2008 to \$4.5 trillion by the end of 2018, while in the UK, listed company debt reached a record £443.2 billion by the end of 2018 (Davies et al., 2022: 54). In Europe and emerging markets debt issuance has followed a similar trajectory. The bonanza of cheap liquidity orchestrated by governments and central banks through the Covid-19 pandemic has only further entrenched this indebtedness. Throughout, money returned to shareholders has grown in step. Discretionary cash flow returned to UK shareholders increased from just over 25 per cent in 1987 to almost 50 per cent in 2014 (Blakeley, 2019: 78), while by 2018, total shareholder pay-outs among FTSE 100 companies was over 100 per cent of net profits, compared with 43 per cent in 2011 (Lawrence et al., 2020: 9). Eurostoxx 600 firms distributed 72 per cent of their net income to shareholders between 2010 and 2018, and S&P 500 firms distributed 87 per cent of net income between 2009 and 2019 (Baker et al., 2020: 1). The peculiar situation of firms returning more to shareholders than they make in net profits, and borrowing on capital markets in order to do so, could be taken as a sign of the rentier constraint the shareholders and investors impose on firms: even in the contemporary conditions of financial abundance, with the threat of exit neutered by the radically diversified portfolios of asset manager capitalism, it is as if wealth holders were dictating terms and extracting a 'rent' from these large companies.

Yet by following the trajectory of leverage power from the conglomerates, through to the raiders, and again today, an alternative account emerges. As Baker et al. (2020) described, there are today many 'hollow firms' that are fundamentally pro-cyclical, drawing credit and investment to reorganise their balance sheets in ever-more risky strategies founded on the optimistic promises of forward-looking claims, bringing income forward and pushing costs back. They are, simply, undertaking strategies of leverage. Rather than build up capital buffers and make their firms more resilient, large corporations have 'run their balance sheet hot', borrowing from banks and capital markets to finance mergers, acquisitions and Intellectual Property purchases, while drawing on creative valuation strategies to best raise payouts to shareholders and keep share prices high.

This work of inflating asset values is different from simply extracting a greater share of output. The 'forward-looking', inflationary nature of their strategies means leveraged power also involves the infrastructural power of valuation practices (Birch and Muniesa, 2020).

As Baines and Hager demonstrated (2021), the biggest and most leveraged firms have turned away from capital investment. Instead, their debts are loaded onto ever thinner portfolios of tangible assets, with promises about future cash flow being secured onto the balance sheet as generous valuations of intangible 'goodwill'. This capacity to manipulate balance sheets, push impairment costs into the future, and – in effect – securitise future cash flow through raising debt demonstrates how leveraged NFCs are helping to construct the conditions of financial abundance within which they operate. The pro-cyclical dynamic witnessed in the conglomerates is again seen here and has the unintended effect of forcing wealth holders – rentier owners – onto a shared terrain and material interest of leveraged-up executives.

Surrounding them are the partner institutions pulled into the orbit of the leveraged firms and compelled to sustain asset price growth. In particular, it has developed alongside the growing significance of the consulting arms of the Big Four accountants: KMPG, Price Waterhouse Coopers, Deloitte, and Ernst & Young. These firms advise managers on how best to improve equity prices and defer impairment costs, while at the same time acting as the auditors that sign off the books and certify the good health of these leveraged companies (Leaver and Martin, 2021). Getting a sense of these more grounded aspects of how financialisation plays out can be difficult from more abstracted readings of structural, rentier power. How the big four accounts have become such crucial players in the engine of leverage, for example, is not easily grasped from notions of creditor power. Yet the turn away from 'productive investment' in the highly leveraged firm has empowered new experts in balance sheet manipulation to play decisive roles in corporate strategy.

These institutions and practices, built from borrower firms, have helped construct the conditions of leveraged, financial abundance that characterises the global economy and sustain a situation where there are now many non-financial firms engaged in Ponzi strategies. As BIS researchers demonstrate, creditors have been instrumentalised by these 'zombie firms', companies that cannot meet debt service costs by profit alone and instead rely on rolling over debt and manipulating their balance sheets. BIS analysis showed that these zombies occupied 2 per cent of all listed NFCs in OECD economies in 1980 and 12 per cent by 2016 (Banerjee and Hofmann, 2018: 70). A high and growing share price is important less for extractive owners than it is to keep cash flow from other lenders streaming in and drawing on the infrastructural power of auditors, accountants, and consultants to help inflate asset prices and keep the cycle of leverage turning.

In this light, the power of finance that programmes of definancialisation seek to overcome is not simply that of the pecuniary rentier but more broadly the power of leverage and the infrastructure mobilised to inflate asset prices.

Beyond ownership: resisting financial power in the age of leverage

Advocates of definancialisation have a welcome goal – the wish to put finance back in its box or, as many put it, make finance the servant of society and not the master of all. The result would be to resurrect the postwar order where manufacturing flourished, jobs were secure, and a growing economy could deliver higher individual and social wages and for the majority of society.[1]

In more prosaic terms, a better financial sector would fulfil its proper purpose as a judicious allocator of capital, channelling savings to productive investment, and thereby growing the economy as a whole. In that way, the macroeconomics of definancialisation is often boilerplate Keynesianism, but it rests on a critical political economy reading of the structural power of rentier owners. Owners – of corporate equity or loanable funds – are able to claim an ever-larger share of output. In this reading, the brutal inequalities of our age are the symptom of the sheer concentration of ownership in today's global political economy (though what has generated that wealth inequality is often cast as exogenous). The claims of owners are then protected, enforced, and reinforced by a legal infrastructure that puts owners ahead of all other stakeholders in society (see Pistor 2022, this volume). Within this, the financial sector works to multiply the claims of owners, protecting and projecting them well into the future and across an ever-wider range of society. Rentiership through ownership and control is – ultimately – a form of accumulation by dispossession, either from the state, from other societies, or the future more broadly. In doing so, rentiers sabotage the proper functioning of the economy and society.

For many critics, this situation is unsustainable. In particular, by eroding the productive basis to which financial claims are notionally attached, rentiers are 'living on borrowed time'. By favouring 'speculative' claims over 'real' productive investment, financialisation has transformed capitalism into an elaborate bubble that can only continue while government and legal authority supports this accumulation through 'jurido-political channels' (Zacarés, 2021: 49).

While the critiques of rentiership, dispossession, and stagnation are urgent and necessary, they risk occluding the power of leverage and the institutions and technologies of valuation that have developed to empower those best able to borrow.

Rather than a fixed 'common pool' of assets from which rentiers are using their legal status as owners and lenders to extract an ever-greater share, the emerging mode of accumulation involves a political economic programme of sustained asset-price inflation that provides highly leveraged borrowers the basis to keep borrowing, strip favoured assets from others, drive up their book value, leverage further, and capture handsome returns for themselves throughout. It is accumulation by inflation, more than it is accumulation solely by law or dispossession.

When financial power is conceptualised in terms of the capacity for generating leverage, rather than the condition of rentiership, the programme for definancialisation changes too. It must extend beyond regulatory and ownership reform to instead work to counter the basis of leverage for some while enhancing it for others.

This chapter has demonstrated how shareholder resources are instrumentalised by leveraged firms to reinforce their financialised strategies and lock in gains for insiders. The majority are excluded from all but expensive consumer borrowing, while a small but significant 'middle class' leverage to buy houses and participate in the asset economy (Adkins et al., 2020). A still smaller stratum saves through their pension and insurance funds, which in turn put their resources into the hands of the asset managers. At each node of the wealth chain the 'dealers in other people's money' are leveraging up to make gains for themselves and bind the material well-being of others to the financial fortunes of themselves. Banks and financial institutions of course do this, but so do financialised, highly leveraged companies.

This presents a challenge for definancialisation advocates that focus on ownership reform as the key step to counter financial power. For example, Thomas Hanna, of the US-based Democracy Collaborative, describes how 'public ownership would convert the rent-seeking concentrations of private financial power into public utilities that work for the common good' (2018: 45). In a similar vein, 'nationalised' asset managers have been advocated as aiding a definancialisation programme by shielding businesses from the short-termist rhythms of finance and allowing for patient investment and real growth. MacFarlane and Gasperin (2020), for example, suggest that a state-owned holding company can 'promote long-term structural transformation and wider public policy objectives' in a way that general shareholders on exogenous financial markets could not. Similarly, there are many who advocate spreading share ownership more widely in society as a means at least to distribute the gains made by stock market inflation and tackling wealth-based inequality.

These are important steps and a necessary part of at least facilitating some redistribution of societal resources. Yet they leave the power of the big leveragers intact and indeed could risk reinforcing the problem. The more stable and predictable creditor and shareholder resources are – and the more people are enrolled into asset price inflation – the easier it is for the large leveragers to source the assets for leveraged growth. Firms that can rely on patient and stable investment from a national investment bank will have a strong basis for then crowding-in private sector finance. Indeed, in some accounts about the boons of national investment banks, that is precisely the point. A politics directed against 'shareholder primacy' and portraying borrower executives as in need of shielding from external rentier financiers risks underestimating how it is in fact the opposite that is often true. Similarly, government contracts involved in the production of nationally owned goods and services often provide the perfect collateral for leveraged firms to issue forward-looking claims and enrich insider managers. The public services industry is plagued by companies, like the now-defunct Carillion, which used their procurement contracts with government to leverage up, outsource, and profit. The regimes of valuation involved unrealistic cost estimations when bidding for contracts, and optimistic income projections, undergirded by accounting and auditing practices that inflated assets so as to allow for further borrowing. Executive insiders gained hugely, as did satellite services of leverage, like the consultants and accountants who advised them, while workers, creditors, government, and taxpayers were fleeced (Wylie, 2020).

Financialised capitalism works on sourcing assets from others, inflating, and leveraging in a recursive cycle. It is why Marois (2021: 154) is correct to say 'there is nothing inherent to public financial institutions making them function in a way that definancialises economies and societies'. Whether the experience of UK-nationally owned Royal Bank of Scotland or the pro-cyclical Sovereign Wealth Funds of Norway or China, 'state capitalism' is as much enrolled into dynamics of financialisation as anything else (Alami and Dixon, 2020).

Yet Marois (2021: 155 original emphasis) also points out there is at least 'the *potential* for society to make them function in definancialising ways [that] slow financial flows channel funds to public goods, prioritise public mandates over profits'. The ambiguity rests on the fact that the rentier power that stems from ownership is not the sole problem. Definancialisation must also confront the differing capacity for leverage and the practices, institutions, and infrastructural power of valuation that embed these differences. This would entail a programme to try and curtail the credit and shareholder equity available to leveraged firms, but also to politicise the institutions like the consultants, auditors, and accounting standards, which help to inflate asset values and provide a basis for leverage.

This would work alongside the existing moves to politicise central bank collateral frameworks and asset purchase programmes. The prices of financial assets included into these central bank interventions are sustained at a higher level, and yields lowered, and in doing so are part of the infrastructure of valuation that inflates asset prices. The research by Matikainen et al. (2017) has challenged the climate impacts of existing collateral frameworks by showing how central banks have favoured the assets of ecologically damaging companies while excluding other more progressive possible alternatives.

Taylor (2022), meanwhile, has examined the very construction of ecological risk valuations and how these inflate 'grey' assets while undervaluing 'green' concerns. His investigation of the construction of actuarial risk has shown the difficulties professional actuaries have had trying to establish climate-related risk as part of their professional jurisdiction. Doing so would allow those risks to make their way into valuations of the financial assets of climate-breaking companies. Yet the relationship of the models of risk management the actuaries currently use are drawn from financial economics, which does not adequately value climate risk into its assumptions. The result is actuaries are fundamentally failing to account for and quantify climate risks in their financial valuation assessments. The effect of course is to construct financial asset prices in a way harmful to societal well-being. The assets of climate-damaging companies are inflated, which by comparison undervalues more sustainable alternatives, locking them out of greater leverage.

Any potential nationally owned asset manager that still operates from the same risk and valuation frameworks as private ones will be undermined in their capacity to challenge financialised outcomes. The infrastructural power of capital market intermediaries is in that sense a crucially important obstacle to the success of any potential definancialisation programme.

This insight could be extended to a broader effort to help de-leverage the debts of the richest, while working to open up debt resources and shift valuation practices in favour of the sectors and firms and models of sustainability currently undervalued and locked out of financial abundance (see Davies et al., 2022). These principles differ fundamentally from the definancialisation programme alluded to in academic and civil society literature. The idea is not to systematically de-leverage so that the real economy investment gets prioritised, and postwar-style economic growth somehow revived. Instead, it is about recognising that leverage and the liquidity that allows leveraged actors to meet the survival constraint are constructed through truly *political* economic means. The valuation process that imbues financial assets with high prices provides the basis for leverage power that then enrols broader society in the most heavily indebted forward-looking economic projects. The consequence is that today asset prices do not have a straightforward relation to the real economy to which they are supposedly founded upon. They are instead heavily mediated by the institutions and practices of valuation, which include state action, that work to construct prices. The Federal Reserve's multitrillion dollar holding of agency mortgage-backed securities, alongside its vast purchase of high-yield risky debt-distressed company assets during the teeth of the Covid-19 emergency, demonstrates the political capacity the leveraged financialised economy creates to sustain asset values independently of real economy conditions. Simply, when institutional heft is put behind some debtors, there is no demonstrable limit on their capacity to survive. The lesson to be gleaned from the era of financialisation – and the power it has granted the biggest debtors – is the true elasticity this involves.

Any counter-project to financialisation would properly need to specify the coordinates of this power and politicise it in ways that ask why liquidity is not extended to the provision of social infrastructure in the way it is more destructive to economic entities. This pulls the analysis out of the realm of ownership reform into something as politically difficult and technically complex. Yet that is precisely what might be necessary.

Conclusion

Financialisation has been a process that has unevenly and in a myriad of ways rewritten the rules of reproduction in the global political economy and altered the basis upon which profits are captured and costs assigned. The inequities and exploitations involved are profound and deeply institutionally embedded. Rather than a regulatory fix or even ownership transformation that simply 'reverses' this history and de-financialises the economy, counter-political programmes need to work from these new rules of leverage power and politicise the valuation processes that sustain it. This necessitates an analysis of financial power that goes beyond the focus on and instead examines how some can enrol other people's capital for strategies of their own enrichment.

This chapter has focused on non-financial companies, but the capacity for leverage has empowered financial institutions, none more so than banks, and indeed some of the largest and most indebted nations. There is significant promise in the emerging literature on leverage, which could benefit from further engagement with the scholarship on valuation and the infrastructural power of the institutions involved.

This is work that is yet to feed into the social movements and political programmes associated with definancialisation. The normative hold of the postwar years of productive, managerial capitalism is still too strong an anchor, and it ends up fuelling an analysis too centred on the restoration of economic growth. A social movement capable of tackling the power of creditors and shareholders must necessarily also take aim at the highly leveraged firms and be accompanied by a technical movement that can build an infrastructure of alternative valuations.

Note

1 That the 'Golden Age' was also built on the exclusion and exploitation of racialised and gendered workers, and colonial extraction, is all too easily overlooked.

References

Abraham F, Cortina JJ and Schmukler SL (2020) *Growth of Global Corporate Debt: Main Facts and Policy Challenges* (Working Paper, September). Washington, DC: World Bank.

Adkins L, Cooper M and Konings M (2020) *Asset Economy*. Cambridge: Polity Press.

Alami I and Dixon AD (2020) State capitalism(s) redux? Theories, tensions, controversies. *Competition & Change* 24(1): 70–94.

Auvray T, Durand C, Rabinovich J, et al. (2021) Corporate financialization's conservation and transformation: From Mark I to Mark II. *Review of Evolutionary Political Economy* 2: 431–457.

Baines J and Hager SB (2021) The great debt divergence and its implications for the covid-19 crisis: Mapping corporate leverage as power. *New Political Economy* 26(5): 885–901.

Baker A, Haslam C, Leaver A, et al. (2020) *Against Hollow Firms: Repurposing the Corporation for a More Resilient Economy*. Centre for Research on Accounting and Finance in Context (CRAFiC).

Ban C and Bohle D (2021) Definancialization, financial repression and policy continuity in East-Central Europe. *Review of International Political Economy* 28(4): 874–897.
Banerjee RN and Hofmann B (2018) The rise of zombie firms: Causes and consequences. Available at: www.bis.org/publ/qtrpdf/r_qt1809g.htm (accessed 9 July 2020).
Beck M, Knafo S and Sgambatti S (2022) Leveraging financial claims: Transatlantic bank struggles and the power of US finance. In: Braun B and Koddenbrock K (eds) *Capital Claims: The Political Economy of Global Finance*. London: Routledge, pp. 33–49.
Bhidé A (1995) *Building the Professional Firm: McKinsey & Co.: 1939–1968*. Boston: Harvard Business School General Management Unit Working Paper (95–010).
Birch K and Muniesa F (eds) (2020) *Assetization: Turning Things into Assets in Technoscientific Capitalism. Inside Technology*. Cambridge, MA and London: The MIT Press.
Blakeley G (2019) *Stolen: How to Save the World from Financialisation*. New edition. London: Repeater Books.
Braun B (2020) Asset manager capitalism as a corporate governance regime. *The American Political Economy: Politics, Markets, and Power* 270.
Braun B (2021) Exit, control, and politics: The structural power of finance under asset manager capitalism. *SocArXiv*. October 12, 2021 doi:10.31235/osf.io/4uesc.
Braun B and Buller A (2021) Titans. *Phenomenal World*, 6 November. Available at: www.phenomenalworld.org/analysis/blackrock-asset-manager-capitalism/ (accessed 6 December 2021).
Chandler AD (1977) *The Visible Hand: The Managerial Revolution in American Business*. 16 print. Cambridge, MA: Belknap Press of Harvard University Press.
Christophers B (2019) How financial giants might come to rule us all. *Jacobin*, 18 June. Available at: https://jacobinmag.com/2019/06/blackrock-fairburn-finance-wall-street-vanguard (accessed 13 December 2021).
Copley, J (2022) *Governing Financialization: The Tangled Politics of Financial Liberalization in Britain*. Oxford: Oxford University Press.
Dagdeviren H and Karwowski E (2022) Impasse or mutation? Austerity and (de)financialisation of local governments in Britain. *Journal of Economic Geography* 22(3): 685–707.
Davies W, Dutta S, Taylor N, and Tazzioli M (2022) *Unprecedented?: How Covid-19 revealed the politics of our economy*. London: Goldsmiths Press.
Dobbin F and Zorn D (2005) Corporate malfeasance and the myth of shareholder value. In: *Political Power and Social Theory*. Bradford: Emerald Group Publishing Limited.
Dutta SJ (2018) Servants of industry? Getting financialisation wrong. *New Socialist*, 19 August. Available at: http://newsocialist.org.uk/servants-of-industry/ (accessed 13 December 2021).
Fama EF and Jensen MC (1983) Separation of ownership and control. *Journal of Law and Economics* 26: 301.
Fligstein N (2002) *The Architecture of Markets: An Economic Sociology of Twenty-First-Century Capitalist Societies*. Princeton, NJ: Princeton University Press.
Foroohar R (2016) *Makers and Takers: The Rise of Finance and the Fall of American Business*. New York: Crown Business.
Fourcade M and Khurana R (2017) The social trajectory of a finance professor and the common sense of capital. *History of Political Economy* 49(2): 347–381.
Friedman M (1970) A Friedman doctrine – the social responsibility of business is to increase its profits. *The New York Times*, 13 September. Available at: www.nytimes.com/1970/09/13/archives/a-friedman-doctrine-the-social-responsibility-of-business-is-to.html (accessed 13 December 2021).
Grieman G (1970) Conglomerate mergers. *Notre Dame Law Review* 45(4): 698.

Hanna T (2018) *The Crisis Next Time: Planning for Public Ownership as an Alternative to Corporate Bank Bailouts*. Democracy Collaborative. Available at: https://thenextsystem.org/learn/stories/crisis-next-time-planning-public-ownership-alternative-corporate-bank-bailouts (accessed 6 December 2021).

Hilferding R (2019) *Finance Capital: A Study in the Latest Phase of Capitalist Development*. London: Routledge.

Jensen MC and Ruback RS (1983) The market for corporate control: The scientific evidence. *Journal of Financial Economics* 11(1): 5–50.

Knafo S (2020) Macro-finance and the financialisation of economic policy. *Finance and Society* 6(1): 87–94.

Knafo S and Dutta SJ (2016) Patient capital in the age of financialized managerialism. *Socio-Economic Review* 14(4): 771–788.

Knafo S and Dutta SJ (2019) The myth of the shareholder revolution and the financialization of the firm. *Review of International Political Economy* 1–24.

Konings M (2007) The institutional foundations of US structural power in international finance: From the re-emergence of global finance to the monetarist turn. *Review of International Political Economy* 15(1): 35–61.

Konings M (2018) The logic of leverage: Reflections on post-foundational political economy. *Finance and Society* 4(2): 205–213.

Krier D (2005) *Speculative Management: Stock Market Power and Corporate Change*. Albany, NY: SUNY Press.

Lapavitsas C (2013) *Profiting without Producing: How Finance Exploits Us All*. London, UK: Verso Books.

Lawrence M, Buller A, Baines J, et al. (2020) *Commoning the Company*. Common Wealth. Available at: www.common-wealth.co.uk/reports/commoning-the-company.

Lazonick W and O'Sullivan M (2000) Maximizing shareholder value: A new ideology for corporate governance. *Economy and Society* 29(1): 13–35.

Leaver A and Martin K (2021) 'Dams and flows': Boundary formation and dislocation in the financialised firm. *Review of Evolutionary Political Economy* 2(3): 403–429.

Linsi L, Hopkin J and Jaupart P (2021) Exporting inequality: US investors and the Americanization of executive pay in the United Kingdom. *Review of International Political Economy* 1–27.

Macfarlane L and Gasperin S (2020) State holding companies: An opportunity for economic transformation? *UCL IIPP Blog*. Available at: https://medium.com/iipp-blog/state-holding-companies-an-opportunity-for-economic-transformation-3604093bab87 (accessed 6 August 2020).

Magdoff H and Sweezy PM (1987) *Stagnation and the Financial Explosion*. New York: NYU Press.

Marois T (2021) *Public Banks: Decarbonisation, Definancialisation and Democratisation*. 1st edition. New York: Cambridge University Press.

Matikainen S, Campiglio E and Zenghelis D (2017) The climate impact of quantitative easing. Policy Paper, Grantham Research Institute on Climate Change and the Environment, London School of Economics and Political Science.

Mazzucato M (2014) De-financialising the real economy. *Financial Times Alphaville*. Available at: http://ftalphaville.ft.com/2014/07/22/1904262/de-financialising-the-real-economy/ (accessed 23 April 2020).

Mazzucato M (2018) *The Value of Everything: Making and Taking in the Global Economy*. London: Allen Lane, an Imprint of Penguin Books.

Mohamed S (2020) Anglo-American corporation and corporate restructuring in post-apartheid South Africa. *International Review of Applied Economics* 34(4): 439–455.

Oatley T and Petrova B (2020, April) The global deregulation hypothesis. *Socio-Economic Review* 20(2): 611–633.

Palladino L (2021) Financialization at work: Shareholder primacy and stagnant wages in the United States. *Competition & Change* 25(3–4): 382–400.

Piketty T (2014) *Capital in the Twenty-First Century* (tran. A Goldhammer). Cambridge, MA: Belknap Press.

Pistor K (2022) The rise of autonomous financial power. In: Braun B and Koddenbrock K (eds) *Capital Claims: The Political Economy of Global Finance*. London: Routledge, pp. 251–263.

Sawyer M (2016) Confronting financialisation. In: Arestis P and Sawyer M (eds) *Financial Liberalisation: Past, Present and Future. International Papers in Political Economy*. Cham: Springer International Publishing, pp. 43–85.

Sgambati S (2019) The art of leverage: A study of bank power, money-making and debt finance. *Review of International Political Economy* 26(2): 287–312.

Sgambati S (2022) Who owes? Class struggle, inequality and the political economy of leverage in the twenty-first century. *Finance and Society*, 8 (1), 1–21.

Stockhammer E, Sgambati S and Nesvetailova A (2021) Financialisation: Continuity and change – introduction to the special issue. *Review of Evolutionary Political Economy* 2: 389–401.

Streeck W (2014) *Buying Time: The Delayed Crisis of Democratic Capitalism*. Brooklyn, NY: Verso.

Taylor N (2022) 'Making financial sense of the future': Actuaries and the management of climate-related financial risk. *New Political Economy*. Online first.

van der Zwan N (2014) Making sense of financialization. *Socio-Economic Review* 12(1): 99–129.

Wylie B (2020) *Bandit Capitalism: Carillion and the Corruption of the British State*. Edinburgh: Birlinn Ltd.

Zacarés JM (2021) Euphoria of the rentier? *New Left Review* (129): 47–67.

4

RELATIONAL CLAIMS

Offshore dollar and sovereign debt

Andrea Binder

Introduction

Allegedly, borrowing in a foreign currency constitutes a sovereign's 'original sin' (Eichengreen and Hausmann, 2005). The Latin American debt crises of 1982 and 1994 epitomise the resulting pain: a lost decade of economic growth and the end of the political regimes that had to answer for the dire consequences. Whether the explanation for committing the original sin is seen to lie in the respective sovereign's lack of alternatives (Eichengreen and Hausmann, 2005) or in the shape of domestic institutions (North and Weingast, 1989; Calomiris and Haber, 2014) scholars converge on one point: foreign currency borrowing ties the debtor nation's hand. If external borrowing gets out of control, the government has little leverage to soften the impact through monetary policy. Neither loose rates nor devaluing the currency helps the problem. The foreign banks claim their money back, often assisted by their governments. It is the creditor who sets the terms of renegotiating debt. The borrowing country can either sign off on these terms or default – two options with often calamitous social, political, and economic consequences (see Tomz and Wright, 2013). In that view, power rests with the claimant alone.

As much as this line of argument is intuitive, it overlooks an important phenomenon in international finance: offshore money. Offshore money took its beginnings in the City of London in the Eurodollar markets of the 1950s. British banks began to provide US-dollar-denominated loans against their US dollar deposits. That is, they began creating US dollars in Europe, hence the term 'Eurodollar' (Helleiner, 1994; Schenk, 1998; Altamura, 2017; Ogle, 2017).

Long treated by international political economy scholars as the historical roots of financial globalisation (Helleiner, 1994; Green, 2016; Braun et al., 2020), the Eurodollar system has gained renewed attention in recent years as a contemporary phenomenon of significant importance (Hardie and Thompson, 2020; Tooze,

DOI: 10.4324/9781003218487-5

2018: chapter 3). Since their invention in the 1950s, the offshore money markets have grown and diversified considerably: the short-term currency markets of the 1950s developed into long-term Eurobond, then mid-term Euroloan markets, and from there into contemporary swap and future interest rate derivatives (O'Malley, 2015; Altamura, 2017).

Irrespective of the nature of the financial instrument, the significance of the Eurodollar lies in the 'bifurcation'[1] of currency and jurisdiction. A standard foreign exchange transaction involves the currency and legal system of a foreign country. It allows, say, the Mexican government to borrow US dollar in New York under the jurisdiction of the United States, the US dollars' home country. The Eurodollar, however, allows the Mexican government to borrow US dollar in the City of London, governed by the laws and regulations of the City of London. The cross-border claim is denominated in US dollar, but enforcement is determined by British law.

In this chapter I argue that because of the legal bifurcation of currency and jurisdiction, borrowing in offshore money markets provides sovereign borrowers with *leverage power* in good times and with an ability to *resist enforcement power* in bad.[2] These additional sources of power are not available to the debtor country in the onshore economy, at home, or abroad.

The distinction between good and bad times is an important one when it comes to sovereign debt. Unlike household or corporate debt, sovereign debt cannot be enforced. Consequently, sovereign credit 'entangles', in the words of Pénet and Flores Zendejas (2021: 2), the fate of borrower and lender country. In good times, repayment is automatic, making the interdependence between creditor and debtor neglectable. In bad times, however, the terms of repayment become contested. Creditors employ varying tactics to defend their claims, while sovereign borrowers aim to limit the damage. It is their very existence that is at stake. No party can get out of the dire situation without the other. Interdependence becomes tangible (Pénet and Zendejas, 2021).

In good times, then, offshore credit provides borrowing countries with more access to US dollar liquidity. Better still, the US dollar liquidity comes at better conditions. Offshore borrowing comes with lower interest rates, a lower regulatory burden, and lower tax rates than in either domestic or foreign onshore markets (Black and Munro, 2010; O'Malley, 2015). Offshore finance bestows the borrower with additional *leverage power*.

In bad times, offshore finance can improve the borrower's negotiation position. For onshore claims, the bank that holds the claim, the governing law, and the currency are all of the same foreign nationality. An offshore claim against a borrower, by contrast, can combine banks, governing law, and currency of different jurisdictions. It therefore creates three principal sets of relationships: that between the borrowing sovereign and the banks that hold the claims; that between the borrowing sovereign and the state that sponsors the laws and regulations governing the claim; and that between the borrower and the issuer country of the currency in which the claim is denominated. All three claims relationships can cross different borders. These complex dependencies make it possible for the sovereign borrower to better *resist enforcement power* of creditors.

Yet offshore money alone does not automatically offer the borrower more power as the contrasting experiences of Mexico and Brazil demonstrates. Whether a sovereign can use offshore finance to its advantage depends on, as we shall see, domestic banking institutions and policies (Binder, 2023).

Also, offshore finance does not turn the debtor–creditor relationship upside down. The sources of power that offshore finance affords are not absolute. They are relative to what is available in the onshore economy. Nevertheless, if used strategically, offshore markets provide the borrower with sources of power not available in the onshore economy. Eurodollar borrowing can far outsize US dollar borrowing, as the case of contemporary Brazil demonstrates. Against this background, the chapter suggests revisiting the dominant notion of claims as one-directional power for creditors and move to a relational understanding instead.

The chapter builds its argument based on a historical comparative analysis of Brazil's and Mexico's engagement with the Eurodollar system. Seen from today's perspective, Brazil and Mexico are most different cases. Brazil is the second-largest emerging market borrower in the offshore money markets (McCauley et al., 2015). Mexico has almost no exposure to the offshore dollar (Binder, 2023). Yet, it has not always been like that.

In the late 1970s, Mexico was one of the largest issuers in the Eurodollar markets (Alvarez, 2015; The New York Times, 1976). Combining primary qualitative data from interviews and descriptive statistics with secondary historical data, the chapter traces in a longitudinal analysis Brazilian and Mexican offshore claims and liabilities from their beginnings in the 1960s to today.

After this introduction, the chapter is divided into three sections. The first provides a conceptual analysis of offshore money, especially the Eurodollar, informing the empirical analysis of Brazilian and Mexican offshore claims and liabilities in the second section. The final section interrogates what the conceptual and empirical findings mean for our understanding of power relationships created by claims.

The nature of offshore money

Most political economists have a paradoxical relationship with money. They explicitly dedicate a theory to the international power it bestows while simultaneously subscribing to a neoclassical notion of money that considers money as politically neutral (see Helleiner and Kirshner, 2009; Cohen, 2015; Norrlof, 2017). However, framing money as politically neutral is itself a political project. The roots of that project reach back all the way to England's coin clipping crisis in the late seventeenth century (Eich, 2020). Today, we can fully grasp offshore money's consequences for borrower power only, if we put back the political into the concept of money that informs our analysis.

Money is a social relation between borrower and lender. As any social relation, it has innate political qualities. Its precise nature is codified by law and distributes power between borrower and lender (Pistor, 2019).

This conception of money builds on the thought of Geoffrey Ingham (2004). Key to his theory of the nature of money is that all money is credit because the only way for the government to create money is by going into debt: the issuing of money shows up on a government's balance sheet as a liability. The corresponding asset is registered on the balance sheet of those who hold the government's debt. Money entangles public and private financial actors – the government, its financiers, and taxpayers – via the central bank's balance sheet. Consequently, the notion of sovereign and private debt as separate categories only reflects a snapshot in a constant flow of money between public and private balance sheets. This is especially the case in countries such as Brazil and Mexico, where the government holds considerable stakes in banks and firms.

This notion of money has two implications for the subsequent empirical analysis. First, assessing balance sheets is used as a means to uncover power relationships. Second, bringing together the government, financiers, and taxpayers as the relational core of credit-money, I understand sovereign debt to be the debt accumulated by all sectors of society: the government, financial institutions, non-financial institutions, and households.[3] This understanding is in tension with the neat categories of ultimate debtors/creditors and financial institutions outlined in the introduction to this book (Braun and Koddenbrock, 2022). Framing sovereign debt as accumulated by all sectors of society reflects better the idea of money as a social relation. But it is also due to two empirical realities that make the separate categories of ultimate debtors – governments, firms, and households – and ultimate international creditors – bond holders, international institutions, banks, and foreign governments – obsolete.

First, it is the very purpose of offshore finance to make the ultimate borrower legally and statistically invisible (Sharman, 2010; Zucman, 2015; Pistor, 2019). Often, we do not know who owes how much to whom. Second, these neat categories may exist in good times, yet they collapse in bad. Once default is on the horizon, claims become the subject of 'sovereign debt diplomacies', as Pénet and Flores Zendejas (2021) put it. The negotiation is, ultimately, about how the costs of default are distributed between debtor and creditor countries internationally and between taxpayers and financiers domestically (Calomiris and Haber, 2014).

Offshore finance

Political economists studying offshore finance long converged around three central features characterising the phenomenon: offshore financial services are exclusively offered to non-residents; they entail zero or low taxation and regulation; and they make financial flows, ownership, and liabilities invisible (Palan et al., 2010; Binder, 2023).

However, as research on offshore finance broadened in past years, so did its notion. Especially economists tend to conceive of offshore finance as any US dollar transaction outside the United States. This broad view highlights the importance of analysing external US dollar markets. Yet, replacing the terms 'foreign' or 'external' with 'offshore' adds limited analytical value. What separates the offshore economy from the onshore economy are not national borders. It is the legal regimes offshore financial centres offer to non-residents. The contracts underlying offshore financial services – whether in the realm of taxation or financial regulation – are deliberately designed to circumvent national laws and to keep the financial flows out of sight (Sharman, 2010; Pistor, 2019). It is these legal differences that make offshore money markets attractive to investors and borrowers alike. They allow a borrower from Mexico to issue debt denominated in US dollar but governed by British law. Given the large volume transacted in offshore dollar markets, even seemingly small variations between regulatory frameworks can make a huge financial difference.[4]

Acknowledging the legal intricacies, the Bank for International Settlements (BIS), when it first started to trace Eurobonds statistically, distinguished between a domestic bond (denominated in US dollar and issued in the United States to US American investors), a foreign bond (denominated in US dollar issued in the United States to foreign investors) and a Eurobond (denominated in US dollar, issued outside the United States, and distributed to foreign investors). Yet, in the 1990s, when prices between onshore and offshore issued bonds converged, the BIS merged the foreign bond and Eurobond statistics into the International Debt Statistics (Gruic and Wooldridge, 2012).

This merge made the Eurobond statistically invisible; the legal differences, however, remain. Eurodollars – whether created through loans or bonds – are private liabilities of globally transacting banks, different to standard US dollars, a public liability by the Federal Reserve Bank (Mehrling, 2015). Eurodollars are US dollars created by *non-resident banks* in offshore financial centres outside the United States.[5] It is not only US dollars that are created in offshore money markets, but other internationalised currencies, such as the euro or the yen, are also created offshore. The analysis's exclusive focus on the US dollar is owed to its outsized importance, especially for emerging market economies. For them, access to the US dollar is the gateway to participating in the international economy.

Money links countries across borders via financial claims, creating hierarchical but interdependent relationships. In the case of offshore money, the underlying relationships are particularly complex and opaque. Untangling the undercurrents of offshore finance helps to better understand the relationship between borrower and creditor power.

The long view on offshore financial claims

Given the dearth of quantitative data, untying the undercurrents of offshore finance can best be achieved by a historical account. This empirical section embeds Brazil's and Mexico's engagement in the Eurodollar markets into its historical context. It combines primary data from qualitative participant interviews and descriptive quantitative statistics from the Bank for International Settlement's locational banking statistics with secondary historical sources.

Good times

Between the early nineteenth and early twentieth century, Mexico and Brazil borrowed in the London Stock Exchange's bond markets in pound sterling, intermediated by London's merchant banks (Flores Zendejas, 2020). Their relationships with these banks thus predate the Eurodollar.

When Eurodollar markets began to emerge in the mid-twentieth century, Brazil and Mexico continued borrowing in London from the same merchant banks as they had done in the past. Yet the debt was now denominated in US dollar instead of British pound. The change of currency denomination had far-reaching consequences. The borrowing was not under US regulation, because it took place in Britain. Yet it was also not under British regulation, for it was denominated in a foreign currency.

In the case of Brazil, borrowing in the nascent offshore money markets took off from 1964 onwards. With very little tax income and limited access to domestic credit, the military government was short of revenue. The central government's dire financial situation was the result of a long-standing conflict between the urban ruling elite and the rural oligarchy over how (and whether) to finance the government, reflected in a small banking system (Calomiris and Haber, 2014). Gétulio Vargas fundamentally reformed that small banking system, in his capacity as authoritarian ruler (1930–1945) and democratically elected president (1950–1954). He used one of the country's oldest domestically owned banks, the *Banco do Brasil*, to finance industrialisation and a growing welfare state. He also turned the *Caixa Econômica Federal* into a government-backed system of saving banks. Vargas also laid the foundations for the *Banco Nacional de Desenvolvimento Econômico e Social* (BNDES), the government-owned development bank. The BNDES provided cheap credit to selected, large companies that provided employment. It was used, both during Vargas' reign and under military rule, to keep popular discontent in check by funding employment-supporting policies that went along with repression. Shaped in this way, the banking system financed the elite and kept popular discontent at bay. Yet it did not help to finance the central government. Instead, the government's leverage power came from the offshore markets.

To engage with these markets, the government developed in 1964 an explicit approach to link domestic banks with the Eurodollar system. This legal framework is still the foundation of the country's offshore dollar transactions today.[6] It is codified in Resolution 63, a legal financial statute in Brazil, and further laws. The framework builds on four pillars.

First, the government limited the engagement in the Eurodollar system to a handful of banks, including *Banco do Brasil* and commercial banks such as *Banco Real* and *Banespa*. Second, Resolution 63 allowed Brazilian banks to borrow US dollar internationally and then pass on the corresponding amount in local currency to industrial and commercial firms (Alvarez, 2020). Third, Resolution 63 regulated the Eurodollar activities of participating banks such that the risks of overleverage and of maturity mismatches were minimised. The remaining risks could be transferred from leveraged corporations and banks onto the central bank's balance sheet. This transfer of risk was done through various mechanisms, including currency swaps and the possibility to deposit US dollars with the Central Bank which took on the related exchange risks and charges of foreign lenders. Finally, the government incentivised banks and large corporations to participate in these markets. For instance, it offered through BNDES subsidised credits to large corporations to give them the leverage needed to engage in offshore borrowing. The government also abandoned reserve requirements for all transactions conducted under Resolution 63 (Frieden, 1987; Alvarez, 2020).

In the 1970s, when petrodollars started to flood the offshore markets, the Brazilian government could borrow in London at negative real rates of interest (Skidmore, 2010: 172) furthering its leverage power. Consequently, the government 'embark[ed] on a gigantic borrowing spree', as Rocha (2002: 6) writes. However, it was not only the Brazilian government that went offshore. To hedge against inflation and other risks, particularly during times of hyperinflation, well-off individuals and corporations routinely used offshore accounts to circumvent capital controls and other regulations.[7] By the 1970s, borrowing offshore had become routine for the Brazilian government, banks, corporations, and wealthy individuals alike. Offshore dollar markets enhanced Brazil's leverage power.

In the case of Mexico, serious engagement with the Eurodollar markets started with a banking reform in 1974 when the Mexican government allowed its banks to internationalise. The impetus for the reform was, as in Brazil, a government in search for liquidity. Initially, the nationalisation of the oil industry in 1938 and other industries in the following years splashed money into the state's coffers. However, over time, inefficiencies in some of the state-owned companies became a strain to the budget (MacLeod, 2005: chapters 2–3). At the same time, costs for co-opting key social groups into loyalty with the autocratic government through patronage and privilege rose. By the 1970s, debt began to outpace revenues. The government urgently needed more and cheaper money than the domestic financiers were willing to provide (Calomiris and Haber, 2014: 331–389). The country's largest commercial banks, first among them *Banamex* and *Bancomer*, used the deregulations to get involved in the Euromarkets. Unlike in the case of Brazil, however, that engagement was not actively shaped by the government. The number of banks that were allowed to enter the offshore money markets were not limited. They could directly lend on US dollars to domestic economic actors. There were no regulations to avoid a mismatch of maturities. The central bank also did not backstop the domestic banks' offshore dollar business. The participation in the Eurodollar markets expanded the leverage power of the government and the banks. Eurodollar banking appeared too much of a win-win situation between the financiers and the government for it to be limited.

The Mexican banks expanded their domestic lending activities between 1977 and 1982 at a rate of almost 40 per cent per year. The largest share of that credit went to the government and was used to finance development (Calomiris and Haber, 2014: chapters 10–11). In September 1976, for instance, the Mexican government issued its largest Eurodollar loan – one of the largest loans issued in that market in 1976 – amounting to US$800 million Eurodollar (The New York Times, 1976). The following year, Mexico topped this record with a Eurodollar loan valuing US$1.2 billion (Riding, 1977). Summing up, between 1970 and 1979, Mexican economic actors issued 322 Eurodollar loans amounting to US$16 billion (Alvarez, 2015).

A third of this overall amount included Mexican banks as intermediaries. That is, with interest rates 40–60 percent lower in the Eurodollar markets compared to domestic borrowing, Mexican banks could borrow cheap offshore via their affiliates in the Caribbean, Switzerland, London and lend at higher prices at home. These transactions were not subject to reserve requirements (Alvarez, 2015). The rents through arbitrage were steep.

Bad times

Mexico's Eurodollar borrowing spree came to a sudden end when oil prices fell sharply in 1982. President José López Portillio (1976–1982) signed a moratorium and negotiated a restructuring of the country's debt to avoid a collapse of the domestic banking system.

The negotiation position of Mexico was determined by two core elements. For one, Mexican banks themselves had claims on the government's offshore dollar debt via their international affiliates. Part of the negotiation over Mexico's sovereign US dollar debt was thus an internal affair.

Second, the international branches and agencies of Mexican banks financed their operations in the interbank Eurodollar markets. That is, international banks had claims on Mexican banks' foreign branches and agencies. As Alvarez (2018) demonstrates, Mexican banks' activity in the offshore interbank market had the potential to raise the country's power to resist creditors' enforcement power. According to the then Governor of the Bank of England, Gordon Richardson, the Mexican banks' offshore interbank market position affected over one thousand banks in financial centres and beyond. At the same time, the Mexican banks' own exposure to their government's offshore dollar debt surpassed the exposure of foreign banks. Consequently, the Mexican government was hard-pressed to save its domestic banks from systematic collapse, which in turn strengthened foreign creditors' claims.

In the end, the willingness to save the domestic banks outweighed Mexico's ability to resist enforcement power. The entanglement of offshore money markets did not strengthen the Mexican government's negotiation position. The government agreed to a fierce domestic structural adjustment program, contributing to a lost decade of economic growth and development.

To stop the withdrawal of domestic capital from the banking system, President Carlos Salinas (1988–1994) re-privatised the banks in 1991. He offered investors unlimited insurance against future losses. That offer was so attractive that the investors paid for the banks on offer three times their book value (Calomiris and Haber, 2014: chapters 10–11). In addition, a new financial instrument was introduced to the moratorium between the Mexican government and its international creditors – the so-called Floating Rate Privatisation Note (Alvarez, 2015). The holders of the note could use it to buy shares in Mexico's reprivatised banks. With this setup, Mexico's commercial banks, especially *Bancomer* and *Banamex*, could again engage with the Eurodollar markets. Less than a decade after the debt crisis, Mexico's leverage power through offshore finance was restored.

With the banks back in Eurodollar intermediation, Mexico's private sector moved from being a net creditor in 1990 to being a net borrower only one year later. The lending of Mexican banks in the Eurocurrency market alone increased from

US$321 million in the third quarter of 1994 to US$2.7 billion in the last quarter of 1994 (Antzoulatos, 2002). So, while the banks' engagement with the offshore money markets stayed the same (i.e. unregulated and without a backstop via the central bank), the final borrower changed. This time, Mexican banks used their funding from the interbank market to provide credit to Mexican firms. The leverage power of offshore had moved from the public to the private sector. When the peso collapsed in December 1994, nearly halving in value against the US dollar, Mexican firms' US-dollar-denominated loans doubled in the space of a few days. They could not serve their debt, and as a result the domestic banks needed to be saved from collapse via their renationalisation. The country was back at square one. Only three years after the bank re-privatisation, the government of Ernesto Zedillo (1994–2000) expropriated the private financiers again, costing the country about 15 per cent of GDP.

This time, however, the president allowed unrestricted foreign bank ownership. It took only a few years for the largest Mexican banks to be owned by foreign investors, particularly from the United States and Spain (Calomiris and Haber, 2014: 331–389). The subsequent liberalisation of the financial sector disrupted banking in Mexico more than the revolution did. Between 1991 and 2013 foreign bank ownership increased from about 1 per cent of assets to 74 per cent. No other country in the world internationalised its banking system more deeply or more rapidly (Haber and Musacchio, 2013).

For Brazil, the effect of the 1982 crisis and the government's response to it differed strongly from Mexico's experience. Here 1982 was not a sovereign solvency crisis. It was a Eurodollar liquidity crisis (Alvarez, 2015, 2020). In the months before the 1982 crisis, Brazilian banks' aggregated onshore US dollar assets in New York (and thus under US jurisdiction) amounted to US$1.9 billion; their offshore assets in London (under British jurisdiction) to US$1.3 billion. Given that these numbers exclude the offshore dollar business in Cayman Islands and the Bahamas, it is fair to assume that already in the early 1980s, onshore and offshore US dollar exposure for Brazil was about equal.

When the crisis hit, for shaping its impact on Brazil, the scope and pattern of onshore and offshore US dollar financing were as important as the degree of their regulation. In Brazil, the key approach to financing was regulated cross-border borrowing under Resolution 63. Unregulated interbank financing through offices in London and other financial centres was secondary. According to Alvarez, the ratio was about 3:1 (Alvarez, 2020). The balance sheets of domestic banks engaging in offshore borrowing were, thanks to the regulations under Resolution 63, resilient to the shock.

Brazil, unlike Mexico, did not face a potential meltdown of its entire banking system. Rather, Brazilian banks struggled with the combination of their exposure to other Latin American countries' external debt and the liquidity squeeze in the Eurodollar markets. The losses in interbank markets were tangible, yet unlike in the case of Mexico, in Brazil they accumulated in just two banks: *Banco do Brasil* and *Banespa* (Alvarez, 2015). A further difference to Mexico was that the internationally active Brazilian banks were not exclusively out there to finance themselves. *Banco Real*, for instance, had accumulated retail US dollar deposits in the United States and in Latin American countries. In fact, prior to the crisis, *Banco Real* was a net lender in the onshore US dollar market. As a result, some Brazilian banks could still find financing in the onshore US markets, despite the crisis in the offshore dollar markets (Alvarez, 2020). As their Mexican counterparts, however, Brazilian banks' foreign offices had no access to emergency funding either through the Federal Reserve in New York or through the Bank of England in London (Binder, 2023, chapters 5 and 6). Given that the banks' liabilities were in US dollar, the only option that the Brazilian authorities saw was to take the commercial banks' liabilities on their balance sheet and to default on the foreign creditors' claims. This decision was in stark contrast to Mexico's approach to serve its debt. Unlike Mexico, Brazil's power to resist was not compromised by the pressure to save the domestic banking system from collapse. Domestic regulation helped the Brazilian government to use the leverage power of offshore finance and to resist enforcement power.

Having defaulted on its obligations, the Brazilian government was excluded from offshore borrowing. Consequently, it devised an approach to financing that meant that the domestic banking system provided long-term credit nearly exclusively to the government. In parallel – building on an approach pioneered in the 1960s, but increased in scale and scope – the government subsidised domestic credit to a selected number of large Brazilian multinational corporations via the BNDES. The subsidies help these firms to get the leverage they need to directly issue debt in the Eurodollar markets. That is, the Brazilian government – again consciously – crafted a link between domestic corporations and the Eurodollar system.[8] The purpose was to preserve offshore leverage power. As in the case of Mexico, it was now the private sector that profited from the leverage power available in the Eurodollar markets.

The transition from government to private sector offshore borrowing was made possible because of the transformation of Brazil's state capitalism in the crisis's aftermath. The state no longer acted as owner, but as shareholder of companies, increasing the trust of international investors (Musacchio Farias and Lazzarini, 2014).

The authorities and corporations considered the setup of this second phase of Eurodollar exposure advantageous because it provided large Brazilian corporations with access funding at lower interest rates than at home.[9] In addition, the Brazilian central bank enhanced the sophistication of its system to backstop Eurodollar borrowing. The system consisted of two main pillars: doubling down on offshoring and building up US dollar reserves.

As discussed earlier, prior to the 1982 crisis Brazil's access to US dollar was about equal to its access to offshore dollar. After 1982, strict financial regulations and litigation law in the United States deterred Brazilian corporates from seeking to issue bonds there. Instead, it went offshore more, profiting from the related leverage power. The country's export-oriented development and its increasing oil revenues helped the government to build up US dollar reserves, to backup offshore borrowing (Alami, 2018). By the early 2000s, Brazil had replaced Mexico as one of the largest emerging market borrowers in the offshore markets, as the subsequent descriptive statistics reveal.

Abdication and arrangement

Statistically, offshore money creation is difficult to trace. For instance, debt issued out of a company's offshore affiliate does not appear in official debt statistics (McCauley et al., 2015). Likewise, the fragmentation of the firm across offshore spaces undermines the measurement of foreign direct investment (FDI).[10] The International Monetary Fund (IMF) estimates that 40 per cent of the world's FDI flow through offshore centres without funding any productive activity – it is, in the words of Damgaard et al. (2019), 'phantom investment'. Nevertheless, to better understand the relationship between offshore money creation and international monetary power, we must make the offshore dollar visible.

The BIS locational banking statistics (LBS) were originally set up to do exactly that. Almost ironically, however, over time the BIS statistics were changed so that the characteristics that, according to the BIS's own definition, separate onshore from offshore transactions have become invisible. The LBS does not contain public information on the residence, booking location and governing jurisdiction for individual transactions, or for aggregate transactions on a bilateral basis. It is therefore difficult to directly quantify the volume of offshore transactions. Given these circumstances, I developed a workaround to nevertheless separate offshore and onshore US dollar based on the LBS. The workaround is described in detail in appendix 1.

Based on this estimation approach, we get the following statistical picture for Brazil's (Figure 4.1) and Mexico's (Figure 4.2) contemporary engagement with the offshore and onshore dollar markets.

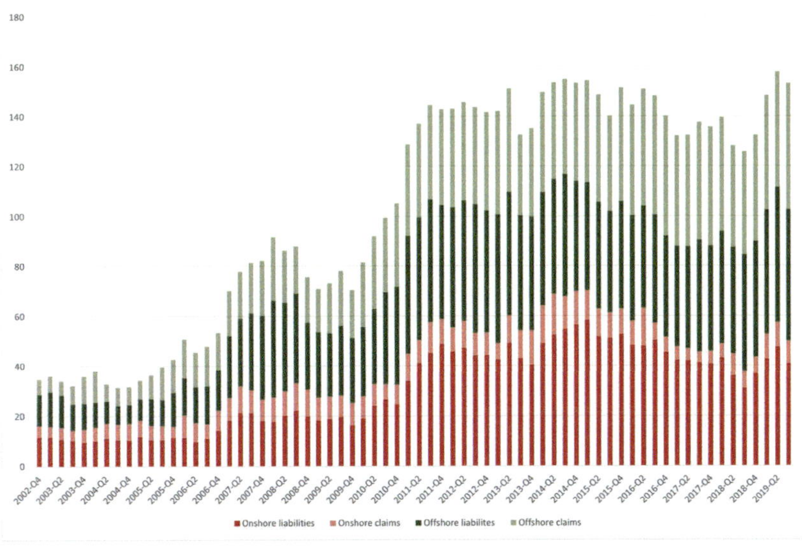

FIGURE 4.1 Brazil: Eurodollar versus US dollar transactions (in billion USD)

Source: BIS locational banking statistics (own calculations)

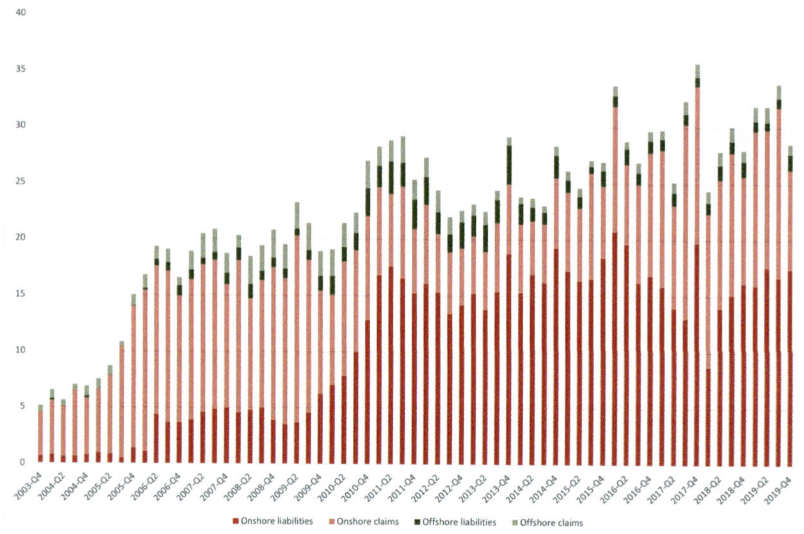

FIGURE 4.2 Mexico: Eurodollar versus US dollar transactions (in billion USD)

Source: BIS locational banking statistics (own calculations)

For Brazil, we can see that the country reports to the BIS since the last quarter of 2002. Figure 4.1 depicts the development of Brazil's claims and liabilities in the offshore dollar markets in relation to its claims and liabilities in the onshore US dollar markets. The red bars represent Brazil's claims (light) and liabilities (dark) towards offshore financial centres denominated in US dollar. The underlying financial flows are created based on the bifurcation of currency (US dollar) and jurisdiction (offshore financial centre). The green bars represent the claims (light) and liabilities (dark) towards the United States. The underlying financial flows are foreign currency borrowing of Brazilian banks with the unity of currency (US dollar) and jurisdiction (United States) intact.

We can observe that Brazil's cross-border transactions denominated in US dollar grew continuously and strongly between 2002 and 2011. Then growth starts to stall. During the full reporting timeframe (2002–2019) liabilities slightly outweigh claims. Relative to the past, Brazil has become a judicious borrower in the offshore and onshore US dollar markets. Contrary to the past, offshore dollar transactions now regularly outweigh onshore dollar transactions. In recent years it is roughly a ratio of 1:2. That is, only a third of Brazil's US-dollar-denominated cross-border transactions are taking place under US jurisdiction. The observable pattern reflects the growing importance of the US dollar in international monetary affairs and Brazil's explicit policy choice on how to deal with it. The Brazilian government and central bank built and refined a framework within which domestic economic actors can engage in the Eurodollar markets. The government supports large corporations to issue debt offshore and built a backstop via growing US dollar reserves. With the global financial crisis, this setup was put to a test. As Figure 4.1 shows, between 2008 and 2009, Brazil's banks and corporations were confronted with a considerable US dollar gap compared to the previous years. The Brazilian central bank responded with a combination of capital controls and swap lines. Swap lines were established internationally with the Federal Reserve and domestically between the central bank and commercial banks. These measures helped to effectively bridge the US dollar gap during the crisis (Allen, 2013: 113–127; Chamon and Garcia, 2016). Consequently, the global financial crisis had comparatively limited negative effects on Brazil's banking sector.[11] In 2009, US dollar credit was still short in the United States, but Eurodollar credit was again flowing freely to Brazil. These flows were mainly driven by supply-side factors. Investors in search for yield in a low-interest environment turned to Brazil and other emerging economies.[12] Brazilian companies happily enjoyed the leverage power as the example of Petrobras, the partially state-owned oil company, shows. In 2009, Petrobras became the largest net issuer of Eurobonds in the world. With two issuances of US$8 billion and US$6 billion between 2009 and 2014, it became one of the most indebted corporations globally (McCauley et al., 2015).

Yet monetary tightening in the United States in 2011 and more strongly in 2013 contributed to an economic crisis in Brazil. Consequently, the central bank set out to defend the private sector's access to US dollar. Between 2013 and 2014, the central bank again provided US dollar swaps to its own banking system from its US dollar reserves. The program amounted to more than US$90 billion or about a quarter of Brazil's total foreign reserves (Chamon and Garcia, 2016). These efforts further pushed the onshore/offshore ratio towards more offshore than onshore transactions.

Tracing Brazil's US-dollar-denominated cross-border transactions onshore and offshore reveals the central importance of the Eurodollar for Brazil's leverage power in a US dollar dominated world. Overtime, Brazil's access to the US dollar became increasingly independent from US jurisdiction. The resulting increased entanglement between several jurisdictions and interlocking balance-sheets across borders also increases Brazil's power to resist enforcement power.

Turning to Mexico, we can see that the country began reporting to the BIS at the end of 2003. Figure 4.2 depicts the development of Mexico's claims and liabilities in the offshore dollar markets in relation to those in the onshore US dollar markets. Again, the red bars represent offshore US dollar claims (light) and liabilities (dark). The financial flows underlying these claims and liabilities are created based on a bifurcation of currency (US dollar) and jurisdiction (offshore financial centre). The green bars depict the onshore claims (light) and liabilities (dark) towards the United States. Here we are observing financial flows where the unity of currency (US dollar) and jurisdiction (United States) are intact.

We can observe that Mexico's cross-border transactions denominated in US dollar behave very differently to those of Brazil. They are on a much lower level, with the collective of all cross-border claims and liabilities, onshore and offshore, peaking at about US$ 35 billion in 2017 compared to about US$150 billion in Brazil in 2019. Likewise, the development over time differs markedly from Brazil's. Cross-border claims and liabilities grew between 2003 and 2006. From 2006 to 2010 they are relatively constant until they start growing again at the end of 2010. From then onwards cross-border transactions are volatile, with some quarters experiencing growth and other quarters shrinkage. In addition, unlike Brazil who is a net-borrower in the onshore and offshore US dollar markets, Mexico was a net-lender between 2003 and 2006. It only started borrowing in US dollar in a somewhat substantial way from 2010 onwards. Most strikingly, however, almost all US dollar transactions take place in the onshore markets. Mexico's exposure to the Eurodollar is marginal. In the words of one interviewee from the *Banco de México*, 'Mexican corporations' cash resides locally or is invested sometimes in some offshore centre, but that is a very small part of it'.[13] Consequently, the 2007–2008 global financial crisis barely affected Mexico's banking system, though it had severe effects on the country's economy.

Mexico's markedly different pattern of exposure to the offshore US dollar markets can be traced back to Ernesto Zedillo's decision, in 1994, to allow foreign ownership of Mexican banks. Subsequently, the ownership of the banking system in Mexico developed from domestic-owned to foreign-owned. At the same time, the issuance of Mexican sovereign debt developed in the opposite direction. Before the Mexican financial crises, 70 to 80 per cent of debt was issued abroad. Today that amount is issued domestically. The ownership structure, though, did not change. Mexico's debt is still foreign owned, since most of it is held by the foreign-owned banks and their pension funds.[14] The big change is that the debt is now denominated in Mexican pesos (Banco de México, 2014). After three decades of offshoring debt with terrible economic, social, and political consequences, Mexico finally stayed clear of the offshore money markets.

Only since the global financial crisis in 2007–2009 Mexican private corporations started to borrow in US dollar again. Mostly driven by supply, Mexican private corporations found it easy to issue US dollar internationally as the US American banks operating in Mexico could provide them with direct access to these markets. That is, an important contemporary reason for economic actors to go offshore – access to US dollar or leverage power not available onshore – is not present in Mexico. Embedded to a considerable extent into the US economy and banking system, Mexico's access to US dollar – where needed – comes through the onshore markets.

In essence, in good times offshore finance provided Brazil and Mexico with the resources not available at home but needed to finance development. In bad times, the potential to resist creditor power did play in favour of the debtors. Yet, as most debt was onshore, other forces prevailed. Mexico's response to the original sin was abdication. Mexico chose a combination of borrowing in its own currency and embedding itself into the US financial banking system. After the 1990s Mexico surrendered, for the time being, the leverage, legal, and resistance power that offshore dollar debt offers in return for more financial stability. The full disintegration of the country's political system after its two successive financial crises in 1982 and 1994 determined this policy choice as much as Mexico's geographical and economic proximity to the United States.

Brazil's answer to 1982 was a functional arrangement. It uses the legal bifurcation of jurisdiction and currency offshore finance offers and thus enhances its leverage power and its ability to resist enforcement power. It manages volatility via regulation, a near-balance of offshore claims and liabilities, and by backstopping its Eurodollar engagement through central bank swaps.

Conclusion

Offshore money's importance lies in the bifurcation of currency and jurisdiction across borders. It provides the borrowing country with leverage power, i.e. access to liquidity at better conditions than available onshore. Better still, it comes with no political strings attached. In addition, the entanglement between the borrowing country, the currencies home country, the offshore jurisdiction, and global lending banks create interdependencies that potentially strengthen the borrowers' ability to resist creditors' enforcement power in case of payment difficulties. However, as the empirical analysis demonstrated these additional sources of powers are not automatic. They depend on domestic institutions, specifically on bank ownership and central bank backstopping.

Mexico allowed a high degree of foreign, especially US ownership, in its banking system, increasing its access to onshore dollar liquidity. One of the prime reasons for countries to go offshore – access to US dollar not available elsewhere – has thus become obsolete. It traded financial stability against the potential sources of power attached to offshore borrowing. Brazil on the other hand, backstops its offshore borrowing with increasing sophistication. It manages the related financial stability to be able to tap the potential sources of power attached to offshore borrowing. This way Brazil created more financial space than would be available onshore.

These findings have implications for how we conceive of sovereign borrowers in the international hierarchy created by claims.

First, comparing Brazil's and Mexico's engagement in the offshore dollar markets demonstrates that offshore finance, once a marginal phenomenon of the international financial system, has become central to it. Any analysis of the international monetary hierarchy must consider the consequences of this development. Second, it is worthwhile to complement the scholarly focus on 'Anglo-America' (Green, 2020) or 'transatlantic finance' (Tooze, 2018: chapter 3) with perspectives on borrowers and on emerging markets. As the case studies demonstrated, deliberate domestic monetary policies make a difference for sovereign borrowing even under adverse conditions such as the Latin American debt crises or the global financial crisis. They demonstrate that sovereign borrowers can be powerful actors, too.

Third, taken together, the centrality of offshore finance and the space for action it provides to borrowing countries highlight, that creditor power is always *relational.*

The relational nature of creditor power stems from the social relationships underpinning money. As the issuance and jurisdiction of money is bifurcated across borders, so are the underlying relationships. Offshore finance creates complex interdependencies between the issuing country (the United States), the country who is providing the laws and regulations (offshore financial centres), global banks (especially in Europe) and borrowers, both public and private. This entanglement constrains anyone actor in its potential courses of action. Yet, the nature and degree of that constraint differs.

The notion of relational creditor power captures the changes taking place in global banking practices; the differing consequences for individual countries related to their history and geography; the actorness of borrowers; and how all of this fluctuates in good times and in bad.

Appendix 1: constructing an estimate for a country's exposure to the Euromarkets

To be considered a part of the Eurodollar system, a transaction must fulfil two conditions: it must be US-dollar-denominated and it must happen between reporting institutions from the case study country and offshore financial institutions from outside the United States. The BIS locational statistics do not allow to breakdown bilateral financial flows by currency. The estimate therefore needs to proceed in two steps. First, I use the BIS locational banking statistics data to determine the share of US-dollar-denominated cross-border transactions between the case study country and the rest of the world. Second, I apply this share to transactions between the case study country and offshore financial centres. In alphabetical order, based on BIS locational banking statistics and completed by European offshore financial centres as identified by Garcia-Bernardo et al. (2017) the jurisdictions' offshore financial centres are noted in Table 4.1.

TABLE 4.1 Offshore financial centres

Caribbean Offshore	*Asian Offshore*	*European Offshore*	*Other Offshore*	*Complemented European Offshore*[15]
Aruba	Hong Kong	Britain	Bahrain	Cyprus
Bahamas	Macao	Gibraltar	Lebanon	Ireland
Barbados	Singapore	Guernsey	Samoa	Liechtenstein
Bermuda		Isle of Men	Vanuatu	Luxemburg
Cayman Islands		Jersey		Malta
Netherlands Antilles				Switzerland
Panama				
West Indies United Kingdom				
Curacao				

Source: Garcia-Bernardo et al. (2017)

Notes

1 The metaphor of bifurcation goes back to Palan (1998) Trying to Have Your Cake and Eating It: How and Why the State System Has Created Offshore. *International Studies Quarterly* 42(4): 625–643.
2 On the concepts of leverage power and enforcement power, see Braun and Koddenbrock (forthcoming), Introduction, pp xx-xx
3 This is also the approach taken by the BIS local banking statistics underlying the chapter's empirical analysis, see appendix 1.
4 Author's telephone interview with financial lawyer, June 2020.
5 For a list of all offshore financial centres considered in the analysis see appendix 1.
6 Author's interview with banker, Rio de Janairo, April 2017.
7 Author's interview with defence lawyer, São Paulo, April 2017.
8 Author's interview with financial expert, Rio de Janeiro, April 2017; author's interview with financial journalist, São Paulo, April 2017.
9 Author's interview with BNDES employee, Rio de Janeiro, April 2017. Author's interview with financial market expert, Rio de Janeiro, April 2017.
10 Reurink and Garcia-Bernardo (forthcoming) this volume,
11 Author's interview with financial sector expert, Rio de Janeiro, April 2017.
12 Author's interview with financial market expert, Mexico City, November 2015. Author's telephone interview with investment banker, May 2017.
13 Author's interview with central bank staff, Mexico City, November 2015
14 Author's interview with central bank staff, Mexico City, November 2015; author's interview with economist, Mexico City, November 2015.
15 Garcia-Bernado et al. (2017) also include Monaco, but as Monaco does not report to the BIS it is excluded here.

References

Alami I (2018) Money power of capital and production of 'New State Spaces': A view from the global South. *New Political Economy* 23(4): 512–529.

Allen B (2013) *International Liquidity and the Financial Crisis*. Cambridge and New York: Cambridge University Press.

Altamura CE (2017) *European Banks and the Rise of International Finance: The Post-Bretton Woods Era*. London and New York: Routledge, Taylor & Francis Group.

Alvarez S (2015) The Mexican debt crisis redux: International interbank markets and financial crisis, 1977–1982. *Financial History Review* 22(1): 79–105.

Alvarez S (2018) A fatal flaw: Domestic Banks and Mexico's International negotiating position in the 1982 debt crisis. *Revista de Historia Económica/Journal of Iberian and Latin American Economic History* 36(3): 337–362.

Alvarez S (2020) *International Banking and Financial Fragility: The Contrasting Experience of Brazil and Mexico in the Lead-up to the 1982 Crisis. Oxford Economic and Social History Working Papers*. Oxford: Oxford University.

Antzoulatos AA (2002) Arbitrage opportunities on the road to stabilization and reform. *Journal of International Money and Finance* 21(7): 1013–1034.

Banco de México (2014) *Financial System Report*. Mexico City.

Binder A (2019) All exclusive: The politics of offshore finance in Mexico. *Review of International Political Economy* 26(2): 313–336.

Binder A (2023) *Offshore Finance and State Power*. Oxford: Oxford University Press.

Black S and Munro A (2010) Why issue bonds offshore? *BIS Working Papers*. Bern: Bank for International Settlements.

Braun B and Koddenbrock K (2022) The three phases of financial power: Leverage, infrastructure, and enforcement. In: Braun B and Koddenbrock K (eds) *Capital Claims: The Political Economy of Global Finance*. London: Routledge, pp. 1–30.

Braun B, Krampf A and Murau S (2020) Financial globalization as positive integration: Monetary technocrats and the Eurodollar market in the 1970s. *Review of International Political Economy*. doi:10.1080/09692290.2020.1740291.1–26.

Calomiris CW and Haber SH (2014) *Fragile by Design: The Political Origins of Banking Crises and Scarce Credit*. Princeton, NJ and Oxford: Princeton University Press.

Chamon M and Garcia M (2016) Capital controls in Brazil: Effective? *Journal of International Money and Finance* 61: 163–187.

Cohen BJ (2015) *Currency Power: Understanding Monetary Rivalry*. Princeton, NJ: Princeton University Press.

Damgaard J, Elkjaer T and Johannesen N (2019) The rise of phantom investments. Empty corporate shells in tax havens undermine tax collection in advanced, emerging market, and developing economies. *Finance and Development* 56(3): 11–13.

Eich S (2020) John Locke and the politics of monetary depoliticization. *Modern Intellectual History* 17(1): 1–28.

Eichengreen BJ and Hausmann R (2005) *Other People's Money Debt Denomination and Financial Instability in Emerging Market Economies*. Chicago, IL: University of Chicago Press.

Flores Zendejas J (2020) Explaining Latin America's persistent defaults: An analysis of the debtor – creditor relations in London, 1822–1914. *Financial History Review* 27(3): 319–339.

Frieden JA (1987) The Brazilian borrowing experience: From miracle to debacle and back. *Latin American Research Review* 22(1): 95–131.

Garcia-Bernardo J, Fichtner J, Takes FW, et al. (2017) Uncovering offshore financial centers: Conduits and sinks in the global corporate ownership network. *Scientific Reports* 7(1).

Green J (2016) Anglo-American development, the Euromarkets, and the deeper origins of neoliberal deregulation. *Review of International Studies* 42(3): 425–449.

Green J (2020) *The Political Economy of the Special Relationship: Anglo-American Development from the Gold Standard to the Financial Crisis*. Princeton, NJ: Princeton University Press.

Gruic B and Wooldridge P (2012) Enhancements to the BIS debt securities statistics. *BIS Quarterly Review* 63–76.

Haber S and Musacchio A (2013) These are the good old days: Foreign entry and the Mexican Banking System.

Hardie I and Thompson H (2020) Taking Europe seriously: European financialization and US monetary power. *Review of International Political Economy*. doi:10.1080/09692290.2020.1769703.1–19.

Helleiner E (1994) *States and the Reemergence of Global Finance: From Bretton Woods to the 1990s*. Ithaca, NY and London: Cornell University Press.

Helleiner E and Kirshner J (2009) *The Future of the Dollar*. Ithaca, NY: Cornell University Press.

Ingham GK (2004) *The Nature of Money*. Cambridge and Malden, MA: Polity.

MacLeod D (2005) *Downsizing the State: Privatization and the Limits of Neoliberal Reform in Mexico*. University Park, PA: Pennsylvania State University Press.

McCauley RN, McGuire P and Sushko V (2015) Dollar credit to emerging market economies. *BIS Quarterly Review* 27–41.

Mehrling P (2015) Elasticity and discipline in the global swap network. *International Journal of Political Economy* 44(4): 311–324.

Musacchio Farias A and Lazzarini SG (2014) *Reinventing State Capitalism: Leviathan in Business, Brazil and Beyond*. Cambridge, MA: Harvard University Press.

Norrlof C (2017) The international political economy of money, macro-money theories and methods. *Review of International Political Economy* 24(4): 718–736.

North DC and Weingast BR (1989) Constitutions and commitment: The evolution of institutions governing public choice in seventeenth-century England. *The Journal of Economic History* 49(4): 803–832.

Ogle V (2017) Archipelago capitalism: Tax havens, offshore money, and the state, 1950s – 1970s. *The American Historical Review* 122(5): 1431–1458.

O'Malley C (2015) *Bonds without Borders: A History of the Eurobond Market*. New York City: Wiley.

Palan R (1998) Trying to have your cake and eating it: How and why the state system has created offshore. *International Studies Quarterly* 42(4): 625–643.

Palan R, Murphy R and Chavagneux C (2010) *Tax Havens: How Globalization Really Works*. Ithaca, NY: Cornell University Press.

Pénet P and Flores Zendejas J (2021) *Sovereign Debt Diplomacies: Rethinking Sovereign Debt from Colonial Empires to Hegemony*. New York: Oxford University Press.

Pénet P and Zendejas JF (2021) *Rethinking Sovereign Debt from Colonial Empires to Hegemony. Sovereign Debt Diplomacies*. Oxford: Oxford University Press.

Pistor K (2019) *The Code of Capital: How the Law Creates Wealth and Inequality*. Princeton, NJ: Princeton University Press.

Reurink A and Garcia-Bernado J (2022) Firm claims: Reinterpreting the global race for foreign direct investement. In Braun B and Koddenbrock K (eds) *Capital Claims: The Political Economy of Global Finance*. London: Routledge, pp. 205–231.

Riding A (1977) Mexico seeks $1.2 billion loan of Eurodollars, its largest ever. *The New York Times*, 9 September, p. 79.

Rocha GM (2002) Neo-dependency in Brazil. *New Left Review* 16: 5–32.

Schenk CR (1998) The origins of the Eurodollar market in London: 1955–1963. *Explorations in Economic History* 35(2): 221–238.

Sharman JC (2010) Offshore and the new international political economy. *Review of International Political Economy* 1–32.

Skidmore TE (2010) *Brazil: Five Centuries of Change*. New York: Oxford University Press.

The New York Times (1976) 18 banks arranging $800 million loan to bolster Mexico. *The New York Times*, 6 October, p. 75.

Tomz M and Wright MLJ (2013) Empirical research on sovereign debt and default. *Annual Review of Economics* 5(1): 247–272.

Tooze JA (2018) *Crashed: How a Decade of Financial Crises Changed the World*. London: Allen Lane.

Zucman G (2015) *The Hidden Wealth of Nations: The Scourge of Tax Havens*. Chicago, IL and London: University of Chicago Press.

5

CLAIMS TO SOVEREIGNTY

MMT as a challenge to money's technical imaginary

Aaron Sahr

Introduction

This chapter begins by recalling two speeches on monetary policy that could not differ more. Both were given by central bank policymakers – one in the middle of Europe, one on the other side of the Atlantic, but at different times. The first speech was delivered at the end of the Second World War by Beardsley Ruml, chairman of the Federal Reserve Bank in New York. A friend and advisor to former US president Herbert Hoover, Ruml had studied statistics and social psychology and worked in academia, in the business world and for a large NGO before ending up in the headquarters of American money. The speech in question appeared in print in 1946. The title 'Taxes for Revenue Are Obsolete' bluntly stated the outrageous thesis that the United States was no longer dependent on tax revenues to pay its federal bills (Ruml, 1946). Instead of waiting until it had taken enough money from citizens, the US government should pay its expenses by creating new money. A powerful nation whose currency was no longer issued as a claim on a scarce commodity such as gold ('fiat money') should not allow itself to be limited in its political decisions by trivialities such as sufficient revenues, Ruml argued.

The second speaker's hair presumably would have stood on end at hearing such an argument. This speech was given in 2012 by Jens Weidmann, an economist who advised the German chancellor Angel Merkel on national and international matters. In 2011, he became the youngest president of the German Bundesbank and thus also one of the European Central Bank's (ECB) decision-makers. Unlike Ruml, Weidmann quoted classic literature, more specifically the German writer Goethe (Weidmann, 2012). In the sequel to *Faust*, Goethe had written a famous passage about financing government spending by creating paper money. Mephistopheles advised a bankrupt emperor to pay his debts with claims on the future economic output of his empire. This legal promise was intended to give the

DOI: 10.4324/9781003218487-6

paper notes purchasing power in the present and make them usable as money; the emperor was of course thrilled.

Weidmann invokes this episode because it is commonly read as a warning against the lure of money creation to finance public spending. Reading the text as a cautionary fable is a kind of culturally entrenched meme (Binswanger, 2014), for the appearance of paper money is deceptive: it is true that bills can initially be settled with mere claims on the future. But then prices rise, because apparently, more and more paper chases fewer and fewer goods. This triggers a vicious spiral that drags everything into the abyss. At least that is how Weidmann presents the matter. In his speech, he warns against the politicisation of money production, because – as he asserts he has learned from Goethe – it inevitably leads to inflation. Politicisation threatens to compromise the very character of money as a neutral medium of exchange.

The employment of 'government printing presses' to finance rising expenditures is commonly associated with failed states and disasters of historic proportions. Nevertheless, Ruml's irritating proposal to politicise money (creation) has recently returned to fiscal and monetary discourse, most prominently in the form of so-called Modern Monetary Theory (MMT). MMT has been discussed in social media as well as traditional public and academic media since the global financial crisis of 2008, with debates intensifying since about 2019. 'Ignored for years', writes the business news service *Bloomberg* in March 2019, 'MMT suddenly finds itself at the centre of America's economic debate' (Holland and Boesler, 2019). Some US senators even called on Congress to officially 'condemn' the theory – probably a unique move, given that parliaments rarely comment on academic conceptual disputes. At the centre of MMT's success is the American economist Stephanie Kelton, who has acted as an economic policy advisor to the Democrats. Her book *The Deficit Myth* became an international bestseller in 2020. In it she echoes Ruml, claiming that the widespread belief in the need for taxes to finance government spending is 'pure fantasy' (Kelton, 2020: 3).

MMT poses a serious challenge to conventional thinking about monetary policy, state financing, and, first and foremost, the role of central banks. This challenge might be misunderstood, in keeping with Weidmann's position, as a diabolical attempt to seduce people into abandoning sound money. However, the aim of this chapter is not to examine MMT as an unremitting debunker of 'myths'. Rather, MMT and Ruml are read as an alternative imaginary of a monetary order, that is, a competing narrative for framing what money is (for). Theories of money occupy key positions within the theoretical architectures that we must draw on for the analysis and critique of economic practices. If one adjusts the meaning of 'money', what is considered fact by some appears to be 'pure fantasy' to others. Theories of money shape what seems possible, sensible, necessary, or insane in terms of monetary policy. The public debates in which democratic societies negotiate their financial possibilities, desires and strategies are structured by imaginaries of monetary orders that draw on theories of money. So today, when MMT and its critics accuse each other of spreading lies and myths in the face of tight state coffers and the huge monetary resources needed to modernise infrastructure, recover from the pandemic troughs, and prepare for climate change, we are in the midst of a political conflict about money itself.

In this chapter, I will address the conventional narrative of the link between money and monetary order (represented here by Weidmann) and contrast it with the MMT narrative. Both draw on an understanding of money as a claim but mean quite different things. The conventional narrative identifies money as a claim to goods. It thus evokes an idea of the monetary order as a means of technically administering these claims (2). This *technical imaginary* shapes the constitution of monetary institutions and monetary policy debates in the present. Within this context, pointing to public financing needs as legitimate reasons for governments to 'print' money appears tantamount to proposing attempted fraud. Central banks are identified as guardians of this administrative setting. Under the smokescreen of a supposedly apolitical monetary order, however, a monetary system has developed that can by no means be considered politically neutral (3). MMT, on the other hand, stands for a fundamentally *political imaginary* of the monetary order. It regards money as a claim to redemption. This claim is ultimately rooted in state rule, which evokes the image of a monetary order as a facility for public provision. MMT's political agenda therefore relies on the utilisation or restoration of monetary sovereignty as a state prerogative and mandate – the re-integration of central banks into the governmental financial apparatus (4). The discursive and institutional hegemony of such a political imaginary would, on the one hand, help to expand the fiscal space in some countries. But it would also expose polities to a new pressure; namely, to find consensual positions on processes of money creation and money destruction (5).

The technical imaginary of the monetary order

Money is a claim – but what kind of claim? In monetary theory there are two fundamentally different answers to this question. This section deals with the conventional answer, which fosters a technical imaginary of the monetary order as an administrative institutional setting that brings money to life and maintains its universal function. This narrative is found in most of economic theory, economic sociology, and public accounts of money. It starts with a fundamentally apolitical understanding of money itself, embedded in an imagination of a monetary order as an enabling context for a universal, hence apolitical function of money. Monetary policy is envisioned as mere administration of a (socio-)technical tool for market exchange. Consequently, as a normative claim resulting from this imaginary, the monetary order is to be kept free from politics (which does not mean, of course, that it is). Money creation, in particular, has been envisioned as a passive instrument best kept out of political quarrels. As a result, central banks are the prime references of this imaginary; they appear as managers of a universal public good.

As Beckert writes drawing on Simmel, a 'sociologically informed theory sees money as a representation of its holder's abstract claim on the commodities produced in an economy. . . . In other words, the possessor of money is owed goods' (Beckert, 2016: 99). Traditionally, economic theory assumes households that produce surpluses and deficits of goods through the division of labour. All economic actors (households) have something to spare and need something else. Those who sell their surplus goods for money do so in the expectation that they will be able to trade the money for other goods from households that were not (necessarily) involved in the initial exchange. Only if holders of money expect to have access to goods does it make sense to hold it at all. This turns money into a generalised entitlement or claim. As a generalised claim on goods, money acts as a tool that coordinates supply and demand. Once such a tool is available, (direct) barter is turned into (indirect) trade. Engaging in a money economy therefore means exchanging goods for things that act as a generalised claim to goods, a claim that is redeemed later. The specificity of modern money in this narrative is that it can function as a claim on goods without providing a good as an incorporated collateral – 'fiat money'.

From this intuitively plausible definition results a certain imaginary of the monetary order as a technical (neutral, apolitical) means of enabling such claims. The value – that is, exchangeability – of money, Beckert continues, can only be explained by the 'the social and political recognition of its owner's claims to a share of the social product' (Beckert, 2016: 99) that 'depends on the existence of a moral atmosphere that facilitates trust in the inherently worthless tokens that are used as money' (Beckert, 2016: 99–102). In short, whether goods *are* owed to someone depends on people's confidence in the abstract claim. The money-stuff can only act as a claim on goods (and, therefore, turn barter into trade) when it can be expected to remain generally accepted, that is, when the 'moral atmosphere' of trust in exchangeability remains intact. What follows from the framing of money as an entitlement to goods is the role assigned to political institutions in traditional national economics, a role that remains to this day: the preservation of these entitlements. Maintenance of this universal 'good' becomes the primary task of monetary institutions. They are responsible for preserving the 'moral atmosphere' in which money holders can trust in the reliability of their claims.

This technical imaginary of the monetary order provided the discursive basis for two macro-models of global monetary institutions that aimed to turn monetary policy into the administration of claim preservation. Both can be read as modes of de-politisation: the decoupling of monetary policy from explicit processes of public governance such as public debates, electoral competition, and parliamentary rule (Kreitner, 2010). The first macro-model is the gold standard. Under the gold standard, the imagination of an apolitical state-of-monetary-affairs was achieved through institutional naturalisation. Paper and book money were to be considered a proxy for a precious metal, thus anchoring money in a given, non-negotiable facticity (Aglietta, 2018). Ideally, every economic value was to be perceived as a reference to gold. Every payment would then be a (symbolised) exchange of one good for another – for gold. With the end of the gold standard, the naturalistic interpretation of the apolitical claim was replaced by another form of objectivation that is based on the notion of risk. The post-metal system of 'managed flexibility' rests, according to Kreitner (2010), on the imagination of the monetary economy as an interactive practice between individuals under conditions of uncertainty. The money economy is imagined as a field full of actors who want to exchange real values with each other and who are subject to uncertainties about nominal values – uncertainties about how much the things being exchanged are worth, about converting these values into equivalence with each other, and about preserving these values. This means that there is an objective and universal necessity for the reduction of uncertainty through the mediator of value – money. Stable prices thus become a condition, a structural prerequisite for the economy to function at all and, as such, a prerequisite for money to *be* money. By withdrawing monetary policy decisions from the struggles of daily politics, or so liberal economists hoped (Skidelsky, 2017), money, as a stable claim on real value, reduces the uncertainty of economic interactions, which is assumed to be a universal 'good' every actor in the economy relies on in the same way. (Political economics has, of course, decisively deconstructed this constitution of monetary policy as a universalist policy; precisely this deconstruction has revealed the dominance of this technical imaginary.)

Based on the technical imaginary, governmental control over monetary issues has deteriorated in the second half of the twentieth century. The administration of monetary policy issues has been placed in the hands of arcane institutions and regimes. Monetary policy frameworks are increasingly handed over to bodies that act in isolation from day-to-day political debates and democratic control. These include, for example, the G8, the IMF, the World Bank, and the OECD, which form a regime of 'low visibility but high impact' that 'is mediated by central bankers more often than politicians' (Kreitner, 2010: 202). At the core of this order is the independent central bank. These banks were trusted to reduce uncertainty through price stability, rather than increasing it through the vagaries of election campaigns and voter opinions. If governments or parliaments were entrusted with the 'technical' control of money, it was assumed, various interest groups would constantly tinker with the value relations of the medium of exchange and thus compromise (like Goethe's emperor) the politically neutral essence of money itself. This would counteract the objective necessity of reducing uncertainty, which – so the idea goes – makes economic practice possible in the first place. The idea of an independent central bank triumphed almost everywhere in the world. The European Central Bank (ECB) was considered a prime example of this technical imaginary. The eurozone states are unable to directly intervene in the ECB's monetary policy decisions. The ECB, in turn, is only allowed to intervene in markets to maintain narrowly defined price policy goals and only in ways that leave value relations untouched to the greatest possible extent.

The norm of price stability is deeply entrenched in the 'apolitical' notion of money as a claim on goods. Throughout the history of monetary ideas, it is often assumed in theory that the value of the claim (how much is actually owed) must be determined by the value of its acquisition. Immanuel Kant already considered it self-evident that a specific sum of money could only be obtained in exchange for a specific effort. This effort would ultimately have to determine how many goods one would receive for the money. For Kant, there was no question that money was only really money if it could buy as much as one invested in its acquisition. This idea is deeply entrenched in mainstream monetary theory. Simmel explicitly defined money as a *substitute* for goods (Simmel, 1989: 222), that is, a surrogate for the goods sold to acquire money, a 'placeholder' (Beckert, 2016: 100). In the first volume of *Capital*, Karl Marx reasoned at length about *true* money being the 'immediate product of labour', meaning that he thought of money as necessarily entering the market through a sale of goods (produced by labour). Money must be the 'product of a sale' that 'represents the realised price of some commodity' (Marx and Engels, 1996: 119). Fiat money threatens to violate the laws of economics, according to Marx, if it does not also arise from the 'transformation' of a commodity (Marx, 1961: 101). But how on earth could fiat money arise from the transformation of a commodity? With these ideas, Kant, Simmel, and Marx in fact laid the groundwork for the contemporary norm of price stability as an expression of an intact and universal 'moral atmosphere'. The norm of price stability seeks to preserve the correspondence between the monetary and economic values available, that is, the values of the claims on goods and the value of the goods themselves. Whoever exchanges a good for a claim must be able to assume that she or he will be given goods of comparable value in return. That is: she or he must assume that the extent of the claim is defined by her or his acquisition. Selling one pound of bread for one dollar can only be counted as a process of substitution if the claim can purchase one pound of bread in the future. If prices are stable, what is given determines what will be received; money can then be thought of as a 'product of a sale'. A monetary policy committed to the goal of price stability thus appeared to be a universalistic policy, that is, a procedure for managing a widely used tool in the interests of the common good. Monetary policy becomes administration, called upon to ensure that everyone is entitled to exactly as many goods as they have (theoretically!) ceded to acquire the claims. Only if prices are stable can money be counted as *real* money, as a substitute, placeholder, or surrogate for surplus goods sold.

The (normative) claim that each money token should be the result of a previously produced and sold good – one could call this the 'primacy of production' – runs through the history of economic ideas right up to contemporary studies in economic sociology, where the economy appears as a process in which goods are first produced, then traded on markets with the help of money, and finally consumed (Swedberg, 2005). 'Production comes "first" in the economic process', Swedberg (2005: 10) writes; real goods are produced and sold, and it is only in the sphere of marked distribution 'where money enters into the picture' (Swedberg, 2005: 12). This positioning of money in the sphere of distribution is accompanied by a (ultimately normative) claim, namely, that money must always be produced in exchange for a good. Mehrling (2011) calls this dominant, interdisciplinary idea the 'economics view'. In it, it is presupposed that the financial possibilities of the present are determined by the economic activity of the past; accordingly, any money creation without prior expansion of the capital stock appears to be a form of fraud.

From this idea is then derived the normative assertion that money (as a claim to goods) can only be legitimately created if there are already goods that can fulfil this claim. Stable prices are read as an indicator of this equilibrium.

Under the hegemonic understanding of monetary policy as a means of managing uncertainty by maintaining price stability, public money creation thus becomes a purely technical instrument in the service of the main goal. This does not mean that central banks do not create money for other reasons, as illustrated by their role as the lenders of last resort. But they must justify these decisions on the political stage in terms of price stability, that is, they are only 'allowed' to produce new claims on goods unless this is justifiable with reference to new (or idle) goods. This justification pressure is encoded in the ECB's mandate (and in the rule of market neutrality as well). Placing public money creation under the dictate of price stability means making money creation dependent on whether goods have already been produced for which additional money is now needed. To say that, strictly speaking, money should only be created when there is deflationary pressure means that one is implicitly referring to precisely this concept of money as a reflection of output that has already been produced. New goods are required to justify the creation of new claims on goods (deflation), and the production of money should cease when there are already too many goods to fulfil the claims made (inflation). (Readers should keep in mind that this refers to political discourse, not to economic causalities.)

We are thus dealing with a way of thinking in which all political claims to money are discredited that deviate from concepts of the mediation of trade through surrogates that reflect past accumulation. Money is considered to be money when it is acquired as a claim on goods against the supplying of goods. Sale and purchase must correspond. This correspondence is established through price stability. The creation of money is only permissible as a means of achieving this goal. The absence of inflation becomes the only legitimate reason for a central bank to create money. That is why the proposal to use money creation to settle accumulating bills appears not only as an attempted manipulation of the value of money but as downright devilry. Maintaining the objective function of money is perceived as the only acceptable task for political institutions. The theory of money as a genuinely non-political claim to goods thus yields a concept of order in which such a claim must be institutionally embedded in a way that makes it appear as neutral as possible. Under this axiom, Ruml's or MMT's proposals would seem to condone fraud – that is, attempts to manipulate what is in fact a quasi-natural tool for market economies.

Neglected powers

Within the technical imaginary of the monetary order, money creation was considered merely an ancillary device for 'hardening' or 'weakening' a currency. 'Leverage power' (Sgambati, 2019; Braun and Koddenbrock, 2022) in public hands became simply an instrument to achieve price stability, which was understood to be the ultimate means of reducing uncertainty in economic transactions. Money creation ceased to be a legitimate topic of (broader) public discourse. It is no coincidence that questions related to distributing and redistributing monetary assets are among the most common and familiar topics of public politics, while the production of money by issuing claims against the banking sector – 'leverage power' – is seen by many as a task for technical experts and financial engineers. In this view, money creation has already been logically subordinated to the general good of price stability and in any case should not be subject to collective decision-making processes.

The reign of the technical imaginary, however, not only legitimised and rationalised the institution of independent central banks. Rather, it also fostered the dismantling of forms of public governance designed to limit private 'leverage power'. Measures such as credit or capital controls that were once in place in most capitalist countries to steer commercial banks' money creation politically were abolished in the neoliberal revolution of the 1970s and 1980s. This non-governance of one of modern society's most crucial infrastructures was legitimated by referring to the idea that as long as independent central banks keep prices stable, the neutral functionality of money would be preserved, no matter what private banks do. In consequence, private money creation was ruled mainly by 'profit maximisation' (Deutsche Bundesbank, 2017: 21). New money is created for profitable transactions, not, for example, for socially useful or macro-economically beneficial ones. Since the 1980s, banks have increasingly created money for trading existing assets and financing financial transactions (Bezemer, 2019; Huber, 2017; Pettifor, 2017). Kohl, for example, shows that in the OECD world and admittedly to varying degrees, the building of new houses has become increasingly decoupled from the trade in real estate (Kohl, 2020). This mirrors what Bezemer calls the 'debt shift', the concentration of private money creation on asset markets (Bezemer, 2019; Bezemer and Samarlna, 2019). Money creation and growth have become detached from each other. In a comparative study of banks in one hundred countries between 1987 and 2014, Beck et al. (2020) show that a 10% increase in money provided on-balance sheet results in a mere 1.12% increase in GDP per capita growth in the long run. Off-balance sheet money provided 0.34% growth per 10% expansion. This is at least noteworthy insofar as the defensive and pejorative reference to the 'printing press', which is often a knee-jerk reaction against the idea of public money creation, articulates a fear of precisely what has occurred with private money production. Those who argue that one cannot pay for expenditures with the printing press are at least implying that such freshly printed money has no countervalue in the economy and is therefore illegitimate. This is precisely Weidmann's argument when he insinuates that political money creation puts more money into the world than goods. The persuasive power of this objection evaporates, however, when one realises that the private banks are experts in this kind of unproductive endeavour. After all, we are looking back on decades in which billions of new dollars, pounds, and euros entered markets without generating appropriate levels of growth. The technical imaginary of the monetary order suggested that price stability would guarantee a reliable coupling of goods and the generalised claims called 'money', this mechanism proved to be inadequate. In fact, the system lacks a functioning mechanism that ensures that money is created when more goods are brought to market, and there is no mechanism that ensures that money creation fosters growth.

Rather than bringing prosperity, unleashing private money creation has created inequality (Bezemer, 2019; Jackson et al., 2014; Pettifor, 2017; Sahr, 2022). Due to the constant financing of proportionally fewer entrepreneurial investments and more and more purchases of assets, the price of these assets has, overall, risen steadily. This development is also referred to as asset price inflation. Globally, the vast majority of these assets are owned by very few, very wealthy households. Therefore, the private sector's unproductive creation of money has mainly increased the wealth of this small group, but not yielded general increases in prosperity to the same extent. The constantly rising asset prices have also led companies to speculate in asset investments instead of investing in new production capacities. It simply became less lucrative for them to invest in employment and production. Thus, private money creation has been partly responsible for the fact that median wages and salaries in the OECD world have risen much more slowly than capital incomes. It is apparent, but can only be alluded to briefly here: the 'apolitical' constitution of money has profound social and economic (and, moreover, ecological) consequences (see Sahr, 2022 for details). The power to create money is more than a mere instrument for weakening or strengthening a currency. Under the impression of the technical imaginary, money served particular interests, while claiming to be a neutral good.

The political imaginary of the monetary order

Ruml's and MMT's positions are articulated in a completely different argumentative context. In this alternative imaginary, money is not a claim to goods, but instead a claim to redemption. This means that it is a claim on an action, not on a thing. The content of the promise embodied by money is the redemption or settlement of the liability itself (Wray, 2012: 262). This axiom has been called a 'credit theory of money'. 'Credit' in 'credit theory' refers neither to 'loan' nor to 'asset'; in this context, the term stands for the fact a money owner is legally empowered to terminate creditor–debtor relationships of the same type (e.g., Wray, 2012; Desan, 2014).

From MMT's perspective, there are two kinds of such relationships involved in our contemporary monetary order, which is based on a 'template' (Ingham, 2020, see Sgambati, 2019) developed in eighteenth-century England. First, there are 'horizontal' credits between private actors; namely, commercial banks and their customers. This refers to the simple fact that bank deposits are liabilities for the bank. They represent legal claims to 'transfer' amounts to other deposits or to deliver cash. To 'transfer' money from one bank account to another, however, means to settle one debt relation (between the payor and her bank) and to create another – between the payee and his bank. Again, this notion of (bank) money as claim should not be confused with the hypothesis that money's value is a promise of future goods, nor with the idea that it is a claim on another asset like cash

(cash, too, comes into existence as a liability of the banking system). In fact, it is about claims to actions: Being the holder of a monetary claim against a bank (i.e., a deposit) brings an actor into a position to settle any debt she might have with the bank – and others. Money is a privileged type of creditor-debtor relationship that allows those on the creditor side to settle other liabilities as well. Commercial bank deposits, for example, settle private debt, that is, debt resulting from retail purchases, rent, employment contracts, and so on.[1] To pay with money for goods and services therefore means that one settles one's own debts by offering other and different debts (i.e., claims against the banking sector); more specifically, by offering 'higher ranking' debts – liabilities that can redeem more types of obligations than the buyer's own promise of redemption.

Bank debt only gains this potential through integration into a political apparatus that recognises the claims as a means of settlement, by law and (or) convention (Bell, 2001; Ingham, 2004; Desan, 2014; Mehrling, 2017; Koddenbrock, 2019). Here, the second type of creditor-debtor relationships enter the picture: 'vertical' claims between rulers and their subjects. Such relationships exist in two directions in modern states: as claims against the government (bonds) and claims of the state against its currency's users – as taxes. Credit theorists who point to the significance of vertical obligations become 'chartalists'. MMT, as a *neo*chartalist school – albeit not the only one – considers both kinds of vertical debts, but especially taxes, to be crucial for the establishment and maintenance of money. Taxes are perceived as a source of the final demand for a national currency. As subjects of a regime, actors always need to settle tax obligations – or face sanctions if they do not. MMT self-identifies as a taxes-drive-money approach; the 'fear of prison' (Hockett and James, 2020), that is, the need to settle vertical obligations in mutual agreement, is the centrepiece of MMT's imaginary of the monetary order. As 'a dollar is a "get-out-of-jail-free-card"' (Hockett and James, 2020: 6), the role of monetary policy is, 'first and foremost, . . . to ensure there's enough dollars for us to avoid prison' (Hockett and James, 2020: 65). Consequently – at least this is the thesis – private liabilities can only acquire monetary value if they are connected to this prison avoidance scheme of public provisioning.

In eighteenth century England, the crown paid its bills by issuing claims against itself (e.g., exchequer bills that could be used to settle claims of the crown). With the establishment of the Bank of England, claims against the empire became the assets of this new facility, while its liabilities were issued as highest-ranking money. From the perspective of MMT, in this template we continue to pay with claims against the state – however, we do this indirectly, as claims against the central bank 'backed' by sovereign bonds. Privately issued claims acting as local means of settlement thus became included in this *substantially political* monetary order through the acknowledgment of private bank debt as partially equivalent to central bank liabilities. In this hierarchical structure of acknowledgment, credits differ mainly according to the degree of their 'moneyness' (Bell, 2001; Ingham, 2004; Bezemer, 2016; Koddenbrock, 2019), that is, the uniqueness and scope of their ability to redeem obligations. Money is thus not studied as a (possibly even 'neutral') instrument to facilitate market interactions but as a political order (Ingham, 2004; Desan, 2014; Braun, 2016; Koddenbrock, 2019) in which private bank liabilities (and, to various degrees, their derivatives), central bank debts, and government bonds and tax obligations are linked by political conventions, legal stipulations, and mutual interests to command resources.

This is the basis for an imaginary of the monetary order that is from the outset political rather than technical. Based on this story, the monetary order can no longer be imagined as a framework that secures the credibility of a set of individual claims on goods. Rather, firstly, money itself appears not a set of assets but as a web of interdependent debts that refer to one another. Secondly, from MMT's point of view, this state-based 'money grid' (Mehrling, 2017) is primarily not a tool that transforms barter into trade; it is a machine enabling the government to move resources and private persons to avoid jail. Since vertical claims (claims against the state, i.e., bonds, but also claims of the state, i.e., taxes) form the pillars on which this machinery rests, the monetary order appears primarily as one of public rule and public provision.

Arguing within a political imaginary of the monetary order, MMT claims monetary sovereignty as a public prerogative. Monetary sovereignty is commonly understood as the territorial control over means of payment in a national jurisdiction (Pistor, 2017). Across the many different definitions, 'the right to create money via the issuance of currency and the right to conduct independent exchange rate and monetary policies emerges as the lowest common denominator from the existing literature' (Zimmermann, 2013: 3; cf. van't Klooster and Murau, 2020). If monetary sovereignty is identified as the right to or a monopoly on issuing the means of exchange, it becomes apparent that the very emergence of modern monetary orders in the eighteenth century was in fact accompanied by the dismantling of that very monopoly. The template of modern money is a 'hybrid' (Weber, 2018: 47) system, in which the right to issue money is shared between public and private banks, forming a resilient 'public-private partnership' (Ingham, 2004, 2020) based on a political 'deal' between capitalist society's stakeholders (Koddenbrock, 2019).

With the political imaginary of the monetary order comes an alternative notion of monetary sovereignty. In Sahr and Müller (forthcoming), we proposed that this distinction should be highlighted by using the term *agential* monetary sovereignty and contrasting it with *territorial* monetary sovereignty. Agential monetary sovereignty does not refer to the right or capacity to influence the value of monetary assets within (inflation) and between (exchange rate) territories, that is, how much goods are, in fact, owed to domestic or foreign money owners. Instead, it refers to the state's own ability to pay. Monetary economies are characterised by an imperative: actors are forced to constantly reproduce their ability to pay (liquidity, i.e., capacity to settle debts) to survive economically. Minsky (2004: 96) has called this the 'survival constraint' (Mehrling, 2017). One could now call all those actors 'monetarily dependent' who must reproduce their own liquidity by accessing the money of others – by selling assets, by borrowing, or by imposing payment obligations. Those who are able to settle their debts without having to resort to pre-existing money with previous owners, in contrast, would be monetarily sovereign.[2] Thus, actors who are monetarily sovereign in the agential sense can *decide* to be able to pay or 'relax their own survival constraint' (Pistor, 2017: 496). This is only possible if one has the power to produce new money for self-determined purposes without being dependent on the consent of others or on material scarcities.

In contrast to the territorial narrative, where monetary sovereignty is (beginning to be) lost with the emergence of modern bank-based money, agential sovereignty only arises with the institutionalisation of the 'template'. As the money supply provided by bank's balance sheets is – in accounting terms – hyperelastic, the extent to which actors can reproduce their ability to pay by creating new money is determined by their 'elasticity space' (Murau, 2020); that is, by how useful claims against said actor are for the banking sector. With government bonds becoming (historically) 'safe assets' and (institutionally) the resource of the highest-ranking money, the state's domestic elasticity space became *potentially* infinitely elastic as well.

Under the reign of the technical imaginary, many countries made it more difficult for their governments to access the money creation capacity of their central bank. A prime example is the eurozone (Mitchell and Fazi, 2017). The ECB is not only not allowed to buy government bonds directly under any circumstances. It is also only permitted to buy them from the secondary market with newly created money (and thus improve the fiscal space of governments) if it can justify this action in terms of its primary objective. From the perspective of the political imaginary of MMT, such a construction does not appear as a dictate of economic reason but rather as a quite bizarre, self-imposed constraint on the public purse – a policy that in any case urgently needs to be corrected.

Now it becomes clear why Ruml's assessment differs so substantially from Weidmann's: In balance sheet terms, central bank money is offset by government debt, which is recorded as central bank assets. When states pay, they pay indirectly with claims against themselves. Central banks can therefore accept new government bonds as assets at any time and credit someone else with new money in return, either to a private bank that deposits a government bond or to the government itself. In both cases, more money is created through government deficit spending. And in the same way, the money disappears again when the government bond is settled and thus deleted from the balance sheet. The reduction of government debt through excess tax revenues thus reduces the money supply. Seen this way, taxes do not finance public expenditure; they reduce the money supply by shrinking central bank's balance sheet. MMT thus proposes a thoroughly political reading of this triad of government debt, money creation, and taxes. They argue in favour of polities to instrumentalize their indebtedness defined by political processes, rather than profitability considerations. Seen in this light, whether taxes have become obsolete for state financing is thus neither a reform proposal disguised as a question, nor an enquiry about a simple fact. It is about an alternative interpretation of the existing monetary system that radically breaks with financial habits of thought that have been practised for decades.

Neglected constraints

Finance means initiating, maintaining, and terminating claims against private and public actors. Each claim, more precisely, has such a 'life cycle' (Braun and Koddenbrock, 2022). The political imaginary represents a subjugation of the central bank claim cycle to fiscal logics. Fiscal (taxes and bonds) and monetary claims (central bank money) should work hand in hand under the political imaginary: The central bank is supposed to use its leverage power to finance public spending. Subsequently, the government is supposed to use its (fiscal) enforcement power to pay off the central bank's claims through taxes. This has – very briefly – two dangers: First, the claim life cycles that take place in the private part of the financial nexus rely on the 'infrastructural power' of central banks for their initiation, maintenance and termination (Braun, 2020). It is questionable whether politicised central banks could still fulfil their goal of keeping claims alive (see also Mertens and Metz, 2022). A central bank operating according to fiscal imperatives may be sabotaging its own efforts to save the private claim cycles from collapse. In terms of power theory, the politicisation of the central bank's leverage power could cannibalise its infrastructural power.

Secondly, politicising the central bank claim life cycle requires a public negotiation of money creation (by the central bank) and money destruction (through taxes). Such an expansion of monetary policy debates is not without risk, as can be illustrated by the euro area. The eurozone as a community of states unites states that are economic competitors with different political cultures, economic strengths and weaknesses, and constellations of interests. Since this top-down institutional unification was supposed to foster political integration of the European population, it depended on finding the lowest common denominators for many tricky political issues (Schelkle, 2017). Ensuring that the ECB could act outside the realm of parliamentary decision-making processes and narrowing its mandate to price stability made European unification possible, precisely because it limited the space for day-to-day political decisions (Höpner and Spielau, 2018). A polity that negotiates its monetary policy concerns under the political imaginary must, in contrast, mediate between interests, build coalitions, and find legitimate compromises with regard to much broader issues. For this would entail not only publicly negotiating the hardness of the currency (technical imaginary) but also what money is to be created for and how it is to be destroyed again (political imaginary). Thus, within the eurozone, the German population would possibly have to support a joint money creation to benefit Greek infrastructure, while the taxes of the successful German export industry would be used to reduce the money supply in times of threatening inflation. It would be difficult to find majorities for this, to say the least. Politicising issues that have so far been excluded from the procedures of political agreement thus creates room for action, but also puts a burden on the entire political system by rising political 'maintenance costs' (Höpner and Spielau, 2018: 160).

Conclusion

It should have become clear that the two speeches cited at the beginning of this chapter that serve us here as placeholders for imaginaries of the monetary order do not merely exemplify two attitudes that would have been adequately described as conflicting preferences for soft or hard currencies. By applying utterly different notions of what kind of claim money is, both positions talk about very different things when they make statements about monetary policy. Under the political imaginary, money is political first and foremost because it is an order for financing public projects. Here, monetary policy is not determined by the *leading* question of how many goods are owed to the holders of monetary claims within a monetary space. The imaginaries imply different basic framings that determine what monetary policy *is about*. While creating money for public purposes seems to be a form of fraud within the technical imaginary, it appears to be the most obvious choice for someone arguing within the political imaginary. Here, monetary policy is essentially the control of a collective apparatus for the purpose of communal provision.

On the one hand, a dethronement of the technical imaginary would increase the room for manoeuvre for many governments. In the face of a lack of prosperity, failing infrastructure, unemployment, pandemics, and the need for measures to protect against and mitigate the climate crisis, the dominance of the technical imaginary must be considered a threat to our global future. The technical imaginary is responsible for the current state of our monetary system and a protector of the few in the guise of the universal common good. On the other hand, its dominance fulfils a function, namely the integration of different goals and interests (Braun, 2016), and, thus, the reduction of political maintenance cost of the monetary system. It remains to be seen whether policies framed and legitimised within the political imaginary would be democratically possible, not only but especially in the eurozone – even if they might be economically or socially beneficial (and at most a little devilish).

Notes

1 For credit theorists, all these interactions should be described and analysed as the creation and settlement of debt, Ingham (2020: 41).
2 Note that the ability to pay is a relative category that varies, for example, between domestic and international contexts. In a US-dollar-dominated world economy, most states' *international* ability to pay is de-facto dependent on income or borrowing.

References

Aglietta M (2018) *Money: 5,000 Years of Debt and Power*. London and New York: Verso.
Beck T, Döttling R, Lambert T, et al. (2020) *Liquidiy Creation, Investment, and Growth*. London: Centre for Economic Policy Research.

Beckert J (2016) *Imagined Futures: Fictional Expectations and Capitalist Dynamics*. Cambridge, MA: Harvard University Press.
Bell S (2001) The role of the state and the hierarchy of money. *Cambridge Journal of Economics* 25(2): 149–163.
Bezemer DJ (2016) Towards an 'Accounting View' on money, banking and the macroeconomy: History, empirics, theory. *Cambridge Journal of Economics* 40(5): 1275–1295.
Bezemer DJ (2019) *Money and Its Uses: Development or Wealth?* Zeist: Triodos.
Bezemer DJ and SamarIna A (2019) *Debt Shift, Financial Development and Income Inequality* (Working Paper No. 646). Amsterdam: De Nederlandsche Bank. doi:10.2139/ssrn.3436782.
Binswanger HC (2014) *Geld und Magie: eine ökonomische Deutung von Goethes Faust*. Hamburg: Murmann.
Braun B (2016) Speaking to the people? Money, trust, and central bank legitimacy in the age of quantitative easing. *Review of International Political Economy* 23(6): 1064–1092.
Braun B (2020) Central banking and the infrastructural power of finance: The case of ECB support for repo and securitization markets. *Socio-Economic Review* 18(2): 395–418.
Braun B and Koddenbrock K (2022) The three phases of financial power: Leverage, infrastructure, and enforcement. In: Braun B and Koddenbrock K (eds) *Capital Claims: The Political Economy of Global Finance*. London: Routledge, pp. 1–30.
Desan C (2014) *Making Money: Coin, Currency, and the Coming of Capitalism*. Oxford: Oxford University Press.
Deutsche Bundesbank (2017) *Monthly Report: April*. Available at: https://www.bundesbank.de/en/publications/reports/monthly-reports/monthly-report-april-2017-667334 (accessed 10 December 2021).
Hockett R and James A (2020) *Money from Nothing: Or, Why We Should Learn to Stop Worrying about Debt and Love the Federal Reserve*. Brookly, NY: Melville House.
Holland B and Boesler M (2019) MMT has been around for decades. Here's why it just caught fire. Available at: www.bloomberg.com/news/articles/2019-03-11/mmt-has-been-around-for-decades-here-s-why-it-just-caught-fire (accessed 10 December 2021).
Höpner M and Spielau A (2018) Better than the euro? The European monetary system (1979–1998). *New Political Economy* 23(2): 160–173.
Huber J (2017) *Sovereign Money: Beyond Reserve Banking*. Cham: Springer International Publishing.
Ingham G (2004) *The Nature of Money*. Cambridge and Malden, MA: Polity.
Ingham G (2020) *Money*. Medford: Polity.
Jackson A, Dyson B and Daly HE (2014) *Modernising Money: Why Our Monetary System Is Broken and How It Can be Fixed*. London: Positive Money.
Kelton S (2020) *The Deficit Myth: Modern Monetary Theory and the Birth of the People's Economy*. New York: Public Affairs.
Koddenbrock K (2019) Money and moneyness: Thoughts on the nature and distributional power of the 'Backbone' of capitalist political economy. *Journal of Cultural Economy* 12(2): 101–118.
Kohl S (2020) Too much mortgage debt? The effect of housing financialization on housing supply and residential capital formation. *Socio-Economic Review* 19(2): 413–440.
Kreitner R (2010) The jurisprudence of global money. *Theoretical Inquiries in Law* 11(1): 177–208.
Marx K (1961) *Zur Kritik der Politischen Ökonomie*. MEW 13. Berlin: Dietz.
Marx K and Engels F (1996) *Capital: Vol. 1*. London: Lawrence & Wishart.
Mehrling P (2011) *The New Lombard Street: How the Fed Became the Dealer of Last Resort*. Princeton, NJ: Princeton University Press.

Mehrling P (2017) Financialization and its discontents. *Finance and Society* 2(2): 138–150.
Mertens D and Metz C (2022) Night of the living debt. Non-performing loans and the politics of making an asset class in Europe. In: Braun B and Koddenbrock K (eds) *Capital Claims: The Political Economy of Global Finance*. London: Routledge, pp. 169–188.
Minsky H (2004) *Induced Investment and Business Cycles*. Cheltenham and Northampton, MA: Edward Elgar.
Mitchell W and Fazi T (2017) *Reclaiming the State: A Progressive Vision of Sovereignty for a Post-Neoliberal World*. London: Pluto Press.
Murau S (2020) *A Macro-Financial Model of the Eurozone Architecture Embedded in the Global Offshore US-Dollar System*. Boston: Boston University, Global Development Policy Center, Global Economic Governance Initiative. doi:10.2312/iass.2020.041.
Pettifor A (2017) *The Production of Money: How to Break the Power of Bankers*. London and New York: Verso.
Pistor K (2017) From territorial to monetary sovereignty. *Theoretical Inquiries in Law* 18(2): 491–517.
Ruml B (1946) Taxes for revenue are obsolete. *American Affairs* I: 35–39.
Sahr A (2022) *Keystroke Capitalism: How Banks Create Money for the Few*. London: Verso.
Sahr A and Müller C (forthcoming) Contested privatisation. On the state of monetary sovereignty in the euro zone. In: Smith C (ed.) *Sovereignty in a Global Perspective*. London: British Academy, pp. 210–234.
Schelkle W (2017) *The Political Economy of Monetary Solidarity: Understanding the Euro Experiment*. Oxford: Oxford University Press.
Sgambati S (2019) The art of leverage: A study of bank power, money-making and debt finance. *Review of International Political Economy* 26(2): 287–312.
Simmel G (1989) *Philosophie des Geldes*. Berlin: Suhrkamp-Verlag.
Skidelsky R (2017) *Money and Government: A Challenge to Mainstream Economics*. London: Penguin Books.
Swedberg R (2005) The economic sociology of capitalism: An introduction and agenda. In: Nee V and Swedberg R (eds) *The Economic Sociology of Capitalism:* Princeton, NJ: Princeton University Press, pp. 3–40.
van't Klooster J and Murau S (2020) Rethinking monetary sovereignty: The global credit money system and the state. Available at: osf.io/preprints/socarxiv/k9qm8 (accessed 10 December 2021).
Weber B (2018) *Democratizing Money: Debating Legitimacy in Monetary Reform Proposals*. Cambridge and New York, NY: Cambridge University Press.
Weidmann J (2012) Begrüßungsrede anlässlich des 18. Kolloquiums des Instituts für bankhistorische Forschung (IBF) Papiergeld – Staatsfinanzierung – Inflation. Traf Goethe ein Kernproblem der Geldpolitik? Available at: www.bundesbank.de/de/presse/reden/begruessungsrede-710686 (accessed 10 December 2021).
Wray LR (2012) *Modern Money Theory: A Primer on Macroeconomics for Sovereign Monetary Systems*. Basingstoke: Palgrave Macmillan.
Zimmermann CD (2013) *A Contemporary Concept of Monetary Sovereignty*. Oxford: OUP.

PART II

Infrastructural power

6

THE NEW GATEKEEPERS OF FINANCIAL CLAIMS

States, passive markets, and the growing power of index providers

Jan Fichtner, Eelke Heemskerk and Johannes Petry

Introduction

In the past, most governments had to brace themselves for the eventuality that 'bond vigilantes' (Arbogast, 2020; Rommerskirchen, 2019) or hedge fund 'wolf packs' (Fichtner, 2013a, 2013b) could suddenly move crucial financial markets in one direction or another. Interest rates of sovereign debt could quickly move up or domestic stock markets could plummet in a short amount of time as 'hot money' rushed in and out of national financial systems, thereby strongly interfering with countries' economic and social policies (Harmes, 1998; Roos, 2019). This was particularly the case for small and developing countries – or 'emerging markets' in the parlance of international investors – because foreign investors mainly from Western countries had enormous assets under management compared to the size of these national economies. In this setup, public international financial institutions, mainly the World Bank and IMF, were often crucial gatekeepers in these processes of capital reallocation and the enforcement of financial claims.

Today, following a set of rapid and fundamental changes in international finance, these same governments face another counterpart that has the power to move markets. These new and powerful kids on the block are the financial firms that create, maintain and sell key stock indexes. Only three of them dominate this growing and highly profitable sector: MSCI, S&P Dow Jones Indices and FTSE Russell, each accounting for about 26% of global index industry revenues; in addition, Bloomberg plays an important role in bond indexes.

In this chapter we will argue and show how the major index providers have become crucial gatekeepers of capital, yielding infrastructural power over international investments. They have become key counterparts to states in global finance, and their central position in the index investing ecosystem confers them the role of new de facto private regulators that exert standard-setting power (Petry

DOI: 10.4324/9781003218487-8

et al., 2021). Through their country classification methodologies, in- and exclusions, and watchlists, index providers are *steering* financial claims whereby they influence domestic financial regulation, investor access and international capital flows in developing countries. Next to the World Bank and IMF, index providers are thus emerging as private authorities that are at times able to impose *de facto* conditionalities.

This has not always been the case, in fact the infrastructural power of index providers only came about after a recent but fundamental shift in the organisation of global finance: the shift from active to passive investing. Since the global financial crisis of 2007–2008 active investors are increasingly being supplanted by the passive investment ecosystem. Passive investment means that asset owners (e.g. pension funds, high-net-worth-individuals or small retail investors) invest their money in financial products that simply replicate well-known benchmark indexes, such as the S&P 500 or the MSCI World Index in the equity segment, and the Bloomberg Barclays Global Aggregate Index or the JPMorgan Emerging Market Bond Index in the fixed income space. The appeal of these passive index funds is that they charge far lower fees than actively managed funds, while generating mostly the same (or higher) returns. As a result, a growing herd of investors has been migrating from active funds to the passive asset management ecosystem.

Between 2006 and 2018, globally about US$3,200 billion have exited actively managed equity funds, while more than US$3,100 billion have entered index equity funds (Sushko and Turner, 2018; Henderson, 2019) – an hitherto unprecedented mass-migration of capital from active to passive funds, which are mostly managed by BlackRock, Vanguard and State Street (Fichtner and Heemskerk, 2020). By mid-2019, the assets of US equity index funds exceeded the assets of actively managed equity funds for the first time (Gittelsohn, 2019). As a result, we have entered what we have called the 'age of passive asset management' (Petry et al., 2021; see also Braun, 2016, 2020; Fichtner et al., 2017; Haberly et al., 2019; Jahnke, 2019). The recent coronavirus pandemic has not reversed this trend – if anything it has accelerated it, as bond index funds have witnessed record inflows in 2020 (Wagner and Ballentine, 2020).

Under this new reality, the role of index providers in the investment chain is fundamentally transformed. In the past, their indexes primarily served informational purposes. An index such as the American S&P 500, the German DAX or the Japanese Nikkei was primarily a numerical representation of a particular stock market. Indexes served as benchmarks against which analysts could gauge the performance of stocks. While the decisions of index providers had some influence on actively managed funds, the rise of passive investing transformed their role profoundly. Index funds in effect delegate their investment decisions to index providers. As a consequence, they de facto 'steer' capital as inclusions of companies or countries to key indexes causes inflows of many billions of US$ while exclusions can lead to large quasi-automatic outflows (Petry et al., 2021). Index investing thus represents a form of 'delegated management'. Crucially, these inclusions and exclusions come with a wide range of discretionary decision making, with a 'flow through effect on the investor's portfolio' (Robertson, 2019: 843). As Howard Marks of Oaktree Capital underscored: 'somebody is making very active decisions about which stocks will be in each "passive" product. . . . The people who create the indexes are deciding which stocks will be invested in' (Alloway et al., 2017).

Index providers have now become crucial gatekeepers in the infrastructure of international financial claims, because they determine the criteria that states, especially emerging markets, have to fulfil to qualify for index membership, while investors are increasingly delegating their investment decision-making power to them. Index providers essentially provide a crucial infrastructure that enables the creation and trading of increasingly passively allocated financial claims (see also Petry, 2021a). Through the infrastructural power they derive from this gatekeeper position, index providers are able to 'standardise' the issuers of capital claims and, as we try to show in what follows, the countries in which these issuers reside. This has far reaching implications because it attributes the three dominant index providers with the power to shape the conditions under which actors are allowed into the global financial system. Historically, such gatekeeper functions in the international financial system were privy to hegemonic or imperial states, in close cooperation with private finance. Since the end of Bretton Woods the IMF and the World Bank have tried to fill this gatekeeper position. In this chapter we argue that today index providers have such a central position in international finance as de facto private regulators which exert standard-setting power that it begs the question to what extent they have become functional equivalents of the Bretton Woods institutions.

This chapter investigates the prominent role that index providers play today in order to better understand what their role may be in the (near) future. In particular we aim to dissect the influence of index providers on domestic financial regulation, investor access and international capital flows. To this end, the following section gives an overview about the development and the characteristics of index providers and elaborates on the role of index providers as intermediaries in financial claims. The third section subsequently discusses how index providers impact states, inter alia via their country classification methodologies, in- and exclusions, and watch-lists. We analyse these developments using secondary literature, financial news and index methodologies, as well as 16 expert interviews with index providers, exchanges and asset managers conducted between July 2017 and September 2019. In the final section we take stock and reflect in order to better determine how the organisation of global financial authority is currently changing. While certainly not similar, we see striking functional equivalents between index providers and the Bretton Woods institutions.

Index providers and financial claims

In essence, indexes are numerical tools that enable the comparative evaluation of (groups of) assets over time. The purpose of indexes is to display the performance of a specific economic entity such as a nation's stock market (S&P 500) in one single number that is relatively easy to understand and comparable over time. As such indexes consist of a series of corresponding dates and numbers, evaluations based on a series of assets (e.g. stock or bond prices) with specific weightings, whose sequence depicts the performance of the evaluated assets (Robertson, 2019). Thereby, indexes demarcate the boundaries of what these entities are: the 500 companies that the S&P 500 evaluates are (perceived as being) synonymous with the US stock market.

Crucially, constructing indexes is not a purely technical exercise. The 'veneer of numerical representation' (Broome and Quirk, 2015: 829) conceals the normative values and assumptions underlying their calculation as index providers have significant discretion in devising their methodologies. Their notions on what constitutes 'good' corporate governance at the level of the firm and a 'favorable' investment environment at the level of (national) markets helps or hinders firms and countries in attracting capital, essentially deciding what is investment-worthy in global financial markets (Petry et al., 2021). By deciding what to include into/exclude from an index and how to calculate these, index providers play an important role as they increasingly define 'the norms of what's considered acceptable in international finance' (Alloway et al., 2017). This combination of standard-setting and legitimate decision-making power means that index providers have gained a position of private authority in capital markets, providing these private financial actors with the capabilities and positions of power as gatekeepers of capital.

This gatekeeper role of index providers in international finance is relatively novel and the last step in a longer period of transition. With the shift in global finance from banks to capital markets, indexes became more relevant as information tools tracking the development of financial markets (Campbell-Verduyn, 2016). First, this led to the emergence of a few indexes as recognised benchmarks by those index providers that had positioned themselves to 'provide the right concept at the right time for the market'.[1] Second, investors wanted to compare performance between markets in a transparent and trustworthy manner. This gave rise to globally comparable equity indexes, for instance by MSCI, which 'investors really like because you can separate the globe into individual, comparable pieces'.[2] Furthermore, in the 1980s derivatives exchanges such as CME in Chicago and LIFFE in London started launching index futures and options, gradually increasing their importance as reference prices for underlying assets (Millo, 2007).

A few index providers enjoyed considerable brand recognition, some indexes became synonymous with the markets they aimed to represent, and index futures enabled risk management for those markets. Moreover, many actively managed funds used them as baselines to compare their performance. Therefore, indexes had at least some influence on asset managers as any deviation from the relevant index could be conceived as a kind of risk management metric. However, indexes only loosely anchored asset allocation as most fund managers had discretion in choosing both the *degree* of replicating an index as well as the *time period* for doing so. As one interviewee noted, back then 'the propagated characteristic of active management was to be different from the index . . . to beat the index'.[3] Hence, the decision-making power of index providers over the composition of their indexes had relatively limited impact as it intermediated capital flows very indirectly. Thus, at that time, the main function of indexes was to provide market information; their exact composition was not yet crucial to investors, listed companies or countries. This changed fundamentally with the rise of passive investing in the mid-2000s. Index providers began to influence capital flows in an *immediate* and *comprehensive* way. Being a central component of the index funds ecosystem conferred them – gradually and only as a side-effect of their business model – a position of growing private authority in financial markets (Petry et al., 2021).

The financial crisis triggered two reinforcing trends that transformed index providers from merely supplying information to exerting authority. First, the global index industry concentrated, which led to a growing power position of the few index providers that remained. The second and more consequential trend was the money mass-migration towards passive investments, which significantly increased the nascent authority of index providers as evermore funds directly tracked their indexes, such as the S&P 500 or the MSCI World. Whereas in the past indexes only loosely anchored fund holdings around a baseline, now they had an instant, 'mechanic' effect on the holdings of passive funds, thereby 'steering' capital flows. Increasingly, investments were not actively managed by fund managers but passively invested into index mutual funds and ETFs (Braun, 2016, 2020; Fichtner, 2020; Fichtner et al., 2017; Haberly et al., 2019; Jahnke, 2019). This makes sense as the vast majority of actively managed funds have not been able to beat benchmark indexes over longer periods of time, while charging substantially higher fees than index funds (SPIVA, 2019).

Today, index providers de facto steer the giant passive investment capital flows. But index providers have a steering effect over active managed funds as well. Established and well-known indexes are increasingly used as direct benchmarks by actively managed funds which measure their performance against these indexes, and which thus are crucial as investment baselines. Benchmarking against indexes has reached enormous proportions: US$14.8 trillion, US$16 trillion and US$8.9 trillion of assets (equities and bonds) was benchmarked against the indexes of MSCI, S&P DJI and FTSE Russell in 2017/18, respectively. This is up from US$7 trillion (MSCI), US$7.1 trillion (S&P DJI) and US$7.1 trillion (FTSE Russell) in 2013 (Petry et al., 2021: 161).[4] Therefore, the rise of passive management also increases the authority of index providers vis-à-vis active management because by steering evermore passive capital index decisions now mechanically move ever larger parts of the markets, creating a 'pull effect' that actively managed funds need to follow.[5] This means that not only passive funds shift their investment according to reclassifications by index providers, but also active funds that are benchmarked against established indexes (Raddatz et al., 2017).

Mediating financial claims

With the ongoing shift from active to passive investing, index providers have become a vital component of a changing global financial system – the 'infrastructure of the infrastructure' of the global economy (Cerny, 1994). From their previous role as mere information providers for capital markets they have become central actors of passive asset management that exert de facto standard-setting power in global financial markets. Index providers have thus become crucial *intermediaries or gatekeepers* in the relationship between states and (increasingly passive) markets. Of course, index providers do not hold financial claims themselves as they do not own stocks or bonds. Instead, similar to listed companies, a separation between the management and the ownership of financial claims is emerging. While big asset managers such as BlackRock, Vanguard and State Street are the de facto owners of these claims (on behalf of end-investors), investment decisions are increasingly taken by index providers on their behalf.

Similar to payment system providers (Nölke, 2022) and clearinghouses (Thiemann, 2022), index providers should therefore be understood as private financial actors that organise the infrastructural arrangements which enable the functioning of financial markets (Petry, 2021a: 584–585). An index can be understood as a formula that specifies which assets are to be held by investors through index funds/ETFs and more indirectly through benchmarking practices. However, as Bernards and Campbell-Verduyn (2019: 783) note, such financial infrastructures 'can confer, extend and enable new forms of governance'. By deciding which assets become parts of these baskets of financial claims amidst increasingly passive investment flows, index providers make decisions about the composition of investors' portfolios.

From a relational perspective the major index providers are intermediaries between the creditors or claim holders and the debtors or claim issuers (see Figure 1.5 in Chapter 1). The ultimate creditors or claim holders here are investors, which for the index providers take the shape and form of 'the' investment community. This community is dominantly Western or Anglo-American in origin although not exclusively. It is up to the index providers to ensure that the indexes they create are considered by the investment community as a fair and proper reflection of 'the market'. This means negotiating a fine line between – for instance – in- and excluding firms based on good corporate governance practices on the one hand or on financial performance on the other.

At the other side of the financial claims which the index providers mediate stand the debtors (or claim issuers) – the firms or governments that seek access to international capital. This is a diverse group compared to the creditor/claim holder side of the equation, and what the major index providers essentially do is to classify which debtors or claim issuers (companies, governments) are of enough 'quality' to grant them the status of index-worthiness. In what follows we are particularly interested in the leverage that index providers thereby have over governments.

Index providers in the hierarchy of global finance

A large literature has focused on international investors and their relationship to national governments (Rommerskirchen, 2015, 2019; Hardie, 2012; Maxfield,

1998; Haggard and Maxfield, 1996). However, this relationship is highly unequal between countries. Some states – most notably the United States – derive power from the global dominance of institutional investors (Konings, 2007, 2009). After all, most large global investors are Anglo-American entities (Fichtner, 2017) and capital markets globally have transformed according to a script provided mainly by US-based financial and political interests (Carroll et al., 2019; Gabor, 2020; Panitch and Konings, 2009). As Konings (2007: 49–50) noted with respect to the Eurodollar markets 'the creation of a highly integrated and liquid financial structure [through US financial institutions] enhanced America's structural power'. Thereby, the Anglo-American investor community facilitates and perpetuates existing power relations and hierarchies within the global economy (Bortz and Kaltenbrunner, 2018), reproducing US financial hegemony (Norrlof, 2010; Panitch and Gindin, 2012; Strange, 1987).

While not necessarily gaining power like the United States, other developed countries can at least thwart the influence of global investors (e.g. Goyer, 2007). While the convergence of national capitalisms in the face of (financial) globalisation was heavily debated in the 1990s and 2000s (Berger and Dore, 1996; Strange, 1997; Lane, 2003), at least with respect to developed countries, some scholars argue that national capitalist diversity among OECD countries has persisted despite global financial pressures (Maxfield et al., 2017; Mosley, 2003; but see, Streeck, 2010; Hay, 2020).

However, this is markedly different for developing and emerging economies. As Mosley (2000: 3) noted, 'in the developing world . . . the influence of financial markets on government policy autonomy is more pronounced'. These countries are situated at the bottom of global financial hierarchies and are much more prone to changing investor sentiments (Alami, 2018; Kaltenbrunner and Painceira, 2018; Naqvi, 2019). As Bonizzi and Kaltenbrunner (2018) argued, the mismatch between institutional investors' USD-denominated claims and emerging market assets facilitates more volatile investment allocation behaviour on behalf of what are often perceived as the most risk-averse international investors. Similarly, high yields make emerging markets also very attractive for more risk-friendly investors such as hedge funds (Musthaq, 2021). Reversely, emerging market governments have a series of incentives to comply with global creditors (see Roos, 2019).

For a long time, the Bretton Woods institutions, the IMF and the World Bank, were important gatekeepers and intermediaries between investors and governments – usually linked to conditionalities that forced countries to adopt liberalization policies. Even though they only injected small amounts of capital into these economies, their investments were seen as votes of confidence by international investors which then often followed suit with more substantial investment flows. Increasingly, however, index providers define what is investment-worthy, and now arguably play a functionally equivalent role in mediating these creditor-debtor (or claim-issuer-claim-holder) interactions.

As the IMF (2017: 55–56) notes, 'a financial claim is an asset that typically entitles the creditor to receive funds or other resources from the debtor under the terms of a liability' where 'each claim is a financial asset that has a corresponding liability' (see also Braun and Koddenbrock, 2022). Importantly, both bonds and equities are therefore considered financial claims between two entities: bonds constitute a claim on the basis of a repayment of credit, while stocks 'represent a claim of the owner on the residual value of the entity after the claims of all creditors have been met' (IMF, 2017: 55). And while these bonds and stocks might be securities issued by emerging market companies, these companies are situated within individual countries which create the rules and regulatory frameworks for their national securities markets and these claims consequently influence national policies.

In the new era of passive asset management the locus of agency has shifted towards index providers as they increasingly decide which companies and countries are included into key benchmark indexes. The major index providers bundle many financial claims in their indexes and therefore are an attractive and powerful counterpart for debtors seeking financial inflows. The traditional dyadic relationship between states and investors is therefore transformed in such a way that index providers now have become key counterparts to states, on behalf of 'the' investment community they 'represent'. By deciding on the demarcations of investment entities, they define what an investment looks like. This applies both to broad investment categories such as 'emerging markets' or 'developed markets' where they define which countries qualify as one or the other as well as to benchmark stock indexes, such as the MSCI World, where they decide the criteria that states, especially emerging markets, have to fulfil to qualify for index membership which influences issues of domestic financial regulation, investor access and international capital flows. How countries are (1) categorised into specific country classifications, under which circumstances they are (2) included or (3) excluded and (4) whether they are put on a watchlist are crucial aspects of this process. The remainder of this chapter investigates these different aspects of how index providers shape the financial claims between states and (passive) markets.

How index providers impact states

Country classifications

Through their country classifications, index providers facilitate the standardisation of financial claims. While indexes are composed of the stocks of individual companies, each of these companies is listed on an exchange, which is situated within a country that creates the rules and regulatory frameworks for its national stock market. By deciding over which stocks or bonds are included into their indexes, the major index providers decide which debtors (i.e. corporations and countries or markets) are allowed in.

This is especially relevant for emerging economies as they bear the brunt of skittish investor behaviour (Bonizzi and Kaltenbrunner, 2018). Through index investing the investment decision to enter or exit markets has been delegated to index providers and their seemingly 'technical' criteria; as one index provider noted 'we look at country classification just as a mechanical tool to access markets'.[6] By reclassifying individual countries, index providers effectively redraw the borders of markets. Moreover, index providers set out the criteria that decide which countries are 'investment-worthy', thereby defining the hierarchy in global financial markets.

For developing countries, being part of an index is important as this attracts international investment into their 'under-developed' stock markets, not only funding their domestically listed companies but also raising their international profile. Index inclusion is an accolade for countries as the inclusion signifies and establishes the international investment community's trust into their economy.[7] As one interviewee noted: 'Obviously for any economy the no.1 aspiration for a government is to create the economic conditions to attract foreign investments. . . . So being included in a broad index is essential.'[8]

But as argued earlier, seemingly objective index calculation is based upon normative assumptions about the nature of markets, which, first and foremost, should be freely accessible for international investors. After all, the composition of the index needs to reflect to a certain extent a status quo in the investment community so that the index is considered to be a valid reflection of 'the' market. By setting out these criteria, index providers thus formalise and shape the norms of global finance. Index providers decide whether to include countries into their indexes and whether to classify them as 'frontier', 'emerging' or 'developed' markets.[9] As one interviewee put it: 'the big index providers, they are setting standards! . . . Before, nobody paid attention, but now so much money follows them, . . . they have a lot of political power!'[10]

While S&P DJI is the world's largest index provider by revenue, this is mainly due to the crucial S&P 500 index. In contrast, MSCI is the largest provider for emerging markets equity indexes (Miyajima and Shim, 2014). In the words of the *Financial Times*, 'MSCI . . . in effect controls the definition of which countries are "emerging markets"' (Authers, 2018). Therefore, MSCI's criteria for inclusion/exclusion are crucial for emerging markets. MSCI's CEO even states that 'there's not a country that doesn't call as soon as a review is announced' (Wigglesworth, 2019). These criteria are set out in MSCI's Market Classification Framework (Table 6.1), comprising three elements: economic development; size and liquidity; and investor access. Economic development is not crucial as a criterion, neither are the size and liquidity requirements (only 2–5 companies need to meet minimum requirements).

Portugal's tiny stock market, for instance, only has a market capitalisation of $89 billion and 36% of GDP, while South Korea has a market capitalisation of $2,333 billion and 133% of GDP with a much more advanced financial system as well as a six times larger GDP. Portugal, however, is classified as a 'developed market' while Korea is an 'emerging market' in MSCI and other index providers' portfolios. Korea's classification is largely the result of offshore restrictions on index trading as KRX, Korea's exchange and provider of the country's benchmark stock index, KOSPI, does not license its index to create offshore derivatives, essentially preventing speculators in offshore markets from influencing the stock price

TABLE 6.1 MSCI Market Classification Framework

	Sustainability of economic development requirements	*Market accessibility criteria*					*Size and liquidity requirements*		
		Openness to foreign ownership	*Ease of capital inflows/outflows*	*Efficiency of operational framework*	*Competitive landscape*	*Stability of the institutional framework*	*# of firms meeting the criteria*	*Firm size (full market capitalisation)*	*Security size (float market capitalisation)*
Frontier Markets	No requirement	At least some	At least partial	Modest	High	Modest	2	$700 million	$53 million
Emerging Markets	No requirement	Significant	Significant	Good and tested	High	Good and tested	3	$1,400 million	$700 million
Developed Markets	Country GNI per capita 25% above the World Bank high income threshold for 3 years	Very high	Very high	Very high	Unrestricted	Very high	5	$2,801 million	$1,400 million

Source: Authors, based on data from MSCI, 2020b

evaluation of Korean companies while investor registration is also cumbersome and no offshore currency market exists (MSCI, 2020a, 2020b; Petry et al., 2021). Investor access is the dealmaker/breaker for country classifications, and it is this criterion on which most indexing decisions are based.[11]

As MSCI (2020b: 2) states, the criterion of market accessibility 'aims to reflect international institutional investors' experience of investing in a given market', and its assessment is 'based on qualitative measures' that MSCI reviews for all markets at least once a year during its Global Market Accessibility Review. This provides MSCI with a great degree of discretion and 'ample space for subjective judgement on whether certain countries should be considered frontier or emerging markets' (Moreolo, 2018); the same applies for their weighting within indexes. While index decisions about company inclusions are often more indirect and not targeted at individual companies, in the case of country reclassifications index providers take a much more proactive role.[12]

In order to affect classifications, countries 'have homework to do' and 'boxes to tick'[13] – simply talking with index providers is not sufficient, 'they really need to make effective changes'.[14] In 2019, an index reclassification of emerging countries resulted in a 'seismic shift' of over US$120 billion in active and passive fund flows (Robertson and Lam, 2019). Hence, in the age of passive investing the reclassification of countries into 'developed', 'emerging' and 'frontier' markets can lead to billions of rapid 'automatic' in- or outflows by funds that track the respective indexes. With the move towards passive investing, the locus of agency between international investors and governments has therefore shifted. As this section argued, the actions and judgements of index providers can have important consequences for states – as is demonstrated in the following subsections.

Country inclusion: China

In June 2017, MSCI decided to (gradually) include China A-shares into its emerging market index which serves as a benchmark for investments worth US$1.8 trillion, followed by FTSE Russell and S&P DJI in 2018. In early 2019, MSCI then announced to quadruple the weighting of Chinese A-shares to 20% using the confident slogan: 'emerging markets may never be the same' (Wright, 2019). By May 2020, index inclusions had steered at least US$180 billion of passive and active investment into China's stock market (Oliver, 2021), with resulting long-term passive inflows estimated at more than US$400 billion over the next decade (He, 2018). This represented a milestone in China's opening process and an 'accolade' for its aspiration to becoming a global financial power and showcased increased recognition from the international investment community. One foreign exchange trader likened it to 'China's ascent into the Champions League' and 'basically the same message to asset managers as [the IMF's] SDR inclusion was to central bankers'.[15]

However, China's index inclusion was a quite contested and political process. Many observers suggested that Chinese regulators had to make concessions, with the main issue being guaranteed investor access to China's relatively closed market. As one interviewee noted:

> MSCI have actually accomplished quite a lot by the inclusion. It's amazing that it was an external, private organization that suddenly gets CSRC [China Securities Regulatory Commission] and government officials to bend and to agree to things that they would have never agreed to in any other circumstances.[16]

As another interviewee highlighted, MSCI has a quasi-regulatory function – 'even though MSCI is not a regulator, companies need to abide by, to respect their rules'.[17] Since the inclusion, MSCI for instance delisted several Chinese companies that suspended the trading of their shares as this violated market accessibility.[18] Over the years, MSCI has been in close contact with the Chinese authorities, advising regulators on how to regulate markets to meet inclusion requirements or informing Chinese companies about MSCI corporate governance standards.[19]

Other observers, however, voiced concerns that the inclusion resulted from pressure by the Chinese government and MSCI's profit expectations through increased access to China.[20] *The Wall Street Journal*, for instance, highlighted that Chinese stock exchanges threatened to cancel MSCI's access to Chinese market data in case of a non-inclusion (Bird, 2019). In addition, this unprecedented inflow of foreign capital will take place according to rules set out by the Chinese state, including a level of surveillance, intervention and market guidance unthinkable in Western markets (Petry, 2020, 2021b). Because of the index inclusion, asset managers were 'forced into China'[21] – with index providers as intermediaries in this relationship.

Whether MSCI or the Chinese government prevailed in this development is still up for debate. What becomes clear, however, is that China's inclusion into MSCI indexes was not a neutral technical exercise but a highly political process with a significant impact on the global allocation of financial assets that requires further investigation. It is important to note that few states have the power to contest index providers, with China (and the United States) as possible exceptions to the rule. Most countries need to comply with their rules due to their integration into global financial circuits – this becomes especially clear when it comes to index exclusions.

Country exclusions: Peru and Argentina

One example for the power of index decisions is the case of Peru which MSCI in 2015 pondered to exclude from their 'emerging market' index and recategorise as 'frontier market'.[22] However, while the MSCI Emerging Markets index serves as a benchmark for funds worth $1.8 trillion, its frontier market index is tracked by only $4–14 billion.[23] Within a day following MSCI's announcement that it was considering moving Peru to its frontier markets index, the Peruvian stock market fell by 5% in one of the largest single-day losses. Cristian Laub, president of the Lima Stock exchange, estimated that in case of a reclassification, within three months $1.5 to $5 billion of international funds would exit the stock market, stating that 'if they tell us we're a frontier market, it will take us between 7–10 years to become an emerging market again; that's why the situation is serious'.[24] In September of 2015, the finance minister of Peru as well as officials from both the central bank and the securities regulator suddenly changed their schedules and took flights to New York for pressing consultations. The urgency of this situation was nicely captured by Alloway et al. (2017):

> What prompted a bevy of Peruvian officials to make the eight-hour journey wasn't a matter of urgent statecraft or diplomacy. Instead, it was a rumor that . . . MSCI might oust the South American country from its . . . emerging-markets index.

Eventually Peru managed to escape this fate by engaging in "roadshows with institutional investors 'to identify what were the necessary measures to strengthen liquidity and implement them'" (Doll, 2019). These measures included the introduction of market maker incentives, changes in trading rules that eased algorithmic trading, enabled short selling and derivative trading and as well as eliminating the capital gains tax.[25] Peru has since been on a watchlist and needs to continue its reform path in order to maintain its 'emerging market' status. What this episode demonstrates is the interlocking relationship between states and index providers, and the increasing private authority exercised by the latter.

Whereas Peru narrowly escaped a downgrade, the case of Argentina tells a different story. After Argentina imposed capital controls to prevent the depletion of foreign-currency reserves amidst a crisis of confidence that fueled dollar outflows, MSCI excluded Argentina from its emerging market index (MSCI, 2009). Since then, the Argentinian government engaged in renewed efforts to convince MSCI to also upgrade locally listed stocks from the frontier to the emerging market category, with measures such as replacing local brokers with global investment banks, upgrading its trading infrastructure and most importantly to 'imitate Peru' (Doll, 2019) – by cosying up to international investors, adhering to their standards, and trying to win back the favour of the major index providers. Further, between December 2015 and January 2017 capital controls were mostly dissolved (Table 6.2). Following these regulatory changes, MSCI reclassified Argentina to the Emerging Markets index during their Semi-Annual Index Review in May 2019,[26] resulting in capital inflows of about $3.8 into Argentina's stock market as estimated by JPMorgan.[27]

As these examples demonstrate, the decisions of index providers to include or exclude countries into an index or move them from one index category to another have significant consequences for both investor capital flows as well as national policies and the design of regulatory frameworks. The major index providers steer capital and negotiate (or in some cases arguably dictate) the conditionalities of financial claims between states and (passive) financial markets.

TABLE 6.2 Regulatory changes in Argentina

Restrictions	*Before December 2015*	*By January 2017*
Minimum period during which investments must stay in the country	365 days	Removed
Mandatory cash deposit applied to USD inflows	30%	Removed
Maximum limit for repatriation of funds from the same of equity securities	USD 500,000 per month	Removed
Approval from the central bank for repatriation of funds	Required and with certain conditions	Removed

Sources: MSCI (2016) *Consultation on a market reclassification proposal for the MSCI Argentina Index*. Retrieved from www.msci.com/documents/1296102/2907491/Argentina+Consultation_FINAL.pdf/9032789b-92c6-45ae-b9a3-d9d78284b8d7; MSCI (2017) *Consultation on a market reclassification proposal for the MSCI Argentina Index*. www.msci.com/documents/1296102/1330218/Argentina_Consultation_Jun17_FINAL.pdf/84f26c98-41a3-4ab5-8117-dd36ea81e7f4

Country watchlists: Korea, Brazil, India and Turkey

Country inclusions and exclusions, however, are only an ultimate solution for index providers to exercise their power. A probably even more effective instrument in their toolkit is placing countries on a watchlist. These watchlists have a dual purpose. On the one hand, they have an encouraging effect on countries that are under consideration for an inclusion or upgrade (e.g. from frontier to emerging market) – if countries' stay on their reform path, they will soon reap the benefits. On the other hand, if countries are 'misbehaving' they will be considered for a downgrade or exclusion and watchlists thus have a disciplinary effect. While in the era of active markets the threat of an investment strike kept states at bay, today the threat of an index reclassification through index providers facilitates this new constitutionalism (Gill and Law, 1989). By placing countries on watchlists for inclusions, exclusions or reclassifications, index providers create incentives for states to comply with their rules, again acting as key gatekeepers.

This is a very similar pattern to the effects of rating outlooks issued by the major credit rating agencies (Sinclair, 2005). Essentially, if a large index provider places a country on a watchlist it has a similar effect as when a rating agency gives a country a negative credit outlook. It is a warning sign to comply with the rules set out by the market authority or to suffer the negative consequences, i.e. the eventual downgrade and the following outflow of investments. Korea, Brazil, India and Turkey, for instance, are on MSCI's 'watchlist' of countries that could be downgraded if they do not ease investor access (MSCI, 2018; Tan and Robertson, 2018), highlighting the need to comply with the rulebook drafted by the major index providers.

In the case of Turkey, a series of bans on stock lending and short selling caused MSCI to consider downgrading Turkey to a 'frontier' market. MSCI noted that these steps 'severely restrict the ability of institutional investors to express active investment views and hedge portfolio risk' and that Turkey might be reclassified 'if the already deteriorating accessibility level of the Turkish equity market were to worsen further'. Emre Akcakmak, a Dubai-based portfolio manager at East Capital, noted that a reclassification as frontier market would be a 'loss of prestige' for Turkey, as 'its place is next to India, South Africa, Indonesia, Thailand – not next to some of the less developed and smaller frontier markets' (Pitel, 2020). While Turkey has not yet been reclassified, its weighting of the MSCI Emerging Market index was reduced from 0.5% in April 2020 to 0.28% in April 2021. This essentially represents a slap on the wrist by the index provider, with a possible reclassification looming in the background that is expected to trigger about $5 billion in total outflows from Turkish equities, including about $2–3 billion from passive investment funds that automatically track the index.

Watchlists have an intermediary function that signal to both investors and governments whether and under what conditions the current investment equilibrium might be changing. Placing a country on a watchlist can also make investors nervous and especially active investors might already exit a market before a possible downgrade, only increasing the pressures on the respective country's government to comply with the investment conditions set out by the major index providers. The threat of a downgrade or the promise of a potential upgrade therefore already influences the actions of states and markets.

Conclusion

In the past, so-called 'bond vigilantes' have frequently impacted sovereign debt markets, demanding higher yields whenever inflation expectations shot up. In their heyday during the 1980s and 1990s they strongly influenced US economic policy; during the Eurozone crisis bond vigilantes drove interest rates up for countries such as Italy and Spain to such an extent that they nearly faced a sovereign default. According to the *Oxford Dictionary*, a vigilante is 'a member of a self-appointed group of citizens who undertake law enforcement in their community without legal authority, typically because the legal agencies are thought to be inadequate.' Bond vigilantes thus can be seen as a kind of financial market 'militia' that takes the law into their own hands, so to speak, in order to punish states that 'live beyond their means.' Packs of bond vigilantes do not follow specific rules and their behaviour is rather erratic. That is why they have also been called 'hot money' in the past. The IMF and World Bank were gatekeepers in this previous setup as much as they stepped in during moments of crises, imposed conditionalities on crisis-ridden countries and injected capital to prevent a worsening of the respective countries' financial position, thereby maintaining the status quo of financial claims between debtors and creditors.

The rise of the index investing ecosystem is slowly but steadily supplanting the species of the bond vigilantes while simultaneously also taking on a role as gatekeepers that is (to some degree) functionally equivalent to the Bretton Woods institutions. First, a global financial habitat dominated by passive index funds is structured by different rules and logics. Foreign money that enters emerging markets via index funds is arguably not erratic, 'hot money' but rather sticky, 'cold' money. Investors in such funds have delegated their investment decisions to the respective index provider and are therefore not able to sell stocks or bonds of individual countries they may perceive as overly risky. What is still possible, though, is that due to an investor panic there is a general rush out of emerging markets. Furthermore, there are indications that index funds make emerging markets more sensitive to financial conditions in the 'Global North' (Converse et al., 2020).

Instead of erratic in- and out-flows into/from single countries, reallocation through indexes occurs in a more orderly fashion, largely determined by the index providers' schedule of market classification and weighting reviews. This may provide developing countries a certain amount of stability, or at least some transparency over investor behaviour. Increasingly, countries are not anymore facing an unpredictable pack of foreign investors but their counterparts are three major Anglo-American index providers whose decisions are more or less rule-based and thus predictive to a certain extent. If vigilantes are aggressive and erratic, the nature of index providers is almost diametrically opposed – rational and relatively rule-based. With a bit of imagination they could be called the new global finance 'bailiffs' – actors which are vested with growing (private) authority that act on behalf of the international investor community.

Most small and developing states are well aware that they have to fulfil the criteria for market accessibility for foreign investors set by the three major index providers. Moreover, states and markets know that the decisions of these index providers to include or exclude countries have become very consequential in this new age of passive investing. Rather than the IMF and World Bank which often only engaged with countries in moments of crises, index providers fulfil their role as gatekeepers more directly and permanently – constantly monitoring markets, their improvements and deviations from the rules set out in their methodologies and acting on these changes in regular intervals. It might be the case that in this new era of passive asset management financial flows in and out of developing countries will become more 'orderly' due to the rising importance of index investing. However, this does not at all mean that the global financial system is becoming less hierarchical – on the contrary, the major index providers are quickly turning into powerful gatekeepers that mediate international financial flows.

Notes

1 Interview: Senior managing director, index provider (Zurich, 23 August 2019).
2 Interview: Business development, exchange (Hong Kong, 19 August 2019).
3 Interview: Head of research, index provider (Frankfurt, 20 August 2019).
4 Moreover, there is a substantial proportion of equity funds that officially are actively managed but do not actually deviate much from their benchmark indexes. This is referred to as 'closet indexing' or 'index hugging', and it is estimated that in the EU between 5–15% of all equity funds could fall into this category (ESMA, 2016).
5 Interview: Head of research, index provider (Frankfurt, 20 August 2019).
6 Interview: Senior managing director, index provider (London, 3 September 2019).
7 Interview: Senior managing director, index provider (London, 3 September 2019).
8 Interview: Senior managing director, index provider (Zurich, 23 August 2019).

9 Country classification schemes are relatively similar: MSCI and S&P DJI (Frontier; Emerging; Developed) and FTSE (Frontier; Secondary Emerging; Advanced Emerging; Developed) (FTSE, 2019; MSCI, 2020b; S&P DJI, 2018).
10 Interview: Business development, index provider (Hong Kong, 27 September 2018).
11 Interview: Research department, index provider (Shanghai, 23 September 2019).
12 Interviews: Head of research, index provider (Frankfurt, 20 August 2019) and senior managing director, index provider (Zurich, 23 August 2019).
13 Interview: Head of research, index provider (Frankfurt, 20 August 2019).
14 Interview: Research department, index provider (Shanghai, 23 September 2019).
15 Interview: FX trading desk, global bank (Frankfurt, 25 January 2018); also, interview: hedge fund manager (Hong Kong, 27 June 2017)
16 Interview: business development, index provider (Hong Kong, 27 September 2018).
17 Interview: International department, exchange (Shanghai, 26 April 2018).
18 Interview: research department, index provider (Shanghai, 23 September 2019).
19 Interviews: international department, exchange (Shanghai, 26 April 2018), general manager, exchange (Hong Kong, 27 September 2018) and research department, index provider (Shanghai, 23 September 2019).
20 Interview: business development, global exchange (Hong Kong, 7 July 2017).
21 Observation: Orient Securities-Hong Kong Exchange Group investor presentation (Hong Kong, 6 July 2017).
22 see: www.msci.com/documents/1296102/2907491/Consultation+on+a+Market+Reclassification+Proposal+for+the+MSCI+Peru+Indexes/691d9a13-48cb-43f4-993b-e2b9f381a248 (last accessed 16 November 2020)
23 There is no exact data available for how many investors track individual indexes, with estimates ranging from $4 billion (https://e.vnexpress.net/news/business/phat-dat-realtor-proposed-to-msci-frontier-market-100-index-4187766.html (last accessed 16 November 2020) to $14 billion (https://perureports.com/lima-stock-exchange-falls-5-on-reclassification-fears/1977/ (last accessed 16 November 2020).
24 see: https://oxfordbusinessgroup.com/overview/tough-times-reforms-under-consideration-are-likely-increase-liquidity-and-trade-volumes (last accessed 16 November 2020).
25 see: https://oxfordbusinessgroup.com/overview/tough-times-reforms-under-consideration-are-likely-increase-liquidity-and-trade-volumes (last accessed 16 November 2020).
26 https://app2.msci.com/eqb/pressreleases/archive/MSCI_May19_QIRPR.pdf
27 www.berettagodoy.com/newsletter/argentina-regains-emerging-market-status/

References

Alami I (2018) Money power of capital and production of 'new state spaces': A view from the global south. *New Political Economy* 23(4): 512–529.

Alloway T, Burger D and Evans R (2017) Index providers rule the world – for now, at least. *Bloomberg*, 27 November. Available at: https://www.bloomberg.com/news/articles/2017-11-27/index-providers-rule-the-world-for-now-at-least (accessed 30 November 2021).

Arbogast T (2020) *Who Are These Bond Vigilantes Anyway? The Political Economy of Sovereign Debt Ownership in the Eurozone* (MPIfG Discussion Paper 20/2). Cologne: Max Planck Institute for the Study of Societies.

Authers J (2018) Indices don't just measure markets – they drive performance. *Financial Times*, 23 June. Available at: https://www.ft.com/content/ebcb8e88-7572-11e8-aa31-31da4279a601 (accessed 30 November 2021).

Berger S and Dore R (eds) (1996) *National Diversity and Global Capitalism*. Ithaca, NY: Cornell University Press.

Bernards N and Campbell-Verduyn M (2019) Understanding technological change in global finance through infrastructures. *Review of International Political Economy* 26(5): 773–789.

Bird M (2019) How China pressured MSCI to add its market to major benchmark. *The Wall Street Journal*, 3 February. Available at: https://www.wsj.com/articles/how-china-pressured-msci-to-add-its-market-to-major-benchmark-11549195201 (accessed 30 November 2021).

Bonizzi B and Kaltenbrunner A (2018) Liability-driven investment and pension fund exposure to emerging markets: A Minskyan analysis. *Environment and Planning A: Economy and Space* 51(2): 420–439.

Bortz P and Kaltenbrunner A (2018) The international dimension of financialization in developing and emerging economies. *Development & Change* 49(2): 375–393.

Braun B (2016) From performativity to political economy: Index investing, ETFs and asset manager capitalism. *New Political Economy* 21(3): 257–273.

Braun B (2020) Central banking and the infrastructural power of finance: The case of ECB support for repo and securitization markets. *Socio-Economic Review* 18(2): 395–418.

Braun B and Koddenbrock K (2022) The three phases of financial power: Leverage, infrastructure, and enforcement. In: Braun B and Koddenbrock K (eds) *Capital Claims: The Political Economy of Global Finance*. London: Routledge, pp. 1–30.

Broome A and Quirk J (2015) Governing the world at a distance: The practice of global benchmarking. *Review of International Studies* 41(5): 819–841.

Campbell-Verduyn M (2016) Merely TINCering around: The shifting private authority of technology, information and news corporations. *Business & Politics* 18(2): 143–170.

Carroll T, Clifton J and Jarvis DSL (2019) Power, leverage and marketization: The diffusion of neoliberalism from north to south and back again. *Globalizations* 16(6): 771–777.

Cerny PG (1994) The infrastructure of the infrastructure? Toward embedded financial orthodoxy in the international political economy. In: Palan RR and Gills B (eds) *Transcending the State-Global Divide a Neostructuralist Agenda in International Relations*. Boulder, CO: Lynne Reinner, pp. 223–249.

Converse N, Levy-Yeyati E and Williams T (2020) How ETFs amplify the global financial cycle in emerging markets. International Finance Discussion Papers 1268. Available at: https://www.federalreserve.gov/econres/ifdp/files/ifdp1268.pdf (accessed 30 November 2021).

Doll IO (2019) Argentina wants MSCI to upgrade local shares to emerging status. *Bloomberg*, 7 January. Available at: https://www.bloomberg.com/news/articles/2019-01-07/argentina-seeks-msci-to-upgrade-local-shares-to-emerging-status (accessed 30 November 2021).

ESMA (2016) ESMA updates on supervisory work on closet index tracking (ESMA/2016/138). Available at: www.esma.europa.eu/sites/default/files/library/2016-138_esma_updates_on_supervisory_work_on_closet_indexing.pdf (accessed 30 November 2021).

Fichtner J (2013a) Hedge funds: Agents of change for financialization. *Critical Perspectives on International Business* 9(4): 358–376.

Fichtner J (2013b) The rise of hedge funds: A story of inequality. *Momentum Quarterly* 2(1): 3–20.

Fichtner J (2017) Perpetual decline or persistent dominance? Uncovering Anglo-America's true structural power in global finance. *Review of International Studies* 43(1): 3–28.

Fichtner J (2020) The rise of institutional investors. In: Mader P, Mertens D and Van der Zwan N (eds) *The Routledge International Handbook of Financialization*. London: Routledge, pp. 265–275.

Fichtner J and Heemskerk EM (2020) The new permanent universal owners: Index funds, patient capital, and the distinction between feeble and forceful stewardship. *Economy & Society* 49(4): 493–515.

Fichtner J, Heemskerk EM and Garcia-Bernardo J (2017) Hidden power of the big three? Passive index funds, re-concentration of corporate ownership, and new financial risk. *Business & Politics* 19(2): 298–326.

FTSE Russell (2019) FTSE equity country classification process. Available at: www.ftse.com/products/downloads/FTSE_Equity_Country_Classification_Paper.pdf (accessed 30 November 2021).

Gabor D (2020) Critical macro-finance: A theoretical lens. *Finance & Society* 6(1).

Gill S and Law D (1989) Global hegemony and the structural power of capital. *International Studies Quarterly* 33(4): 475–499.

Gittelsohn J (2019) End of era: Passive equity funds surpass active in epic shift. *Bloomberg*, 11 September. Available at: https://www.bloomberg.com/news/articles/2019-09-11/passive-u-s-equity-funds-eclipse-active-in-epic-industry-shift (accessed 30 November 2021).

Goyer M (2007) Capital mobility, varieties of institutional investors, and the transforming stability of corporate governance in France and Germany. In: Hancké B, Rhodes M and Thatcher M (eds) *Beyond Varieties of Capitalism: Conflict, Contradictions, and Complementarities in the European Economy*. Oxford: Oxford University Press, pp. 195–219.

Haberly D, MacDonald-Korth D, Urban M and Wojcik D (2019) Asset management as a digital platform industry: A global financial network perspective. *Geoforum* 106: 167–181.

Haggard S and Maxfield S (1996) The political economy of financial internationalization in the developing world. *International Organization* 50(1): 35–68.

Hardie I (2012) *Financialization and Government Borrowing Capacity in Emerging Markets*. Basingstoke: Palgrave Macmillan.

Harmes A (1998) Institutional investors and the reproduction of neoliberalism. *Review of International Political Economy* 5(1): 92–121.

Hay C (2020) Does capitalism (still) come in varieties? *Review of International Political Economy* 27(2): 302–319.

He L (2018) US$400 billion expected to flow into Chinese stocks after MSCI inclusion. *South China Morning Post*, 15 May. Available at: https://www.scmp.com/business/companies/article/2146084/us400-billion-expected-flow-chinese-stocks-after-msci-inclusion (accessed 30 November 2021).

Henderson R (2019) JP Morgan edges closer to zero fees in a push for passive. *Financial Times*, 11 March. Available at: www.msci.com/documents/1296102/1332381/MSCI+Announcement+-+Feb+18+2009.pdf/fa1d2571-4d61-4541-93a0-9b1d47ed1f2d (accessed 30 November 2021).

IMF (2017) *Monetary and Financial Statistics Manual and Compilation Guide*. Washington, DC: International Monetary Fund.

Jahnke P (2019) Ownership concentration and institutional investors' governance through voice and exit. *Business & Politics* 21(3): 327–350.

Kaltenbrunner A and Painceira JP (2018) Subordinated financial integration and financialisation in emerging capitalist economies: The Brazilian experience. *New Political Economy* 23(3): 290–313.

Konings M (2007) The institutional foundations of US structural power in international finance: From the re-emergence of global finance to the monetarist turn. *Review of International Political Economy* 15(1): 35–61.

Konings M (2009) The construction of US financial power. *Review of International Studies* 35(1): 69–94.

Lane C (2003) Changes in corporate governance of German corporations: Convergence to the anglo-american model? *Competition & Change* 7(2–3): 79–100.

Maxfield S (1998) Effects of international portfolio flows on government policy choice. In: Kahler M (ed.) *Capital Flows and Financial Crises*. Ithaca, NY: Cornell University Press, pp. 69–92.

Maxfield S, Winecoff WK and Young KL (2017) An empirical investigation of the financialization convergence hypothesis. *Review of International Political Economy* 24(6): 1004–1029.

Millo Y (2007) Making things deliverable: The origins of index-based derivatives. *The Sociological Review* 55(2): 196–214.

Miyajima K and Shim I (2014). Asset managers in emerging market economies. *BIS Quarterly Review*, September, pp. 19–34.

Moreolo CS (2018) Don't doubt the power of index providers. *Investment Pensions Europe*, 18 February. Available at: https://www.ipe.com/analysis/opinion/dont-doubt-the-power-of-index-providers/10022946.article (accessed 30 November 2021).

Mosley L (2000) Room to move: International financial markets and national welfare states. *International Organization* 54(4): 737–773.

Mosley L (2003) *Global Capital and National Governments*. Cambridge: Cambridge University Press.

MSCI (2009) MSCI Barra announcement on the status of the MSCI Argentina and Pakistan Indices. Available at: www.msci.com/documents/1296102/1332381/MSCI+Announcement+-+Feb+18 + 2009.pdf/fa1d2571-4d61-4541-93a0-9b1d47ed1f2d (accessed 30 November 2021).

MSCI (2016) Consultation on a market reclassification proposal for the MSCI Argentina Index. Available at: www.msci.com/documents/1296102/2907491/Argentina+Consultation_FINAL.pdf/9032789b-92c6-45ae-b9a3-d9d78284b8d7 (accessed 30 November 2021).

MSCI (2017) Consultation on a market reclassification proposal for the MSCI Argentina Index. Available at: www.msci.com/documents/1296102/1330218/Argentina_Consultation_Jun17_FINAL.pdf/84f26c98-41a3-4ab5-8117-dd36ea81e7f4 (accessed 30 November 2021).

MSCI (2018) MSCI market classification framework: Consultation on potential methodology enhancements. Available at: www.msci.com/documents/1296102/1330218/Market+Classification+Consultation+%28Final%29.pdf/081f2dcb-f2f5-a93b-f529-0b5aaa5847d5 (accessed 30 November 2021).

MSCI (2020a) MSCI global market accessibility review. Available at: www.msci.com/documents/1296102/1330218/MSCI_2020_Global_Market_Accessibility_Review_Report.pdf/78a73a91-af3d-cf21-94e8-1cc2c159d2ce (accessed 30 November 2021).

MSCI (2020b) MSCI market classification framework. Available at: www.msci.com/documents/1296102/1330218/MSCI_Market_Classification_Framework_2020.pdf (accessed 30 November 2021).

Musthaq F (2021) Development finance or financial accumulation for asset managers?: The perils of the global shadow banking system in developing countries. *New Political Economy* 26(4): 554–573.

Naqvi N (2019) Manias, panics and crashes in emerging markets: An empirical investigation of the post-2008 crisis period. *New Political Economy* 24(6): 759–779.

Nölke A (2022) Geoeconomic infrastructures: Building Chinese-Russian alternatives to SWIFT. In: Braun B and Koddenbrock K (eds) *Capital Claims: The Political Economy of Global Finance*. London: Routledge, p. 246–277.

Norrlof C (2010) *America's Global Advantage: US Hegemony and International Cooperation*. Cambridge: Cambridge University Press.

Oliver L (2021) Are you being left behind? Institutions are not waiting on MSCI China A-Share inclusion. *KraneShares Blog*, 13 May. Available at: https://kraneshares.com/are-you-being-left-behind-institutions-are-not-waiting-on-msci-china-a-share-inclusion/ (accessed 30 November 2021).

Panitch L and Gindin S (2012) *The Making of Global Capitalism: The Political Economy of American Empire*. London: Verso.
Panitch L and Konings M (eds) (2009) *American Empire and the Political Economy of Global Finance*. Basingstoke: Palgrave Macmillan.
Petry J (2020) Financialization with Chinese characteristics? Exchanges, control and capital markets in authoritarian capitalism. *Economy & Society* 49(2): 213–238.
Petry J (2021a) From national marketplaces to global providers of financial infrastructures: Exchanges, infrastructure & power in global finance. *New Political Economy* 26(4): 574–597.
Petry J (2021b) Same same, but different: Varieties of capital markets, Chinese state capitalism & the global financial order. *Competition & Change* 25(5): 605–630.
Petry J, Fichtner J and Heemskerk E (2021) Steering capital: The growing private authority of index providers in the age of passive asset management. *Review of International Political Economy* 28(1): 152–176.
Petry J, Koddenbrock K and Nölke A (2021) State capitalism and capital markets: Comparing securities exchanges in emerging markets. *Environment and Planning A: Economy and Space*. Epub ahead of print 4 October. doi:10.1177/0308518X211047599.
Pitel L (2020) Turkey faces threat of MSCI downgrade to 'frontier' market. *Financial Times*, 24 June. Available at: https://www.ft.com/content/dca643f7-ae94-4498-8856-b6ba2f96981b (accessed 30 November 2021).
Raddatz C, Schmukler SL and Williams T (2017) International asset allocations and capital flows: The benchmark effect. *Journal of International Economics* 108: 413–430.
Robertson AZ (2019) Passive in name only: Delegated management and 'index' investing. *Yale Journal on Regulation* 36(2): 795–851.
Robertson B and Lam E (2019) UBS sees $121 billion of EM flows amid 'seismic' index shifts. *Bloomberg*, 11 February. Available at: https://www.bloomberg.com/news/articles/2019-02-11/ubs-sees-121-billion-of-em-flows-amid-seismic-index-shifts (accessed 30 November 2021).
Rommerskirchen C (2015) Debt and punishment: Market discipline in the Eurozone. *New Political Economy* 20(5): 752–782.
Rommerskirchen C (2019) *EU Fiscal Policy Coordination in Hard Times: Free Riders on the Storm*. Oxford: Oxford University Press.
Roos JE (2019) *Why Not Default? The Political Economy of Sovereign Debt*. Princeton, NJ: Princeton University Press.
S&P DJI (2018) Country classification methodology. Available at: https://us.spindices.com/documents/index-policies/methodology-country-classification.pdf (accessed 30 November 2021).
Sinclair TJ (2005) *The New Masters of Capital: American Bond Rating Agencies and the Politics of Creditworthiness*. Ithaca, NY: Cornell University Press.
SPIVA (2019) SPIVA U.S. year-end 2018. *S&P Indices Versus Active Database*. Available at: https://us.spindices.com/spiva/ (accessed 30 November 2021).
Strange S (1987) The persistent myth of lost hegemony. *International Organization* 41(4): 551–574.
Strange S (1997) The future of global capitalism; or, will divergence persist? In: Crouch C and Streeck W (eds) *Political Economy of Modern Capitalism: Mapping Convergence and Diversity*. London: SAGE Publications, pp. 172–191.
Streeck W (2010) E pluribus unum? Varieties and commonalities of capitalism. Max Planck Institute for the Study of Societies, MPIfG Discussion Paper, 10/12. Available at: https://papers.ssrn.com/sol3/papers.cfm?abstract_id=1805522 (accessed 30 November 2021).
Sushko V and Turner G (2018) The implications of passive investing for securities markets. *BIS Quarterly Review*, pp. 113–131.

Tan A and Robertson B (2018) MSCI weighs capping India, Brazil weights over investor access. *Bloomberg*, 30 May. Available at: https://www.bqprime.com/global-economics/msci-weighs-capping-india-brazil-weights-over-investor-access (accessed 30 November 2021).

Thiemann M (2022) The benefits of network centrality: Central counterparties, the enforceability of claims and the securing of extra-profits. In: Braun B and Koddenbrock K (eds) *Capital Claims: The Political Economy of Global Finance*. London: Routledge, pp. XX–XX.

Wagner C and Ballentine C (2020) Record $170 billion has flooded into bond ETFs thanks to fed. *Bloomberg*, 12 October. Available at: https://www.bloomberg.com/news/articles/2020-10-12/bond-etfs-go-from-roughed-up-to-record-inflows-thanks-to-the-fed (accessed 30 November 2021).

Wigglesworth R (2019) MSCI chief looks beyond traditional indices for growth. *Financial Times*, 31 July. Available at: https://www.ft.com/content/8781d88e-b1ed-11e9-8cb2-799a3a8cf37b (accessed 30 November 2021).

Wright C (2019) MSCI China reweighting a big deal – but not that big. *Euromoney*, 1 March. Available at: https://www.euromoney.com/article/b1dbtqkccxw6w9/msci-china-reweighting-a-big-deal-but-not-that-big (accessed 30 November 2021).

7

THE BENEFITS OF NETWORK CENTRALITY

Central counterparties, the enforceability of claims, and the securing of extra-profits

Matthias Thiemann

Introduction

Derivatives, financial claims to future revenue flows, have become the hallmark of financialized capitalism (Helleiner et al., 2018). They are central elements of private risk management systems that allow financial actors to address financial market volatility (Bryan and Rafferty, 2006, 2007; Esposito, 2013; Lockwood, 2015). The expansion of derivatives, claims on revenue flows derived from developments in underlying assets, has been facilitated by the rise of financial economics, which helped to move speculation on future price developments away from the notion of gambling and towards the notion of informed-risk taking (De Goede, 2004). These theories also permitted the building of financial infrastructures, which embed these financial formulaes into market practices (MacKenzie and Millo, 2003; MacKenzie, 2009), facilitating the expansion of stock exchanges, such as the Chicago Board of Exchanges or the Chicago Mercantile Exchange to offer the trading of stock options, futures and foreign exchange and interest rate swaps (MacKenzie, 2006).

Derivatives allow their claim holders to hedge against an uncertain future (Esposito, 2013), permitting the creation of calculability amidst a volatile financial environment. A central condition to make these futures calculable for individual agents, however, is that the counterparty to the derivative and its claim on future flows of revenue does not default, thereby guaranteeing the enforceability of these claims. If the counterparty does default, all the calculations regarding the volatilities of asset classes and their correlations, based upon which market agents build a hedged portfolio are obsolete, as a new, largely uncalculable problem enters into the calculations.[1] For a financial system based on the calculation and pricing of future contingencies, the systemic question hence arises which agent is willing and capable to provide the system with this kind of stability, absorbing not only the risks inherent in the contracts entered, but also the risk of default by any single

DOI: 10.4324/9781003218487-9

counterparty ? Which actor is able to provide a guarantee of low, quasi-zero counterparty risks, i.e. a low probability of default to others in the face of such uncertainty? The system of financial risk management is by necessity based on certain central agents, whose balance sheets are capable of shouldering these volatilities of financial capitalism, providing stability to the system in return (Tucker, 2014).[2]

While large dealer banks held this highly profitable position before the financial crisis, capitalizing on their large balance sheets and their too-big to fail status (Kane, 2009), this status came under question after the cataclysmic experience of the Lehman Brothers default in 2008. Subsequently, financial regulators worldwide chose to elevate central counterparties (CCPs) to the role of anchors of systemic stability, making these agents into central nodes of financialized capitalism (Genito, 2019). Strengthening the resilience of these CCPs would become a core pillar of regulatory interventions post-crisis (Tucker, 2011), as regulators sought to reconstruct, rather than abolish shadow banking (Birk and Thiemann, 2020; Braun, 2020; Endrejat and Thiemann, 2020; Gabor and Ban, 2016; Thiemann, 2014, 2018). In this regulatory project of creating resilient market-based finance, CCPs were to be the ever-present other. Removing counterparty risks from the equation, their presence guarantees the possibility for calculated risk-taking by private agents. In this sense, their newly won status at the center of trading claims on the future can best be understood as part of the regulatory attempt to make empirical financial markets behave in line with financial theory, allowing the insurance against all possible risks to become a reality (MacKenzie, 2006).

As I will argue, this new regulatory regime, its legal provisions as well as the implicit and explicit liquidity support by central banks reduce the likelihood of a CCP default towards zero. We show that this de facto status of non-bankruptcy gives rise to a risk-reward distribution between the different members of the clearing business which favors CCPs over clearing member banks. It also leaves systemic risks largely with central banks, which are forced to provide liquidity to these entities in the case of systemic turmoil. These facts invite us to reflect on the role of regulators and their legal interventions on the status and profitability of financial market agents. To make sense of these dynamics, we suggest to revisit the theory of the coding of capital (Pistor, 2019) and the structural factors which underlie the power of claim-making (Braun and Koddenbrock, 2022, this volume), embedding them within a legal theory of finance (Pistor, 2013). Based on this analysis, the extra-profits generated by CCPs become a structural feature, inscribed in the regulatory positioning of these entities in the financial system post-crisis. This positioning can only be understood if one takes into account regulators' desire to stabilize a vision of "resilient market based finance" (FSB, 2015), which incentivized the clearing of derivatives in order to maintain a system of private risk management (Lockwood, 2018).

The rise of CCPs post-crisis

Pre-crisis, the structural problem of how to exclude counter-party default risks was solved through the balance sheets of the Too-big-to fail banks, such as Deutsche

Bank and investment banks, such as Lehman Brothers. These entities were essentially absorbing the counterparty risks of other contractual partners on their balance sheet for a fee, using their large balance sheets to equilibrate these risks, applying the law of large numbers and the calculus of financial economics to balance different claims and net them on their balance sheet. This activity was enabled by the fact that these large dealer banks, could accumulate a critical mass of deals on their balance sheets They could do so because they could provide much of their balance sheets free or almost free of regulatory charges to their clients, while accumulating systemic risks in the process (s. Thiemann et al., 2018). In part at least, their business model was to cash in in their too-big to fail status with clients, their low counterparty risk being implicitly linked to their systemic size (s. Kane, 1988, 2009 for a general reflection on the regulatory advantages of this status).

This risk taking was hence not only largely free of regulatory charges and highly profitable,[3] but also based on the implicit public backstop by public authorities, validating a notion of shadow banking which points to the persistent involvement of banks' balance sheet, backstopped by central banks (Claessens and Ratnovski, 2014). This era of a largely unregulated market for derivatives, which were mostly offered in the form of over-the counter derivatives by broker-dealers ran into problems during the 2007/2008 crisis (Duffie, 2018; Eren, 2014), culminating in the failure of Lehman brothers in 2008. Disentangling the swaps and derivatives book of Lehman proved extremely difficult for supervisors in the event of the default,[4] aggravating the uncertainty over where the actual losses were located and hence fueling contagion in financial markets, which were no longer able to assess counter-party risks (Swedberg, 2012). At the same time, a different actor in the realm of netting counterparty risks proved much more resilient, hence posing less problems for supervisors and becoming a supposed solution for regulators' conundrum of how to deal with derivatives markets after the financial crisis (Bulfone and Smolenska, 2020).

Central CounterParties had little to no losses during the crisis and proved remarkably resilient during the financial market turmoil (FSF, 2007). This is why regulators pinned their hopes to solve the problem of too interconnected to fail on CCPs, with regulation bringing about the rise of CCPs in financial markets (G20, 2009; Cerezetti et al., 2019). Holding the promise of unbundling the financial system post-financial crisis, helping to overcome the problem of too connected to fail, they themselves would become too big to fail in the process (Chamorro-Courtland, 2012; Krahnen and Pelizzon, 2016).

Before the final regulatory decisions regarding the mandatory clearing came into force in 2012, CCPs were a backwater of financial markets, a rather unimportant niche player which did provide useful services but was by no means dominating the clearing of derivatives or repo-transactions. Post-2012, CCPs experienced strong balance sheet growth (Duffie, 2016), so much so that they became major profit centers for their owners, large stock exchanges (Petry, 2020). With the obligation for mandatory clearing for most derivatives, an idea endorsed in 2009 by the G20 and implemented by 2010 in the United States (Dodd-Frank legislation) and

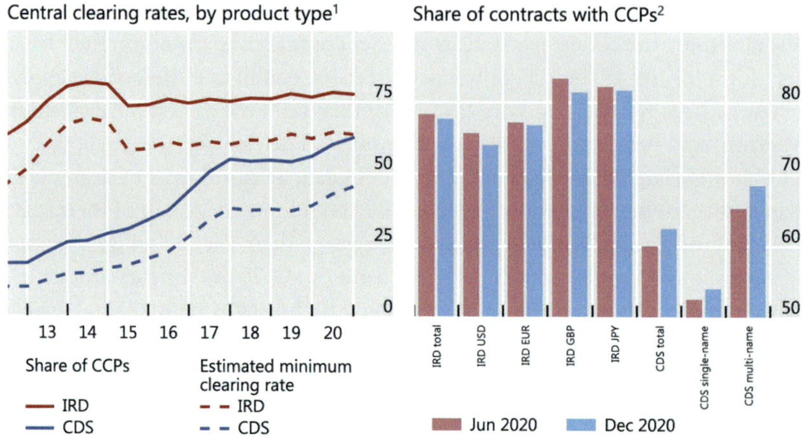

FIGURE 7.1 Growth of central clearing for different asset classes

Source: BIS (2021: 4).

2012 in the EU (European Market Infrastructure Regulation), Over-The Counter FX-derivatives, credit swaps and the clearing of repo-trades increasingly migrated to CCPs (see Figure 7.1). As a consequence of this growth, almost 80% of interest rate derivatives and more than 55% of Credit Default Swaps worldwide were cleared with CCPs in 2021 (BIS, 2021, for prior numbers, s. Aramonte and Huang, 2019: 88)

With this growth of business volume, came an increase in profitability and employment linked to post-trade operations (Huang, 2019; Huang and Takats, 2020), which meant that the presence and expansions of CCPs suddenly become a major asset for financial centers.[5] Their profitability, with an average of 36% is more than three times the average profitability of banks, which since 2010 hovers around 10% (Huang and Takats, 2020: 7).[6] To fully understand the basis of these large profits and its link to regulatory interventions, we need to first turn to the particular business model of CCPs and the role membership banks play in it.

Description of the business model of CCPs and their profitability

Central counterparties, most of which are today owned by stock exchanges, are in the business of entering into counterparty agreements, whereby they assume the counterparty risk of another entity for a fee. Entering into a counterparty agreement, clients have to post collateral based on initial margins and have to provide additional collateral when the volatility of their contracts increases (called variable margins). The advantage for their clients is that it allows corporate clients to reduce collateral needed to secure their positions, as CCPs are assuming a large portfolio of e.g. derivative contracts, allowing for certain of the risks of these derivative

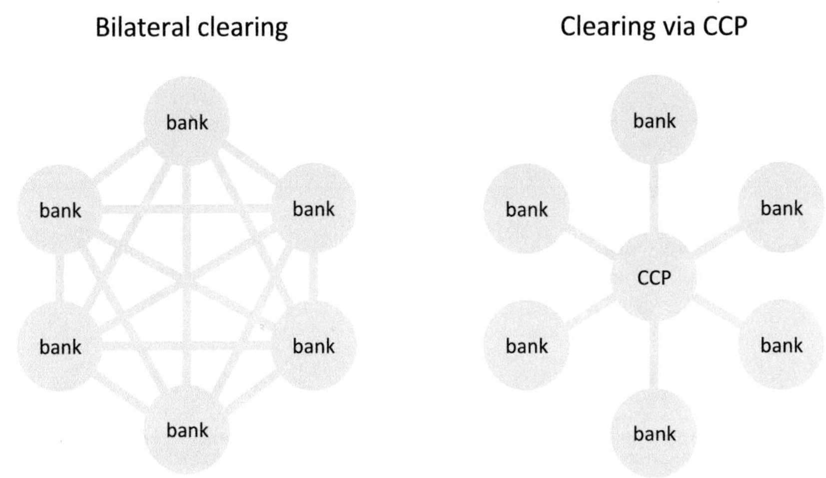

FIGURE 7.2 Simplified graphical representation of the effect of CCPs on the structure of the financial system

Source: Friedrich et al., 2017

positions to net out. This netting of collateral for corporate clients also reduces overall requirements for collateral for the system as a whole, which became a crucial concern in the context of the post-crisis regulatory move to an ever-more collateral intensive financial system (Gabor, 2016). Entering into these agreements also provides certainty to clients with respect to their risk calculations if the CCP can be deemed "bankruptcy proof," as this allows the elimination of any counterparty risks. As such, CCPs stand in between prior business partners and replace them as the central node in a web of derivative contracts (Figure 7.2).

Given that the capacity of CCPs to manage these financial risks depends to a large degree on the size of their portfolio of trades which allows the application of the law of large numbers (statistical regularities only hold for a large number of trades) and hence of private risk management techniques based on financial economics, there is a network effect inherent to the business of CCPs.[7] Due to this structural characteristic of the business model of CCPs, the business of CCPs is usually based on large volumes of trades, realizing a low profit margin. This aspect of the business of CCPs means that the high profitability of CCPs can only be realized by applying a high leverage, using little of own risk bearing capital to the overall volume of trades. This means that CCPs generally only carry a minuscule amount of core capital with respect to their overall business, seeking to maximize the risks they assume given a limited amount of core capital (interview former CCP risk manager, 2018; Huang, 2019; Huang and Takats, 2020).

This thin layer of equity by CCPs, coupled with the question of the resilience of these entities was a point of concern for regulators as they were seeking to transform shadow banking into "resilient market based financing" (FSB, 2015).

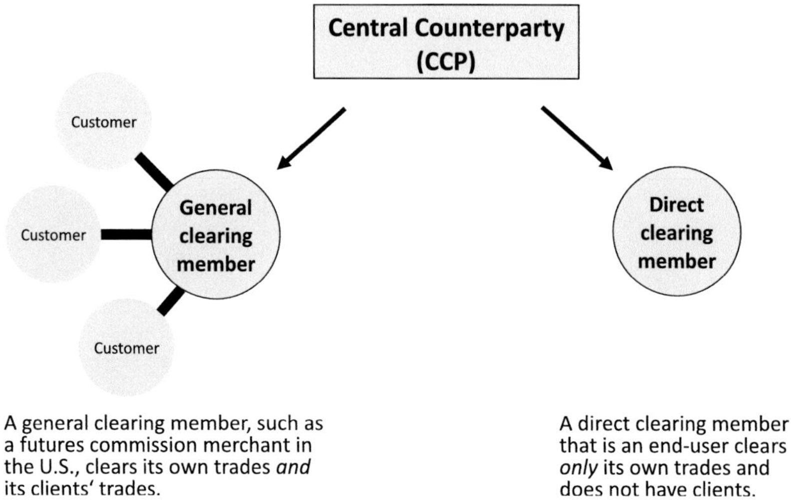

FIGURE 7.3 Actual business model of CCPs, including general clearing members

Source: Own representations

This was linked to a second aspect, possibly the biggest regulatory headache, which was the persistant entanglement of banks and CCPs in the business of clearing derivatives and repo-markets. This inextricable intertwinement becomes evident, once one zooms into the way the clearing business of CCPs is actually organized, revealing the much larger role of general clearing member banks than the initial simplified graph revealed (see Figure 7.3).

The largest general clearing members of a CCP depicted earlier are clearing member banks, which in turn collect the derivatives of their customers, which they clear for them with the CCP. In this way, large banks de facto share the business of clearing with CCPs, which pre-crisis was the domain of the large dealer banks alone. In other words, large general clearing member banks offer their clients netting agreements, and they in turn enter into netting agreements with a CCP, reducing the amount of necessary collateral posted at each step of the way, allowing both central clearing member banks as well as CCPs to use less collateral than the one initially posted by end clients. This continuing business linkage between CCPs and large banks can best be appreciated when looking at the example of LCH Clearnet in London, the largest CCP in Europe which invited the large banks into a profit sharing agreement to attract their business (s. e.g. Stafford, 2013). In the context of Brexit, its contender in Europe, the German CCP Eurex did the same in 2017 to attract Euro-denominated FX derivatives to their own trading platform (s. Jones, 2020).

This facet provides us with a slightly different graphical understanding of the clearing business in concentric cicles, where CCPs stand at the center of the clearing business, surrounded by clearing banks, which collect and channel the derivative trades of their end clients. A CCP is dependent in its business model on its clearing member banks, which collect the trades their clients have entered into and subsequently transfer them to the CCP for clearing. This interlinkage between central counterparties and clearing member banks invites a constant struggle between CCPs and banks over which entity carries how much risk of default of counterparties and which entity gains from ensuring the enforceability of these claims.[8] CCPs, which usually are owned by stock exchanges hence stand in a permanent relationship of both competition and cooperation with their large member banks, collaborating in the collection of derivatives for netting, while vying to appropriate as much of the fee business for themselves and delegating as much as possible of the risks to the commercial banks. It is in the context of this struggle over profits and risks of the business of netting derivative trades that regulators have crucially intervened.

Regulatory interventions post-crisis

To ensure the viability of CCPs, regulators have insisted on installing three lines of defense (CPMI-IOSCO, 2012). Given the fact that CCPs themselves have very limited core capital, these interventions regarding the risks CCPs accumulate mean that their clearing member banks de facto carry a large part of the burden. In this respect, the first line of defense is the collateral posted by the defaulting member of the CCP (Huang and Takats, 2020: 5), which are based on the netting calculations of the CCP risk models. The second line of defense, called "skin in the game" is based on the sliver of equity of CCP itself, which is often backed up by contingent capital contributions of the stock exchange behind them, that is capital which will be made available by the stock exchange, should the skin in the game be used up (howver not all of it is available for the second line-of defence). The third line of defense regards the central clearing member banks' prefunded resources, such as default fund contributions and the possibility for a call on surviving member banks to provide resources to secure the functioning of the CCP (Huang and Takats, 2020: 5).

The actual distribution of possible losses among these different lines of defense and the size of the contribution of each of these members involved in the netting of collateral has been heatedly debated, with regulators taking the final decisions only recently. In the end, the regulator-imposed distribution of losses and allocation of risk bearing capital meant that the 39 largest CCPs around the globe in 2019 had equity of only 5 billion dollars, when collateral provided for margin requirements equalled 700 billion dollars and default funds by member banks consisted of more than 100 billion dollars (Huang and Takats, 2020: 6). Regulatory decision-making which led to this distribution, we argue, has been shaped by regulator's project of transforming shadow banking into resilient market-based finance, and hence the perceived need to ensure the viability of CCPs at all times. If the vagaries and volatilities of the shadow banking system were to be brought under control, this implied the guarantee of persistent trading of risk unaffected by the default of central nodes in the network of financial contracts, a truly utopian aspect of the regulation of shadow banking (Kessler and Wilhelm, 2013). Uncluttering this network and replacing dealer banks with CCPs yet at the same time meant that CCPs themselves were not allowed to default.

This impossibility of default, inscribed in the regulatory project has led to considerations in regulatory circles that CCPs are de facto public infrastructures, a fact which in 2010 led to the public discussion whether CCPs should not be public infrastructures tout court (interview, Bundesbank official involved in the discussions, June 2016). Yet, in the end the decision was taken to maintain the private status of these entities, inscribing the private ownership of the quasi-public institution CCP at the heart of this regulatory program, much in line with Pagliari's finding of the prevalence of private risk management systems in the context of post-crisis reforms (Pagliari, 2012). The contradiction this status entails and how they were resolved can best be observed in the regulatory work on the CCP recovery and resolution directives as well as the intervention of central banks in the process.

To make sense of these dynamics, we propose to combine and advance the theory of law in finance (Pistor, 2013), which points to the malleability of legal constraints at the apex of the financial system with the general legal theory of capital as "coded" assets, which links the profitability and valuation of assets to the legal properties of assets (Pistor, 2019). Going beyond this proposition, we point to the legal coding of the organizational form which is not only shaped by private lawyering, but also by regulatory projects and hence public law, providing infrastructural power to CCPs in the process (Braun and Koddenbrock, 2022, this volume).

Theory: hierarchical financial space and the coding of capital

The first leg of our theoretical tool kit, the legal theory of finance emphasizes that the centrality of actors in financial system is crucial for the probability of the flexibility of the law when they encounter problems (Pistor, 2013). It states that the more central you are in the financial system, that is to say the higher up you are placed in the hierarchy of the system (Mehrling, 2012), the more likely the public rules of bankruptcy are to be relaxed when the system enters into financial troubles (for an empirical analysis of this dynamic in the financial crisis, s. Mehrling, 2010; Pistor, 2013). Pointing to the central hybridity of the financial system, erected in the interplay between private and public actors, this theory points out that the survival constraints which structures bankruptcy law will not be applied and emergency liquidity assistance will be forthcoming to actors deemed too important to fail. This theoretical "encoding" of systemic risk into legal considerations regarding bankruptcy proceedings hence crucially links the fate of financial entities to their position within the financial system.

The second leg of the theory consists in pointing to the legal composition of assets as claims to future revenue flows which are enshrined in private law (Pistor, 2019; Braun and Koddenbrock, 2022; this volume). It is the work of private lawyers which codes these assets in such a way that their owners gain priority on claims, that the enforceability of claims is secured and, that if possible, they can escape bankruptcy proceedings. Such lawyering might involve the shielding of such assets from other claimants by evoking organizational forms, such as the trust to protect real estate and other assets. The attachment of these properties provides these assets with a durability and fungibility which secures their holders crucial advantages in the struggle for extra-profits. Shifting the risk-reward profile of these assets, it increases their value as capital to the holder of these assets. Our proposal is to meld and advance both of these theories and to include the role of public regulatory projects to make sense of the case of the heightened profitability and durability of CCPs.

Here, we would like to point out that the notion of capital, as recently advanced by Pistor (2019), explicitly includes the modern corporate form. Capital is not always free-floating in the form of freely tradable assets, which are traded to become more durable. Instead, capital can become fixed in the corporate form, whereby it becomes equity, which posits a non-tradable claim on future revenues of a corporate entity. Many of the same considerations regarding the durability of that capital still apply, yet they are now applied to the corporate form itself, concerning its modalities of survival, the revenue streams and risks it is exposed to and/or the existence of other entities, be they public or private which de facto assume these risks and/or rewards. One consequence of this move is that it is now not only private law and the ingenuity of the masters of the code which can generate advantages for particular factions of capital. Instead, such advantages can also be generated through stipulations in public law regarding the risk and reward profile certain corporate forms are subjected to (Djelic, 2013). Their work can create legal corporate forms which de facto shield the owner of these corporate forms from the risks of bankruptcy (for the case of "entails" protecting aristocrats' real estate, see Pistor, 2019: 37f).

Expanding the realm of analysis to public law allows us to not only focus on the agency of private lawyers, but also public lawmakers and regulators, which pursue their own goals of statecraft, when shaping these legal stipulations regarding corporate forms.[9] This analytical shift throws into the spotlight the possibility of the alliances of regulators and private blocks of capital in the pursuit of certain "state projects" (Quinn, 2017; Ozgode, 2021). In the case at hand, the regulatory project consists in establishing CCPs as a central pillar of the project of the transformation of shadow banking into "resilient market based financing" (FSB, 2015), which finds its expression in crucial stipulations in public law. It is, we will argue these legal stipulations, which are an expression of the central position CCPs have gained in this regulatory project of making "market-based finance" resilient. In the pursuit of this regulatory project, CCPs have been elevated towards the status of indispensable infrastructures, a quasi-public utility which nevertheless remain in private ownership, which in turn secures extra-profits for those holding the equity of these entities.

It is this "infrastructural power" now held by CCPs which is the foundation of these extra-profits, which are based on a legal re-ordering of the risks and rewards of the enterprise of clearing derivatives contracts and repo-contracts. This legal re-ordering was enacted by an alliance of regulators and CCPs in favor of the latter, de facto forcing large commercial banks, which act as member banks of these CCPs to carry a larger part of the risks of the clearing business. Understanding the actual realized profitability of a business enterprise as the outcome of the distribution of risk and rewards of certain activities, it is the fine-tuning of both of these components that explain why by 2018, CCPs were on average more than three times as profitable as large commerciam member banks (Huang and Takats, 2020: 6).

Fundamental contradiction of the private status of CCPs in the current regulatory framework

CCPs are supposed to be the ever-present other in the vision of market-based finance, those entities which permit the elimination of counter-party risk. At the same time, CCPs are privately owned entities, most often owned by stock exchanges which are hence supposed to be subject to market discipline of failure. This hybrid status, and the linkage of CCPs to both commercial banks as clearing member banks on the one hand and the regulatory initiatives to increase the resilience on the other hand led to two frictions. On one level, there was the fight between banks and CCPs over who should bear the costs of precaution, that is to say who should provide how much loss absorption capacity in terms of equity and collateral to deal with the daily fluctuations of asset classes? On the other hand, the question arose who should bear the costs if events in financial markets spiralled out of control and what were to be the security valves which would allow the continued services of the CCP?

These issues were negotiated in the context of the EU regulation of CCP Recovery and Resolution, which was completed in December 2020. Seeking to determine how the repercussions of market turmoil, caused for example by the default of a large member bank could be cushioned to prevent disruptions in the functioning of CCPs, this regulation sought to establish ex ante the distribution of losses in case of emergency. In the background of these questions, the more fundamental question lurked with respect to the issue whether a CCP could ever even be allowed to fail. Given their central status to regulatory reforms, had they not become a public infrastructure, like an electricity grid which cannot be turned off (s. Nabilou and Asimakopoulos, 2020)? This question posed itself with a dramatic virulence in the negotiations over the resolution directive, which envisioned the modalities of resolving a failed CCP to prevent the failure of such a CCP to further disrupt the market in a situation most likely already characterized by severe financial market turmoil (for a financial practitioner perspective on the outcomes of these fights, s. Cerezetti et al., 2019).

The fight over the burden-sharing in recovery and resolution

The question how to make CCPs resilient to financial market turmoil rose to the top of the regulatory agenda after at the G20 Summit in Pittsburgh in

September 2009 decided that "all standardised OTC derivative contracts should be traded on exchanges or electronic trading platforms, where appropriate, and cleared through central counterparties by end 2012 at the latest" (FSB, 2010). Subsequently, the FSB coordinated with the international association of capital market regulators IOSCO and the Committee on Payments and Settlement Systems (CPSS; later to be renamed the Committee on Payment Systems and Market Infrastructures (CPMI)) to generate the Principles for Financial Market Infrastructures, published in April 2012. While these principles were a first attempt to coordinate globally on the safe regulation of CCPs, the question of how to organize recovery and resolution of these entities was not yet decided.

Instead, several working groups were formed, seeking to generate a regulatory framework that would secure these market infrastructures. The work of these working groups was documented in the recovery report October 2014 and then updated through regulatory guidance in July 2017 (CPMI-IOSCO, 2017). Such guidance then still needed to be translated into national or European regulation, in turn inviting struggles over the question of how to allocate possible losses in moments when the viability of CCPs is in critical danger. For the case of the EU, these negotiations started after the enactment of the European Market Infrastructure Regulation (EMIR), implementing the PFMIs in 2012 and lasted well more than half a decade. In the EU, it took the institutions almost five years to find agreement on the CCP Recovery and Resolution framework proposed by the European Commission in 2016. Without going into too much detail, one can argue that banks largely lost the fight over the attribution of risks, as it is not CCPs but mainly banks have to bear the burden of potential losses in the case of recovery.

The PFMI required the establishment of an "end-of-waterfall" structure for a CCP, "which comprised a layer of unfunded contributions from members, the haircutting of variation margin (often for a defined period, or up to a cap) and, as a last resort, the 'tear-up' of cleared contracts" (Cerezetti et al., 2019: 14). This configuration grants CCPs the right to allocate losses to clearing member banks in case of a recovery situation, giving them access to member's capital, the collateral they provide and in extremis the right to tear up contracts which cannot be reassigned to other member banks (ISDA, 2021). This means that clearing member banks are liable with their collateral and as contributing members to the CCP are bearing much of the risks the CCP is exposed to. While CCPs also had had to raise their "skin in the game" (capital at risk) following these new rules,[10] their equity continues to only be a sliver of what is needed to bear the risks (Huang and Takats, 2020). This distribution of losses in the recovery situation to us is the strongest sign of the positioning of regulators on the side of CCPs. Why do we see this distribution of risk and rewards? We submit that it is because the viability of CCPs has been deemed crucial, in particular by central banks which exerted pressure in the background as they provide the liquidity to central counter-parties in case of market turmoil.

These reforms, implemented against the complaints of clearing member banks basically allow CCPs to charge for clearing and netting trades, in effect removing counterparty risks while allowing the CCP to shift a big part of the risks of their actual business to clearing member banks. This structural one-sidedness of reforms, based on the centrality of CCP's, deemed crucial for the regulatory project continued with respect to the crafting of the Resolution directive. Here, the goal was to ensure that in resolution, a CCP can perform its function, as the resolution authority takes the CCP into receivership (Cerezetti et al., 2019: 13). The reason for that is that different CCPs operate with different netting systems, implying that the transfer of trades to a new CCP would most likely produce new margin calls for concerned parties (Cerezetti et al., 2019: 14). To avoid this from happening, resolution authorities have the right in case of systemic crisis to annul option contracts, based on the no creditor worse off clause. This implies that if a trade endangers the viability of a CCP, the resolution authority can cancel such a trade against the will of a clearing bank. To do so, it only needs to be able to make the case that annuling the trade makes "no creditor worse off" (Art. 21(1)(c) CCP RRR), which is guaranteeed by the fact that the default of a large CCPs will always be a systemic event (Cerezetti et al., 2019).

This role of regulators in resolution regulation points to the underlying problem inherent in the resolution of CCPs. From the beginning, the goal of regulators working on resolution was to be able to resolve a CCP in an orderly manner, securing financial stability in the short run while imposing market discipline in the long run (FSB, 2010). Yet, given the new centrality of CCPs in the reordered financial system, the question arises whether such a default is actually a possibility? Here, expert interviews with technocrats of the ECB firmly came down on the negative side, but only in off-the record interviews. The arguments invoked refer to the fact that you cannot turn off a CCP in a crisis, just like you cannot turn off the provider of an electricity grid. This public infrastructure status of CCP's means that default, the real life basis of "market discipline" is a utopia regulators cannot risk to become a reality.

Conclusion: the unresolved contradiction of the private status of CCPs

While the enforceability of claims is essential for capitalism, the enforceability of options is essential for financialized capitalism.[11] If it cannot be secured on a broad level, it risks the breakdown of a technique of hedging future events and their potential negative outcomes based on a private risk calculus (Esposito, 2013), a breakdown which the Great Financial Crisis confirmed can have highly deleterious consequences. In the context of the attempt to reconstruct this system of financialized capitalism post-crisis (Birk and Thiemann, 2020), we observe the rise of CCPs, standing at the center of the regulatory attempt to engineer a system of "resilient market based finance." In the context of these interventions, CCPs have become a cornerstone of today's financial markets, persistently achieving above-average profits. As we have tried to show, the power of CCPs to achieve these above-average profits is caused by their newly gained network centrality in the financial system (Friedrich and Thiemann, 2017).

Securing the enforceability of claims, CCPs have secured for themselves a profitable stream of business without the risk of default. Acting as a quasi-public infrastructure, whose functioning needs to be secured at all times, their private status secures profits for their owners, the large stock exchanges.

This new status of network centrality is not the outcome of "organic" market developments, but is instead the outcome of the regulatory project of "resilient market based finance" (FSB, 2015) pursued by regulators since the financial crisis. This project installed CCPs as those agents that secure the space of calculability, which forms the foundation of the the trading of claims based on contingent futures. The negotiations and outcome of the recovery and resolution regime for CCPs reflect the importance of this financial actor and their function for regulators, in particular central banks which are bound to provide liquidity assistance to CCPs in case market turmoil requires it. The current arrangement, which secures recovery of CCPs at all costs can hence be understood as an outcome of public actors' interest, which decisively intervened in the struggle between competing private factions of finance capital. Concomitantly, the resolution regime for CCPs is best understood as a "placeholder" (Riles, 2011), a stand in for a solution which de facto cannot be found, as CCPs cannot be allowed to default. In the end, resolution is a prospect to be prevented under all possible scenarios for large CCPs.

The theoretical implication in the context of this book is that based on the leverage and infrastructural power they have come to accumulate over the last decade, CCPs have managed to secure a profitable stream of income for themselves. A quintessential element in this development is the regulatory project pursued by regulators in the context of post-crisis reforms. Seeking to ensure the enforceability of options, this regulatory project needed to find an ever-present other, an entity which could be credibly trusted to always be there. This structural necessity undergirds their particular legal status. This finding provokes important follow up questions in terms of the political economy of financial market regulation. First and foremost, if CCPs are indeed an infrastructure necessary for the functioning of financial markets, whose functioning needs to be ensured at all times, on what normative claim can their private status rest? If it is the superiority of private actors to enact private risk management techniques, then how can this be squared with the fact that they de facto cannot be allowed to go bankrupt? The current way to resolve these difficult questions is by installing a legal placeholder, which states that these entities can be resolved and hope that the tail-event never arises.

This strategy, pretending to have found a solution, while not having one prevents the debate about larger questions regarding the political economy of financialized capitalism. It masks the persistence of a central bank "put" on CCPs (Singh, 2012), a public backstop by central banks which will provide liquidity to CCPs if financial market volatility proves too strong to handle. This de facto institutional set-up means that this form of risk management, pressing volatilities and uncertainties into a calculable form (Bryan and Rafferty, 2007) requires quasi-public infrastructures, which themselves escape private risk management and instead depend on the provision of a public backstop. But if central banks always need to backstop these infrastructures during episodes of systemic turmoil, the question poses itself how much control central banks actually exert over their behavior in normal times? On a more abstract level, the public needs to ask whether this infrastructure that guarantees the enforcement of private claims on future developments is set-up in a way that benefits the public at large, or whether the public is merely and unwittingly underwriting the accumulation of systemic risks, the actualization of which it will pay dearly through the central bank backstop. Only by making these features of financialized capitalism explicit, namely its reliance on quasi-public infrastructures currently in private ownership can we hope to have a debate on these issues.

Notes

1 This uncalculable nature of counterparty risks is captured in the concept of systemic risk linked to the « too connected to fail » metaphor, which has by now become a cornerstone motivating post-crisis financial regulation (s. Ibrocevic and Thiemann, 2018; Thiemann et al., 2021).

2 As recent crises suggest, this status is de facto fulfilled by central banks, which position private agents in between their interventions and the market. Tucker himself pursues this theme in his speech, only in the inverted order, asking whether CCPs might become the new central banks, whereas we will argue that central banks have become the new CCPs. This fact requires political debate, which we will seek to open up in the conclusion.

3 Bespoke OTC derivatives were the source of large profits, a highly concentrated market pre-crisis, with basically the 5 large dealer-banks sharing the market pre-2008 (s. Duffie et al., 2010)

4 It eventually took years to resolve the trading book (Swedberg, 2012)

5 This heightened status of CCPs is well reflected in the struggle over the divorce of the UK from EU financial market regulations during the Brexit debate, with the struggle over the clearing of Euro denominated FX derivatives becoming a major battle in the political debate (s. Friedrich et al., 2018; James and Quaglia, 2021)

6 While this number is driven by the outstandiing profitability of ICE, even without ICE, CCP profitability is more than double as high as bank profitability.

7 The larger the client base and the portfolio size of CCPs, the more netting is possible, allowing certain CCPs to undercut their less developed competitors in terms of margining requirements, even leading to the possibility of predatory margining (Krahnen and Pelizzon, 2016), whereby CCPs consciously underprice risks in their collateral requirements to gain market share.

8 Imagine for example one of the clearing banks to default, the question then arises: who is going to shoulder the risk, the CCPs or member banks?

9 Pistor's own work on these issues points to lawyers in the UK, which acted on behalf of the interests of landed real estate until the mid 19th century. However, she does not consider the possibility that these agents pursue projects other than those in the interests of the ruling class.

10 A key point of contention in the negotiations in the EU was whether to increase the CCP's "skin in the game", by introducing a second layer of CCP's own resources which are to be absorbed losses prior to further cash calls or variation margins gains haircutting (VMGH). Such an increase in the potential burden imposed on CCPs, however, is only apparent, where there is a safety valve in the form of short-term investment. In other words, if the CCP invests its assets long-term, losses are allocated straight to the clearing members (Art. 9(15)(c) CCP RRR).

11 Options understood here as particular claims to hedge against future volatility.

References

Aramonte S and Huang W (2019) OTC derivatives: Euro exposures rise and central clearing advances. *BIS Quarterly Review* 83–93.

Bank for International Settlement (BIS) (2021) Statistical release: OTC derivatives at end-December 2020. Available at: www.bis.org/publ/otc_hy2105.pdf (accessed 13 December 2021).

Birk M and Thiemann M (2020) Open for business. Entrepreneurial central banks and the cultivation of liquidity. *New Political Economy* 25(2): 267–283.

Braun B (2020) Central banking and the infrastructural power of finance: The case of ECB support for repo and securitization markets. *Socio-Economic Review* 18(2): 395–418.

Braun B and Koddenbrock K (2022) The three phases of financial power: Leverage, infrastructure, and enforcement. In: Braun B and Koddenbrock K (eds) *Capital Claims: The Political Economy of Global Finance*. London: Routledge, pp. 1–30.

Bryan D and Rafferty M (2006) *Capitalism with Derivatives: A Political Economy of Financial Derivatives, Capital and Class*. London: Palgrave Macmillan.

Bryan D and Rafferty M (2007) Financial derivatives and the theory of money. *Economy and Society* 36(1): 134–158.

Bulfone F and Smolenska A (2020) The internal and external centralisation of Capital Markets Union regulatory structures: The case of Central Counterparties. In: Heritier A and Schoeller M (eds) *Governing Finance in Europe-A Centralisation of Rulemaking?* Cheltenham: Edward Elgar, pp. 52–78.

Cerezetti F, Cruz Lopez J, Manning M and Murphy D (2019) Who pays? Who gains? Central counterparty resource provision in the post-Pittsburgh world. *Journal of Financial Market Infrastructures* 7(3): 1–24.

Chamorro-Courtland C (2012) The trillion dollar question: Can a central bank bail out a central counterparty clearing house which is "too big to fail"?. *Brooklyn Journal of Corporate, Financial & Commercial Law* 6(2): 433–485.

Claessen S and Ratnovski L (2014) *What is Shadow Banking? (IMF Working Paper No. 14/25)*. Washington: IMF Press.

CPMI-IOSCO (2012) Principles for financial market infrastructures. Available at: www.bis.org/cpmi/publ/d101a.pdf (accessed 14 December 2021).

CPMI-IOSCO (2017) Recovery of financial market infrastructures October 2014 (Revised July 2017). Available at: www.bis.org/cpmi/publ/d162.pdf (accessed 13 December 2021).

De Goede M (2004) Repoliticizing financial risk. *Economy and Society* 33(2): 197–217.

Djelic M-L (2013). When limited liability was (still) an issue: Mobilization and politics of signification in 19th-century England. *Organization Studies* 34(5–6): 595–621.

Duffie D (2016) Financial regulatory reform after the crisis: An assessment. Post-conference version. In: *2016 ECB Forum on Central Banking*, Sintra, 27–29 June.

Duffie D (2018) Financial regulatory reform after the crisis: An assessment. *Management Science* 64(10): 4835–4857.

Duffie D, Ada L and Lubke T (2010) *Policy perspectives on OTC derivatives market infrastructure. FRB of New York Staff Report*. New York: Federal Reserve Bank of New York.

Endrejat V and Thiemann M (2020) Reconstructing the shadow banking chain. *Competition and Change* 24(3–4): 225–247.

Eren E (2014) Intermediary funding liquidity and rehypothecation as determinants of repo haircuts and interest rates. In: *27th Australasian Finance and Banking Conference*, Sydney, 16–18 December.

Esposito E (2013) *The Future of Futures*. London: Edward Elgar.

Financial Stability Board (FSB) (2010) Implementing OTC derivatives market reforms. Available at: www.fsb.org/wp-content/uploads/r_101025.pdf (accessed 14 December 2021).

Financial Stability Board (FSB) (2015) Transforming shadow banking into resilient market-based finance: An overview of progress. Available at: www.fsb.org/wp-content/uploads/shadow_banking_overview_of_progress_2015.pdf (accessed 14 December 2021).

Financial Stability Forum (FSF) (2007) FSF Working Group on market and institutional resilience preliminary report to the G7 Finance Ministers and Central Bank Governors 15th of October. Available at: www.fsb.org/wp-content/uploads/r_0710a.pdf (accessed 14 December 2021).

Friedrich J, Resch C, Thiemann M (2018) If you do it, do it right: The need for a common European supervisory architecture for CCPs. SAFE Policy Letter No. 70. Frankfurt/Main: Leibniz Institute for Financial Research SAFE.

Friedrich J and Thiemann M (2017) Capital markets union: The need for common laws and common supervision. *Vierteljahrshefte zur Wirtschaftsforschung* 86(2): 61–75.

Gabor D (2016) The (impossible) repo trinity: The political economy of repo markets. *Review of International Political Economy* 23(6): 967–1000.

Gabor D and Ban C (2016) Banking on bonds. The new links between states and markets. *JCMS: Journal of Common Market Studies* 54(3): 617–635.

Genito L (2019) Mandatory clearing: The infrastructural authority of central counterparty clearing houses in the OTC derivatives market. *Review of International Political Economy* 26(5): 938–962.

G20 (2009) G20 leaders statement: The Pittsburgh Summit. Available at: www.g20.utoronto.ca/2009/2009communique0925.html (accessed 14 December 2021).

Helleiner E, Pagliari S and Spagna I (2018) Governing the world's biggest market: The politics of derivatives regulation after the 2008 crisis. In: Helleiner E, Pagliari S and Spagna (eds) *Governing the World's Biggest Market: The Politics of Derivatives Regulation after the 2008 Crisis*. Oxford: Oxford University Press, pp. 1–26.

Huang W (2019) *Central Counterparty Capitalization and Misaligned Incentives* (BIS Working Papers No 767). Basel: Bank for International Settlements.

Huang W and Takats E (2020) *Model Risk at Central Counterparties: Is Skin-Inthe-Game a Game Changer?* (BIS Working Papers No 866). Basel: Bank for International Settlements.

Ibrocevic E and Thiemann M (2018) *All Ideas Are Equal, But Some Are More Equal Than Others* (SAFE Working Paper 214). Frankfurt/Main: Leibniz Institute for Financial Research SAFE.

ISDA (2021) Partial Tear-Up: Comparison to other rebalancing tools and how the tool could evolve. Available at: www.isda.org/a/vxDgE/Partial-Tear-Up.pdf (accessed 14 December 2021).

James S and Quaglia L (2021) Brexit and the political economy of euro-denominated clearing. *Review of International Political Economy* 28(3): 505–523.

Jones H (2020) Eurex senses Brexit momentum in euro clearing battle with London. *Reuters*, 26 February.

Kane E (1988) Interaction of financial and regulatory innovation. *The American Economic Review* 78(2): 328–334.

Kane E (2009) Ectracting nontransparent safety-net subsidies by strategically expanding and contracting a financial institutions' accounting balance sheet. *Journal of Financial Services Research* 36(2): 161–168.

Kessler O and Wilhelm V (2013) Financialization and the three utopias of shadow banking. *Competition and Change* 17(3): 248–264.

Krahnen JP and Pelizzon L (2016) *"Predatory" Margins and the Regulation and Supervision of Central Counterparty Clearing Houses (CCPs)* (SAFE White Paper Series 41). Frankfurt/Main: Leibniz Institute for Financial Research SAFE.

Lockwood E (2015) Predicting the unpredictable: Value-at-risk, performativity and the politics of financial uncertainty. *Review of International Political Economy* 22(4): 719–756.

Lockwood E (2018) The politics and practices of central clearing in OTC derivatives markets. In: Helleiner E, Pagliari S and Spagna (eds) *Governing the World's Biggest Market: The Politics of Derivatives Regulation after the 2008 Crisis*. Oxford: Oxford University Press, pp. 168–198.

MacKenzie D (2006) *An Engine, not a Camera. How Financial Models Shape Markets*. Cambridge, MA: MIT Press.

MacKenzie D (2009) *Material Markets. How Economic Agents Are Constructed*. Oxford: Oxford University Press.

MacKenzie D and Millo Y (2003) Constructing a market, performing theory: The historical sociology of a financial dervatives exchange. *American Journal of Sociology* 109(1): 107–145.

Mehrling P (2010) *The New Lombard Street*. Princeton, NJ: Princeton University Press.

Mehrling P (2012) Hierarchies in finance. In: Taylor L, Rezai A and Michl T (eds) *Social Fairness and Economics. Economic Essays in the Spirit of Duncan Foley*. London: Routledge, pp. 394–404.

Nabilou H and Asimakopoulos IG (2020) In CCP we trust . . . or do we? Assessing the regulation of central clearing counterparties in Europe. *Capital Markets Law Journal* 15(1): 70–97.

Ozgode O (2021) The emergence of systemic risk: The Federal Reserve, bailouts, and monetary government at the limits. *Socio-Economic Review*. Epub ahead of print 15 February. doi:10.1093/ser/mwaa053.

Pagliari S (2012) Who governs finance? The shifting public – private divide in the regulation of derivatives, rating agencies and hedge funds. *European Law Journal* 18(1): 44–61.

Petry J (2020) Security exchanges: Subjects and agents of financialization. In: Mader P, D Mertens and van der Zwan N (eds) *The Routledge International Handbook of Financialization*. London and New York: Palgrave, pp. 253–264.

Pistor K (2013) A legal theory of finance. *Journal of Comparative Economics* 41(2): 315–330.

Pistor K (2019) *The Code of Capital*. Princeton, NJ: Princeton University Press.

Quinn S (2017) "The Miracles of Bookkeeping": How budget politics link fiscal policies and financial markets. *American Journal of Sociology* 123(1): 48–85.

Riles A (2011) *Collateral Knowledge*. Ithaca, NY: Cornell University Press.

Singh M (2012) Puts in the Shadow (IMF Working Paper No. 12/229). Washington, DC: IMF Press.

Stafford P (2013) LSE earns more from profit-sharing deal at clearing house. *Financial Times*, 13 November. Available at https://www.ft.com/content/2ee2ccf0-4c5a-11e3-923d-00144feabdc0, last accessed august 8th 2022,

Swedberg R (2012) The role of confidence in finance. In: Knorr-Cetina K and Preda A (eds) *Oxford Handbook of the Sociology of Finance*. Oxford: Oxford University Press, pp. 529–545.

Thiemann M (2014) In the shadow of Basel: How competitive politics bred the crisis. *Review of International Political Economy* 21(6): 1203–1239.

Thiemann M (2018) *The Growth of Shadow Banking, a Comparative Institutional Analysis*. Cambridge: Cambridge University Press.

Thiemann M, Birk M and Friedrich J (2018) Much ado about nothing? Macro-prudential ideas and the post-crisis regulation of shadow banking. *KZfSS Kölner Zeitschrift für Soziologie und Sozialpsychologie* 70(1): 259–286.

Thiemann M, Melches CR and Ibrocevic E (2021) Measuring and mitigating systemic risks: How the forging of new alliances between central bank and academic economists legitimize the transnational macroprudential agenda. *Review of International Political Economy* 28(6): 1433–1458.

Tucker P (2011) Clearing houses as system risk managers. Available at: www.bankofengland.co.uk/speech/2011/clearing-houses-as-system-risk-managers-speech-by-paul-tucker (accessed 14 December 2021).

Tucker P (2014) Are clearing houses the new central banks? In: *Over-the-counter derivatives symposium*, Chicago, IL,11 April.

8

GEOECONOMIC INFRASTRUCTURES

Building Chinese-Russian alternatives to SWIFT

Andreas Nölke

Introduction: the contestation of cross-border infrastructures for the trading of claims

For financialization to work properly, it requires well-established cross-border infrastructures. Crucial parts of these infrastructures are payment systems. Payment systems are necessary for claim creation as well as claim enforcement, and in particular for claim trading, the core elements of the financialization process (Braun and Koddenbrock, 2022, this volume). Payment systems need financial messaging services, in order to manage the system of clearing and settlement of a multitude of transactions. During the decades after the Second World War, the limited amount of cross-border bank transactions relied in a very cumbersome, costly and not always reliable manner on sending telegrams for messaging. The intensification of financialization in the 1970s went hand-in-hand with the establishment of the SWIFT (Society for Worldwide Interbank Financial Telecommunications) association, in order to authorize cross-border transactions, authenticate parties and record exchanges in a much more efficient way. International payment infrastructures have increasingly become important for the global economy, given the tremendous rise of transnational capital flows since the 1990s (Braun and Koddenbrock, 2022, this volume).[1]

During the last decades, the Belgium-based SWIFT has established itself as the dominant institution for the recording of cross-border financial transactions. More recently, however, this dominance has been challenged by some large emerging markets. In March 2019, the Russian Parliament has approved the use of the Bank of Russia's SPFS (System for Transfer of Financial Messages) for cross-border use. Iran, Venezuela and Turkey have indicated their intention to use the system, joined by Belarus in 2021. Already in 2015, China had launched its CIPS (China International Payments System), with strongly increasing transactions – and a messaging

DOI: 10.4324/9781003218487-10

system independent from SWIFT – during the last couple of years. More recently, both countries are reported to have started to explore options to link the two systems, together with India (Daye, 2019). Moreover, the November 2019 meeting of the BRICS Business council in Brasilia has discussed options to put a BRICS-wide payment system into place (Emmanuel, 2019). In India, a parliamentary committee recently has reiterated the call for an alternative to SWIFT (Mandavia, 2021).

How can we explain the emergence of alternative financial messaging systems – or even complete alternative payment systems? The activities of large emerging economies with regard to cross-border financial transaction signaling are not without reasons. When Russia-NATO-tensions started to rise again around the turn of the year 2021/22 around a Russian military build-up close to the border of Ukraine, an exclusion of Russia from SWIFT was one of the Western threats most frequently discussed (Faulconbridge, 2021; Shagina, 2021; Smith, 2022). In September 2021, the European Parliament (EP) had called that the "EU should be ready to use its leverage and call for the exclusion of Russia from the SWIFT payment system to deter Russian authorities from engaging in further aggressive behaviour" (EP, 2021), echoing previous EP resolutions threatening the exclusion of Russia from SWIFT (Götz, 2021). Already in the context of the 2014 Crimea crisis, debates about Western sanctions against Russia included the threat to disconnect the country from SWIFT and had led to the development of the SPFS system. During the year 2020, decoupling of China from SWIFT was at the focus of discussions in the United States on how to react to human rights issues with regard to the Uyghur population in China as well as the repression of the protest movement in Hong Kong (O'Toole, 2020). However, China and Russia were not the first to disagree with the US government's handling of SWIFT. A first "SWIFT affair" ranged between 2006 and 2010, when the EU strongly disagreed with the utilization of its data on European citizens within the US "Terrorism Financing Tracking Programme" (De Goede, 2012). Moreover, the specific background of the Russia-China initiatives mentioned above were US (and later EU) sanctions against Iran that used the latter's exclusion from SWIFT as a bargaining chip during the negotiations over Iran's nuclear program, the second SWIFT affair. The 2012–2015 financial sanctions imposed on Iran – with the decoupling from SWIFT as "icing on the cake" of previous (more important) measures against Iranian banks (O'Toole, 2020) – are estimated to have led to a loss of $241.73 billion of Iranian GDP, equalizing 64.8 percent of Iranian GDP in 2012 (Majd, 2018: 189). In November 2018, SWIFT again suspended the access of Iranian banks from its message system.

In spite of the potentially wide-ranging implications of the current challenges of the global payment system for the future of the financial sector, the problem has mostly been ignored in the literature on global finance. Generally, SWIFT has hardly been studied in any comprehensive way (for notable exceptions see the insider accounts by Scott and Zachariadis, 2014 as well as Leibbrandt and de Terán, 2021). Moreover, most studies put the "second SWIFT affair" in the context of interstate relations, in particular challenges to US global political and military hegemony (Caytas, 2017; Farrell and Newman, 2019; Gjoza, 2019). As far as the economic side of things is covered, the focus mostly is on the importance of SWIFT – and its alternatives – for the international trade of countries that are facing US economic sanctions (Arnold, 2016; Geranmayeh and Lafont Rapnouil, 2019). More recently, the second SWIFT affair has been analyzed from the perspective of critical infrastructure studies, highlighting how this type of infrastructure is rooted in colonial structures (De Goede, 2021). However, the importance of the SWIFT affairs for the functioning of the global financial system so far only has been mentioned in passing (Dörry et al., 2018; Westermeier, 2020). In order to address this research gap, I will first establish the geoeconomic context of current struggles over SWIFT. Next, I will highlight the importance of cross-border payment signaling infrastructures for the trading of financial claims. In a third step, I will study the reasons for the challenge of the established global payment infrastructures through China and Russia in a more comprehensive way. The conclusion focuses on implications for the future of financialization.

Conceptual framework: alternatives to SWIFT between neo-liberal and state-capitalist financialization

Why is the development of alternatives to SWIFT important for the creation, trading and enforcement of claims? The existence of a well-working alternative global financial messaging system would not by itself put limits on conventional cross-border financialization. So far, the main purpose of the alternative Russian system is to support trade in goods in spite of economic sanctions. The Chinese system mainly was established to support the global utilization of the Renminbi as a lead currency. Moreover, it is not a safe bet to count on a joint approach of the BRICS. The early successes of the establishment of the Contingent Reserve Arrangement and of the New Development Bank (both in 2014) may be misleading. Clearly, there are "limits to the BRICS' challenge . . . in global finance", as the case of the difficult establishment of an alternative BRICS credit rating agency indicates (Helleiner and Wang, 2018).

Still, let us imagine a future where a much larger share of the cross-border trading of claims takes place in the regions covered by the alternative Chinese and Russian systems. How would this affect the future of financialization? A study of the Chinese financial sector provides us with a clue regarding the likely direction of events. By looking at the role of stock exchanges in China, Johannes Petry (2020, 2021a) has identified the contours of "financialization with Chinese characteristics". The latter carries a number of features that may look quite unusual to students of financialization in the West. In a state-capitalist system of financialization, speculation is discouraged by trading rules, regulatory oversight harsh and based on a comprehensive monitoring system, the trading of financial claims slow and state control pervasive, often including capital controls (Petry, 2020: 221). Recently, the canceled IPO of "Ant Financial", announced to become the largest initial public offering ever (with a volume of 37 billion US$), has given a demonstration of the operations of a state-capitalist financial system, although (or even because) the context is not transparent. Apparently, the Chinese regulators intended to send a clear signal with regard to the primacy of the state over even the most useful financial sector operations (FT, 2020).

Based on these observations, we have developed a more general juxtaposition between the ideal typical forms of financialization currently dominating in the West which are based on hands-off "neo-liberal capital markets", and an alternative form of financialization based on "state-capitalist capital markets" (Petry et al., 2021).[2] Although China so far is the most clear-cut case of a state-capitalist financialization, we are witnessing the emergence of state-capitalist features of financialization in other large emerging economies as well. Examples include strong state control over stock exchanges in Korea, Russia and India, the utilization of commodity pricing power via derivatives marketplaces by Russia and India, or lengthy application processes for potential foreign investors in India and Korea (Petry et al., 2021). A China- or Russia-led alternative payment system would fit these features very well, by allowing national governments a much higher control over cross-border payments. Moreover, it would reduce the vulnerability of these governments regarding US-led sanctions via the SWIFT system.

Correspondingly, the United States' attempt to use SWIFT for "weaponized interdependence" (Farrell and Newman, 2019) clearly comes at a cost. Astute observers already have warned against the "unintended consequences" of this behavior many years ago, for example with regard to the development of alternative systems such as SPFS (Jones and Whitworth, 2014). In the context of the Russia-Ukraine tensions 2021/2022 these warnings have been intensified, highlighting that a disconnection of Russia from SWIFT would allow the Chinese governments to learn how to deal with this type of challenge. Moreover, it might lead to a loss of US deterrence towards Russia and China, if SWIFT disconnection does not have the effects desired by the US government (Smith, 2022). In a more general perspective, the erosion of institutions such as SWIFT may also hurt the US financial system, as "the extension of US infrastructural power aboard diminishes state capacity at home" (Weiss and Thurbon, 2018). The core issue here is the importance of a global financial system based on the dollar for the financing of the huge US current account deficit (Schwartz, 2019). Correspondingly, the Republicans' think tank "Defense Priorities" is already "counting the cost of financial warfare" and asks for "recalibrating sanctions policy to preserve US financial hegemony" (Gjoza, 2019), whereas the more bipartisan think tank "Center for a New American Security" echoes this concern and fears a "move away from dollar-based clearing and payments" (Harrell and Rosenberg, 2019). Similar concerns have been voiced by the US Treasury during the Obama, Trump and Biden administrations (Wong and Nelson, 2021: 13; Shagina, 2022: 3). Given the ongoing debates about using decoupling from SWIFT against Russia, it does not seem likely that these warnings will be heeded. Correspondingly, large emerging markets will continue to develop cross-border payment systems that they can control themselves.

In a broader perspective, it is not without irony that severe future limits to the Western model of financialization – i.e. a replacement of neo-liberal capital markets by state-capitalist capital markets in large parts of the world – may be the unintended consequence of US foreign policy considerations. This mirrors the fact that an important part of the emergence of financialization in the United States was the unintended consequence of US domestic policy considerations (Krippner, 2011). In contrast, major financial crises, including the burst of the dotcom bubble and the global financial crisis, and the related efforts for financial sector reregulation, so far were unable to impose severe limits on the established neoliberal mode of financialization.

The importance of global payment message infrastructures for the trading of claims

The emergence of financialization as a system of increased creation, circulation and enforcement of claims often is linked to domestic financial liberalization within the United States (Krippner, 2011). During the 1970s, high demand for fiscal support and limited resources for the latter gave rise to initiatives for a liberalization of formerly strictly regulated domestic financial markets in the United States. Importantly, this account of the original emergence of financialization highlights the importance of "unintended consequences", e.g. financialization as a by-product of other purposes, instead of purposeful lobbying by private financial sector institutions. However, there is a second aspect of the emergence of financialization that tends to be neglected in large parts of the debate about its historical emergence. Financialization was not only a process of domestic liberalization of the financial sector in the United States, but also a process of the intensification of the cross-border trading of claims. Were financialization limited to the United States – or a parallel process taking place simultaneously (but unconnected) in a number of economies – it would be much less powerful. Instead, it has become a strongly hierarchical undertaking within the global economy, leading to manifold relations of dependence (Kvangraven et al., 2021; Koddenbrock et al., 2022).

As far as the emergence of cross-border dimension of financialization has been covered in the literature, the focus usually is on capital account liberalization and the dissolution of capital controls during the late 1970s and the 1980s, followed by the "Big Bang" in the UK and EU financial liberalization (e.g. Helleiner, 1995). Only more recently it has been established that important origins of the phenomenon we call financialization today date back to the late 1950s and the 1960s. Importantly, the evolution of liability management, i.e. the practice of New York banks to raise funds via short-term loans on money markets – instead of relying on deposits or their own capital – took place in the 1960s, indicating a historical turn away from traditional deposit banking (Beck and Knafo, 2020: 142–143; Beck et al., 2022). An important source of this funding were the offshore money markets that evolved in the London Eurodollar markets of the 1950s and expanded during the 1970s, based on a common act of the state and finance in the UK (Braun et al., 2021; Binder, 2022). Arguably, not only the domestic evolution of financialization, but also its cross-border evolution around the US–UK financial systems were not "politics as organized combat" by powerful private sector financial lobbying for deregulation (Oatley and Petrova, 2016, 2020), but rather a form of "public-private infrastructural entanglements" (Braun et al., 2021), with an important role for unintended consequences.

While these accounts undoubtedly point towards the core contributions for the historical emergence of financialization, some important technical aspects of its current operation might be unnoticed, in particular the crucial importance of the centralization of financial activities and its supporting organizations (Oatley and Petrova, 2020: 8). However, most recently a debate on the "infrastructures of global finance" (Bernards and Campbell-Verduyn, 2019; Westermeier, 2020; De Goede, 2021) has made up for this shortcoming, sometimes echoing an earlier discussion on the role of "coordination service firms" for financialization (Nölke, 2003; Nölke and Perry, 2007; Kruck, 2011). Next to the earlier discussion on rating agencies, auditing companies and accounting standard-setters, now also asset managers, index providers, clearing houses, central securities depositories, investor arbitration courts and stock exchanges are recognized as crucial infrastructures for the functioning of the system of creating, trading and enforcing claims (Braun, 2016; Fichtner et al., 2017; Krarup, 2019; Petry, 2021b; Dafe and Williams, 2022, this volume; Fichtner et al., 2022, this volume; Thiemann, 2022, this volume). The global payments message system is another one of these infrastructures. Interestingly, the dominant coordination service firm with regard to a cross-border infrastructure (SWIFT) is based in Belgium and not in an Anglo-American financial centre, which usually dominate global finance (Fichtner, 2017; Green and Gruin, 2021). Correspondingly, the US government cannot exercise informal influence, but has to use more overt forms of pressure. This may explain why US policies on SWIFT have found such a global audience, leading to the two "SWIFT affairs" (so far).

Elements of the cross-border payments process

In order to understand the importance of the global payments message infrastructure (and the importance of SWIFT in the latter), we first have to understand the payment process, a neglected topic of Political Economy research (but see Brandl and Dieterich, 2021). The payment process consists of a number of electronic messages between financial institutions, intermediating the process between the originator (the sender) to the beneficiary (the recipient) of the payment (US Treasury, 2006; Wong and Nelson, 2021). In between the two, there are the originator's and the beneficiary's financial institutions (unless both originator and beneficiary use the same institution) and usually some kind of financial infrastructure. The most simple fund transfer takes place between two customers of the same financial institution: the originator instructs the institution and the institution implements the payment by making entries in its accounting system. If two different financial institutions (usually: banks) are involved, some kind of infrastructure is necessary, sometimes also involving a separate financial messaging system (such as SWIFT).

Given the wide variety of payments (and payment systems), it makes sense to distinguish several sub-types (Bech and Hancock, 2020: 22–28): Usually, retail and wholesale payments are covered by different systems. "Retail" refers to a large number of small payments, typically for purchasing goods and services. Retail payment systems can either be private or public. The trading of claims – such as securities – usually is part of the "wholesale" sector, where there is a much smaller number of much larger transactions (and a central role for SWIFT in cross-border transactions, as we will see later). Very often these transactions have to be settled at a specific day or even a particular time of the day.

In order to understand the role of SWIFT in the broader system of trading of claims, we also need to distinguish between "clearing" and "settlement". The latter refers to the actual transfer of funds. However, given the large number of individual transactions (usually transmitted in batches of payment instructions) very often these transactions have to be reconciled between the financial institutions before settlement. Clearing refers to the process of transmission of transactions as well as their reconciliation. It can take place bilaterally between two banks, but more frequently is organized via automated clearing houses (ACHs).[3] A third important distinction is between "real-time gross" and "deferred net" settlement (and hybrids combining the two). In a "real-time gross settlement" (RTGS) system, each payment is settled individually as soon as it enters the system. This system requires a high degree of liquidity, in contrast to a "deferred net settlement" (DNS) system that carries a higher settlement risk, but is cheaper. In the latter system, payments are settled on a net basis at the end of a pre-defined period of time. Wholesale payments such as those involved in most of the trading of claims usually are operated via RTGS systems. The most important RTGS system is the (US-only) Fedwire Funds Service, operated by the US Fed and going back to 1918. The most important payment system for the wholesale cross-border trading of claims is the US-based CHIPS (Clearing House Interbank Payment System), a private organization established 1974 that specializes on clearing and settlement of high value payments (such as bank loans and securities), based on a hybrid DNS-RTGS system. Both Fedwire and CHIPS create a wealth of payment messages, but a comprehensive control over these data also requires access to SWIFT, given the importance of the latter in cross-border transfers.

Cross-border transfers are more complicated than domestic transfers. Usually, they operate via the system of "correspondence banking", although the latter is not exclusive to cross-border transfers: "Correspondent banking is an arrangement, where one bank (the correspondent) holds deposits owned by other banks (the respondents) and provides payments and other services to them" (Bech and Hancock, 2020: 32). While some origins of the principle of correspondence banking date back to about 1400, the system has been established since the late 1800s (Rice et al., 2020: 38). Given that by far not all banks internationally have a correspondence relationship, the actual transfer of funds can take on a chain relationship. Here the originator instructs his/her financial institution, the latter uses a financial infrastructure (for clearing and settling) to turn to a respondent bank (in the country of the originator), which turns to a correspondent bank (cross-border) that uses a financial infrastructure (for clearing and settling) to turn to the financial institution of the beneficiary. Correspondence banking, however, is retreating slowly, but steadily. We have seen a reduction of about 20% in the number of correspondent banks between 2011 and 2018, in spite of rising values of payments (Rice et al., 2020: 38). The main reason is decreasing profitability, particularly because of increasing regulatory requirements, e.g. with regard to money laundering, tax havens and terrorist financing. Other factors are technological advances with regard to alternative cross-border payment systems. Some of these advances are also important for an understanding of alternatives to SWIFT.

Recent technological innovations in cross-border payment systems

Recently, we have witnessed a considerable degree of innovation with regard to cross-border payments, given that the latter usually are far more expensive, slower and "opaque" than domestic payments, and that the system of correspondence banking is gradually retreating (Bech and Hancock, 2020: 31). Three types of alternatives can be distinguished (Bech and Hancock, 2020: 33–34; see also Brandl and Dieterich, 2021):

(1) "Closed loop" (or in-house) payment systems, where one organization (exclusively) provides the services to both originator and beneficiary. The most well known of these services are Western Union and MoneyGram. AliPay and WeChat Pay provide a very large closed loop system of payments within China. They have started to partner up with overseas payment organizations in order to allow their Chinese clients the utilization of their services during overseas travel. Even more recently, fintechs such as Revolut and Transferwise have developed very cost efficient cross-border payment services for often used currency pairs. They use local accounts in both currencies. As soon as the originator pays an amount to the account of the fintech in his country of residence, the fintech account in the country of residence of the beneficiary credits an equivalent amount. A real currency conversion is not necessary.

(2) "Infrastructures" either build a cross-border payment system anew, or link established payment systems across borders in order to replace correspondence banking. If we do not count a single currency system such as the Single Euro Payments Area (SEPA), the most important case of the latter is the "Direto a México" system that links the US FedACH system with the Mexican real time gross settlement (RTGS) system, in order to make remittances to Mexico cheaper and faster. Some smaller systems operate in Africa, such as the East African Payment System or are under development such as the Arab Regional Payment System.

(3) "Peer-to-peer" systems cut out any financial intermediary between originator and beneficiary. Most are still at the stage of development, but some are

> already operational. The two most important sub-types are "stablecoins" such as Facebook's Libra (now called "Diem") and "central bank digital currencies" (CBDC) such as the digital Renminbi. Although the prime function of the latter is to support domestic payments, the improvement of cross-border payments also ranges among the targets of CBDC initiatives.

The systems depicted here are all full-fledged payment systems, including not only financial messaging (such as SWIFT) but also clearing and settling. Thus, SWIFT is only one part of the payment system (correspondence banking) for cross-border fund transfers, which is also losing importance overall. Why is SWIFT still important enough to cause major political friction?

A business perspective on cross-border payments mainly focuses on the cost, functionality and speed of the latter – and on the mass of retail payments, such as remittances, purchases of overseas tourists or simple payments for goods and services. These payments are at the focus of most of the innovations mentioned earlier. A political perspective, in contrast, focuses on the payment messaging system and on wholesale transactions, where correspondence banking still is dominant:

> From a financial intelligence perspective, it is the information about the transaction rather than the movement of the actual funds that advances the effort to combat illicit finance. The payment instructions themselves identify the parties to the transaction and sometimes even more detailed information.
> *(US Treasury, 2006: 58)*

Payment data are the crucial resource at stake (Westermeier, 2020). Over the last decades, the United States has used its financial system not only to track illicit finance but also increasingly so as a foreign policy weapon. Correspondingly, the United States was interested to learn not only about Fedwire and CHIPS payment messages (both under US control) but also about SWIFT payment messages. Many fund transfers also combine SWIFT messages and Fedwire, or SWIFT messages and CHIPS for parts of their transactions, particularly those crossing borders (US Treasury, 2006: 64). This leads to the question how SWIFT has achieved this important position in financial messaging.

The historical evolution of cross-border financial messaging and the role of SWIFT

As long as the financial sector largely remained within borders, the need for a cross-border electronic payment message system – and for US access to the latter – was limited. However, during the early 1970s, the traditional communication systems supporting correspondent banking services increasingly appeared to be too limited for catering increasing cross-border financial transactions. Telecommunication in banking exists since the 1840s. Trans-border messaging was strongly supported by the first trans-Atlantic submarine cable in 1866. Telegrams were replaced by telex, i.e. combined with typewriter keyboards from the 1930s onwards. Still, transferring funds via telex was a very cumbersome procedure, with one cross-border financial transaction requiring up to ten telex messages. Moreover, the international telex network increasingly was congested and messages suffered from a lack of standardization and security (Scott and Zachariadis, 2014: 10–13).

When cross-border financialization started to take off during the late 1960s and early 1970s, European banks were under more pressure for developing a financial messaging system than their US counterparts since the latter already had access to wide (domestic) payments network. Moreover, the most important financial transactions in Europe necessarily very often have to take place across borders, therefore providing a strong incentive for European banks to come up with pan-European "clubs" in order to develop platforms for cross-border banking, including the "European Banks' International Company" (EBIC) and the "Associated Banks of Europe Corporation". These clubs were instrumental in assembling 68 banks from the United States and European countries for "The Banks' International Message Switching Project" that was the basis for the foundation of SWIFT on May 3, 1973 in Belgium (Scott and Zachariadis, 2014: 13–16). US banks were also motivated to join SWIFT by the development of the proprietary "Machine Readable Telegraphic Input" (MARTI) system by the First National City Bank of New York (later Citibank), since they may have gotten dependent on the latter – and therefore on a close competitor (Farrell and Newman, 2019: 59).

SWIFT works as a member-owned cooperative society under Belgian law, owned and controlled by its shareholders, mainly banks, securities broker-dealers and institutional investors. Today, more than 2.400 institutions range as owners of SWIFT (Wong and Nelson, 2021: 3). SWIFT is a private infrastructure and charges its users for messages as well as additional services, and returns its surplus to its members by discounts and rebates. Shareholding is based on the principle that ownership should be proportional to the usage of SWIFT's services and shareholding is reallocated every three years (Scott and Zachariadis, 2014: 29–33; Wong and Nelson, 2021: 3). The appointment of SWIFT board directors is based on the ranking of countries with regard to shareholdings, leading to a board composition with 10 members from the EU, 2 each from Switzerland, the United Kingdom and the United States, and one each from Australia, Canada, China, Japan, Russia, Singapore and South Africa at the end of 2019 (SWIFT, 2020: 29). The strong representation of European countries still mirrors the historical emergence of SWIFT and does not respond to the strongly growing importance of large emerging markets – similar to other private coordination service firms such as the International Accounting Standards Board (Nölke, 2015). Twenty-five central banks provide an additional level of SWIFT oversight, led by the National Bank of Belgium (Wong and Nelson, 2021: 3).

Since the launch of SWIFT in 1977, its main function is to communicate payment instructions across borders, but without the actual clearing and settlement. For this communication function, SWIFT has achieved a globally dominating position for wholesale operations (which are most relevant for the trading of claims). About half of its messages relate to securities transactions (SWIFT, 2019: 3). More recently, the fintech Ripple has tried to establish a faster wholesale alternative to correspondence banking with SWIFT, based on distributed ledger technology, but it still only covers a very small fraction of the market, similar to J.P. Morgan's Liink information sharing system (Wong and Nelson, 2021: 8). This is also because SWIFT has countered these initiatives with a faster and more transparent alternative to its traditional service, called "gpi" (global payments innovation) and will implement another speed-enhancing platform in late 2022. Correspondingly, the "infrastructural power" (Schwartz, 2019; Weiss and Thurbon, 2018; Braun and Koddenbrock, 2022, this volume) of SWIFT with regard to cross-border wholesale payments still is undisputed. More than 90% of the $140 trillion of cross-border transmissions in 2020 – equivalent to 152 percent of global GDP – were signaled via SWIFT (The Economist, 2021). However, political conflicts may change SWIFT's undisputed status in the future.

The conflicts over SWIFT and the China-Russia challenge

SWIFT operated smoothly and largely unnoticed by political economists for decades. Its important role for the hierarchy of the global financial system only became obvious when the United States became interested into SWIFT data after the terrorist attacks of 11 September 2001. Earlier attempts to get access to SWIFT data by the Financial Action Task Force were roundly turned down during the 1990s (Scott and Zachariadis, 2014: 127–129; Farrell and Newman, 2019: 66–67). After 9–11, however, the US Treasury stepped up the pressure and threatened SWIFT into cooperation with the Terrorist Finance Tracking Program (TFTP) by issuing subpoenas. This was possible because SWIFT operated a data center in the United States where all messages were stored for 124 days (De Goede, 2012: 216). The disclosure of data to the US Treasury became publicly known by US media coverage in 2006, triggering the "first SWIFT affair". Subsequently, SWIFT came under massive fire by the Belgian government and the European Union, for the violation of data protection laws. In response to the criticism, SWIFT undertook a series of adjustments starting in 2007, including splitting up its messaging infrastructures in two parts, one dealing with intra-European activity and one dealing with global activity. Whereas the latter is processed both in its US and European data centers (located in the Netherlands and, since 2009, Switzerland), the former is exclusively processed in the European data centers (Scott and Zachariadis, 2014: 129–131). In addition, a formal international agreement between the European Union and the United States now regulates the US access to SWIFT data for counter-terrorism operations (Thießen and Jehmlich, 2018: 7). The first SWIFT affair, however, was not concluded by these adjustments and continued well into 2011, in particular as it became a basis of struggles for authority within the European Union (De Goede, 2012).

The "second SWIFT affair", now in the field of geopolitics and not in counter-terrorism, started briefly thereafter (Scott and Zachariadis, 2014: 133–135). In 2012, a US-based advocacy group called "United Against Nuclear Iran" started a campaign against SWIFT, arguing that SWIFT's continued operations with Iranian member banks as well as other Iranian institutions was in violation with sanctions imposed on Iran by the EU and the United States. The US Senate Banking Committee subsequently passed legislation permitting sanctions against SWIFT, if the latter would continue to service Iranian financial institutions. Very quickly thereafter, SWIFT signaled that it would be willing to implement whatever sanctions structure the EU and the United States were coming up with. Based on an EU regulation prohibiting the provision of financial messaging services to sanction institutions, SWIFT complied and cut off 24 Iranian institutions from the global financial signaling system in March 2012, not only a watershed decision in its history, but implicating itself as a geopolitical weapon.[4] Since Iran " 'de-SWIFTing' was readily recognized as the single most effective sanction currently in existence on a macro scale" – or as the "nuclear option" (Caytas, 2017: 14). However, this terminology is exaggerating the role of SWIFT in case of Iran, given that decoupling was only the "icing on the cake", after the already existing US sanctions against any bank still transacting with Iran (O'Toole, 2020; Smith, 2022). The latter are the most powerful instrument, since the US government is authorized to impose heavy fines (e.g. nine Billion Dollar against BNP Paribas in 2014) or even withdraw the US license of any bank that conducts business via any of its subsidiaries with states blacklisted by the United States (Götz, 2021). Most Iranian institutions were temporarily reconnected with SWIFT in 2016, based on the "Joint Comprehensive Deal of Action", also called the "Iran deal", concluded between Iran, the permanent five members of the UN Security Council, Germany and the EU. Bringing the Iranian institutions back into the global financial system was a key bargaining chip in these negotiations (Farrell and Newman, 2019: 69).

The Iran actions, however, were not the end of considerations to employ SWIFT for geopolitical purposes, but rather the beginning. The next case was the Crimea crisis in 2014, refreshed by the Russia-Ukraine tensions in 2021/22. After the Crimea annexation, the US government suggested cutting off Russia from SWIFT. However, SWIFT did not give in. Still, Russia took this episode as a warning and developed its own SPFS (System for Transfer of Financial Messages) for cross-border use, particularly as the threat resurfaced repeatedly during 2014/2015 (Xu, 2020). The SPFS is modelled on the example of SWIFT, runs parallel to the latter and is supposed to step in completely if Russia would be cut off from SWIFT. So far, it is mainly limited to the utilization within Russia, but the Russian government is keenly promoting the system at international summits such as those of the Shanghai Cooperation Organization and of the BRICS. In 2019, the government of Venezuela reportedly has been considering to join the Russian system, due to worries of a new round of sanctions that would also involve exclusion from SWIFT (Laya and Andrianova, 2019). Also in 2019, Iran has linked its newly developed payment signaling system SEPAM to the Russian system (Financial Tribune, 2019). Next to developing SPFS, Russia also took further precautionary measures to shield itself against potential financial sanctions, for example by accumulating huge amounts of foreign reserves and by comprehensively spreading a Russian credit card systems ("Mir") that would limit the repercussions of a cut off from Mastercard and

Visa for Russian consumers (Gricius, 2020). Russia also is developing a digital rouble that is independent from SWIFT (see later), with the launch of a prototype in the internationally isolated Crimea region in early 2022 (Shagina, 2022: 5). While a disconnection from SWIFT based on Western sanctions still would lead to short term capital outflows, currency volatility and a lot of inconvenience for transactions with Russia (e.g. moving back to telex for financial messaging), the mid-term impact seems to be manageable (Shagina, 2021; Smith, 2022).

The EU countries similarly developed an appetite for the utilization of SWIFT as an economic sanction mechanism. Based on a UN Report that some UN-sanctioned North Korean banks still were able to utilize the system of correspondence banking, the Belgian government instructed SWIFT to bar these banks from its system in 2017 (FT, 2017). SWIFT complied and even disconnected all other North Korean banks (Wong and Nelson, 2021: 14). Again, a private infrastructure that provides a public good has de-facto been nationalized for geopolitical purposes. The Iran problem also came back. In 2018, the Trump government – in contrast to European countries – pulled out of the Iran deal and threatened to introduce sanctions against the SWIFT board if the institution continued to cooperate with Iran (Thießen and Jehmlich, 2018: 4). In spite of the absence of any legal US authority over SWIFT, the Belgian institution gave in and delisted Iranian institutions again, citing concerns about the stability of the global financial system (Götz, 2021; Wong and Nelson, 2021: 13). Subsequently, some European countries tried to resist US pressure by coming up with an alternative system for transactions with Iran. Since European banks do not dare to undertake any transactions with Iranian banks, due to the threat of US sanctions (access to the US financial system simply is too important), France, Germany and the UK have come up with an alternative cross-border platform called INSTEX (Instrument in Support of Trade Exchanges), circumventing the remit of US sanctions. So far, the utilization of INSTEX has remained limited to a simple barter trade platform – and even as such, it is very limited, because the sale of Iranian oil or gas is excluded, in order "not to irritate the US too much" (von Hein, 2020: 1). Correspondingly, Iran was only able to offer goods such as carpets and pistachios, while the European exporters limited their offers to humanitarian goods such as medical products – the focus of the first (and so far only) transaction in March 2020. Alternative EU options to circumvent US sanctions do exist in principle, but have not been implemented (Thießen and Jehmlich, 2018: 8–10).

Potentially far more wide-ranging than the Russian or the European response to the second SWIFT affair, however, is the Chinese one. Since 2015, China has been operating the "Cross-Border Interbank Payment System" (CIPS). The latter is not only a financial messaging system such as SWIFT, but a complete payment system, also incorporating clearing and settlement. It still uses SWIFT for cross-border financial messaging, but can also be operated without SWIFT, if necessary. So far, the volume of payments processed within CIPS is rather limited, less than 2 per cent of the US CHIPS system (Yeung, 2020). Correspondingly, China is "astute enough not to challenge SWIFT until the CIPS has matured, but no doubt one day the challenge will come" (Prasad, 2017: 116). CIPS is part of a general shift in China's global policies during the last years. At the core of the Chinese strategy is the concept of "global connectivity" (Godehardt, 2020). In practice, this strategy envisages not only the creation of spatial but also digital infrastructures centered on China. Given the potential threat to be decoupled from the Western financial infrastructure, China seems to have decided that working within the existing institutions (e.g. by setting up a data storage center "Finance Gateway Information Service" in China in cooperation with SWIFT in 2021) alone is not sufficient and needs to be complemented by developing a new set of China-centered institutions. Correspondingly, the China challenge for Western predominance is not only a military or political, but also an economic one.

More recently, the China payment system issue appears to heat up again in the context of growing tensions between China and the United States that did not stop after the change in US leadership from Trump to Biden. Given the threat of a bipartisan US consensus on the need to put a brake on the rise of China, the Chinese government apparently has stepped up its efforts to promote the alternative payment system. In order to avoid being hurt by potential US sanctions too badly, the Bank of China has advised the country's banks to avoid SWIFT messaging (Pymnts, 2020). Moreover, it has intensified its activities to establish a Chinese central bank digital currency (CBDC) as an alternative system for cross-border payments (Greene, 2021). With regard to the latter, CBDCs not only work without SWIFT, but also without the system of correspondence banking – based on a very prominent role for US banks – altogether. In the future, the digital Renminbi (also called "digital yuan", DCEP or e-CNY) should not only be used for domestic retail payments by consumers (currently its main purpose), but also for the wholesale cross-border trading of claims. China hopes to exploit the first-mover status of the Chinese CBDC, the first among the major currencies. However, for many market participants a digital Renminbi might be equally 'toxic' as the physical Renminbi (Kärnfelt, 2020; Shagina, 2021, 2022). Therefore, even more important than the broadening of the utilization of the digital Renminbi is the Chinese support for global CBDC standards and particularly for a multi-CBDC arrangement (a project called "mBridge"). The latter could provide a very cheap and fast alternative to the SWIFT-based system for cross-border payments in the future (Auer et al., 2021). Therefore, it could undermine both the role of the US dollar as global lead currency and of US surveillance of the global cross-border trading of claims (Campbell, 2021; Lewis and Li, 2021). Moreover, the proliferation of CBDCs could also lead to the proliferation of sophisticated capital controls, given that the latter become easy to implement with the high degree of state control over the utilization of this type of digital currencies (Greene, 2021). Fintech innovations such as CBDCs combine financialization with neo-statist authoritarian capitalism in a seamless way (Gruin, 2019, 2021; Gruin and Knaack, 2020). This observation finally leads to the question whether the establishment of alternative financial signaling systems – or the shift to a multi-CBDC arrangement for cross-border payments – has the potential to change the over-all nature of financialization in the future.

Conclusion: alternatives to SWIFT and the future of financialization

So far, the Chinese alternative to SWIFT has only attracted a limited number of users. However, these numbers are rising fast. A Nikkei survey, e.g., indicates an 80% increase of payment settlements based on CIPS between 2017 and 2018, particularly from countries under US sanctions, such as Russia and Turkey, as well as countries involved in the Belt and Road Initiative (Nikkei, 2019). The number of CIPS participants exploded from 195 in October 2015 to 1.189 in May 2021 (Wong and Nelson, 2021: 9–10). Moreover, the alternative system is being utilized in an economic region that currently is growing much faster than the traditional center of the global economy covered by SWIFT. The COVID-pandemic only seems to strengthen this tendency.

The politicization or even "weaponization" of SWIFT has intensified the development and application of central bank digital currencies as an alternative to the existing payment system for the cross border trading of claims, not only for retail payments. State-capitalist economies such as China play the lead role with regard to these alternative systems, particularly with regard to the utilization of central bank digital currencies for cross border transfers. These currencies allow for a high degree of state control, including an easy implementation of capital controls. Correspondingly, the future of global finance may not be general "de-financialization" (Dutta, 2022, this volume), but a coexistence of neo-liberal and state-capitalist modes of financialization (Petry et al., 2021).

Next to state-capitalist features of alternative financial systems, the simple fact of a proliferation of competing payment infrastructures constitute an effect of how alternatives to SWIFT may negatively affect the currently dominant model of the creation, trading and enforcement of claims. So far, this system is based on a very high degree of centralization of its infrastructures, under Anglo-American control (Fichtner, 2017). An obvious politicization leading to a set of competing infrastructures might weaken this important feature of financialization, a development that is clearly worrying US think tanks such as Carnegie (Greene, 2021).

Taken together, the demise of neo-liberal cross-border financialization that may stem from the emergence of alternatives to SWIFT looks like another case of unintended consequence of political actions with other purposes. When the US government started to use SWIFT as a weapon, it certainly did not contemplate the eventual consequences this move may have for neo-liberal financialization more generally. It is not without irony that the process of neo-liberal financialization may both start and end with unintended consequences.

Notes

1 The idea for this paper stems from a research initiative on "Non-Western financial infrastructures" taken by Oliver Kessler in 2019. A big 'thank you' to Oliver, as well as to the other participants of the Erfurt meeting, in particular Nadine Godehardt and Steffen Murau! I'm also very grateful to Andrea Binder, Benjamin Braun, Kai Koddenbrock, Caroline Metz and other participants at the 'Capital Claims' authors'

workshop in November 2020 and to Carola Westermeier for suggestions on previous versions of the paper. The comments received at a panel on 'Domestic Responses to International Capital Mobility Flows' at the 2021 Annual Convention of the International Studies Association were also very useful and I'm much obliged to Xiaoye She and Alexandre Ramos Coelho. The paper is part of the project "Finanzialisierung und Staatskapitalismus: Die Steuerung der Kapitalmärkte in den BRICSS", together with Johannes Petry (PI), Robin Jaspert and Kai Koddenbrock, supported by the German Research Council (DFG) under the grant number NO 855/7–1 (https://statecapfinance.com/).

2 For a similar juxtaposition between China's "neo-statist" and Anglo-American "neoliberal" financialization see Gruin, 2019, 2021; Gruin and Knaack, 2020.

3 The clearing of payments should not be confused with the clearing of derivative contracts, although there are some striking parallels, such as the importance of privately owned entities as quasi-public infrastructures (see Thiemann, this volume).

4 I should mention, however, that the use of SWIFT as a geopolitical weapon is not primarily geared at stopping the trading of claims. By excluding banks and other financial institutions from the SWIFT network, not only wholesale transactions (most important for the trading of claims) are made more difficult, but also retail ones, such as the simple purchase of goods (such as oil and gas) and services. The latter effect is potentially even more sensitive on the side of the recipients of the sanctions. Still, SWIFT-related sanctions do not discriminate between the types of transactions and therefore also affect the trading of claims that is at the focus of this book.

References

Arnold A (2016) The true costs of financial sanctions. *Survival* 58(3): 77–100.

Auer R, Haene P and Holden H (2021) *Multi-CBDC Arrangements and the Future of Cross-border Payments* (BIS Paper No. 115). Basle: Bank for International Settlements.

Bech M and Hancock J (2020) Innovations in payments. *BIS Quarterly Review* 21–36.

Beck M and Knafo S (2020) Financialization and the uses of history. In: Mader P, Merstens D and van der Zwan N (eds) *The Routledge International Handbook of Financialization*. London: Routledge, pp. 136–146.

Beck M, Knafo S and Sgambati S (2022) Leveraging financial claims: How banks dominate global finance. In: Braun B and Koddenbrock K (eds) *Capital Claims: Power and Global Finance*. London: Routledge, pp. 33–49.

Bernards N and Campbell-Verduyn M (2019) Understanding technological change in global finance through infrastructures. *Review of International Political Economy* 26(5): 773–789.

Binder A (2022) Whose claims? Borrower power in offshore dollar markets. In: Braun B and Koddenbrock K (eds) *Capital Claims: Power and Global Finance*. London: Routledge, pp. 69–87.

Brandl B and Dieterich L (2021) The exclusive nature of global payments infrastructures: The significance of major banks and the role of tech-driven companies. *Review of International Political Economy*.

Braun B (2016) From performativity to political economy: Index investing, ETFs and asset manager capitalism. *New Political Economy* 21(3): 257–273.

Braun B and Koddenbrock K (2022) The three phases of financial power: Leverage, infrastructure, and enforcement. In: Braun B and Koddenbrock K (eds) *Capital Claims: Power and Global Finance*. London: Routledge, pp. 1–30.

Braun B, Krampf A and Murau S (2021) Financial globalization as positive integration: Monetary technocrats and the eurodollar market in the 1970s. *Review of International Political Economy* 28(4): 794–819.

Campbell C (2021) How China's digital currency could challenge the almighty dollar. *Time Magazin*, 11 August. Available at: https://time.com/6084146/china-digital-rmb-currency/ (accessed 14 December 2021).

Caytas J (2017) Weaponizing finance: US and European options, tools and policies. Available at: https://papers.ssrn.com/sol3/papers.cfm?abstract_id=2988373 (accessed 14 December 2021).

Dafe F and Williams Z (2022) Financial claims in the unequal world of investor-state arbitration. In: Braun B and Koddenbrock K (eds) *Capital Claims: Power and Global Finance*. London: Routledge, pp. XX.

Daye C (2019) Payments linkage by China, Russia and India can challenge SWIFT hegemony. *Global Times*, 2 October. Available at: https://www.globaltimes.cn/content/1168382.shtml (accessed 20 November 2021).

De Goede M (2012) The SWIFT affair and the global politics of European security. *JCMS/Journal of Common Market Studies* 50(2): 214–230.

De Goede M (2021) Finance/security infrastructures. *Review of International Political Economy* 28(2): 351–368.

Dörry S, Robinson G and Derudder B (2018) There is no alternative: SWIFT as infrastructure intermediary in global financial markets. Financial Geography Working Paper Series No. 22, Luxemburg/Gent.

Dutta S (2022) Countering financial claims: On the political economy of de-financialization. In: Braun B and Koddenbrock K (eds) *Capital Claims: Power and Global Finance*. London: Routledge, pp. 50–68.

Emmanuel OO (2019) BRICS business council greenlights the launch of a single cryptocurrency system. *BTC Manager*, 15 November. Available at: https://btcmanager.com/brics-business-council-single-cryptocurrency-payment-system/ (accessed 23 November 2020).

EP (2021) *European Parliament Recommendation of 16 September 2021 to the Council, the Commission and the Vice President of the Commission/High Representative of the Union for Foreign Affairs and Security Policy on the Direction of EU-Russia Political Relations (2021/2042(INI))*. Brussels: European Parliament.

Farrell H and Newman AL (2019) Weaponized interdependence: How global economic networks shape state coercion. *International Security* 44(1): 42–79.

Faulconbridge G (2021) West could cut off Russia from SWIFT, sanction nord stream, Latvia Says. *Reutters*, 8 December. Available at: https://www.reuters.com/world/europe/west-could-cut-russia-swift-sanction-nord-stream-latvia-says-2021-12-07/ (accessed 8 August 2022).

Fichtner J (2017) Perpetual decline or persistent dominance? Uncovering Anglo-America's true structural power in global finance. *Review of International Studies* 43(1): 3–28.

Fichtner J, Heemskerk EM and Garcia-Bernardo J (2017) Hidden power of the big three? Passive index funds, re-concentration of corporate ownership, and new financial risk. *Business & Politics* 19(2): 298–326.

Fichtner J, Heemskerk EM and Petry J (2022) The new gatekeepers of financial claims: The authority of global index providers. In: Braun B and Koddenbrock K (eds) *Capital Claims: Power and Global Finance*. London: Routledge, pp. 107–128.

Financial Tribune (2019) Banks in Iran, Russia connected via non-SWIFT financial messaging service. *Financial Tribune*, 17 September. Available at: https://financialtribune.com/articles/business-and-markets/99912/banks-in-iran-russia-connected-via-non-swift-financial-messaging (accessed 23 November 2020).

FT (2017) North Korean banks barred from Swift transaction system. *Financial Times*, 8 March. Available at: https://www.ft.com/content/69dd9512-03d9-11e7-ace0-1ce02ef0def9 (accessed 8 August 2022).

FT (2020) Alibaba founder loses magic touch with China's power elite. *Financial Times*, 7–8 November, p. 11.

Geranmayeh E and Lafont Rapnouil M (2019) *Meeting the Challenge of Secondary Sanctions*. Berlin: European Council on Foreign Relations.

Gjoza E (2019) *Counting the Cost of Financial Warfare: Recalibrating Sanctions Policy to Preserve US Financial Hegemony*. Washington, DC: Defense Priorities.

Godehardt N (2020) Wie China Weltpolitik formt: Die Logik von Pekings Außenpolitik. *SWP-Studie 19*. Berlin: Stiftung Wissenschaft und Politik.

Götz R (2021) Nukleare Option oder leere Drohung? SWIFT-Ausschluss Russlands als Santion. In: *Zeitschrift-Osteuropa Blog*. Available at: https://zeitschrift-osteuropa.de/blog/nukleare-option-oder-leere-drohung/ (accessed 1 February 2022).

Green J and Gruin J (2021) RMB transnationalization and the infrastructural power of international financial centres. *Review of International Political Economy* 28(2): 1028–1054.

Greene R (2021) *Beijing's Global Ambitions for Central Bank Digital Currencies Are Growing Clearer*. New York: Carnegie Endowment for International Peace.

Gricius G (2020) Russia's new soft power: The Mir Card system. *Journal of Liberty and International Affairs* 6(2): 32–44.

Gruin J (2019) Financializing authoritarian capitalism: Chinese fintech and the institutional foundations of algorithmic governance. *Finance and Society* 5(2): 84–104.

Gruin J (2021) The epistemic evolution of market authority: Big data, blockchain and China's neostatist challenge to neoliberalism. *Competition & Change* 25(5): 580–604.

Gruin J and Knaack P (2020) Not just another shadow bank: Chinese authoritarian capitalism and the 'developmental' promise of digital financial innovation. *New Political Economy* 25(3): 370–387.

Harrell PE and Rosenberg E (2019) *Economic Dominance, Financial Technology, and the Future of U.S. Economic Coercion*. Washington, DC: Center for a New American Security.

Helleiner E (1995) Explaining the globalization of financial markets: Bringing states back in. *Review of International Political Economy* 2(2): 415–441.

Helleiner E and Wang H (2018) Limits to the BRICS' challenge: Credit rating reform and institutional innovation in global finance. *Review of International Political Economy* 25(5): 573–595.

Jones E and Whitworth A (2014) The unintended consequences of European sanctions on Russia. *Survival* 56(5): 21–30.

Kärnfelt M (2020) *The Digital Yuan Will Only Lend a Minor Boost to Internationalization of the Currency*. Berlin: MERICS. Available at: https://merics.org/en/short-analysis/digital-yuan-will-only-lend-minor-boost-internationalization-currency (accessed 1 February 2022).

Koddenbrock, K, Kvangraven, I and Sylla, N (2022) Beyond financialization: The longue durée of finance and production in the Global South. *Cambridge Journal of Economics* (in print)

Krarup T (2019) Between competition and centralization: The new infrastructures of European finance. *Economy and Society* 48(1): 107–126.

Krippner G (2011) *Capitalizing on Crisis: The Political Origins of the Rise of Finance*. Cambridge, MA: Harvard University Press.

Kruck A (2011) *Private Ratings, Public Regulations: Credit Rating Agencies and Global Financial Governance*. Houndmills: Palgrave Macmillan.

Kvangraven IH, Koddenbrock K and Sylla NS (2021) Financial subordination and uneven financialization in 21st century Africa. *Community Development Journal* 56(1): 119–140.

Laya P and Andrianova A (2019) Weary of sanctions, venezuela mulls using Russian payments system. *Bloomberg*, 16 July. Available at: https://www.bloomberg.com/news/

articles/2019-07-16/weary-of-sanctions-venezuela-mulls-using-russian-payment-system (accessed 23 November 2021).

Leibbrandt G and de Terán N (2021) *The Pay Off: How Changing the Way We Pay Changes Everything*. London: Elliott and Thompson.

Lewis R and Li L (2021) Can De-coupling from the US dollar De-fang US secondary sanctions. In: *China Legal Commentary Channel*. Available at: www.lexology.com/library/detail.aspx?g=fe2079d2-46b7-4976-8305-ba297b55742c (accessed 1 February 2022).

Majd M (2018) The cost of a SWIFT kick: Estimating the cost of financial sanctions on Iran. In: Epstein GE (ed.) *The Political Economy of International Finance in an Age of Inequality: Soft Currencies, Hard Landings*. Cheltenham: Edward Elgar, pp. 175–191.

Mandavia M (2021) Need an Indian alternative to SWIFT payment system. *The Economic Times*, 24 November. Available at: https://economictimes.indiatimes.com/tech/technology/need-an-indian-alternative-to-swift-payment-system-parliamentary-committee/articleshow/87878879.cms (accessed 14 December 2021).

Nikkei (2019) Rise of the Yuan: China-based payment settlements jump 80%, 20 May. Available at: https://asia.nikkei.com/Business/Markets/Rise-of-the-yuan-China-based-payment-settlements-jump-80 (accessed 23 November 2020).

Nölke A (2003) *Private International Norms in Global Economic Governance: Coordination Service Firms and Corporate Governance* (Working Papers Political Science No. 6). Amsterdam: Vrije Universiteit.

Nölke A (2015) Rising powers and transnational private governance: The international accounting standards board. In: Lesage D and van de Graaf T (eds) *Rising Powers and Multilateral Institutions*. Houndmills: Palgrave, pp. 96–116.

Nölke A and Perry J (2007) Coordination service firms and the erosion of rhenish capitalism. In: Overbeek H, van Apeldoorn B and Nölke A (eds) *The Transnational Politics of Corporate Governance Regulation*. London: Routledge, pp. 121–140.

Oatley T and Petrova B (2016) *Banker for the world: Global capital and America's financialization*. Unpublished manuscript. Available at: https://ucrpoliticaleconomy.ucr.edu/wp-content/uploads/2013/09/Oatley.Financialization.UCR_.pdf (accessed 10 December 2021).

Oatley T and Petrova P (2020) The global deregulation hypothesis. *Socio-Economic Review* 20(2): 611–633.

O'Toole B (2020) Don't believe the SWIFT China sanctions hype. In: *New Atlanticist*. Available at: www.atlanticcouncil.org/blogs/new-atlanticist/dont-believe-the-swift-china-sanctions-hype/ (accessed 14 December 2021).

Petry J (2020) Financialization with Chinese characteristics: Exchanges, control and capital markets in authoritarian capitalism. *Economy & Society* 49(2): 213–238.

Petry J (2021a) Same same, but different: Varieties of capital markets, Chinese state capitalism and the global order. *Competition & Change* 25(5): 605–630.

Petry J (2021b) From national marketplaces to global providers of financial infrastructures: Exchanges, infrastructures and structural power in global finance. *New Political Economy* 26(4): 574–597.

Petry J, Koddenbrock K and Nölke A (2021) State capitalism and capital markets: Comparing securities exchanges in emerging markets. *EPA: Economy and Space*.

Prasad ES (2017) *Gaining Currency: The Rise of the Renminbi*. Oxford: Oxford University Press.

Pymnts (2020) Bank of China advises country's banks to avoid SWIFT messaging. *Pymnts*, 29 July. Available at: www.pymnts.com/news/international/2020/bank-of-china-advises-banks-to-avoid-swift-messaging/ (accessed 23 November 2020).

Rice T, von Peter G and Boar G (2020) On the global retreat of correspondent banks. *BIS Quarterly Review* 37–52.

Schwartz HM (2019) American hegemony: Intellectual property rights, dollar centrality, and infrastructural power. *Review of International Political Economy* 26(3): 490–519.

Scott SV and Zachariadis M (2014) *The Society for Worldwide Interbank Financial Telecommunication (SWIFT): Cooperative Governance for Network Innovation, Standards, and Community*. London: Routledge.

Shagina M (2021) *How Disastrous Would Disconnection from SWIFT be for Russia*. Moscow: Carnegie Foundation. Available at: https://carnegiemoscow.org/commentary/84634 (accessed 1 February 2022).

Shagina M (2022) *Central Bank Digital Currencies and the Implications for the Global Financial Infrastructure* (FIIA Briefing Paper 329). Helsinki: Finnish Institute of International Affairs.

Smith AM (2022) SWIFT and certain punishment for Russia? There Are better ways to Deter Moscow than threatening its banking access. *Foreign Affairs*. Available at: www.foreignaffairs.com/articles/ukraine/2022-01-04/swift-and-certain-punishment-russia (accessed 1 February 2022).

SWIFT (2019) *SWIFT in Figures December 2019 YTD*. La Hulpe: SWIFT.

SWIFT (2020) *Annual Review 2019*. La Hulpe: SWIFT.

The Economist (2021) The race to define cross-border finance. *The Economist*, 23 October. Available at: https://www.economist.com/finance-and-economics/the-race-to-redefine-cross-border-finance/21805736 (accessed December 13, 2021).

Thießen F and Jehmlich T (2018) *Iran-Sanktionen, internationaler Zahlungsverkehr und Reformvorschläge aus europäischer Sicht* (Chemnitz Economic Papers No. 23). Chemnitz: Universität Chemnnitz.

Thiemann M (2022) The benefits of network centrality: Central Counterparties, the enforceability of claims and the securing of extra-profits. In: Braun B and Koddenbrock K (eds) *Capital Claims: Power and Global Finance*. London: Routledge, pp. 129–146.

US Treasury (2006) *Feasibility of a Cross-border Electronic Funds Transfer Reporting System under the Bank Secrecy Act, US Department of the Treasury*. Washington, DC: Financial Crimes Enforcement Network.

Von Hein M (2020) EU-Iran INSTEX Trade channel remains pipe dream. *DW*, 31 January. Available at: https://www.dw.com/en/eu-iran-instex-trade-channel-remains-pipe-dream/a-52168576 (accessed 23 November, 2020).

Weiss L and Thurbon E (2018) Power paradox: How the extension of US infrastructural power abroad diminishes state capacity at home. *Review of International Political Economy* 25(6): 779–810.

Westermeier C (2020) Money is data: The platformization of financial transactions. *Information, Communication & Society* 23(14): 2047–2063.

Wong L and Nelson RB (2021) *International Financial Messaging Systems*. Washington, DC: Congressional Research Service.

Xu W (2020) The SWIFT system: A focus on the US-Russia financial confrontation. Available at: https://russiancouncil.ru/en/analytics-and-comments/analytics/the-swift-system-a-focus-on-the-u-s-russia-financial-confrontation/ (accessed 23 November 2020).

Yeung K (2020) How the US uses the dollar payments system to impose sanctions on a global scale. *South China Morning Post*, 25 August. Available at: https://www.scmp.com/economy/china-economy/article/3098691/how-us-uses-dollar-payments-system-impose-sanctions-global (accessed 8 August 2022).

PART III

Enforcement power

9

NIGHT OF THE LIVING DEBT

Non-performing loans and the politics of making an asset class in Europe

Daniel Mertens and Caroline Metz

Introduction

In the midst of another shockwave stemming from the Covid-19 pandemic in November 2021, the European Union completed a legislative process to promote the cross-border trading of non-performing loans (NPLs). The timing was critical. The economic fallout from the pandemic had raised concerns about debtors' ability to repay their loans, subsequently hitting banks' balance sheets. In late 2020, the European Central Bank already anticipated that NPLs – loans that are in or close to default – held by Euro Area banks could reach €1.4 trillion, "well above the levels of the 2008 financial and 2011 EU sovereign debt crises" (Enria, 2020). Policy-makers and technocrats highlighted the need to design "effective NPL resolution policies for the post-COVID-19 world" (Ari et al., 2020), such as bolstering the sale of defaulting debts by institutionalizing a market currently worth €100–200bn annually in Europe (Deloitte, 2019). Both the urgency in building the legal foundations for trading such 'non-performing' claims and the size of the market have, however, not yet led to much reflection in the study of the politics of finance and financialization; a gap this chapter seeks to close.

Interestingly, there is no legal agreement as to what makes a loan 'non-performing', but an authoritative definition categorizes as NPLs loans that are 90 days past due, or loans where the debtor is assessed as "unlikely to pay its credit obligations in full without realisation of collateral" (EBA, 2019: 10). Importantly, the appellation 'non-performing' reveals that NPLs are considered from a creditor's perspective, rather than a debtor's perspective. Indeed, a loan is 'performing' when it continuously accrues the creditor or issuer of the loan (e.g. a bank) profitable cash flows in the form of regular payment of principal and interest. When these payments become irregular, late or non-existent, the loans become 'non-performing'. In other words, a non-performing loan is a financial claim that does not 'perform'

DOI: 10.4324/9781003218487-12

its role of bringing about regular cash flows to the issuer of the loan. Although high NPL ratios can disrupt a bank's overall profitability and reputation – key to market confidence and shareholders' returns – these faulty claims can still be traded. To make good returns out of NPLs, buyers need only to wait for their prices to be so deeply discounted that even small recoveries on their initial value, partly via legal enforcement strategies to 'revive' claims presumed 'dead', make for profit. Those investors, in sum, prey on debt crises to profit from defaults.

These phenomena raise several political economy questions in line with this book's focus on capital claims: How are defaulting debts – failed debt claims from a bank's perspective – kept alive and traded in Europe? Who benefits from these 'living debts' markets and how does this play into the politics of debt? To answer these questions, this chapter examines the political processes unfolding around the trading and enforcement of private debt claims through two case studies. The first traces the assetization of loan portfolios, particularly non-performing mortgage debt, in Germany during the run-up to the 2008 financial crisis. There, the combination of market-building efforts and open contestation in the face of financial globalization resulted in the introduction of (limited) legal debtor protection as a condition for further market expansion. The second case takes us past the 2008 crisis, when the ratio of NPLs reached a new high in Europe. Seen as a make-or-break for the EU's distressed banking systems, these faulty claims became a booming asset class allowing debt collectors and investment funds to make fresh rounds of profits, in a context of supranational 'quiet politics' largely silent over the fate of debtors. Both cases show how particular political mobilizations, rather than inherent (im)moral or (un)profitable qualities of specific types of debt relations, make the trading and enforcement of debt claims possible. To underline how we think this contributes to scholarly reflections on finance as the power-laden creation, trading and enforcement of claims, we begin with conceptually reflecting on private debt claims in the context of this book's theoretical framework.

Debt, power, and disruption

One of this book's premises is that understanding the resilience of financial capitalism requires an analysis of power at each of the three stages of the life cycle of financial claims – as claims are created, traded and enforced (see Braun and Koddenbrock, 2022, this volume). As we seek to make sense of the puzzle that defaulting and thus seemingly untradeable debt claims can have a second life – and a profitable one at that – we resort to two types of power that are at play in the legal infrastructure connecting the financial sector and debtors: *creditor power* and *enforcement power*.

Although debt, including plain consumer debt, is often represented "as a technical and equal exchange of money between a creditor and a debtor", it is a form of power "tied to powerful class-based interests" (Roberts and Soederberg, 2014: 558; 662). Depending on the amounts lent or borrowed, debt can expand the power position of either party. Yet debt often works as a disciplinary device for creditors –

owners of wealth – over borrowers in need of capital or purchasing power; this is what we refer to as *creditor power*. For instance, creditors hold the power to grant the loan or not, to draft the legal contract (over which they generally have greater knowledge than debtors), and, within the boundaries of the law, to dictate the terms and conditions of the loan (amount, collateral, duration, interest rate, penalty fees, etc.). Finally, and key to our case studies, creditor power entails *enforcement power*, which can be outsourced to debt recovery or debt servicing agents, and ultimately involves the legal arm of the state, i.e. the judiciary system (bailiffs, courts, judges, etc., and in extreme cases the prison system) (Roberts, 2014).

As Pistor (2013: 317) notes, the law is not the same for all: it is "binding on the periphery and relatively more elastic at the apex". The law tends to serve (and can be amended if it does not) those already in situations of power, whereas individuals and firms that are least powerful must serve the purpose of repayment or face being deprived of their possessions (collateral), and/or face social and judicial consequences (Langley, 2008). To go beyond this imbalance encoded in law and capture how creditor and enforcement power over debtors prevails throughout the life cycle of debt claims, we need to dive deeper into the workings of debt claims in practice, and interrogate what happens when the normal functioning of claims is disrupted. Disruptions of private debt claims can work two ways: first, by disturbing the expected earnings associated with a claim; second, by unsettling the social obligation underlying the claim.

Claiming profits

Debt contracts typically provide for a creditor to receive payment of principal together with an interest at some agreed-upon future point, while debtors can get immediate purchasing power with the caveat that they will pay back a larger sum in the future. Since the 1990s, financial globalization and rising demand for yield-carrying assets have facilitated an enormous expansion of such debt contracts, leading to an unprecedented growth in cross-borders claims and the inclusion of ever more people and institutions in a global circuit of capital. In many cases, this process required the transformation of formerly local debt contracts into tradeable financial assets, as evident in the financialization of mortgages (Aalbers, 2008; Quinn, 2019).

However, although the increasingly complex, global and financialized nature of debt markets gives an appearance of distance between a financial investors and initial debtors, credit must "return to its place of origin for recovery, namely, to the debtor", because ultimately the success of any debt product "depends on a future gamble that the debtor can access enough funds to repay the loan" (Soederberg, 2014: 44). What happens, then, if the debtor has not been paying for months, and is unlikely to do so in the future? What if both creditor and enforcement powers fail to bring about the expected results?

These so-called *distressed*, *impaired* or *troubled* assets, because of their interrupted cash flows, are not simply loss-inducing for banks, they are also losing much of their value from a wider financial perspective. The 2008 financial crisis was a case in point, when waves of defaults on subprime loans triggered losses on mortgage-based structured instruments so unexpected that they led to paralyzing uncertainty and illiquidity in financial markets. Non-performing loans, which are *already known* to be in or near default thus appear to be unlikely candidates for fresh rounds of value creation. Yet, it is precisely the case that NPLs have been increasingly traded among financial actors, forming the basis for new types of financial marketization and accumulation.

This is because assetization and trading is based on the valuation of assets as regards their expected earning power in the future (Birch and Muniesa, 2020), which entails probabilities for both the resumption of repayment and the enforcement of claims through other means, like foreclosure. *Creditor power* then rests on the ability to stabilize earnings and mobilize *enforcement power* or have the opportunity to sell claims to those who can (better) exercise such powers. However, the fact that NPLs can be sold quickly raises moral questions – should one be able to seek profits from debtors' financial hardship? Morality, in fact, is an important facet of the conceptualization of debt.

Claiming morality

As Calder (1999: 73) notes in his history of consumer credit in the United States, the "moral nature of debt looms at least as large as the economics of borrowed money". Debt as a power relation regularly entails the "moral downgrading" of the debtor, and claim creation "establishes hierarchies in material resources and moral character. When one party struggles to fulfil its obligations, moral regulation intensifies" (Fourcade and Woll, 2013: 604). This can be seen in the 'debts-must-be-repaid' norm that protects creditors' interests. At the same time, creditors also have obligations such as due diligence and securing some form of trust in a (usually long-term) relationship, to which they may be held accountable from debtors. This opens opportunities for negotiations, emphasizing that debt claims contain a dimension of reciprocity, often based on local social interactions (Carruthers and Ariovich, 2010). In other words, disruptions in repayment can also trigger expectations regarding legitimate behavior of the parties involved.

Importantly, such moral considerations may just become as relevant as earning expectations in attempts to govern credit relations or build a legal infrastructure for tradeable debts. According to the interest groups literature, a higher degree of public and media attention – also known as salience – tends to weaken the bargaining position of 'business power' to the benefit of 'non-corporate interests' i.e. civil society. By contrast, 'quiet politics' or low salience tends to favor business influence (Culpepper, 2011; Woll, 2013; Orban, 2016). Salience and the potential for 'noisy politics' are not inherent to a particular issue but are contingent on the historical context and on how a variety of actors (do not) draw attention to a topic, targeting specific elected officials or technocrats. Morality, thus, can be an important point of debates in 'noisy politics', but such considerations are more easily ignored in technocratic policymaking where 'expertise' – often from the industry – is seen as the ultimate basis for 'rational' policymaking. Put differently, the moral aspects of debt can potentially be a power resource for both creditors and debtors, though historically it has mostly worked against debtors (Dyson, 2014).

Our understanding of debt as power combined with these reflections on the profitability and morality of debt give us a lever to answer our initial questions about how non-performing loans became an asset class and what political processes undergirded their trading and enforcement over time in two successive contexts.

Trading the untradeable? Transnational finance and the politics of NPLs in Germany

Germany lends itself to an explorative case study because before the dotcom-bubble had burst in 2001, there had been neither a developed market for, nor a political debate about, large-scale loan trading, NPLs or securitization (apart from covered bonds). However, between 2001 and 2008, the German political economy closely resembles a burning lens for understanding the politics of making private debt an asset class, as it became the largest European market for NPLs. The entry of new financial actors and practices, processes of regulatory liberalization and subsequent political contestation illustrates an attempt both to *catch up with* and *reign in* liberal finance in the context of a self-proclaimed 'social market economy' – a dynamic that Engelen and Konings (2010) have coined 'contested financialization'. Here, we zoom in on the politics of mortgage debt and NPLs in that period, showing how political mobilizations around profitability and moralization shaped the political economy of financialization and reform.

Market-building and the political foundations of trading debt

The political project of establishing secondary markets for private debt claims began around the turn of the century when both the financial industry and the government became increasingly concerned about the competitiveness of the German financial sector. The latter had one of the lowest profitability rates across the EU as well as increasing borrowers' default rates after the Reunification credit boom came to a halt, leading to a low-salience emerging consensus among government officials and the banking sector to build markets for asset-backed securities. However, despite political efforts to facilitate securitization and increase profitability, legal requirements lagged behind. In particular, uncertainty prevailed about how the rights of (new) claim owners – owners of specific tranches of claims – to enforce debt claims and valorize collateral could be transposed into the German legal context. Since borrower default rates and balance sheet risks were fueling the recession, German banks turned to plain credit sales as an alternative, which, unlike asset-backed securities, are not tranched and do not entail different risk classes, but are simply packages or single transactions of outstanding debt claims.

The first major loan portfolio transactions took place in 2003, mainly involving NPLs. According to Deutsche Bank Research, that year German banks sold claims worth €1.5bn. In 2004, the amount had made a five-fold increase to €7.6bn, the annual volume on which the market plateaued over the next years. At least two thirds of this were accounted for by mortgages, i.e. secured debt, but the role of corporate NPLs and unsecured (consumer) loans began to grow. The dominance of real estate-backed transactions (both residential and commercial) was based on the assessment that such collateral was both undervalued (and so were the loans) and easier to valorize than, say, corporate inventories. Importantly, however, the loan transactions involved more than just NPLs. Estimates suggest that around one third of traded mortgages did not show signs of distress, presumably to achieve higher prices through mixed packaging (DB Research, 2007).

The overall volume of NPL and loan portfolio traded an estimated €14.4bn in 2006, with rising demand allowing investors to realize profits in an increasingly liquid market, and enabling more debt-financed acquisitions. In fact, as the German economy picked up again after 2005, Germany became Europe's largest NPL market, attracting investors mainly from the United States: large private equity funds, which had collected billions from institutional investors – mostly pension funds – to take risks in the emerging German loan portfolio market, as well as global investment banks (Köchling, 2013). Their business strategy involved the valuation of loan portfolios by their potential earning power, which involved the growth of an auxiliary business sector that would extract a further share of the value from the original loan agreement, including law firms for transaction management and due diligence, and servicing firms or departments for loan administration and the varied enforcement tasks (creditor-debtor negotiations and debt collection, debt restructuring, on-selling, liquidation of collateral and foreclosures).[1] After all, profits would not only be made through the acquisition of an assumingly undervalued loan portfolio, but also through rationalized asset management and standardized valorization schemes, arguably more advanced among those US financial firms. Crucially, tax incentives and further liberalization reforms had allowed such new financial actors to operate in Germany, based on the argument that their participation in these markets would both stabilize the banking system and stimulate economic growth, making an increase in debt trading evidence of internalizing financial globalization (Soederberg et al., 2005). Therefore, by 2007 market observers and participants had begun to talk about (non-performing) loan portfolios as an "established asset class" (DB Research, 2007).

Still, regulatory uncertainty around the trading of loan portfolios was only gradually receding, and legal debates thrived over the lawfulness of credit sales, potentially hurting bank secrecy and data protection regulations. The German federal court had cleared a number of regional court judgements in favor of 'the market', but the boom in legal commentary on these and the broader issues surrounding credit sales (Schalast et al., 2006; Schimansky, 2008 for an overview) suggests that the struggle for the 'right legal coding of capital', in Pistor's (2019) terms, was in full force, attempting to establish a ranking of claim holders.[2] However, the struggle

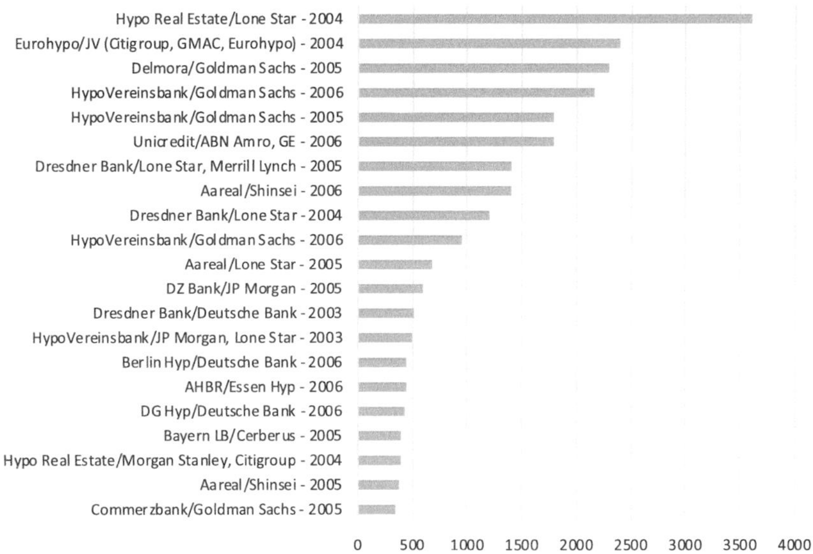

FIGURE 9.1 The largest loan portfolio transactions in Germany, in million EUR, 2003–2006 (Seller/Buyer – Year)

Source: Own adaptation of Deutsche Bank Research, 2007: 7; does not include Lone Star acquisition of AHBR from the German trade union holding company

was not confined to legal commentary. Particular claim enforcement practices provoked public debate, and a discussion over who sold and bought these loans came to bear on the unfolding political and regulatory process. The political implications of trading and enforcing debt – from Lone Star to 'locusts' and the Risk Limitation Act

The political contestation that arose from the establishment of a loan portfolio market in Germany can be traced back to a number of tensions that included the perceived mismatch between relationship lending and debt trading, the claim enforcement strategies of some new asset owners, and the prevalent public discourse around foreign investors in Germany at the time. Starting with the landscape of sellers and buyers to flesh out these tensions, two initial observations are noteworthy. First, as Figure 9.1 shows, the majority of investors came from abroad and predominantly the United States. Both investment banks such as Goldman Sachs, JP Morgan and Citigroup, and investment funds such as Lone Star engaged in major transactions.[3] On the selling side were mostly private commercial banks, who were also among the few who engaged with the first proper German securitization vehicles. Public or cooperative banks are missing from this figure, but the regionally-operating *Sparkassen* were active in small-scale transactions, which quickly provoked public outrage. The main reasons were that they were seen as institutions with a public mission to secure financial services for a local community and thereby representatives of relationship lending. Credit sales on their part were therefore seen as violating the trust element in creditor-debtor relations and implied a rapid loss of reputation. Soon, both the legal uncertainties and the moral economy around claim trading and enforcement produced 'noisy politics', leading to legislative intervention.

Moralizing capital claims and the political economy of reform

"Yeah, that was just ruthless, sleek, overlooking anything humane." This sentence originates from a distressed debtor who was confronted with Hudson, the service provider of Lone Star Funds. Hudson allegedly forced the sale of a couple's two houses, which were acquired by another subsidiary of Lone Star who then re-sold both properties for a price approximately 50% higher than the auctioned price, said to be taxed in an offshore jurisdiction (SWR, 2008). In other words, NPL investors were realizing expected earning power with the support of various legal frameworks. Such reports of both public and private media outlets became trending in 2006–2008. These helped shape the perception that the new owners of debt claims would swiftly capitalize on borrowers' distress. Industry representatives were quick to emphasize media misrepresentation of market behavior and that only defaulting borrowers could be pressured to foreclosure, while also maintaining that such practices on average serve a better allocation of risk and capital in an economy (cf. DB Research, 2007; Köchling, 2013). Legal scholars came to explain that the new claim owners would in principle have the same obligations as the initial lender, but were apparently exploiting legal loopholes to realize short-term profits and, in cases of slight payment delays, ruling out negotiations with debtors over rescheduling (Bredow and Vogel, 2008).

The emerging debate on credit sales to foreign and in particular US investors heavily increased 'moral salience' and fell on fruitful political ground for two reasons. First, the turbulences in the US housing finance market slowly became apparent; second, the public had become attuned to a vulgar political critique of Anglo-American investor practices through the social-democratic imagery of private equity firms as "swarms of locusts".[4] The figure that came to occupy the NPL debate was, however, the alleged victim of new transnationalized financial practices, claim trading and enforcement – the '*Häuslebauer*'. Best understood as the husband of the 'Swabian housewife', he uses credit cautiously for building the family home in the economic heartland of Germany. A close reading of parliamentary hearings and debates shows that this framing resonated with the then ruling Christian Democrats, who bemoaned that with a local bank one could 'have a talk' in a critical situation, but not so with English-speaking credit purchasers (*Bundestag*, 11 Oct 2007, p. 12266). Relatedly, the Social Democrats emphasized the responsibility of banks in settling the credit relation as the borrower had "decided in favor of a specific credit institute and trusts that this institute remains their contractual partner" (ibid., p. 12267).

As the ruling coalition's position took form around the notion of "credit transactions are a matter of trust" (*Bundesrat*, 14 March 2008, Protocol 842, p. 74), it reminisced of a past when "even simple debt obligations had to be performed by the original parties to the contract" (Pistor, 2019: 15). The entry of financial investors and the possibility of trading debt claims with the legal right to enforce a claim was seemingly met with unease since the buyers of NPLs or loan portfolios would not be interested in a long-term customer relationship but in the short-term realization of profits. Highlighting relationship lending, policymakers then connected borrower protection to the protection of the famed *Mittelstand*, but in line with their earlier sponsoring of SME securitization accepted the argument that the market entry of foreign investors would be beneficial for growth and risk allocation. Legal commentary was more inclined to discuss the power relations in enforcement proceedings, arguing existing legal norms could be 'weaponized' by financial investors seeking to realize earnings early (Schimansky, 2008: 1050f).

The servicing and debt collecting industry responded to public accusations by founding the Federal Association for Debt Purchase and Servicing (BKS) in 2007 – whose vice-president was the CEO of Lone Star Germany – following the example of similar US and British Associations, which were founded in the mid-1990s (Palenker, 2019). The Association was set up to advance their core market through standardization and respond to public sentiment by public relation management and self-regulation, but mainly lobby for an easing of legal requirements for their business. The stakes of the financial industry became clear in a public hearing of the German parliament's Finance Committee, where 18 out of 45 statements came from financial associations or individual financial companies, among them Lone Star. Only three statements came from consumer or labor representatives, six from other industry or employer associations and 17 from individual legal experts with varying political or industry alignments.[5]

The legislative debate concluded with the passing of the Risk Limitation Act, which became effective on 19 August 2008, less than four weeks before Lehman Brothers filed for bankruptcy and the loan portfolio and securitization markets effectively froze. The Act included a number of provisions about claim trading and financial investors' practices, emphasized borrower protections focusing on consumers and workers. It entailed, *inter alia*, obligations to inform borrowers about the possibility of loan sales when entering the loan agreement, and imposed restrictions on mortgage termination as well as enforcement activity, particularly by bolstering compensation claims for borrowers.

While it certainly strengthened debtor rights through 'noisy politics', the Act came out as a middle-of-the-road-approach wedded to a broader creditor-friendly institutional set-up, eventually providing the legal infrastructure for claim trading and enforcement. Consequently, the Risk Limitation Act was rather well received among finance specialists, since it did not repeal market mechanisms, but provided legal certainty for further transactions (Köchling, 2013). Debtor-friendly court decisions such as one by the German regional court of Hamburg, which had judged immediate foreclosures to be illegal means of claim enforcement through third-party investors, were also cashed in by higher court authorities, and Lone Star set up a new fund with the German loan portfolio market as a key investment location (Börsen-Zeitung, 2008).

Non-performing loans on banks' balance sheets grew in the shadow of the global financial crisis, and sales were made to the same pre-crisis investors, namely Lone Star, US Bancorp, PIMCO and Blackstone (PWC, 2012), who epitomized the excess liquidity of institutional capital. But according to the World Bank, the share of NPLs on German banks' balance sheets before Covid-19 was only around a third of the 2005 value. The credit industry itself has argued that the German market for NPLs operates below potential, not only because the broadly beneficial economic situation for the German economy over the past 10 years has led to lower default rates, but some banks remain concerned about reputation losses when selling large packages of loans, in part as a consequence of the morally-laden discourse of the 2000s. Against this backdrop, the trading and servicing industry increasingly looked at the wider European (distressed) loan market (Brogt and Dzieciol, 2017). Both the regulatory activity and the politics had clearly moved to the intergovernmental and supranational level after the financial and Euro Area crises, somewhat transnationalizing the politics of making private debt an asset class – one more reason to shift our analytical focus too.

Trading the untradeable. Distressed debt markets in post-crisis Europe

Taking us after the global financial crisis, this second case study provides a succinct political economy of the European distressed debt market, analyzing how seemingly untradeable financial claims have continued to be the basis for financialization, while European institutions act to facilitate debt trading rather than protect debtors.

NPLs volumes soared following the 2008 crisis, when increasing numbers of households and companies were unable to keep up with their debt payments. In 2012–2013, about 7% of all European loans were non-performing, up from below 3% in 2008. In 2013 the stock of NPLs in Europe reached €1 trillion. Although this level subsequently decreased, European banks still held €636 bn of NPLs in 2019, with mortgages and unsecured consumer loans making up a third of this amount (European Commission, 2019). With renewed economic hardship induced by the Covid-19 pandemic, the ratio of NPLs began to rise again in Europe. These trends hide disparities within the region, from less than 1% of NPLs in Sweden to 39% in Greece in 2019 (EBA, 2019: 8). Households in several countries were hard-hit by the austerity-fueled recession: 15–20% of household loans were non-performing in Ireland and Italy in 2016 (ECB, 2017), but this reached about half of households in Greece and Cyprus – for an EU average of 4.3% (KPMG, 2018).

Trading distressed debts

From 2011 onwards, Europe saw a steady rise in NPL transactions. In fact, the NPL stock decrease on European banks' balance sheets after 2013 is largely attributed to NPL sales and securitizations in secondary markets (EBA, 2019: 8).[6] Between 2014 and 2017, NPL transaction reached €100–150 bn per year (Mourmouras,

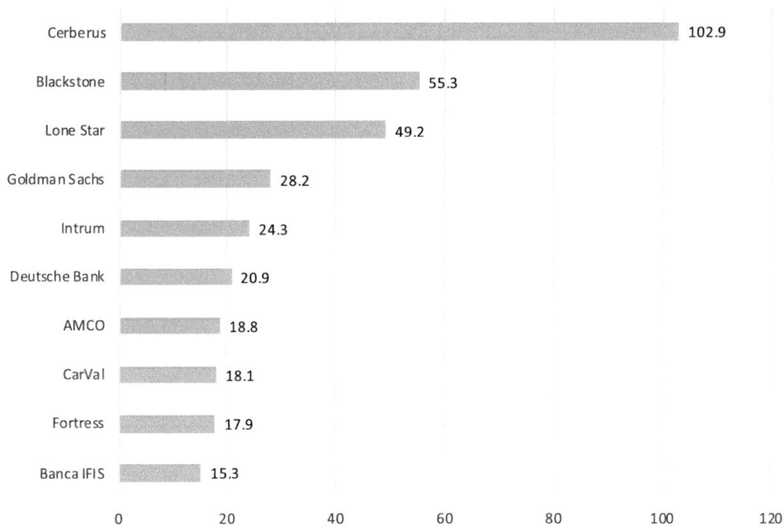

FIGURE 9.2 Top ten buyers of European NPLs 2014–2019, volume in billion EUR

Source: own adaption of Deloitte, 2019: 7

2019). 2018 was a record year, with 207 transactions (together worth €205 bn) completed across Europe – mostly in Italy and Spain, followed by Portugal and Ireland, with Greece and Cyprus deemed the next booming marketplaces (Debtwire, 2018).

NPL sellers are, essentially, European banks under pressure to deal with their NPLs, and (semi) publicly managed asset management companies set up specifically to dispose of toxic assets following the financial crisis. The top sellers of NPLs in Europe in 2014–2019 included three of these so-called 'bad banks', as well as Spanish, Italian, Irish, English, Portuguese and German banks (Deloitte, 2019). The 'buy-side' of the NPL market is composed of debt *purchasers* and debt *servicers*, who have become closely intertwined.[7] Buyers of – or rather, investors in – NPLs are predominantly private equity funds and asset management funds owned by large investment banks, whose investment is driven by large 'cash pools' in search for yield. As in the German case, Cerberus, Blackstone, Lone Star and Goldman Sachs have been top buyers of European NPLs (see Figure 9.2).

How, then, can 'non-performing' loans constitute profitable investments? A central strategy for investors is to wait for pressure to mount on NPL-loaded banks, so that eventually NPLs are sold (very) cheap: 40–50% discount for mortgages and up to 90–95% for unsecured consumer loans (European Commission, 2018b: 14). Returns are maximized using a combination of the following: recovering value on the debt – via enforcement methods – superior to the price paid to buy it; re-selling the debt at a higher price later on; in the case of loans secured with property, repossessing the properties and selling/renting/operating them at a profit. Logically, the higher the discount, the easier it is to make a return on investment. Another important factor when it comes to mortgages is real estate prices – investors bet they will go up after the purchase, increasing the assets' market value (Byrne, 2015a).

These strategies have paid off, with distressed debt investors posting high profit margins. The expected rate of return among European NPL investors is 10–15% (Ashurst, 2017), but private equity funds such as Blackstone, Apollo or Oaktree often hit 40–55% profit margins (European Commission, 2018b). Lone Star, identified in our first case study as one of the US equity funds buying up German mortgages in the 2000s, consistently posted average annual net returns of 20% (Forbes, 2016). Lone Star, in fact, was the third top buyer of European NPLs in 2014–2019 (Deloitte, 2019). However, the fact that Lone Star became the ultimate creditor of thousands of European debtors, as illustrated later, has raised concerns.

Political implications of distressed debt trading – the case of Lone Star (again)

In 2018, Irish bank Permanent TSB, majority-owned by the Irish state, was under pressure to significantly reduce its NPL ratio. It decided to sell a €2.1bn distressed loans portfolio for €1.35bn – a 38% discount – to Start Mortgages, an affiliate of Lone Star, which contained 10,700 NPLs linked to Buy-To-Let and residential properties (PTSB, 2018). Rating agency DBRS (2018) upgraded the bank's rating in December 2018 as the "significant reduction" of NPLs would allow it "to grow profitability".

Although the bank's CEO Jeremy Masding affirmed that customers would "continue to be afforded the protection" of existing regulations after the sale (PTSB, 2018), the deal was controversial in Ireland, with headline-grabbing accusations that the Irish government was "outsourcing evictions during the worst housing and homelessness crisis" in Irish history (Irish Mirror, 2018). The Irish Mortgage Holders Organization said it was "reprehensible that Irish families have been thrown to vultures by a bank which only exists from State support and funds from the taxpayer" and warned that Lone Star would be unlikely to agree deals on arrears or renegotiate the terms of the loans, but would rather seek to repossess the homes (Irish Times, 2018). In late 2018, Masding was heard by the Irish Parliament's Finance Committee for the third time regarding the transactions. He argued that NPL markets were "the least worst [*sic*] alternative" to deal with high NPL levels, and stressed that the "tsunami of repossessions" feared by critics had never materialized (Joint Committee, 2018). Michael McGrath, a politician of Ireland's Republican Party Fianna Fáil, found it suspicious that Start Mortgages and Lone Star refused to answer questions about how they would handle "loans that are intrinsic to people's day-to-day lives", and emphasized "the level of stress, anxiety and mental health issues" this was causing debtors (ibid).

The controversy surrounding Lone Star did not come out of the blue. In 2015 already, New York Attorney General Eric Schneiderman opened an investigation into a Lone Star affiliate over its "heavy-handed mortgage-servicing tactics, including aggressive foreclosures" (Forbes, 2016). In 2016, news emerged that thousands of mortgages issued by Irish Nationwide and bought by Lone Star were "worth up to €90m more than the deeply discounted price [that Lone Star] paid to buy them" from the state's bad bank IBRC which had taken on Irish Nationwide's book (The Times, 2016). The homeowners involved "were denied the chance to buy out their mortgages when they were put up for sale" (ibid). That same year, Lone Star owner John Grayken was ranked the second wealthiest private equity manager worldwide, with a $6.3 bn net worth (Forbes, 2016), outlining the sheer inequalities of the distressed debt market and the ever more distant debtor-creditor relationship that underpin it.

One issue, then, is that private equity funds, because they are not banks and are newly systemic actors in European distressed debt markets, are not governed by banking regulation or dedicated legal framework. A mere focus on this *lack of regulation*, however, misses a crucial point: the bad debt market operated by global investment funds "could not take place without a political and regulatory environment which facilitate[s] them" (Byrne, 2015b: 10).

The European politics of distressed debt markets

Financial regulators have had NPLs on their radar for several years. Yet the EU is less concerned with NPLs in and of themselves as it is with NPL build-ups on banks' balance sheets and their implications for banks' profitability. As such, the EU sees NPL markets as a good way for banks to 'manage' their NPLs.

In March 2018, as part of an NPLs Action Plan, the Commission issued a Directive proposal intended to remove "undue impediments" to distressed debt markets, i.e. to establish common rules for loan servicers and purchasers and facilitate cross-border NPL transactions in the EU (European Commission, 2018a). The Directive was eventually slightly amended as part of the regular EU legislative process, but the initial proposal reveals that the Commission intended to support the marketization of NPLs, without due consideration for debtors' rights.

First, the Directive proposal set out some rules on the authorization of credit servicers, but did not provide equivalent requirements for debt purchasers, although they can also "enforce credit". These purchasers-servicers, then, were allowed to enforce debt claims (corporate debt for non-EU investors, and all debts including mortgages and consumer loans for EU investors) without needing to comply with the requirements applying to servicers. In addition, the proposal prohibited national governments from putting in place any other requirements for purchasers and servicers.[8] In practice, this meant that existing national-level rules going beyond those of the Directive would have to be removed. For example, in twelve member states investors must receive authorization from a central bank or a supervisor to purchase NPLs. In some countries a banking license is required, and in others only financial entities are allowed to buy NPLs (European Commission, 2018b:19). Although "motivation for authorisation requirements in some cases is based on debtor or data protection concerns" (ibid), such requirements were to be removed under the new framework, because the Commission "consider[ed] that those specific rules constitute[d] a barrier for business" (BEUC, 2018). By the same token, the proposal prevented states to implement any future regulate the market.

The Commission's legislative proposal, in sum, was not merely an attempt to harmonize rules across the EU; it is a clear example of downwards harmonization whereby the EU effectively intends to ban any *more* or *other* regulation. As policy advisor for The Left Group in the European Parliament Emma Clancy (2019) puts it, the key risk was that the Directive would "take away the right of EU member states to place regulations and restrictions on vulture funds and debt collectors", as the Risk Limitation Act of 2008 did to some extent in Germany. Altogether, this cast doubts on the credibility of the Commission's claims that its NPL markets legislation was adequately considering consumers' interests.

Indeed, the power imbalance that exists between a creditor and a debtor (Roberts and Soederberg, 2014) is exacerbated in the case of NPLs, where both sellers and buyers have an interest in strong enforcement measures: sellers because that means higher selling prices, and buyers because that means better recovery on loan value, and hence return on investment. As an industry memo explains, NPLs often do not "generate any payments by the debtors that are made willingly" and it is thus "incumbent upon the servicer to take active steps to resolve the NPLs and generate a cash flow" (Ropes and Gray, 2016). Without strict regulation and supervision, efforts of debt purchasers and collectors to extract payments from distressed borrowers can lead to abusive practices, as was reported in several countries (BEUC, 2018; Porino, 2020). Given this sharp conflict of interest between debtors and secondary creditors and servicers, a lack of adequate regulation of secondary purchasers and servicers can be a threat to debtors' protection.

Unsurprisingly, then, the Impact Assessment of the Directive proposal predicted that the impact on borrowers would range from 'quite negative' to 'very negative'. In other words, the Commission's own 'audit services' expected that the proposed changes would have *only negative impacts on debtors*. As a European Parliament briefing put it, such a "welfare shift from borrowers and supervisors to the benefit of investors and loan servicers" would "seem to go against the Commission policy on consumer protection" (EPRS, 2019: 5). The Commission, it appears, was much more closely aligned with the wishes of European financial lobby organizations. In its response to the Commission's public consultation on NPLs, the Association for Financial Markets in Europe warned for instance against the erosion of creditor and enforcement power:

> debtor protection . . . should be measured against other relevant considerations so that any such provisions do not result in increased costs and longer time frames for resolution/enforcement, which could have a negative effect on the price at which banks can sell their NPLs" (AFME, 2017).

Members of AFME include numerous banks sellers of NPLs, but also Blackstone, Goldman Sachs, and Deutsche Bank, respectively the second, fourth, and sixth top buyers of NPLs in 2014–2019 (see Figure 9.2).

In fact, looking at *who responded* to the NPL consultation might partly explain why the Commission, as per its Directive proposal, promoted secondary markets for NPLs that would benefit financial actors over debtors. Of the 50 respondents, 37 represented corporate interests, and among these, 30 directly represented financial sectors' interests (European Commission, 2017). That is, 60% of the material submitted to the consultation emanated from the financial sector itself. Banking interests were represented by at least 15 organizations, including individual banks, national lobby associations (the banking associations of Austria, France, Germany, Italy, the Netherlands and Spain) and EU-level lobby associations such as AFME, European Banking Federation, European Savings and Retail Banking Group, or European Mortgage Federation.

Individual financial firms are also likely to be over-represented in the consultation, because they had the opportunity to respond both directly and via multiple membership organizations. For example, UniCredit responded directly to the consultation as a bank; but it is also a member of the Italian Banking Association, itself a member of the European Banking Federation, both of whom responded to the consultation. In addition, UniCredit is a member of AFME, Loan Market Association, Europe Commercial Real Estate Finance Council, and European Mortgage Federation – who all responded to the consultation. More qualitative research is needed to assess how involved UniCredit and other banks were in the shaping of various associations' responses, but it is striking that at least 7 responses to the consultation (out of 50) are likely to represent the interests of a large bank like UniCredit.

On the other hand, only three organizations representing workers, consumers or civil society shared their views in that consultation. One of them, the non-profit organization Finance Watch (2018), recommended that any proposition to expand NPL markets should include "high levels of consumer protection in debt collection practices". The European consumer organization BEUC (2018) went further, arguing that "market actors who maximize their profits on the back of vulnerable consumers and businesses should . . . face restrictions". Despites these dissident voices, however, the initial debate on the NPL markets Directive remained largely circumscribed to EU regulators and industry representatives, far removed from mainstream media attention and the daily concerns of EU citizens. Such 'quiet politics' help to explain why moral questions attached to the trading and enforcement of debt – especially in situations where local debtors cannot meet their payment obligations, and distant buyers make hefty profits – have only marginally arisen into the public debate, leaving the door open for 'industry experts' to argue for market 'fixes' to what could be seen as a much wider socioeconomic over-indebtedness issue.

The scope of this study does not allow to draw conclusions on the next stages of negotiations at the European Parliament and Council, where parliamentarians and policymakers accountable to their electorate could potentially make political noise about NPL markets and consumer protection. However, the European Commission's 'quiet politics' regulatory efforts to promote financialization, in alignment with much of the financial industry, is a key element explaining how zombie debt claims are kept (profitably) alive – often to the detriment of debtors.

Conclusion: shining new light on the living debt

This chapter sought to make sense of the puzzling fact that seemingly untradeable – dead – debt claims have become a viable asset class over the past 20 years in Europe. In our two case studies we showed how crises-cum-financial globalization made for profitable opportunities to trade non-performing loans, followed by political debates and quests for a legal infrastructure that mediated between concerns over financial stability, profitability and social obligations inscribed in debt relations. Legislative action, first nationally, then supranationally, ultimately institutionalized new ways to make defaulting debt obligations tradable and enforceable, mitigating the disruption to creditors' earning expectations and enabling new financial actors to capitalize on struggling debtors.

At the same time, the cases differ in their politics. The German case exemplified a process of emerging *moral salience* where policymakers became sensitive to voters' concerns in an environment of 'noisy' financial politics. The European case, meanwhile, was rather a case of *moral silence*. There, the 'quiet' politics of the EU – geared towards market construction and banks' profitability, and involving a legislative process initially removed from electorates but open to business influence (see Lemoine and Piganiol, 2022, this volume) – allowed narrow but powerful financial interests to win the day over moral considerations focused on debtors' rights. In neither case, however, could the power of debtors to halt repayment or mobilize around presumed illegitimate financial practices (Ravelli, 2019; García-Lamarca, forthcoming) weigh fundamentally against financial actors' creditor and enforcement power, able to rely on a wide array of debt collection practices underpinned by creditor-friendly financial regulation and insolvency regimes.

Altogether, the sale and securitization of defaulting debts as well as regulatory changes aimed at easing these transactions form part of the ongoing assetization and marketization of debt defaults. Through this, 'classic' bank-customer claim relations are broken, and new ones arise, whereby ever more distant investors-turned-creditors attempt to recover (some of the) value dictated by the terms of the initial bank-customer claim contract. Debtors find themselves enrolled in transnational financial market transactions which bring significant profits to global investment funds and banking conglomerates, (North American) private equity funds and debt collectors. Thus, even when financialized capitalism runs into its own contradictions, appearing as NPL crises endangering banks' own profitability, financialization continues to be the fix of choice.

However, there are alternatives to the financialization of distressed debts. Debtors could be allowed "to purchase their own debt at the discounted price, instead of it being sold to third-parties" (BEUC, 2018). More broadly, fundamental political-economic changes are needed to ensure that decent standards of living do not depend on access to credit, and that capital markets expansion is no longer an EU priority. Without such paradigmatic shifts, the radical altering of ingrained practices of 'credit' and 'debt' remains in the far distance – meanwhile, dead or alive, financialized claims 'are coming to get us'.

Notes

1 Special servicing firms who often belong to the investors, such as Hudson Advisors (Lonestar) or Servicing Advisors Deutschland (Citigroup, Eurohypo, GMAC).
2 Within the scope of this chapter it is impossible to trace the legal arguments, law firms, judges and scholars involved, but a network analysis of 'claims about claims' could be a fruitful law and political economy research endeavour opening the black box of legal struggle.
3 Since the German legal framework did not straightforwardly allow non-bank institutions such as private equity and hedge funds to handle mortgages and other loans, some investors such as Cerberus and Lone Star also acquired German banks to circumvent regulatory barriers and obtain greater regulatory flexibility to restructure loan conditions (Schalast et al., 2006).
4 The locust imagery was introduced by former SPD chairman Franz Müntefering in 2004, mainly alluding to private equity investments in German companies through leveraged buy-outs. However, the SPD itself was responsible for providing key legislative requirements for these funds to become active in Germany.
5 Sourced from http://webarchiv.bundestag.de/archive/2008/0213/ausschuesse/a07/anhoerungen/082/Stellungnahmen/index.html; last accessed 28 January 2021.
6 Other ways for banks to deal with NPLs include 'write-offs, collateral repossession, collateral liquidation, cash collections' (EBA, 2019: 16).
7 The loan servicing industry in Europe has grown significantly over the past decade, having average profit margins of about 18% per year (European Commission, 2018b). Further research is warranted as to how this may affect debt collection practices and debtors' rights.
8 Articles 5 and 15.2 (European Commission, 2018a)

References

Aalbers MB (2008) The financialization of home and the mortgage market crisis. *Competition and Change* 12(2): 148–166.

AFME (2017) Consultation response. Available at: www.afme.eu/globalassets/downloads/consultation-responses/afme-ppa-response-to-consultation-on-secondary-markets-for-non-performing-loans-and-distressed-assets.pdf (accessed 1 December 2021).

Ari A, Chen S and Ratnovski L (2020) COVID-19 and non-performing loans: lessons from past crises. ECB Research Bulletin No.71. Frankfurt: ECB.

Ashurst (2017) Greek NPL momentum builds, 4 December. Available at: www.ashurst.com/en/news-and-insights/insights/greek-npl-momentum-builds/ (accessed 1 December 2021).

BEUC (2018) The European Commission's proposal is a bad deal for distressed borrowers. Available at: www.beuc.eu/publications/beuc-x-2018-068_secondary_market_for_non-performing_loans.pdf (accessed 1 December 2021).

Birch K and Muniesa F (2020) *Assetization: Turning Things into Assets in Technoscientific Capitalism*. Boston, MA: MIT Press.

Börsen-Zeitung (2008) Lone Star wappnet sich für neue Kreditkäufe. No. 19, 29 January, p. 4.

Brady N (2016). Lone Star in quick home loan profits. The Times, 27 November. Available at: www.thetimes.co.uk/article/lone-star-in-quick-home-loan-profits-js30g35hj (accessed 1 December 2021).

Braun B and Koddenbrock K (2022) The three phases of financial power: Leverage, infrastructure, and enforcement. In: Braun B and Koddenbrock K (eds) *Capital Claims: The Political Economy of Global Finance*. London: Routledge, pp. 1–30.

Bredow GM and Vogel H (2008) *Kreditverkäufe in der Praxis – Missbrauchsfälle und aktuelle Reformansätze* (Working Paper No. 82). Frankfurt: Institute for Law and Finance.

Brogt T and Dzieciol J (2017) Der NPL-Markt in Deutschland und Europa: Wohin führt der Weg? *Immobilien & Finanzierung* 13: 436–438.

Byrne M (2015a) Bad banks: The urban implications of asset management companies. *Urban Research & Practice* 8(2): 255–266.

Byrne M (2015b) From Puerto Rico to the Dublin Docklands; Vulture funds and debt in Ireland and the Global South. Report, Debt and Development Coalition Ireland (DDCI).

Calder L (1999) *Financing the American Dream. A Cultural History of Consumer Credit*. Princeton, NJ: Princeton University Press.

Carruthers B and Ariovich L (2010) *Money and Credit. A Sociological Approach*. Cambridge: Polity.

Clancy E (2019) Brussels' plan for bad loans is a second bailout for the banks, 18 April. Available at: https://emmaclancy.com/2019/04/18/brussels-plan-for-bad-loans-is-a-second-bailout-for-the-banks/ (accessed 1 December 2021).

Culpepper PD (2011) *Quiet Politics and Business Power. Corporate Control in Europe and Japan*. Cambridge: Cambridge University Press.

DB Research (2007) *"Notleidende Kredite" – eine etablierte Assetklasse. Der Handel mit Kreditportfolios in Deutschland*. Frankfurt: Deutsche Bank Research.

DBRS (2018). Rating Report – Permanent TSB Group Holdings plc, 19 December. Available at: www.permanenttsbgroup.ie/sites/tsb/files/rating-pdf/dbrs/2018.12.19-Ratings-Report.pdf (accessed 1 December 2021).

Debtwire (2018). European NPLs-FY18. An overview of the non-performing loan market. Available at: www.debtwire.com/pdf/EuropeanNPLFY18!.pdf (accessed 1 December 2021).

Deloitte (2019). Deleveraging Europe. Available at: https://www2.deloitte.com/content/dam/Deloitte/uk/Documents/corporate-finance/deloitte-uk-deleveraging-europe-2019.pdf (accessed 1 December 2021).

Dyson K (2014) *States, Debt and Power*. Oxford: Oxford University Press.

EBA (2019) *EBA Report on NPLs*. Paris: European Banking Authority.

ECB (2017) *Stocktake of National Supervisory Practices and Legal Frameworks Related to NPLs*. Frankfurt: European Central Bank.

Engelen E and Konings M (2010) Financial capitalims resurgent: Comparative institutionalism and the challenges of financialization. In: Morgan G, et al. (eds) *The Oxford Handbook of Comparative Institutional Analysis*. Oxford: Oxford University Press, pp. 601–624.

Enria A (2020). ECB: The EU needs a regional 'bad bank'. *Financial Times*, 26 October. Available at: www.ft.com/content/cc3a9a51-4d9a-4c73-9ff0-9f623ecf4065 (accessed 1 December 2021).

EPRS (2019) Credit servicers, credit purchasers and the recovery of collateral. EU Legislation in Progress Brief. European Parliamentary Research Service. Available at: www.europarl.europa.eu/RegData/etudes/BRIE/2019/635514/EPRS_BRI(2019)635514_EN.pdf (accessed 1 December 2021).

European Commission (2017) Public consultation on the development of secondary markets for non-performing loans and distressed assets and protection of secured creditors from borrowers' default. Available at: https://ec.europa.eu/info/consultations/finance-2017-non-performing-loans_en (accessed 1 December 2021).

European Commission (2018a) Proposal for a Directive of the European Parliament and of the Council on credit servicers, credit purchasers and the recovery of collateral. COM(2018) 135 final, Brussels, 14 March.

European Commission (2018b) Impact assessment. The development of secondary markets for non-performing loans by removing undue impediments to loan servicing by third parties and the transfer of loans (Part 1/2). SWD(2018) 75 final. Commission Staff Working Document, Brussels, 14 March.

European Commission (2019) Fourth Progress Report on the reduction of non-performing loans and further risk reduction in the Banking Union. Communication from the Commission. COM/2019/278 final. Brussels, 12 June.

Finance Watch (2018) 'Would you mind holding this for me?' Finance Watch Policy Brief, June. Available at: www.finance-watch.org/wp-content/uploads/2018/08/Finance-Watch-Policy-Brief-NPLs-June-2018.pdf (accessed 1 December 2021).

Forbes (2016). The billionaire banker in the shadows, 1 March. Available at: www.forbes.com/sites/nathanvardi/2016/03/01/the-billionaire-banker-in-the-shadows/?sh=3fb4e86a4a84 (accessed 1 December 2021).

Fourcade M and Woll C (2013) Moral categories in the financial crisis. Introduction. *Socio-Economic Review* 11(3): 601–627.

García-Lamarca M (forthcoming) *Non-Performing Loans, Non-Performing People: Life and Struggle with Mortgage Debt in Spain*. Athens, GA: University of Georgia Press.

Irish Mirror (2018) Campaigner warns of 'civil resistance' as fury grows over sale of Permanent TSB mortgages to vulture funds, 8 August. Available at: www.irishmirror.ie/news/irish-news/campaigner-warns-civil-resistance-fury-1304727 (accessed 1 December 2021).

Irish Times (2018) Shares in permanent TSB up 4.3% as it sells home loans, 31 July. Available at: www.irishtimes.com/business/financial-services/shares-in-permanent-tsb-up-4-3-as-it-sells-home-loans-1.3582035 (accessed 1 December 2021).

Joint Committee (2018) Sale of property loans (project glas) by permanent TSB: Discussion, 11 October. Available at: www.oireachtas.ie/en/debates/debate/joint_committee_on_finance_public_expenditure_and_reform_and_taoiseach/2018-10-11/3/ (accessed 1 December 2021).

Köchling M (2013) Der NPL-Markt in Deutschland: Marktentwicklung, Klassifizierung und Marktbeteiligte. In: Köchling M and Schalast C (eds) *Grundlagen des NPL-Geschäfts*. Frankfurt: Frankfurt School Verlag, pp. 15–42.

KPMG (2018) Non-performing loans in Europe. What are the solutions? Available at: https://assets.kpmg.com/content/dam/kpmg/xx/pdf/2017/05/non-performing-loans-in-europe.pdf (accessed 1 December 2021).

Langley P (2008) *The Everyday Life of Global Finance. Saving and Borrowing in Anglo-America*. Oxford: Oxford University Press.

Lemoine B and Piganiol M (2022) Claiming Greece: Technocracies of privatization and financial claims on public assets. In: Braun B and Koddenbrock K (eds) *Capital Claims: The Political Economy of Global Finance*. London: Routledge, pp. 232–247.

Mourmouras I (2019) Speech at the investors' conference on Greek & Cypriot NPLs, 13 February. Available at: www.bankofgreece.gr/en/news-and-media/press-office/news-list/news?announcement=40be6e37-c13c-4dd4-9b79-d810b151c45c (accessed 1 December 2021).

Orban A (2016) Mobilizing moral boundaries: The politics of derivatives reform in the US. *New Political Economy* 21(6): 555–573.

Palenker NR (2019) *Loan-to-Own. Schuldenbasierte Übernahmen in Zeiten moderner Restrukturierungen und mangelnder Gläubigertransparenz*. Baden-Baden: Nomos.

Pistor K (2013) A legal theory of finance. *Journal of Comparative Economics* 41(2): 315–330.

Pistor K (2019) *The Code of Capital*. Princeton, NJ: Princeton University Press.

Porino G (2020) Debt collection: Europe could end unjustifiable and wide-spread malpractices, 9 February. Available at: www.finance-watch.org/debt-collection-europe-could-end-unjustifiable-and-wide-spread-malpractices/ (accessed 1 December 2021).

PTSB (2018) Sale of non-performing loan portfolio, 31 July. Available at: www.permanenttsbgroup.ie/sale-non-performing-loan-portfolio (accessed 1 December 2021).

PWC 2012: Issue 4: A growing non core asset market - European outlook for non core and non performing loan portfolios. Available at: https://store.pwc.de/de/publications/issue-4-a-growing-non-core-asset-market-european-outlook-for-non-core-and-non-performing-loan-portfolios (accessed 1 December 2021).

Quinn SL (2019) *American Bonds. How Credit Markets Shaped a Nation.* Princeton, NJ: Princeton University Press.

Ravelli Q (2019) Debt struggles: How financial markets gave birth to a working-class movement. *Socio-Economic Review* 19(2): 441–468.

Roberts A (2014) Doing borrowed time: The state, the law and the coercive governance of 'undeserving' debtors. *Critical Sociology* 40(5): 669–687.

Roberts A and Soederberg S (2014) Politicizing debt and denaturalizing the 'new normal'. *Critical Sociology* 40(5): 657–668.

Ropes & Gray (2016) Non-performing loans and securitisation in Europe, 7 April. Available at: www.ropesgray.com/en/newsroom/alerts/2016/April/Non-Performing-Loans-and-Securitisation-in-Europe (accessed 1 December 2021).

Schalast C, Ockens K, Jobe C and Safran R (ed.) (2006) Work-out und servicing von notleidenden Krediten. HfB Working Paper No. 76.

Schimansky H (2008) Verkauf von Kreditforderungen und Unterwerfung unter die sofortige Zwangsvollstreckung. *Zeitschrift für Wirtschafts- und Bankrecht* 23: 1049–1052.

Soederberg S (2014) *Debtfare States and the Poverty Industry. Money, Discipline and the Surplus Population.* Oxon: Routledge.

Soederberg S, Menz G and Cerny PG (eds) (2005) *Internalizing Globalization. The Rise of Neoliberalism and the Decline of National Varieties of Capitalism.* Basingstoke: Palgrave Macmillan.

SWR (2008) Wie Heuschrecken in Deutschland Hausbesitzer abzocken, 26 May. Available at: https://www.swr.de/report/skrupellose-geschaefte-wie-heuschrecken-in-deutschland-hausbesitzer-abzocken/-/id=233454/did=3507778/nid=233454/wgmpye/index.html (accessed 1 December 2021).

Woll C (2013) Lobbying under pressure: The effect of salience on European Union Hedge fund regulation. *Journal of Common Market Studies* 51(3): 555–572.

10

THE FINANCIALIZATION OF INVESTOR-STATE DISPUTE SETTLEMENT

Florence Dafe and Zoe Phillips Williams

Introduction

The growing role and power of finance in economic life is by now widely recognized by political economy scholars working in the broadly defined space of financialization. However, these analyses have, until recently, tended to focus on the impact of finance on the domestic level. Work that has looked at financialization at the international level has most often had as its unit of analysis global financial institutions. In this chapter, we look instead at the ways in litigation finance also commonly known as third-party funding (TPF), has transformed the decentralized international investment protection regime. As we will see, firms located in the financial sector gather funds from other investors in order to finance litigation in the sphere of international investment. The international investment regime, comprising investment treaties and contracts, and investor-state dispute settlement (ISDS), has as its express purpose the de-localization of disputes between state governments and foreign investors. The financialization of ISDS is nonetheless historically rooted in legal changes in key domestic jurisdictions, and today shapes the relationships between an array of private (financiers, law firms, and investor-claimants) and public (respondent-state) actors. Thus, while we follow Pistor (2019) in identifying the ways in which states provide the legal framework for financial activity, or claims, to take place, this chapter also identifies the ways in which finance, in turn, shapes the functioning of one area of law.

International investment agreements (IIAs) are signed by states but extend important rights to private actors. Specifically, these treaties allow investors (the claimants) from one signatory state to sue the government of another signatory state (the respondent) before an international tribunal for alleged treaty violations. These violations may be any state measure or action: from the outright expropriation of an investment project, to the passing of more stringent environmental

DOI: 10.4324/9781003218487-13

regulations. While these treaties contain language that is similar to that of many free trade agreements and WTO law, the form of dispute settlement much more closely resembles that of private commercial arbitration, and successful claimants are awarded monetary damages, paid by the respondent state.

As discussed at further length later, the use of arbitration by foreign investors became increasingly common in the late 1990s. During this time, a growing number of states were hit with claims in response to a widening array of policy measures, and many of the world's largest international law firms, such as White & Case, Jones Day and Hogan Lovells, to name a few, expanded their investment arbitration business. Approximately a decade later, we witnessed the emergence of TPF of investment arbitration in which financiers shoulder the costs[1] of launching an arbitral claim against a state, generally in exchange for a share of any eventual monetary award obtained by the investor. In this way, TPF of ISDS is one iteration of the broader practice of litigation funding in which an actor "that has no interest in the underlying merits of a dispute but provides funding or resources for the purpose of financing the legal costs and expenses of an international arbitration" (ICCA, 2018: 1).

Through this practice, third-party funders not only create a claim on a share of any future awards from the arbitration proceedings but also support the enforcement of the claims of international investors vis-à-vis sovereign states by supplying the long-term financing investors require to shoulder the considerable costs of international arbitration proceedings, which usually take several years. Thus, this incursion of finance into this relatively niche area of international law has turned these legal claims into financial claims, transforming the decisions of international arbitrators into a new asset class, to be invested in and traded as any other. This development also further alters the power dynamic between states and private economic actors – in this case foreign investors. Indeed, TPF helps foreign investors keep their legal, and financial, claims against states "alive" in situations in which, absent funding, this might not be the case. This is because the presence of funding available to investor-claimants alters the distribution of risk in the system, providing funds to investors to launch their legal claims, which they would otherwise have to pay out of pocket. This potentially makes investors more likely to bring claims, even if these are frivolous (lacking in legal merit) or more importantly, "marginal" – that is, claims that do not fit the pattern of, for example, outright expropriation of an investors' assets, but involve "highly complex questions of public policies, preferences, and competing rights and obligations and are not cases in which the government was acting in bad faith or for discriminatory purposes (Güven and Johnson, 2019: 24). These marginal claims can then push the boundaries of the use of ISDS ever deeper into true public-policy decision-making. This increase in the ability of investors to bring claims may in turn make respondent states more likely to settle, and more wary, in the future, of taking measures which may negatively affect investors, even if these are in the interest of other actors, or constituents other than foreign investors. (Güven and Johnson, 2019).

Explaining the rise of TPF of ISDS

TPF of investment arbitration claims against states appears to be an increasingly common occurrence. While a lack of transparency requirements in most investment treaties and arbitral rules makes it difficult to ascertain the extent of its use, as we have written elsewhere, both funders and lawyers alike assert that funding arrangements are quickly becoming routine (Dafe and Williams, 2020). What explains the rise of this practice?

One necessary condition for the rise of TPF is, of course, a sufficiently active investment arbitration regime, a condition which has undoubtedly been met over the last decade and a half. While the first investment treaties were signed in the 1960s, the signing and ratification of BITs took off in the late 1980s and early 1990s, as states competed for investment, and international actors advised developing and transition economies that these treaties would attract investment (Elkins et al., 2006; Poulsen, 2015). A "boom" in arbitration followed about a decade later, and 2018 saw the highest number of new cases registered at the International Centre for the Settlement of Investment Disputes (ICSID) (UNCTAD, 2019). While investment arbitration was initially conceived of as a tool for investors in politically unstable, post-colonial states, its use has greatly expanded in recent years, even as outright expropriations have become rare (Pandya, 2014). Now, investors routinely challenge regulatory measures, including those taken by OECD countries; indeed, countries such as Canada and Spain are amongst the most frequent respondent states (Bonnitcha and Williams, 2019; UNCTAD, n.d.). There is thus a large enough universe of cases to attract funder interest in arbitral claims as an asset class (Dafe and Williams, 2020).

The development of the TPF industry also required legal changes in key jurisdictions. While not traditionally facing restrictions in countries with a civil law tradition, since the middle ages, common law jurisdictions have prohibited the practices of champerty and maintenance – the support by a third party of litigation in which they have no "legitimate" concern, and the financial gain from such a case (Barker, 2011: 8). While TPF could easily be considered to contravene rules prohibiting champerty and maintenance, its legal status was cemented in the UK by a 2005 Court of Appeal ruling and 2009 report written by Justice Jackson. Specifically, the latter clarified that if funders complied with any future regulation of the practice, agreements between funders and litigants would "not be overturned on the grounds of maintenance and champerty" (Jackson, 2009: 124). From the UK, the practice spread to the United States, and more recently, has been permitted for international arbitration in the Asian arbitration hubs of Singapore and Hong Kong, and as both scholars and industry insiders argue, this is largely the result of competition among jurisdictions to attract arbitration business (Steinitz, 2011; Dafe and Williams, 2020). As we've discussed elsewhere, funders understood these changes, particularly in the UK, to be a turning point, giving them confidence to invest in litigation finance (Dafe and Williams, 2020). This is in large part because while investment arbitration takes place beyond state jurisdiction, the enforcement of arbitral awards (and thus the procedure for funders to recoup their investment in the event that a respondent state fails to pay the award in a timely fashion) takes place through domestic courts.[2] This, along with the need to ensure that funding contracts can be enforced against the claimant, requires the legality of TPF in relevant domestic jurisdictions. Happily, for the industry, states have, to date, been content for the litigation finance industry to be largely self-regulating (Dafe and Williams, 2020).

While the arbitration boom, and concurrent legal developments have facilitated it, to truly understand the emergence of TPF we must be able to account both for the demand and the supply of funding. With regard to the former, proponents of the practice claim that TPF provides a means of access to justice for claimants who otherwise cannot afford the (increasingly high) costs of arbitration (Steinitz, 2011). Indeed, in our discussions with funders, we frequently heard that TPF made it possible for investors, particularly those whose investment had been destroyed by state measures and were thus "impecunious", to have access to this form of dispute settlement (Dafe and Williams, 2020). While this is certainly true for some investors who enter into funding arrangements, the decision to supply funding is made based on funders' assessment of the relative risk and reward of funding an investment claim, rather than concerns for the investor's ability to access justice. Moreover, we find evidence that TPF is increasingly being sold to, and used by claimants as a "corporate finance tool" whether or not they are able to cover the costs of arbitration (Dafe and Williams, 2020: 11). Therefore, it is necessary to look at the "supply side" of the capital flowing into litigation to have a full understanding of the emergence of this phenomenon.

The timing of the take-off of TPF – when increasing numbers of financiers were establishing themselves as litigation funders – suggests one possible cause for this supply of capital: the global financial crisis. Indeed, a significant number of funds were established in the years immediately following the crisis (Dafe and Williams, 2020), possibly providing access to litigation for crisis-hit investors who have had fewer resources to devote to any arbitral proceedings during this period, increasing the demand for funding. Indeed, many funders we've spoken to, as well as industry observers, identified the global financial crisis as a potential explanation for the rise of TPF of investment arbitration.

However, a focus on the global financial crisis as the central explanatory factor in the rise of TPF would miss that the practice is, rather, an example of the much broader historical economic trend of financialization which describes the broad shift from production- to finance-led growth (Epstein, 2005). This shift is both a cause and a consequence of the growth in supply of capital, which in turn looks for and perhaps creates vehicles for investment. TPF is one such vehicle and one that has continued to be attractive to investors in the post-crisis era as both assets that are uncorrelated with the market, and an investment that has the possibility for very large returns, even in a low interest rate environment (Dafe and Williams, 2020). Moreover, domestic jurisdictions that are not unfriendly to TPF, as well as an international regime which allows for the enforcement of arbitral awards, means that investing in ISDS claims is additionally appealing to investors as states "usually pay up in the end" (Dafe and Williams, 2020: 13).

The financialization of ISDS

What are the implications of the rise of TPF? It is fair to say that a silent revolution is occurring within the investment protection regime. Finance, in alliance with legal professionals, has become an important player in the creation, trading and enforcement of investment treaty claims. What this amounts to is a financialization of ISDS, which we, following Braun and Koddenbrock (2022), define as a process by which the number and value, the tradability, and the enforceability of cross-border financial claims increases in the realm of international investment. There are three main dynamics which allow finance to assume such a central role in the monetization of investment treaty claims, which we will discuss in turn. First is the alignment of the interests of funders, the legal industry and investors due to joint material benefits. Second is the imperative to earn a return on the large amount of capital amassed by the TPF industry. Third is the lack of concerted state action to limit the role of finance in ISDS.

The alignment of the interests of funders, the legal industry and investors

While the gains may not be distributed evenly among private agents, there is broad agreement that financiers, the legal industry and investors benefit materially from the rise of TPF in ISDS, as is also evident in a win-win narrative promoted by private agents (Dafe and Williams, 2020: 10).

In light of the growth of players in the sector and the increase in the number of cases in which funding is secured, finance, along with law firms, emerges as a clear beneficiary. Given the lack of transparency regarding the number and terms of funding arrangements, it is difficult to establish precisely how much the funding industry has gained. Yet extant data suggests that returns have been considerable over the past decade. A much-publicized case, *Teinver versus Argentina*, involves Burford Capital, an international investment firm and likely the biggest player in the industry, which in 2018 made $107 million dollars from selling its share of an investment treaty arbitration award to an unknown institutional investor. Burford had been involved as a third-party funder in a case brought against the government of Argentina after it had nationalized two Argentine airlines (Güven and Johnson, 2019). By selling its share of the claim, Burford secured a 722% return on its invested capital, amounting to a profit of $94 million (Burford Capital, 2019). In another highly profitable case, Tenor Capital Management provided $76 million in a lawsuit of the Canadian mining firm Crystallex International Corp waged against Venezuela for expropriating a gold mine. The funder proposed to pay Crystallex's general corporate expenses, as well as the costs of pursuing the ICSID arbitration. In return, the funder would receive 35% of the net proceeds of any arbitral award or settlement (Omnibridgeway, 2017). When Crystallex won the award, Tenor was promised an $800 million-dollar pay day, a ten-fold return on its investment (Hals, 2018). While these may be idiosyncratic cases we find in our expert interviews that it is not unusual that funders, while taking some risk, might enjoy returns ten times over their investments and that litigation finance outperforms many specialized investment vehicles (Dafe and Williams, 2020: 9).

But financiers are not the only private agents that benefit from the availability of TPF. The legal industry and the large investors who are the claimants in the arbitration benefit as well. With regard to investors, the share of the award they receive may be significantly smaller when they use TPF as opposed to when they do not. In the case *Crystallex v. Venezuela*,[3] the funding agreement Crystallex signed specified that the funder, Tenor Capital, which eventually provided $76 million to fund the litigation, would receive at least 70 percent of any payments Crystallex could collect from Venezuela, once Crystallex paid off Tenor's loan and other creditors (Hals, 2018).

Nonetheless, TPF may still be attractive for investors given the significant costs that are involved in bringing an investment claim against a state. As discussed earlier, without financial support, arbitration may be prohibitively costly for some firms, especially if they are financially distressed (Dafe and Williams, 2020: 17). That said, TPF is, as we have discussed elsewhere, more widely available and thus more prevalent for large claims (i.e., the size of the damages alleged by the investor) which naturally tend to involve larger investors. The reason for this is that, due to profit considerations, funders rule out cases they consider meritorious when the size of the investment provided would be below a certain amount (Dafe and Williams, 2020). As a result, it is not only small financially distressed investors that seek TPF. Instead, it has also become common for large, liquid investors to turn to TPF because it allows them to remove the costs of the arbitration from their balance sheet or spread or reallocate the risk involved in bringing a claim (Dafe and Williams, 2020: 17; Norton Rose Fulbright, 2016). The reliance on TPF can thus also be seen as a response to the pressures of shareholder capitalism to avoid a concentration of costs and the risks on the balance sheet.

Initially, law firms greeted the arrival of TPF with skepticism. Lawyers were concerned about the legality of TPF and whether funders would become their competitors (Dafe and Williams, 2020: 23). Over time, however, the legal industry embraced TPF on that grounds that funders serve as a means of increasing the number of cases they are able to take on. In fact, it has become quite common for lawyers to offer potential claimants not only legal advice but also to recommend and match claimants and funders in an effort to help arrange for TPF (Kalyanpur and Newman, 2021; Dafe and Williams, 2020: 24). An important enabler of the rapprochement between funders and law firms were what Kalyanpur and Newman (2021) refer to as "cross-field interactions" between lawyers and funders. More specifically, the funding industry has heavily recruited from international law firms, made deliberate efforts to reach out to law firms and promote the use of TPF, and institutionalized such interactions through regular exchange.

What has emerged is that over time, the interests of funders, the legal industry and investors as claimants have become increasingly aligned, with the former two players in some cases forming a symbiotic relationship, where the growth of one type of actor feeds the growth of the other. In fact, TPF has not only become widely accepted and used, but a significant portion of the profits associated with the practice of ISDS are now derived from TPF. This mirrors the central claim in the literature that in a context of financialization, an important share of profits is derived from financial activities as opposed to productive investment (Krippner, 2005; Orhangazi, 2008; Arrighi, 2004).

The profit-maximization imperative

The financialization of ISDS is, however, not only reflected in the increase in the relative importance of income generated through financial activities as a share of total profit-generating activities in ISDS, but also in the ways in which financial institutions shape the process of ISDS when they provide funding. More specifically, the imperative to earn a return on the large amount of capital amassed by the TPF industry helps to explain how finance has come to play such a central role in the creation, trading and enforcement of investment treaty claims.

With the emergence of funders, whose business model consists of deploying the capital they control and maximizing the profits from their deployment, financial logics have increasingly come to shape the funding of cases and thus an important part of ISDS practice. There are three main facets of the dominance of financial logics. First, there is lack of respondent funding. Second, TPF has begun to rely on more complex financial instruments and strategies, mimicking investment banks. Third, it has become common that funders assume an active role in the cases, increasingly their involvement in mechanism of claims enforcement.

Quite glaringly, state-side funding has been very limited to date, with only a few examples of respondent-side funding, which diverge in several respects from the more common cases of claimant funding. In a case receiving high publicity, the Bloomberg Foundation and its Campaign for Tobacco-Free Kids provided financial support and technical assistance to the government of Uruguay for its defense against the tobacco company Philip Morris in the ICSID case *Philip Morris v. Uruguay*[4] in which Philip Morris challenged state regulations requiring plain packaging of tobacco products (Sahani, 2017). In the case *RSM Production Corporation versus Grenada*, the Russian oil company Global Petroleum, which had a competing interest in the oil exploration rights that had been revoked from RSM, helped to fund Grenada's defence (Honlet, 2015; ICCA, 2018: 23–24). In both cases, however, the funder had an independent financial or non-financial interest in the outcome. Usually, however, TPF is provided solely to claimants. We found that among the 16 major funders we interviewed all save one smaller entity expressed doubts about the prospects for respondent funding by commercial third parties (Dafe and Williams, 2020: 5). The reason are unresolved questions about how contracts would be designed given that only investors can act as claimants and are thus the only party which can be awarded monetary damages. States, as it is often noted, can only "not lose" an arbitration, and there is no obvious source of return on investing in a respondent state's litigation costs.

With regard to the use of financial instruments and strategies, a secondary market for claims has emerged. Burford, a major funder, is particularly active in the secondary market, as is for instance evident in *Teinver v Argentina*.[5] Teinver concerned the expropriation of two airlines owned by a Spanish firm, and ultimately involved a long and complex fight about damages. Teinver claimed the highest value it reasonably could, while the government of Argentina asserted that the airlines were so badly run that they were valueless. Even before the World Bank arbitral tribunal settled on a value in the middle (Burford, 2019: 33), Burford, which had funded the claim, sold its entitlement to the Teinver award for $107 million against a $13 million investment (Güven and Johnson, 2019: 8).

Another example of the introduction of financial instruments in ISDS is the increasingly common practice of portfolio financing. In portfolio financing, a funder takes a financial interest in a basket of claims, which may be focused around the same claimant, or around the same law firm. This practice thus relies on the cross-collateralization of several different claims lessening funders' exposure to risk should a single case be lost (Dafe and Williams, 2020: 16). For the funder, this is a strategy to diversify its investment risk. For the claimant, that may result in better terms of the funding arrangement.

The second facet of the increasing dominance of financial logics in ISDS is that funders assume an increasingly active role in the ISDS cases. In particular, funders tend to analyze material related to the case to determine whether it is viable and should move forward, and later exercise influence in the process of arbitration by supporting or opposing strategies by the claimant in the arbitration, as they have insights into the proceedings and key documents (Dafe and Williams, 2020: 16). In *Teinver v. Argentina*, for instance, the funding agreement specified that Burford had a right of access to information relating to the case (Jus Mundi, 2019). States have tried to reduce the role of funders in the arbitration process by raising objections with tribunals against a continuous exchange of information between funders and claimants, as happened, ultimately without success, in *Teinver v. Argentina*. In a case in which the US energy company EuroGas initiated arbitration proceedings against Slovakia over revoked rights to one of the world's largest talc deposits, Slovakia also sought a ruling from the tribunal that the third-party funder would not have access to any confidential information in the case (Hepburn, 2015). The claimants, meanwhile, saw no need for a special provision on confidentiality, arguing that the funder would be bound by the same requirements as any other person involved in the case. For Slovakia, though, the funder was not involved in the case, but was equivalent to a member of the public, which justified an order that the parties' confidential information would not be shared with them. Ultimately, the funder, whose identity has not been published, maintained its access to information on the proceedings of the case because the tribunal sided with the claimants, ruling that the funder would "have the normal obligations of confidentiality".

Moreover, funders may also exercise pressure to not settle a case below a certain amount keeping claims alive until a minimum level of profit can be generated.[6] In some cases, this is done by structuring their returns in such a way that it does not make financial sense for the claimant to ever settle below a certain amount (Dafe and Williams, 2020: 16). In others the funding agreement specifies a minimum amount for settlement. In *Teinver v. Argentina*, for instance, the agreement between Burford and the claimants specified that "any settlement agreement for an amount at least equal to USD 250 million shall be accepted with no need of a further agreement on the part of the claimants" (Jus Mundi, 2019). When Argentina argued that such a provision amounted to an improper interference by Burford in the arbitration, the tribunal ruled that the provision was "no more than an agreement between the parties to the Funding Agreement on what a reasonable settlement amount would be". In light of funders' access to confidential documents related to the case, the transfer of a substantial share of the proceeds from an award to funders when the claimants win the case, and that funding agreements rule out some actions or options for claimants and their lawyers while encouraging others, it is not surprising that states have often accused funders of exercising undue influence over arbitral proceedings.

Finally, it may sometimes be difficult to draw a clear line between funders and claimant. For instance, in *Teinver v. Argentina*, where the funding agreement specified amounts for settlement and gave rise to an exchange of letters between the insolvency administrators of the claimant and Burford regarding the entitlement to the proceeds of the award, the respondent argued that the funders had become the real party in the arbitration (Jus Mundi, 2019). In another case, *Gabriel Resources Ltd v. Romania*, Tenor Capital Management, which financed Canadian company Gabriel Resources' $4.4 billion claim against Romania, following the alleged expropriation of a mining project, Tenor was granted the right to appoint a nominee to Gabriel's board as part of the funding agreement (Gabriel, 2016). While it is debatable to what extent funders have become the real beneficiaries of third-party-funded investment arbitration, there is broad agreement that financiers have become an important third actor in a system which was originally based around two, namely states and investors.

The other side of the coin: states and TPF

One party that has largely been absent from our discussion so far is the state, or rather the international community of states. States have played a central role as facilitators of the rise of finance in ISDS. As outlined earlier, states have created an enabling legal environment, especially by dropping champerty and maintenance laws, both in an effort to respond to concerns about access to justice and in an effort to compete as attractive hubs for international arbitration as in the case of Singapore and Hong Kong (Dafe and Williams, 2020). More broadly, Pistor (2019) argues for the role of the state in facilitating private investment, as providers of the legal infrastructure which allows and protects investment and in our case, for third-party-funded claims.

In addition, states have facilitated the emergence of a large supply of investable capital that turns to TPF in its search for profitable investment opportunities in two ways. First, by reducing state welfare spending as part of the shift towards asset-based welfare (Bonizzi and Churchill, 2017; Gabor, 2018). This policy increased the funds that institutional investors and their asset managers control and need to deploy, fuelling the search for profitable investment outlets. Second, the decline in tax rates and failure to cooperate on a global level to address tax evasion and avoidance has contributed to the increasing concentration of wealth has allowed elites and large corporations to accumulate funds, which they seek to invest profitably (Lysandrou, 2011; Hager, 2015).

But it is not only the actions of individual states that have facilitated the financialization of ISDS, but also the lack of concerted, collective action in response to the increasingly prominent role of finance in the investment protection regime. In particular, concerted state action to increase transparency in regard to TPF in ISDS lacking, despite the fact that respondent states often request, during arbitral proceedings, that the use of funding, the identity of funders and the terms of the funding agreement should be disclosed.[7] While ISDS tribunals have frequently sided with respondents that TPF and the names of funders have to be disclosed, tribunals have tended to rule in favor of claimants that the disclosure of the terms of funding is not relevant to the arbitration. At the institutional level, we witness a similar dynamic. Two major international organizations for arbitration, namely the ICC through the new 2021 ICC arbitration rules (ICC, 2020) and ICSID through its fourth working paper (ICSID, 2020) have mandated the disclosure of the presence and identity of a third-party funder, but do not generally require disclosure of the specific terms of the funding agreement.

For respondent states, this lack of transparency is a concern for two main reasons. One is security for costs. Having become aware of the fact that claimants are using TPF in the ISDS arbitration, states have often raised concerns that the use of TPF could be an indication that the claimant lacked the funds to finance the costs of the proceedings, which they might have to bear should they lose the arbitration. To ascertain whether claimants are sufficiently liquid to shoulder the costs of the arbitration, states have sometimes requested that tribunals ask claimants to provide a deposit or to disclose the terms of the funding agreement in order to determine whether the agreement provides funds to the claimant if they lose they case. Through disclosure, respondent states can reduce the risks of a "hit and run" arbitration, where a funder pays for a claimant to bring a case but is not liable to pay the state's costs if the claimant loses.

Quite often, however, arbitral tribunals tend to assign the burden of proof that a claimant is unable to shoulder the state's costs if it loses to respondent states as the parties requesting greater transparency or a deposit from the claimant (Leventhal, 2018). In an arbitration between Bolivia and Bermuda-based mining company South American Silver, the tribunal ruled that the mere existence of a funding agreement does not evince the impossibility of payment, or insolvency, and thus did not request any additional efforts from the claimants to respond to concerns about security of costs (Jaramillo, 2016). While there exist cases in which the tribunal asked the claimants to deposit a certain amount of funds as security, produce evidence of an adverse costs insurance, or share the funding agreement, cases where tribunals ordered the disclosure of funding agreements, as occurred in *Manuel García Armas v. Venezuela* (Leventhal, 2018), remain the exception.

Besides security for costs there is a second reason why transparency in relation to TPF is a key concern for states as respondents, namely conflicts of interests. As delineated earlier, in some cases funders have come to play an activist role in the arbitration proceedings and disclosing the identity of the funder and the terms of the funding agreement may help to establish the extent to which funders strengthen the hand of claimants and are involved in key decisions during the proceedings. The greater the extent of funder involvement, the greater the risk that concerns other than protecting the investment of a claimant shape the position of the claimant in the arbitration. Moreover, transparency in TPF might help to reveal whether there are conflicts of interests among arbitrators. For example, in an arbitration case involving the energy company Canepa Green Energy Opportunities and Spain, the state sought to disqualify the arbitrator of the claimant on the grounds that he had sat on the Investment Committee of the funder Harbour Litigation Funding Limited at the time when Harbour funded Canepa in another case, without initially disclosing it (Bohmer, 2019). Ultimately, the tribunal ruled that neither the failure of the arbitrator to disclose his relationship with the funder nor the actual relationship with Harbour were sufficient to disqualify the arbitrator from the tribunal.

A recent case involving an American businessman, Mr. Amorrortu, who lodged an arbitration claim under the Peru-USA Trade Promotion Agreement, also illustrates the efforts by individual states to enhance transparency to achieve security of costs and reduce the risk of conflicts of interests. In *Bacilio Amorrortu v. Peru* an UNCITRAL tribunal ordered the disclosure of the identity of the claimant's third-party funder, but declined Peru's request that the terms of the funding arrangement should be revealed (IA Reporter, 2020). Peru had asked for an order that the claimant: (i) disclose his funder's identity; (ii) confirm that the funding terms includes payment of a potential adverse costs award; and (iii) provide copies of the funding terms relevant to a potential costs award as well as to the funder's say over the proceedings (Bohmer, 2019). Peru explained that this information was needed in order to assess any potential conflicts of interest, and also to clarify the basis for a potential security for costs application. The arbitrators noted that they were "unwilling" to infer a lack of funds from the mere fact that the claimant had opted to use a third-party funder. According to the tribunal, there are "numerous other reasons" for seeking third-party funding beyond impecuniosity, such as risk management and validation by an objective third party (Bohmer, 2019). While the tribunal ordered that the "identity" of the third-party funder should be disclosed to both the tribunal and the respondent in order to determine potential conflicts of interest, but argued that the claimant, was under no duty to demonstrate that he was free to reach a settlement or make other procedural decisions. In fact, the tribunal argued that the application raised a "potentially important 'access to justice' issue" and that, if the claimant met the jurisdictional requirements then "there is no additional requirement that he prove financial capacity to meet any potential adverse costs award or that he is the master of his own litigation".

What emerges from these empirical examples is that states as respondents have individually sought to increase transparency in TPF in ISDS, but have as a group thus far failed to set rules that address the gap in transparency, and thus to specify the limits of the role that finance plays in the creation, trading and enforcement of investment treaty claims. In fact, as concerted state action has not been forthcoming, major organizations like the ICC and ICSID have developed rules that limit transparency, though this increases the risks of exacerbating the inequities inherent to a legal regime that is already weighted in favor of private interests.

Conclusion

In this chapter, we have situated the TPF of international investment arbitration claims within the broader trend of financialization. As a case study, the TPF of ISDS is instructive, as it demonstrates that financial actors, in an increasingly cooperative and mutually beneficial relationship with international legal actors, play an integral role in the enforcement of financial claims against sovereign states. The role funders play in ISDS is thus similar to the role which Lemoine and Piganiol (2022) identify for the Greek bureaucracy in privatizations to support debt repayment. In doing so, this chapter shows that the role and enforcement power of finance has also increased in this relatively niche and decentralized area of international law.

The rise of TPF within this regime has had profound impact on the practice of ISDS, introducing a third actor – financiers – into a system that was designed to include only investors and states. As described in the third section, TPF has created new relationships between the private actors within the system, over time aligning the interests of funders, law firms and investor-claimants. This has allowed funders, in an exercise of enforcement power, to have a greater influence on decision-making in the context of legal proceedings, potentially impacting the size of the monetary claims against states and shaping incentives around the settlement of disputes. As only claimants, and not states, can reasonably expect to access funding for ISDS cases, the incursion of finance into the investment protection regime arguably further shifts the balance in favour of private rather than public interests. While the goal of this paper was to increase our understanding of the reasons for the rise of TPF, it nonetheless helps us anticipate the ways in which the insertion of financial interests into this legal system may shape its functioning in ways that, as mentioned in the introduction, further put states on the "back foot" when fighting these legal claims, increasing the risk tolerance of investors to bring claims that may, for example, touch on areas of public policy and the economic and political interests of a wide array of domestic actors in the respondent state. Thus, in general terms, by increasing the ability of investors to keep their claims against respondent states "alive", TPF lowers the risk they face in doing so, TPF further skews the ISDS system in favour of private interests.

Of course, legal changes in key jurisdictions and lack of concerted push to regulate the industry either domestically or in international fora have created a friendly environment for the industry; thus states may be both the victims and the facilitators of financialization. As also Binder highlights in this volume, states have exercised agency, not least by changing the law, in shaping the relationship between borrowers and creditors. Now, some states are ringing the alarm about TPF in ISDS, and as discussed earlier, make attempts to curtail the practice in the context of individual ISDS proceedings. However, this approach leaves states to rely on arbitrators to, for example, require claimants to disclose their funding relationships in the context of asking for security for costs. More broadly, there has been a lack of coherent action taken by states, to date, to address the practice, and given the alignment of interests between the funding and arbitration industries, it is unsurprising that arbitral fora have continued the trend of only lightly regulating the practice of TPF in investment arbitration. Nonetheless, there is currently an opportunity for more a more concerted effort to regulate or rein in the practice of TPF of ISDS if states so choose – the ongoing UNCITRAL Working Group on ISDS reform. It remains to be seen if this opportunity will be seized.

Notes

1 These costs include paying for legal counsel, as well as the arbitrator fees and costs associated with the nuts and bolts of running what tends to be a several years-long legal process.
2 This is facilitated by an international agreement, the New York Convention. Signatories of the Convention empower their own domestic courts to enforce arbitral awards if the respondent state does not voluntarily pay what the tribunal determines is owed to the investor. In practice, this means that assets of the recalcitrant respondent state can be seized and awarded to the investor by domestic courts in any country that has signed the Convention.
3 Crystallex International Corporation v. Bolivarian Republic of Venezuela, ICSID Case No. ARB(AF)/11/2
4 Philip Morris Brands Sàrl, Philip Morris Products S.A. and Abal Hermanos S.A. v. Oriental Republic of Uruguay, ICSID Case No. ARB/10/7 (formerly FTR Holding SA, Philip Morris Products S.A. and Abal Hermanos S.A. v. Oriental Republic of Uruguay).
5 Teinver S.A., Transportes de Cercanías S.A. and Autobuses Urbanos del Sur S.A. v. The Argentine Republic, ICSID Case No. ARB/09/1
6 About one third of all publicly known arbitral claims are settled before they reach the final award stage. The terms of these settlements are generally confidential but many likely involve a payment to the investor.
7 See for instance Honlet Honlet J-C (2015) Recent decisions on third-party funding in investment arbitration. *ICSID Review – Foreign Investment Law Journal* 30(3): 699–712., Jaramillo Jaramillo EZ (2016) *PCA Case No. 2013–15. Procedural Order No. 10.* Available at: www.italaw.com/sites/default/files/case-documents/italaw7176.pdf (accessed 13 November 2021) and Charlotin (2017).

References

Arrighi G (2004) *The Long Twentieth Century. Money, Power, and the Origins of Our Times.* New York: Verso.

Barker GR (2011) *Third Party Litigation Funding in Australia and Europe* (Working Paper No. 2). Canberraq: Centre for Law and Economics, ANU College of Law.

Binder A (2022) In good times and in bad: Offshore dollar markets and the international monetary power of borrowers. In: Braun B and Koddenbrock K (eds) *Capital Claims: The Politica Economy of Global Finance*. London: Routledge, pp. 121–148.

Bohmer L (2019) Analysis: In newly-obtained ruling, tribunal considers that arbitrator's relationship to litigation funder must be disclosed, but non-disclosure does not, by itself, warrant disqualification; Spain responds by bringing a second challenge this week. Available at: www.iareporter.com/articles/analysis-in-newly-obtained-ruling-tribunal-considers-that-arbitrators-relationship-to-litigation-funder-must-be-disclosed-but-non-disclosure-does-not-by-itself-warrant-disqualification/ (accessed 12 August 2022).

Bonizzi B and Churchill J (2017) Pension funds and financialisation in the European union. *Revista De Economía Mundial* 46: 71–90.

Bonnitcha J and Williams Z (2019) Politically motivated conduct in investment treaty arbitration. Available at: www.iisd.org/itn/2019/04/23/politically-motivated-conduct-in-investment-treaty-arbitration-jonathan-bonnitcha-zoe-williams/ (accessed 12 August 2022).

Braun B and Koddenbrock K (2022) The three phases of financial power: Leverage, infrastructure, and enforcement. In: Braun B and Koddenbrock K (eds) *Capital Claims: The Politica Economy of Global Finance*. London: Routledge, pp. 17–61.

Burford (2019) Annual report 2018. Available at: www.burfordcapital.com/media/1526/bur-31172-annual-report-2018-web.pdf (accessed 12 August 2022).

Burford Capital (2019) Burford Capital announces successful conclusion to Teinver annulment applications. Available at: www.burfordcapital.com/newsroom/burford-capital-announces-successful-conclusion-to-teinver-annulment-applications/ (accessed 14 October 2021).

Charlotin D (2017) Arbitrators express doubts about a right to security for costs, but bankrupt claimant's "after-the-event" insurance policy obviates any need to rule definitively. Available at: www.iareporter.com/articles/arbitrators-express-doubts-about-a-right-to-security-for-costs-but-bankrupt-claimants-after-the-event-insurance-policy-obviates-any-need-to-rule-definitively-on-respondents-request/ (accessed 12 August 2022).

Dafe F and Williams Z (2020) Banking on courts: Financialization and the rise of third-party funding in investment arbitration. *Review of International Political Economy* 28(5). doi:10.1080/09692290.2020.1764378.1–23.

Elkins Z, Guzman AT and Simmons BA (2006) Competing for capital: The diffusion of bilateral investment treaties, 1960–2000. *International Organization* 60(4): 811–846.

Epstein GA (2005) Introduction: Financialization and the world economy. In Epstein GA (ed.) *Financialization and the World Economy*. Cheltenham: Edward Elgar Publishing.

Gabor D (2018) *Understanding the Financialisation of International Development Through 11 FAQs*. Washington DC: Heinrich Böll Stiftung North America.

Gabriel (2016) Press release. Closing of private placement. Available at: www.gabrielresources.com/documents/GBU_closingofprivateplacement_140716_close_filing.pdf (accessed 13 November).

Güven B and Johnson L (2019) The policy implications of third-party funding in investor-state dispute settlement. Columbia Center on Sustainable Investment, CCSI Working Paper (5). New York.

Hager SB (2015) Corporate ownership of the public debt: Mapping the new aristocracy of finance. *Socio-Economic Review* 13(3): 505–523.

Hals T (2018) Want to Sue Venezuela for millions? These firms can help, for a price. Available at: www.reuters.com/article/us-venezuela-lawsuits-finance-insight-idUSKCN1OK0EP (accessed 12 August 2022).

Hepburn J (2015) ICSID tribunal orders identification of third-party funder, but denies state's request for security for costs and claimants' request for provisional measures. Available at: https://www.iareporter.com/articles/icsid-tribunal-orders-identification-of-third-party-funder-but-denies-states-request-for-security-for-costs-and-claimants-request-for-provisional-measures/ (accessed 12 August 2022).

Honlet J-C (2015) Recent decisions on third-party funding in investment arbitration. *ICSID Review – Foreign Investment Law Journal* 30(3): 699–712.

IA Reporter (2020) Amorrortu v. Peru. Available at: www.iareporter.com/arbitration-cases/amorrortu-v-peru/ (accessed 13 November).

ICC (2020) 2021 Arbitration rules. Available at: https://iccwbo.org/dispute-resolution-services/arbitration/rules-of-arbitration/rules-of-arbitration-2021/#article_11 (accessed 13 November).

ICCA (2018) *Report of the ICCA-Queen Mary Task Force on Third Party Funding in International Arbitration*. The Hague: International Council for Commercial Arbitration.

ICSID (2020) Proposal for amendment of ICSID Rules (Working Paper No. 4). Available at: https://icsid.worldbank.org/sites/default/files/documents/WP_4_Vol_1_En.pdf (accessed 22 August 2022).

Jackson R (2009) Review of civil litigation costs: Final report. London: Ministry of Justice.

Jaramillo EZ (2016) PCA case no. 2013–15. Procedural order no. 10. Available at: www.italaw.com/sites/default/files/case-documents/italaw7176.pdf (accessed 13 November).

Jus Mundi (2019) Teinver v. Argentina. Available at: https://jusmundi.com/en/document/decision/en-teinver-s-a-transportes-de-cercanias-s-a-and-autobuses-urbanos-del-sur-s-a-v-argentine-republic-annulment-proceeding-thursday-21st-december-2017 (accessed 13 November).

Kalyanpur N and Newman AL (2021) The financialization of international law. *Perspectives on Politics* 19(3): 773–790.

Lemoine B and Piganiol M (2022) Claiming Greece: Technocracies of privatization and financial claims on public assets. In: Braun B and Koddenbrock K (eds) *Capital CLAIMS: The Politica Economy of Global Finance*. London: Routledge, pp. 363–386.

Leventhal AG (2018) Towards an exceptio fundati? Assessing a (potentially) emerging exception for third party funding in investment treaty decisions on security for costs in the wake of Armas v. Venezuela. Available at: http://arbitrationblog.kluwerarbitration.com/2018/09/18/assessing-a-potentially-emerging-exception-for-third-party-funding-in-investment-treaty-decisions-on-security-for-costs-in-the-wake-of-armas-v-venezuela/ (accessed 13 November).

Lysandrou P (2011) Global inequality as one of the root causes of the financial crisis: A suggested explanation. *Economy and Society* 40(3): 323–344.

Norton Rose Fulbright (2016) International arbitration report. Available at: www.nortonrosefulbright.com/files/international-arbitration-report-issue-7-142408.pdf (accessed 13 November).

Omnibridgeway (2017) Litigation funding paves way for Crystallex's $1.4B award against Venezuela. Available at: https://omnibridgeway.com/insights/blog/blog-posts/blog-details/global/2016/04/06/third-party-funding-paves-way-for-crystallex-s-$1.4b-award-against-venezuela (accessed 13 November).

Orhangazi Ö (2008) Financialisation and capital accumulation in the non-financial corporate sector: A theoretical and empirical investigation on the US economy: 1973–2003. *Cambridge Journal of Economics* 32(6): 863–886.

Pandya SS (2014) Democratization and foreign direct investment liberalization, 1970–2000. *International Studies Quarterly* 58(3): 475–488.

Pistor K (2019) *Code of Capital: How the Law Creates Wealth and Inequality*. Princeton, NJ: Princeton University Press.

Poulsen LNS (2015) *Bounded Rationality and Economic Diplomacy: The Politics of Investment Treaties in Developing Countries*. Cambridge: Cambridge University Press.

Sahani VS (2017) Revealing not-for-profit third-party funders in investment arbitration. Available at: https://oxia.ouplaw.com/page/565 (accessed 13 November).

Steinitz M (2011) Whose claim is this anyway – third-party litigation funding. *Minnesota Law Review* 95: 1268–1338.

UNCTAD (2019) Investment policy hub. Available at: https://investmentpolicy.unctad.org/investment-dispute-settlement (accessed 21 March).

UNCTAD (n.d.) Investment dispute settlement navigator. Available at: www.nzz.ch/international/trumps-friedensplan-fuer-nahost-die-neusten-entwicklungen-ld.1536711#subtitle-was-sieht-trumps-nahostplan-vor-second (accessed 16 November).

11

FIRM CLAIMS

Reinterpreting the global race for foreign direct investment

*Arjan Reurink and Javier Garcia-Bernardo**

Acknowledgments

This project has received funding from the European Research Council (ERC) under the European Union's Horizon 2020 research and innovation programme (grant agreement number 638946). We thank Saila Stausholm for providing the data on the number of employees at the Big Four accounting firms. We also thank Milan Babic and the other members of the CORPNET research group, as well as Benjamin Braun, Sandy Hager, Marina Hübner, Lukas Arndt, Bruno Casella and Richard Bolwijn for useful suggestions and comments.

Introduction

One major class of cross-border financial claims in today's economy is what is commonly referred to as foreign direct investment (FDI). FDI is generally operationalized as any long-term equity or debt investment, made by a transnational corporation (TNC), in a foreign subsidiary, affiliate, or branch, whereby the investing TNC is in a position to exercise a sufficient degree of direct control over the organization and management of that subsidiary or branch.[1] Since the 1990s, the dollar-value of global FDI claims has increased exponentially. Annual flows of global FDI have expanded from $205 billion in 1990 to $1.4 trillion in 2017 (Figure 11.1(A)). The worldwide stock of FDI has expanded accordingly. Whereas in 1990 it stood at $2.2 trillion, in 2017 this figure has risen to $31.5 trillion (Figure 11.1(B)).

Motivated by the anticipated benefits from incoming FDI,[2] national governments across the globe have become increasingly preoccupied with improving the attractiveness of their countries' investment climates in order to outcompete other countries in the global race for FDI (Cerny, 1990; Elkins et al., 2006; Jensen, 2008; Porter, 1990; Stopford et al., 1991; Thomas, 2010). Such international

DOI: 10.4324/9781003218487-14

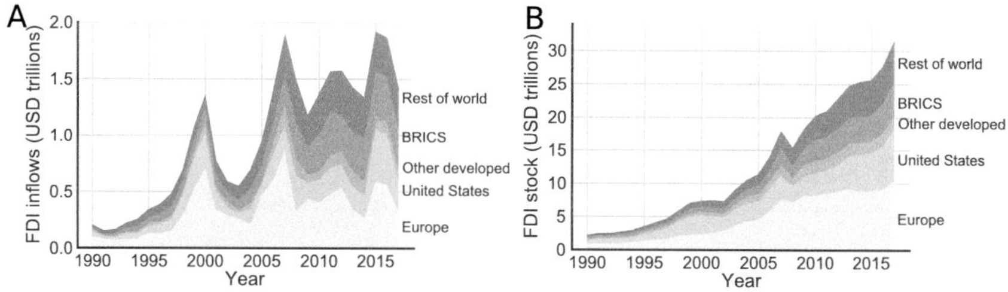

FIGURE 11.1 The increasing importance of foreign direct investment

Source: Notes: (A) FDI inflows by region (B) FDI stock by region.

Data: All FDI data was collected from the UNCTAD World Investment Report (2018).

competition for FDI presents one of the main dynamics in contemporary capitalism and, accordingly, has become a key research focus of scholars studying the international political economy (IPE).

Typically, IPE research on this global race for FDI interprets the global surge in FDI flows and stocks as a reflection of the internationalization of TNCs' production processes. In search of cost savings, talent, and access to lucrative markets, large firms increasingly started to unbundle, outsource and relocate part of their productive activities offshore. Potential host country governments, enthused by the prospect of jobs, economic growth, and productivity gains, further encouraged the international expansion and fragmentation of firms by luring foreign firms into their territories with generous tax breaks, subsidies, and other kinds of investment incentives. Thus understood, the surge in global FDI since the 1990s reflects the unbundling and internationalization of TNCs' production processes and constitutes an important driver of economic development around the globe.

In this chapter, we argue that this particular productivist understanding of the global race for FDI is unsatisfactory for two reasons. First, it does not adequately account for the fact that not all FDI is the same. There is important heterogeneity in the type of productive activities funded through FDI flows, with each type of activity responding to different country characteristics and generating distinct economic and political benefits for the countries hosting it. Compare, for instance, a TNC's investment in a manufacturing plant in Slovakia with the relocation of its regional headquarter to the Netherlands. Both the institutional features required to attract those investments and the benefits that the host countries can expect to reap from them are fundamentally different. If we as IPE scholars want to get the story about the global race for FDI right, it is crucial that we account for this heterogeneity, both in our conceptual thinking and in our operationalizations.

Second, by conceiving FDI exclusively as a source of funding for productive activities, the conventional IPE understanding of FDI overlooks the fact that a significant share of global FDI today does not reflect TNC investments in productive operations, but a rearrangement of legal claims on the future value generated by

TNCs' already funded operations.[3] The claims perspective laid out in the introduction to this volume helps to make sense of this. Whenever an investor-firm makes a direct investment into a foreign subsidiary, it provides not only the financial means for that subsidiary to carry out productive activities, it simultaneously creates a claim on the future value generated through those activities.[4] These claims, however, are not absolute; they are challenged by competing claims, including those coming from host and home countries' tax authorities. TNCs adopt a range of legal-financial strategies to undermine the enforcement of these competing tax claims on the future value generated by their global subsidiaries. Crucially, these strategies revolve around the use of holding companies located in jurisdictions whose legal and tax frameworks confer on FDI-investors certain privileges that have the effect of increasing the "firmness" of their claims *vis-à-vis* those of the tax authorities of the countries in which their productive activities are located. Effectively, then, TNCs use holding companies as vehicles for exercising financial *enforcement power* (see Braun and Koddenbrock, 2022, this volume). To get things right in our analyses of the global race for FDI, it is therefore crucially important to analytically separate FDI into productive subsidiaries from FDI into holding companies and to distinguish between countries' capacity and motivations to attract these two different types of corporate entities.

We address these conceptual and methodological concerns by developing a new understanding and measurement of FDI. To this end, we first trace a process of corporate restructuring that we refer to as the "great fragmentation of the firm". Doing so leads us to conceptually distinguish between five categories of FDI. Namely, FDI in: manufacturing affiliates, shared service centers, R&D facilities, intermediate holding companies, and top holding companies. We then develop a novel method for measuring those various categories of FDI. This allows us to then show for each of these categories of FDI which EU member states are most successful in attracting it, what macro-institutional and tax arrangements they rely on for doing so, and what benefits they receive from it in terms of tax revenues and job creation.

The great fragmentation of the firm

The impressive expansion of global FDI in recent decades has been a symptom of a fundamental reorganization during that period of the architecture of TNCs. This reorganization, we propose, is best understood not just in terms of a fragmentation and geographical dispersion of TNCs' productive activities, but also of their legal-financial structure. We will refer to this dual process of fragmentation as the *great fragmentation of the firm*.

Conceptually, the great fragmentation of the firm can be thought of as transpiring on two levels of corporate organization. At the *productive level*, the notion of the great fragmentation of the firm captures the unbundling and geographical dispersion of TNCs' productive activities. This level of the great fragmentation has been well-documented in the International Business and Management literature as well as the Political Economy literature on Global Value Chains and Global

Production Networks. This body of literature discusses how, driven by growing demands to maximize shareholder value, and facilitated by advances in information and communication technology (ICT) and gradual reductions in trade and investment barriers, from the 1980s onwards large firms increasingly began to unbundle, outsource and relocate part of their operational activities offshore. Over time, these processes have resulted in the emergence of global value chains through which large TNCs, so-called "lead firms", organize and coordinate their productive operations across geographies (Gereffi et al., 2005; Coe et al., 2008). Most salient in this regard, both politically and in terms of scholarly interest, has been the relocation of TNCs' manufacturing activities to low labor-cost countries (Blinder, 2006).

However, the offshoring of operational activities has not been confined to manufacturing activities. Since the second half of the 1990s, TNCs have increasingly been unbundling, outsourcing and offshoring business support services as well (McIvor, 2010). The offshoring of business support services has involved not only back office and support operations, such as human resource management, legal services, and accounting (Wilson, 1995), but also front-office operations such as customer support (Breathnach, 2000) and even research and development activities (Dachs et al., 2014). As of recently, the unbundling and geographical dispersion of TNCs operational activities has also come to affect those functions that traditionally were combined in the TNC's global corporate headquarter (Desai, 2009). For example, TNCs' global treasury and financing function might be separated from other headquarter functions to be performed by a separate legal entity operating from a jurisdiction that provides the optimal institutional environment for the performance of that specific function. Similarly, strategic management might be offshored to jurisdictions that provide large pools of managerial talent and that are conveniently located in the proximity of major markets.

At the *legal-financial level* of corporate organization, the great fragmentation of the firm involves processes of legal restructuring and financial innovation that enable firms to strengthen their claims on the future value created through their globalized operational activities. This dimension of the great fragmentation is currently being explored in the emerging literature on Global Wealth Chains (Bryan et al., 2017; Seabrooke and Wigan, 2017). Based on our reading of this literature, we distinguish three important features of the rethinking of the legal-financial organization of the corporate group. A first feature has been the interposition of (intermediate) holding companies in group ownership structures. These are companies that engage in narrowly defined activities such as the holding of equity or debt stakes in group subsidiaries or the holding of rights to the (sub)licensing of intellectual property. The use of holding companies has increased significantly since the 1990s. For example, assets held by intermediate holding companies in the Netherlands have increased from under 1.8 EUR trillion in 2006 to 3.8 EUR trillions in 2015.[5] For Germany, assets held by intermediate holdings increased by 1400% from 1989 to 2001 (Weichenrieder et al., 2008).

A second feature has been the rearrangements of important value-creating assets, especially intellectual property such as copyrights, patents, and trademarks, across group subsidiaries. Through intra-group transactions and cost-contribution agreements, either ownership of the intellectual property assets themselves, or (parts of) the rights to the income streams generated by those assets are transferred to group holding companies established especially for the purpose of holding those assets.

A third feature concerns innovative approaches to intra-group financing arrangements, often supporting a strategy called "earnings stripping". In the case of earnings stripping, subsidiaries located in high-tax jurisdictions are financed by subsidiaries located in low-tax jurisdictions. The interest on the debt paid by the subsidiary in the high-tax jurisdiction reduces the taxable profits reported in that jurisdiction and increases the taxable profits in the low-tax jurisdiction – thus transferring the claims on the profits from the high-tax to the low-tax jurisdiction.

The anatomy and geographical dispersion of corporate groups

Over the last couple of decades, the operational and legal-financial fragmentation of the TNC has resulted in a transformation of the large firm from a functionally diverse, but legally and jurisdictionally contained enterprise to a multi-subsidiary corporate group, in which different functions are fulfilled by specific subsidiaries that often exist as separate legal entities in different jurisdictions. A typical TNC, or corporate group,[6] nowadays has dozens, if not hundreds of subsidiaries, each of which fulfills a specific role in the broader scheme of the corporate group[7] (Figure 11.2). Although the constellation and specific functions of individual

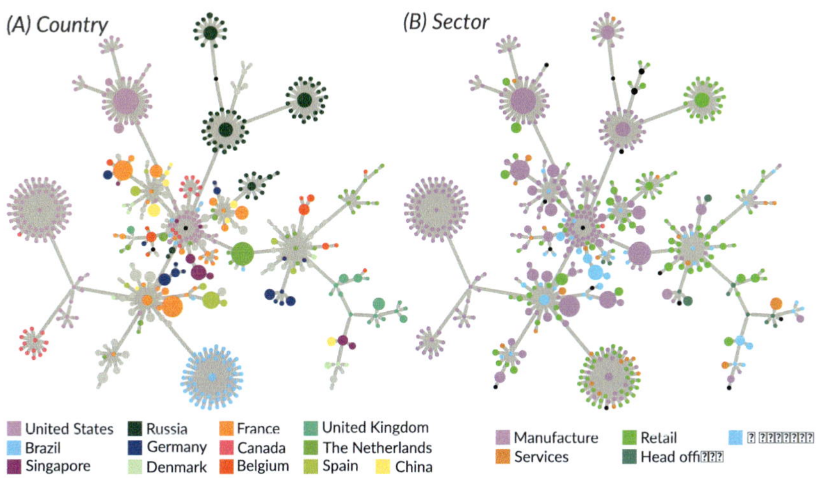

FIGURE 11.2 Corporate structure of a large food company

Source: Notes: Nodes represent different subsidiaries, connected by ownership relationships. Colors indicate (A) country of incorporation, and (B) type of entity. Node size indicates turnover reported by the entity.

Data: Orbis (Bureau van Dijk)

subsidiaries are idiosyncratic and unique for each corporate group, for analytical purposes we distinguish between five broad types of subsidiaries. These are *manufacturing affiliates; shared service centers; R&D facilities, top holding companies;* and *intermediate holding companies*. Next, we discuss for each of these types of subsidiaries the kinds of activities they engage in, their specific function in the broader scheme of the corporate group, and the macro-institutional arrangements and tax incentives that can be expected to attract these types of activities.

Manufacturing affiliates

A first type of subsidiary is the manufacturing affiliate. Beginning in the 1960s, and increasingly so with the gradual abandonment of international trade and capital barriers in the 1980s and 1990s, TNCs began to outsource and relocate parts of their manufacturing operations to foreign locales. Initially, such relocations primarily involved the most routine and labor-intensive of TNCs' manufacturing operations and were driven above all by a search for labor cost advantages (Lewin and Peeters, 2006). Over time, however, TNCs increasingly began to relocate more complex tasks and have moved beyond cost savings to consider such things as worker skills, infrastructure, and government trade and investment policies (Ellram et al., 2013).

In addition to the benefit of low labor costs and other institutional factors, manufacturing affiliates often make use of special regimes available in the new host country. Such "special economic zones" typically offer a combination of tax and tariff incentives and may even exclude firms operating in those zones from labor, environmental and ownership regulations that apply to firms operating elsewhere in the country (Farole et al., 2011).

Shared service centers

A second cluster of group subsidiaries consist of shared service centers. These are subsidiaries that provide centralized support services to other group entities. This may involve both low value-adding back-office operations, such as information technology, human resource management and accounting, as well as higher value-adding services, such as procurement, marketing, sales and distribution. Some firms have opted for an outsourcing strategy, in which specific services (mostly the lower value-adding back-office operations) are provided by a third party service provider. A trend in recent years, however, has been for TNCs to centralize and "in-source" some or all business support activities and have them performed by a captive entity (Lewin and Peeters, 2006; Bondarouk, 2014).[8] This entity, known as a "shared service center" (SSC), then provides the services to other group entities. Such an SSC may serve the entire corporate group or selected group entities operating in a specific geographical region or line of business.

Two considerations may lie behind the establishment of shared service centers. The first is cost reduction. SSCs allow corporate groups to benefit from economies of scale and avoid duplication of services across subsidiaries. Moreover, when located in jurisdictions that provide inexpensive labor, the establishment of SSCs can result in substantial savings on labor costs (Lewin and Peeters, 2006). An increasingly important driver for the growing use of SSCs, however, is a desire to source new organizational capabilities (Lewin and Peeters, 2006). TNCs increasingly discover that offshoring technical, professional and administrative activities allows them to tap into new pools of highly qualified staff (Lewin and Volberda, 2011).[9] Regardless of which of these considerations prevails, the successful implementation of SSCs relies heavily on the availability of good transportation and ICT infrastructure and the availability of an English speaking workforce (Doh et al., 2009). Taxes, on the other hand, appear to play only a secondary role in TNCs' decisions on where to locate their SSCs. A survey conducted by management consulting firm Deloitte amongst 311 large firms that had established over 1,000 SSCs found that 70% of companies do not take taxation into consideration when choosing the location of their SSCs. We expect that this might be partly explained by the fact that SSCs are often run as cost, rather than profit centers and thus make little or no taxable profits. Still, 17% of companies setting up SSCs do so with the objective to reduce their global tax burden – for instance through transfer pricing strategies.[10]

Research and development (R&D) facilities

A third cluster of group subsidiaries consists of TNCs' R&D facilities. These are subsidiaries that are responsible for TNCs' product innovations. Although up until the 1990s these activities used to be performed in the context and proximity of TNCs' global headquarters (Patel and Pavitt, 1991), increasingly TNCs are relocating them across jurisdictions (Dachs et al., 2014).

Existing literature identifies three main motives underlying the internationalization of TNCs' R&D activities (Carlsson, 2006). The first is for TNCs to adapt the design and development of their goods and services to the specific needs of local markets (Fors and Zejan, 2012). This is typically done for markets that are especially important for a firm's sales figures. Another motive for the relocation of R&D facilities is to bring them in closer proximity to TNC's previously offshored manufacturing operations. Finally, a third, and increasingly prominent, motive underlying the relocation of R&D activities away from TNCs' home country is a desire to establish a presence in highly innovative regions and cities (Florida, 1997). TNCs relocating their R&D activities to such regions do so to get access to local talent and knowledge. Important considerations taken into account by TNCs seeking to tap into local innovative capacities are the availability of highly qualified personnel and a high density of universities and other types of research institutions (Cantwell and Piscitello, 2002; Dachs et al., 2014). The cost of R&D personnel appears to be of only minor importance in the R&D location decision (Dachs et al., 2014). Instead, TNCs value countries, and regions within countries, that provide for attractive living conditions that make it easy to attract additional knowledge workers from abroad (Malecki, 1987).

Although there appears to be consensus in the literature that macro-institutional factors dominate TNCs' R&D offshoring decisions, tax incentives are said to play a role as well (Hines, 1994; Cantwell and Mudambi, 2000). Tax incentives for R&D activities may involve tax credits for R&D expenditures or so-called patent or innovation boxes, whereby income emanating from qualifying IP is taxed at a reduced rate (Evers et al., 2015). Especially the latter type of incentive has become widely used in Europe over the last decade. As of June 2017, 14 European jurisdictions had introduced some form of innovation box.[11] Moreover, to attract foreign high-skilled workers, and thus increase their attractiveness as a location for TNCs' R&D activities, some jurisdictions have implemented temporary tax reductions for personal income taxes for foreign knowledge workers.

Top holding companies

The fourth cluster of group subsidiaries we identify are top holding companies. Top holding companies are companies that appear at the apex of a corporate group's ownership structure and therefore are often referred to as the group's "global ultimate owner" (GUO). These entities play a key role in the legal-financial organization of the group. The location of the top holding company generally determines the legal home of a corporate group and thereby not only the company law under which it operates, but in many cases also its tax residency.[12] Since a large fraction of profits are typically transferred to the top holding company, the tax residency of that company is a key factor in determining the consolidated tax rate of the group (Dischinger et al., 2014). For publicly listed TNCs, the top holding company is also the legal entity whose shares are traded on a stock exchange and thus administers the group's relationship with its external shareholders. This means that the tax regime of the jurisdiction in which the top holding is domiciled determines how dividend payments to shareholders are taxed.

Not all top holdings, however, are the same. The traditional top holding company would be domiciled in the jurisdiction from which the group originated[13] and not only fulfill a key role in the legal-financial organization of the corporate group, but also act as the group's global headquarters, meaning that it performs most or all of the corporate functions responsible for the orchestration of the group's global value chains: strategic management, shared services, and compliance and reporting (Baaij et al., 2015). In today's fragmented TNC, these functions are increasingly unbundled and relocated to jurisdictions that provide the optimal conditions for the performance of those specific functions (Desai, 2009; Baaij et al., 2015). Examples of traditional headquarter functions that TNCs may detach from their top holding and relocate across borders are the staff function (resulting in the establishment of SSCs), the group financing and treasury function (resulting in group financing companies – see next subsection), and the strategic management function (resulting in divisional and regional headquarters – see next subsection).

Given the large impact of the tax regime that applies to a top holding on the overall tax burden of a corporate group, TNCs have large incentives to transfer their top holding to a jurisdiction with low corporate income tax rates, low or non-existing withholding taxes on dividend payments to shareholders, and/or a favourable company law framework (Voget, 2011; Baaij et al., 2015). In the period 1997–2007, 6% of all multinationals relocated their headquarters to another jurisdiction by means of corporate inversions or mergers with a foreign firm (Voget, 2011). Over 50 percent of US multinationals that relocated their headquarters to another jurisdiction by means of corporate inversions in the period 1990–2016, did so to countries with no corporate income tax – mainly the Cayman Islands, Bermuda and the British Virgin Islands (Slangen et al., 2017). Transferring the top holding to another jurisdiction may have other non-tax related benefits as well. For instance, it has been suggested that top holding relocations may enable TNCs to improve communication and knowledge exchange with investors (Birkinshaw et al., 2006), and give them access to new pools of managerial talent (Baaij et al., 2015).

Intermediate holding companies

These are holding companies that may positioned anywhere under the top holding in a corporate group's ownership structure. Intermediate holding companies appear in different forms and may be used for a number of purposes. One such purpose is to minimize the impact of claims coming from home or host countries' tax authorities on the value that is created by the TNC's operating subsidiaries. To achieve this, debt or equity investments in the foreign subsidiary are not held directly by the parent company, but indirectly through an intermediate holding company, or "conduit" entity. Returns made on those investments are then channeled back to the parent company through the conduit entity in the form of interest or dividend payments. Through such interest payments, TNCs can shift parts of their tax base from the host country to a third country in which that tax base usually qualifies for generous tax exemptions, or is taxed at a (very) low rate. Channeling interest and dividend payments through intermediate holding companies also allows TNCs to benefit from favorable provisions in the tax treaty that has been negotiated between the host country of the operating subsidiary and the country in which the intermediate holding company is located. Such provisions may include reduced withholding tax rates on dividend- or interest payments – reducing the tax claims of the host state on those transactions.

Intermediate holding companies may also be used for royalty transactions. Such "royalty conduits" may receive royalty payments because they are the legal owner of an intellectual property asset itself or because they own the economic rights to the royalty income generated by the asset due to a licensing agreement with the group entity that legally owns the asset (Maine and Nguyen, 2017). Either way, these agreements reduce the tax base of the subsidiary in the host country, thus negating the scope of host governments' tax claims on the value generated by the operating subsidiary. The described dividend-, interest-, and royalty conduit functions may also be combined in a single intermediate holding company.

The archetypical intermediate holding company is one that has few employees and plays only a minor role in managing and directing group activities. This may be different, however, in the case of intermediate holding companies that combine pure holding activities (i.e. the holding and administering of assets, be they financial, tangible, or intangible assets) with strategic, coordinating or capital management functions. The best example of such multifunctional intermediate holding companies are regional headquarters. Regional headquarters are typically designed to both hold the equity capital of operational subsidiaries active in the relevant region and to engage in strategic decision-making and coordinating functions regarding the TNC's activities in that region. It is also not uncommon for a regional headquarters to accommodate a shared service center offering business support services to operating subsidiaries in that specific region. Another example is the group financing company, sometimes also referred to as the group's treasury. These are entities that are responsible for the management of intra-group financial transactions, such as intra-group lending, group liquidity management, hedging, and other financial operations that had traditionally been part of the finance function of the corporate headquarter.

A number of institutional features can make a jurisdiction an especially attractive location for the establishment of intermediate holding companies and/or regional headquarters. One is the availability of the institutional infrastructure necessary to support intermediate holdings companies: a stable and efficient state apparatus, sufficiently advanced ICT infrastructure, and the availability of knowledgeable tax advisors, trust firms, and other types of business services (Eicke, 2009; Wójcik, 2013). For group treasuries, having access to deep and developed capital markets may represent an important consideration (Eicke, 2009). Perhaps even more important for TNCs' decisions where to locate their intermediate holding companies, however, are the specificities of a jurisdiction's tax regime. One such specificity is the absence of withholding taxes on outgoing and incoming dividend, interest and royalty payments, or the availability of reduced rates on such payments. Typically, therefore, intermediate holding companies are located in jurisdictions that provide TNCs with access to an extensive network of bilateral tax treaties, enabling them to significantly reduce the tax costs of funneling payments through a specific jurisdiction (Weyzig, 2013). Other aspects of a country's tax regime that TNCs may consider in the location decision for their intermediate holding companies are the administrative burden created by tax compliance and the existence and enforcement of anti-avoidance provisions. Finally, the availability of investment treaties with countries in which an envisioned holding company's subsidiaries are located may further increase the attractiveness of a jurisdiction as a location for an intermediate holding company.

The representation of the anatomy of the contemporary firm sketched in the previous paragraphs is, of course, a highly stylized one. Explicitly distinguishing between FDI in these five different types of operations does, however, provide a degree of analytical traction that has been missing in previous analyses of international competition for FDI. In the ensuing analysis we exploit this analytical traction to develop a more sophisticated understanding of this phenomenon. Specifically, we answer three simple questions: Which EU countries attract which types of FDI? What institutional and tax arrangements do they use to do so? And what are the benefits they receive from doing so in terms of tax revenues and employment creation?

Analytical approach, data and visualization

Analytical approach

To answer these questions we conducted a two-step analysis. In a first step we determined for each of the five categories of FDI identified in the third section which EU member states[14] are most successful in attracting those activities. Because the available data on FDI does not distinguish between the different types of investment projects that are financed by the FDI flows, we constructed a set of indicators that gauge the intensity of the economic phenomena and activities associated with each type of FDI. Throughout the remainder of the article we denote these indicators as *activity indicators*.

In a second step, we collected a range of *macro-institutional* and *tax policy indicators* to understand which macro-institutional features and tax policies may be associated with those countries that are most successful in attracting the different categories of FDI. For example, based on our reading of the literature, we include labor costs and corporate income tax rates as possible determinants of foreign direct investments in manufacturing affiliates, while we include the availability of low withholding taxes as a possible determinant for investments in intermediate holding companies. Throughout the ensuing text, we label our indicators using square brackets (e.g. [Governance]).

The motivations for our indicators and the exact operationalization of each indicator can be found in Table A.1 and Section A.4 in the Online Appendix (www.routledge.com/9781032111193).

Data

To construct our indicators we use a combination of macro (country-level) and micro (firm-level) statistics. Macro statistics were collected from Eurostat, World Bank Open Data, the International Bureau of Fiscal Documentation, and UNCTADstat. Since we obtain the majority of our indicators from Eurostat, we generally lack data on Switzerland. Micro statistics were collected from the Orbis database. Orbis collects information on over 250 million public and private firms worldwide from official country registrars and other country collection agencies, and it is a frequently used source of data (Vitali et al., 2011; Johannesen et al., 2016; Garcia-Bernardo et al., 2017) that offers good coverage for EU's firms (Garcia-Bernardo and Takes, 2017). All indicators were calculated as the mean value for the period 2007–2017, or a subset of the period when data was not available for all years. Our selection of the 2007–2017 period reflects two considerations. The first is purely pragmatic; this is the only period for which all databases provide data. The second is that our activity indicators reflect stocks of FDI, rather than flows. This implies that each indicator reflects investments accumulated prior to the period. Because, as stated in the introduction, we decided to focus our analysis on non-financial corporations, we restricted the Orbis and Eurostat data to include only non-financial corporations. For a complete description of all the indicators, including sources, time data availability and descriptive statistics see Tables A.1–A.6 in the Online Appendix as well as the Supplementary Methods section. In order to ensure replicability and cumulative knowledge-building, all our indicators and *Python* code are available in the Online Appendix: www.routledge.com/9781032111193 under Creative Commons Attribution-ShareAlike 4.0 license.

Visualization of the results

Normalization

Our visualization strategy assigns a color to a numerical value, where blue corresponds to low values and red corresponds to high values. Using the same matching between colors and numerical values in all variables would be infeasible since the range of our variables varies by several orders of magnitude. While the average tax rate of multinationals is 0.18 (± 0.07), the average time to complete and submit taxes is 192.2 (± 99) days. In order to visualize the results effectively, we need to normalize all variables so that they lie in the same range. A common normalization strategy (StandardScaler) is to subtract the mean and divide by the standard deviation, which standardizes all variables to have mean equal to zero and standard deviation equal to one. However, this strategy is not robust to outliers – such as Malta with an FDI stock 16 times the size of its GDP. Instead, we use another normalization strategy (RobustScaler) where we subtract the median and divide by the interquartile range – the range between the 1st quartile (25th percentile) and the 3rd quartile (75th percentile) (Figure 11.4A). Figure 11.4B visualizes the data on FDI flows in 2017 (Figure A.1 in the Online Appendix) using both RobustScaler and StandardScaler. When using RobustScaler we are able to see both the outliers (Malta and Cyprus) and countries attracting high FDI stocks (Belgium or Netherlands) in red, while for the StandardScaler strategy only the outliers are visible.

Clustering

We use the activity indicators to identify countries that compete for a specific category of FDI. We make use of a clustering algorithm to guide our interpretation of the results. The clustering algorithm calculates the distance between two countries based on the differences between all activity indicators. For instance, in Figure 11.3B there are two variables (RobustScaler and StandardScaler). There is a

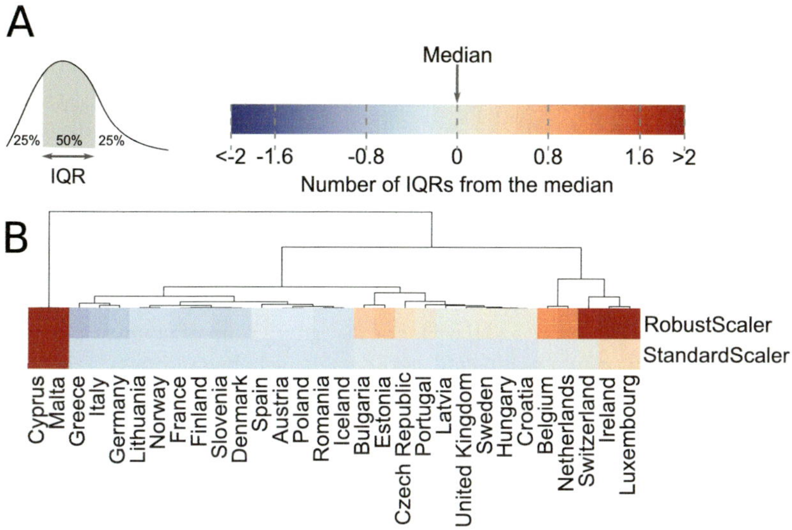

FIGURE 11.3 Visualization of our results

Source: Notes: (A) Example of the interquartile range (IQR) and the color scheme used throughout the analysis. (B) Example of the FDI stock by country using two normalization strategies. Note that the outliers (Malta and Cyprus) reduce the range of countries visible with the StandardScaler strategy.

Data: All FDI data was collected from the UNCTAD World Investment Report (2018).

small distance between two countries if they have similar values for both variables. The algorithm then constructs a tree, where countries appear in adjacent branches if the distance between them is small – e.g. Cyprus and Malta, or Luxembourg, Ireland, Switzerland, the Netherlands and Belgium.

To arrange countries into groups, many different clustering algorithms can be used. Each of these techniques uses its own distance formulas, and thus yields different results. In order to avoid cherry-picking a clustering technique that produces "meaningful" results, we apply the default algorithm and use the results only as a starting point, on the basis of which we then cluster the countries manually. The initial clustering is provided in Figure A.2 in the Online Appendix. A detailed explanation of the clustering algorithm and its possible variations is provided in the Supplementary Methods.

Results

Manufacturing affiliates

We first identified those countries that attract disproportionate amounts of TNCs' manufacturing affiliates. We found a prominent cluster of countries composed of Romania, Hungary, Poland, Slovakia, Czechia, Estonia, Malta and Bulgaria

(Figure 11.4A). All these countries engage primarily in low value-adding manufacturing activities in which they show high levels of wage-adjusted productivity. Moreover, this cluster of countries receives greenfield investment flows in the manufacturing sector of 2.0% (±0.8%) of their GDP, which contrasts with the 0.4% (±0.3%) received by all other countries[15] There is, however, a broad distinction within this cluster between those countries in which a large fraction of the labor force is employed in foreign owned companies in the manufacturing sector and those for which this fraction is much smaller (Figure 11.4B). In Malta, Romania, Estonia, Hungary, Slovakia, and Czechia the number is 6.9% (±1.8), whereas for Poland and Bulgaria it is 3.7% (±0.5%). For the latter group of countries, however, a number of factors might partly explain these relatively low numbers. For Poland, the country's large population size has a significant downward effect on the percentage of the labor force employed by foreign firms. The raw number of jobs created in that country, however, is 680,000, considerably higher than the numbers for countries of similar size, such as Spain and Italy (386,000 and 429,000 respectively). For Bulgaria, the size of greenfield investment suggests that a future increase in the number of jobs in foreign-owned manufacturing operations can be expected.

We next moved to the macro-institutional and tax arrangements associated with the countries previously identified (Figure 11.4C). As anticipated, since we assume cost reductions to be the primary motivation for the offshoring of manufacturing operations, all countries previously identified score low on all macro-institutional indicators when compared with the EU average. As Figure 11.4C shows, labor costs are especially low in Romania and Bulgaria. These countries' exceptionally low labor costs may be an important factor in explaining why since 2007, the year they joined the European Union, these countries have been the largest recipients of greenfield FDI in manufacturing activities. Regarding the tax indicators (which, in Figure 11.4C are separated from the macro-institutional indicators by a thin white line), we see that all the identified countries have corporate income tax rates that are significantly lower than those for most other European countries, with the notable exceptions of Ireland and Cyprus. They also all stand out both in terms of the number of tax incentives targeted specifically to investments in manufacturing activities and in terms of the low levels of withholding taxes that they levy on outbound dividend payments. We also observe that all countries that attract manufacturing affiliates, except Slovakia and Czechia, had signed large numbers of investment treaties, but not tax treaties, with Western Europe before they entered the European Union. This suggests that withholding tax considerations are secondary to the securing of property rights in TNCs' decisions where to locate their offshored manufacturing activities.

Shared service centers

We next identified countries that attract disproportionate numbers of TNCs' SSCs. Here we identified three clusters of countries that do so (Figure 11.5A). All countries in those three clusters (with the notable exceptions of Poland and Bulgaria, which we will discuss later), see a relatively large fraction of their labor

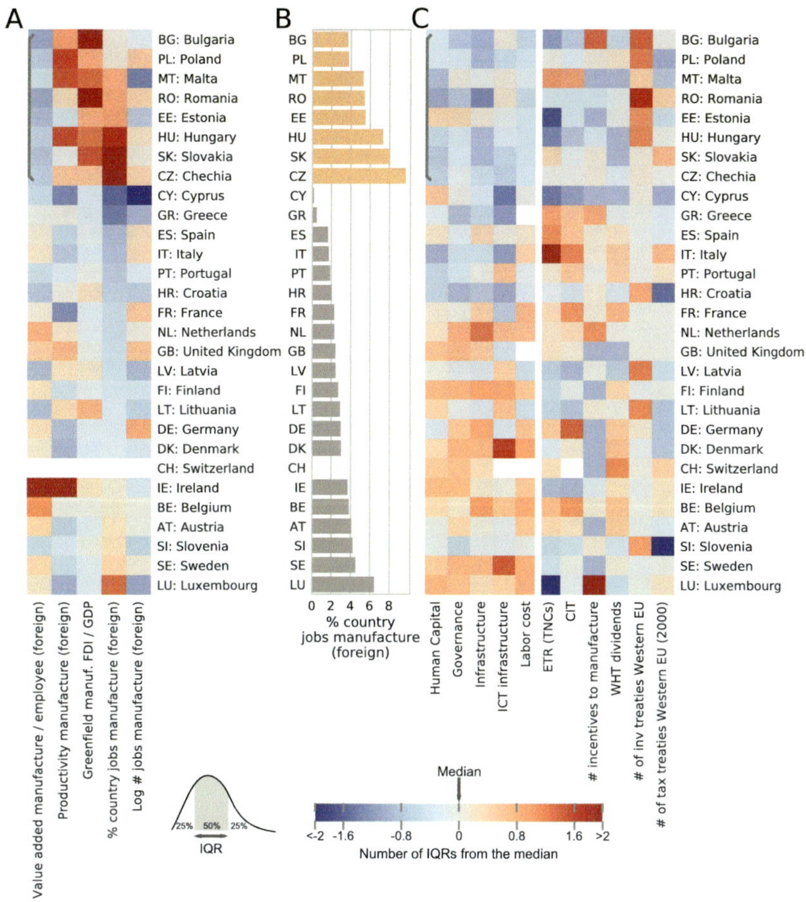

FIGURE 11.4 Manufacturing affiliates

Source: Notes: (A) Activity indicators, (B) benefits, and (C) macro-institutional features and tax incentives associated with attracting manufacturing affiliates. The identified clusters of countries are marked with a gray bracket (A, C) and different shades of orange (B). Countries are sorted according to their assigned cluster.

Data: Eurostat, World Bank Open Data, the International Bureau of Fiscal Documentation, and UNCTADstat (see Table A.1 in the Online Appendix).

force employed in foreign owned SSCs. The first cluster, consisting of the Netherlands, Ireland, United Kingdom and Luxembourg attracts high value-adding SSC activities, has high wage-adjusted productivity and receives large amounts of greenfield investments in SSC activities. The second cluster, composed of Finland, Austria, Belgium and Sweden, also attracts high value-adding SSC activities but shows lower wage-adjusted productivity and also somewhat lower levels of greenfield investment in SSCs. We interpret this difference as the second cluster being

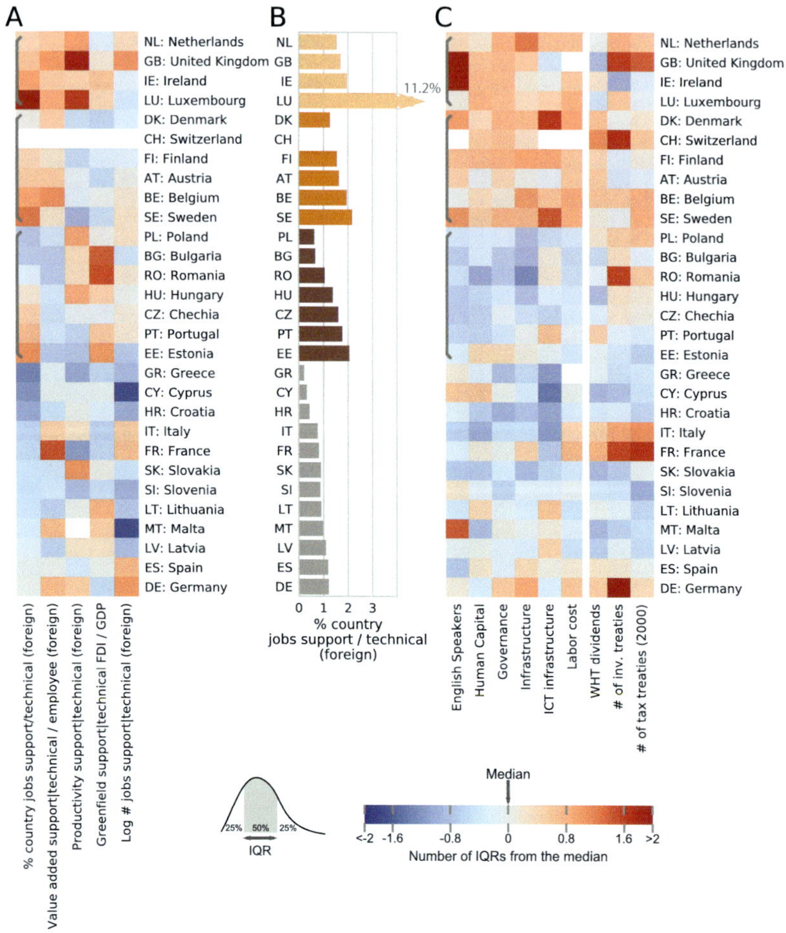

FIGURE 11.5 Shared service centers

Source: (A) Activity indicators, (B) benefits, and (C) macro-institutional features and tax incentives associated with attracting shared service centers. The three identified clusters of countries are marked with gray brackets (A, C) and different shades of orange (B). Countries are sorted according to their assigned cluster.

Data: Eurostat, World Bank Open Data, the International Bureau of Fiscal Documentation, and UNCTADstat (see Table A.1 in the Online Appendix).

somewhat less attractive as a location for TNCs' high value-adding SSC operations and therefore attracting fewer such operations. The third cluster, composed of Poland, Bulgaria, Romania, Hungary, Czechia, Portugal and Estonia, is characterized by low value-adding activities but high levels of adjusted productivity. In this third cluster, foreign owned SSCs employ 1.3% (±0.5%) of the labor force, compared to 4.1% (±4.7%) and 1.7% (±0.3) for the first and second clusters respectively

(Figure 11.5B). However, Bulgaria receives the second highest flows of greenfield FDI and we thus expect employment numbers to increase in the following years. In the case of Poland, the large size of their labor force causes a downward bias in the share of the labor force employed in foreign owned SSCs. In fact, the raw number of workers in foreign owned SSCs in Poland (372,000) is two to four times higher than the number for Romania (183,000), Portugal (107,000), Czechia (102,000) and Hungary (78,000).

Looking at the macro-institutional and tax policies associated with the countries in those three clusters (Figure 11.5B), we make the following observations. High value-adding SSC activities (first and second clusters) take place in countries that combine high levels of human capital, governance and infrastructure with an expensive, but highly productive labor force, while the contrary is true for low value-adding activities (third cluster). Similar to the manufacturing case, tax considerations appear to be secondary to macro-institutional determinants in TNCs' decisions where to locate their SSC activities. We assume this to be a result of the fact that most SSCs are run as cost centers and therefore do not make substantial amounts of taxable profits.

R&D facilities

Thirdly, we identified countries that attract disproportionate amounts of TNCs' R&D facilities. We found two clusters of such countries (Figure 11.6A). The first consists of a heterogeneous group of highly developed countries. All countries in this cluster have a large R&D sector, evidenced by the large share of their labor force employed in corporate R&D facilities and the large numbers of patent applications by both domestic and foreign firms. Moreover, these countries all display high levels of R&D expenditure financed from abroad, which indicates that a significant proportion of R&D operations in those countries is conducted by foreign owned firms. This is further confirmed by the fact that, corrected for the size of their economies, these countries show high numbers of patent applications by foreign owned companies. Three countries within this cluster (Belgium, Ireland and the United Kingdom) distinguish themselves from the others in that foreign owned firms account for 42–45% of all patent applications in those countries – compared with 16–31% in the rest of the cluster. The second cluster consists of Hungary, Bulgaria and Czechia. Compared to the first cluster, R&D takes a much less prominent role in these countries' economies, as evidenced by the much lower fraction of their labor forces employed in R&D operations as well as the low number of patent applications by domestic firms (Figure 11.6B). They do, however, receive high values of foreign R&D expenditure, suggesting that foreign firms see them as suitable locations for their offshored R&D activities nevertheless.

To get a deeper understanding of the differences between the two clusters, we then looked at the macro-institutional and tax features of these countries. For the first cluster of highly developed countries, fluency in English, ICT infrastructure, graduates in science and technology and quality of life highly correlate with

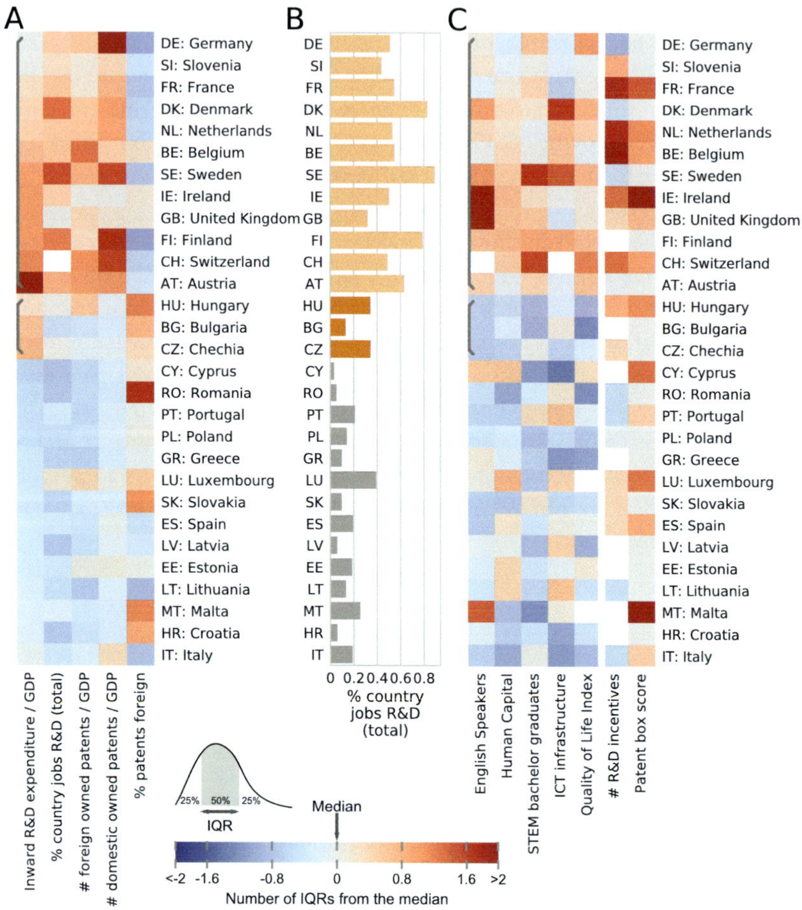

FIGURE 11.6 R&D facilities

Source: (A) Activity indicators, (B) benefits, and (C) macro-institutional features and tax incentives associated with attracting R&D facilities. The two identified clusters of countries are marked with gray brackets (A, C) and different shades of orange. Countries are sorted according to their assigned cluster.

Data: Eurostat, World Bank Open Data, the International Bureau of Fiscal Documentation, and UNCTADstat (see Table A.1 in the Online Appendix).

foreign owned R&D activities (Figure 11.6C). This was expected, since TNCs operate R&D facilities in those countries where the skills are located. The top three countries by foreign R&D investment (Austria, Switzerland and Finland) rank 4th, 2nd, and 3rd for quality of life and 6th, 3rd and 2nd for graduates in science and technology. For the second cluster of countries, low labor costs appear to dominate over other indicators. Most likely, the fact that these countries see comparably large amounts of their total R&D expenditures come from foreign owned companies and see a large percentage of their domestic patent applications come from foreign owned companies as well, is due to the prominent presence of foreign owned manufacturing activities in those countries. As explained in the section on Research and Development facilities above (pp 211–212), one motivation for TNCs to relocate some of their R&D activities is to have them in the proximity of their already offshored manufacturing operations. Finally we found that R&D incentives (with the notable exception of the patent box) are correlated with R&D activity. However, we also found a number of countries (i.e. Sweden, Austria or Denmark) that offer only a small number of R&D incentives but nevertheless attract high levels of foreign R&D investments. This indicates that tax considerations play only a secondary role to the availability of talent in those countries.

Top holdings

We identified two clusters of countries that attract disproportionate amounts of TNCs' top holding companies (Figure 11.7A). The first cluster is composed of the three smallest EU member states: Cyprus, Luxembourg and Malta. The second is composed of Ireland, Switzerland, the Netherlands and the United Kingdom.[16] Both clusters attract disproportionate amounts of top holding companies, but countries in the first cluster attract the highest numbers relative to the sizes of their GDPs. Countries in the first cluster also seem to enjoy more significant benefits from hosting top holdings, at least as far as tax revenues are concerned. They raise tax revenues of 5.4% (±0.3%) of their GDP from corporations, compared with 2.5% (±0.5%) in other European countries (Figure 11.7B). The main difference between the two clusters, however, concerns the profit rate of foreign firms (Figure 11.7A). The profit rate in the first cluster is 511,000 (±230,000) €/employee,[17] significantly higher than the profit rates in the second cluster (59,000 ±7,530 €/employee) and all other countries (69,000 ±38,000€/employee). Furthermore, the three clusters differ from each other in terms of their differential score on the difference in profit rates between multinational and domestic companies. For the first cluster this difference stands at 135,000 (±187,000) €/employee, for the second at 17,000 (±23,000) €/employee, and for the third at -59,000 (±36,000) €/employee. For all other countries this difference stands at -58,000 (±44,000) €/employee.

The difference between the countries in the first and second cluster becomes more pronounced when their scores on the macro-institutional and tax indicators are considered (Figure 11.7C). Most importantly, the effective tax rates (ETRs) for countries in the second cluster are significantly higher than those for countries in the first cluster. We find the median ETR for companies with revenues higher than one million dollars to be 3.9% in Luxembourg, 9.8% in Cyprus, 28.0% in Malta, and 20.6% (±6.0%) in all other European countries. In the Maltese case, however, the effective tax rate excludes an up to six-sevenths refund to shareholders on the tax paid. Including this refund in the calculation would bring the ETR down to 4–8%. Moreover, the low ETRs that multinationals pay in these countries do not necessarily apply to domestic companies. We found that the tax paid by TNCs in countries that belong to the first cluster is up to 11 percentage points lower than

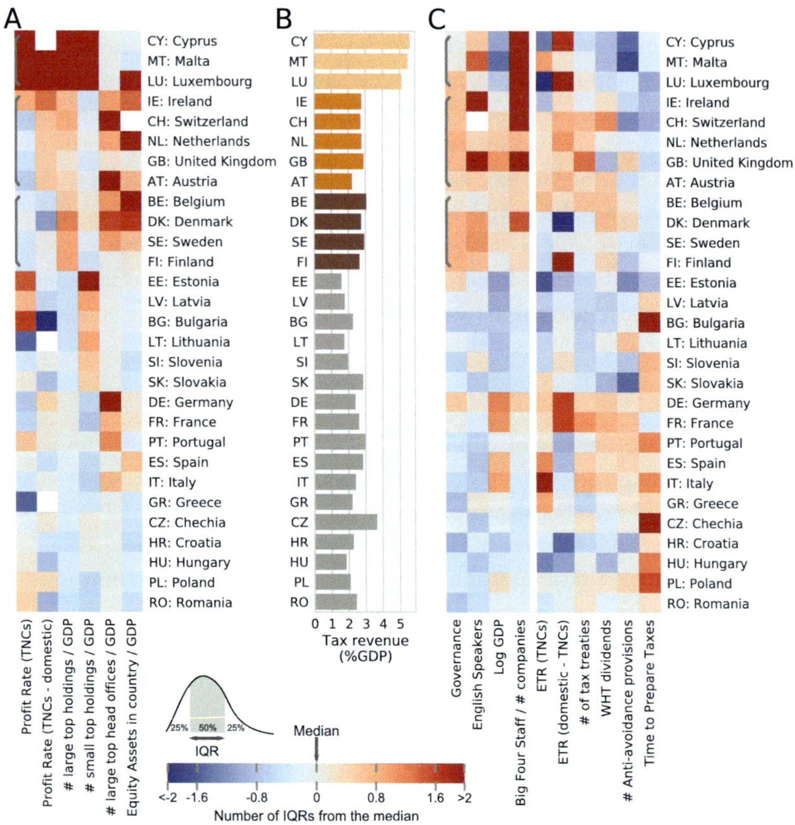

FIGURE 11.7 Top holdings

Source: (A) Activity indicators, (B) benefits, and (C) macro-institutional features and tax incentives associated with attracting top holdings. The three identified clusters of countries are marked with gray brackets (A, C) and different shades of orange. Countries are sorted according to their assigned cluster.

Data: Eurostat, World Bank Open Data, the International Bureau of Fiscal Documentation, and UNCTADstat (see Table A.1 in the Online Appendix).

the tax paid by their domestic counterparts. We interpret our finding that countries in the first cluster combine low effective tax rates with relatively high profit rates of multinationals, and above those of domestic companies, as an indication that TNCs locate their top holding in those countries primarily for reasons of tax planning. Countries in the second cluster, with lower profit rates of multinationals, larger economies, a higher score on the governance indicator, and higher effective tax rates for multinationals, seem to be able to attract a larger fraction of top holdings that are not exclusively motivated by tax planning considerations, meaning, for example, actual global or regional headquarters. Another difference between the three clusters concerns the absence of an extensive network of tax treaties in the first one. We interpret the apparent unwillingness of countries to sign tax treaties with countries in the first cluster as another indication that TNCs locate their top holdings in Cyprus, Malta, and Luxembourg mainly to reduce their tax burden. For countries in the second and third cluster, on the other hand, we interpret their ability to sign tax treaties with large numbers of countries as an indication that the top holdings located in those countries are perceived as more legitimate by potential treaty partners. Finally, our results further suggest that countries may increase their attractiveness as a location for TNCs' top holding companies by offering low withholding taxes on dividends and providing for a lenient and efficient tax legislation (low number of anti-avoidance provisions and short time needed to prepare taxes).[18]

Intermediate holdings

Lastly, we identified three clusters of countries that attract disproportionate amounts of intermediate holding companies, or conduits (Figure 11.8A). The first cluster is composed of Hungary, Malta and Cyprus. Countries in this cluster are all specialized in one type of intermediate holding company. Cyprus operates as a pure dividend conduit, as evidenced by its high value of conduit investment. Hungary and Malta attract disproportionally large payments for the use of intellectual property, reflecting their status as preferred jurisdictions for royalty conduits. The second cluster is composed of a prominent group of multi-purpose countries: Luxembourg, Netherlands, Switzerland, Ireland, Belgium and the United Kingdom. All countries in this group exhibit high values for all types of holding activities. For the case of the United Kingdom, its large GDP – 3.4 times higher than the second largest country in the cluster – downplays the importance of the country as a conduit jurisdiction. The third cluster we identified consists of four countries that attract moderate amounts of holding companies: Finland, Sweden, Austria and Denmark. Countries in this group are frequently used as dividend conduits, and occasionally as royalty and interest conduits.

We next analyzed the macro-institutional indicators correlated with the clusters (Figure 11.8C). We found that countries in the second and third clusters have good governance, a highly developed ICT and financial infrastructure, and a large presence of the Big Four. Contrary, countries in the first cluster exhibit comparatively lower levels of governance and infrastructure (at similar levels than Spain or France), which suggest that tax determinants may be the key to their success. Indeed, we found that all three countries have no withholding taxes, a low number of anti-avoidance provisions, and the most generous patent boxes in Europe. The patent box in Hungary (established in 2003) offers a tax rate of 5% on qualifying royalty income, the Maltese patent box (established in 2010) provides a full exemption for all qualifying royalty income, and the Cyprus patent box (established in 2013) offers an 80% exemption in gross profits (tax rate below 2.5%).

The second cluster of countries is also characterized by the presence of a generous patent box, and either the presence of the notional interest deduction or

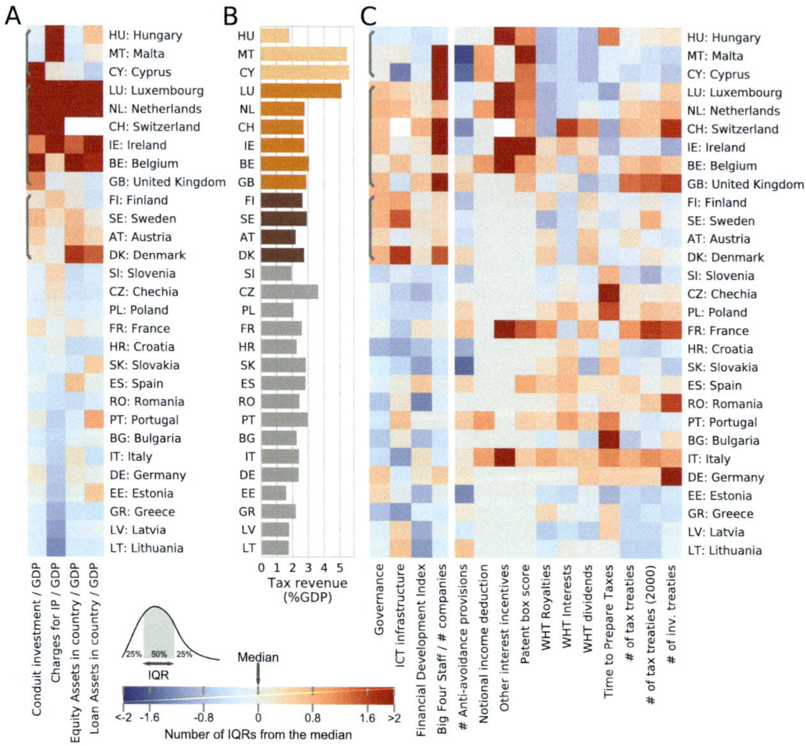

FIGURE 11.8 Intermediate holdings

Source: (A) Activity indicators, (B) benefits, and (C) macro-institutional features and tax incentives associated with attracting intermediate holdings. The two identified clusters of countries are marked with gray brackets (A, C) and different shades of orange. Countries are sorted according to their assigned cluster.

Data: Eurostat, World Bank Open Data, the International Bureau of Fiscal Documentation, and UNCTADstat (see Table A.1 in the Online Appendix).

another tax incentive targeting group interest payments. The high correlation between the patent box score and the success to attract royalty holdings indicates that royalty holdings (but not R&D activities) are attracted to places with generous patent boxes, which is consistent with the literature on patent location (Karkinsky and Riedel, 2012; Evers et al., 2015). Moreover, the correlation between the presence of measures granting special tax treatment for interest income and the loans held by non-financial corporations in a country indicates that interest holdings may be attracted to places with generous interest incentives. Moreover, countries in this group have either no or low withholding taxes (Luxembourg and the Netherlands), or an extensive network of tax treaties (Switzerland, Belgium, United Kingdom). The only exception is Ireland, with moderate withholding taxes and a relatively shallow network of tax treaties. However, withholding taxes in Ireland can be avoided by using a holding company in a third EU country that has an extensive network of tax treaties, since intra-group payments in the EU are exempt from withholding taxes. Countries in this second cluster also have a large network of investment treaties, ensuring investor rights and increasing the attractiveness of a country for dividend holdings. Finally, countries in the third cluster are characterized by the highest levels of governance, reduced regulation and incentives, evidenced by the lack of anti-avoidance provisions and interest incentives.

Conclusion

In this paper, we challenged the monolithic and productivist understanding of FDI that underpins most IPE analyses of the global race for FDI. Specifically, we argued that global patterns of FDI stocks and flows, as well as the strategies countries adopt to position their economies in those patterns, can only be fully understood by conceiving of FDI not just as the channeling of past savings accumulated in one jurisdiction towards new productive activities in another jurisdiction, but also as a legal contract that entitles the investor-firm to lay claim on the future value generated through those activities.

By putting the legal and future-oriented nature of FDI front and center, the claims perspective on FDI directs our attention towards the strategies investor-firms adopt to bolster the strength of their claims on future value generated through the activities of their operating subsidiaries *vis-à-vis* those of the tax authorities in which the TNC operates. These strategies revolve around the use of holding companies located in jurisdictions whose legal and tax frameworks confer on FDI-investors certain privileges that have the effect of reducing the scope of those tax authorities' claims on future value generated by the TNC's operating subsidiaries.

To address these conceptual and methodological concerns we first traced the *great fragmentation of the firm* to distinguish between five different categories of FDI – namely, foreign investments in manufacturing affiliates, shared service centers, R&D facilities, intermediate holding companies (conduits) and top holding companies (sinks). Using a combination of micro and macro statistics, we then showed for each category of FDI which EU member states are most successful in attracting it and identified some of the benefits they obtain from doing so. We also identified a range of macro-institutional and tax indicators present in countries that attract these different categories of FDI.

The mapping exercise presented in this paper showed that a small group of EU member states (Luxembourg, the Netherlands, Switzerland, Ireland, Belgium, the United Kingdom, Malta and Cyprus) has developed the institutional infrastructure on which TNCs rely for their tax planning strategies. These countries thus appear to be in the global race for FDI not just to attract investments in productive activities, but at least partially also to attract TNCs' holding companies, which are established primarily for the purpose of undermining other countries' capacity to enforce their tax claims on the value generated through TNCs' productive activities in those countries.

Notes

* The order of the authors has been randomized. Both authors contributed equally to this work.
1 Typically, the criterion of 'a sufficient degree of direct control' is operationalized as a holding of 10% of the voting shares in the subsidiary (OECD, 2009).
2 Amongst others, these include concrete short-term benefits, such as increased tax revenues, growing employment, and GDP growth, as well as more intangible long-term ones, such as knowledge spillover effects, productivity gains, and a reduction of current account deficits.
3 It has been estimated that such 'Phantom FDI' accounts for almost 40% of total global FDI (Damgaard et al., 2019). Moreover, a large share of global FDI reflects merely takeover of already existing productive activities (M&A), and thus merely represents a transfer of control over activities as well as claims on the future value produced by these activities (trading claims).
4 In this chapter we focus on the trading of FDI-related claims. However, in the context of this edited volume it might be relevant to note that these claims can be traded as well. Indeed, a significant share of global FDI flows reflects corporate takeovers, and thus a transfer of already existing claims on future value created by productive activities.
5 Data on Special Financial Institutions from De Nederlandsche Bank.
6 Throughout this article we use the terms "transnational corporation" (TNC), "multinational" and "corporate group" interchangeably.
7 The function may even be so specific that it pertains only to a particular transaction and a limited period of time. If such subsidiaries are not dissolved after their specific purpose has dissipated, this may, over time, result in their becoming obsolete; an artefact of the past.
8 See also: https://www2.deloitte.com/content/dam/Deloitte/dk/Documents/finance/SSC-Handbook-%20Hit-the-Road.pdf
9 See also www.pwc.de/de/finanzdienstleistungen/assets/pwc_studie_financial_shared_service_centers.pdf
10 For example, Starbucks' centralized procurement SSC, located in the Netherlands, played an important role in the tax planning strategy the company had adopted in order to minimize the tax burden on its European operations (Kleinbard, 2013).
11 These are Belgium, Cyprus, France, Hungary, Ireland, Italy, Liechtenstein, Luxembourg, Malta, the Netherlands, Portugal, Spain, the canton of Nidwalden in Switzerland, and the UK (Chen et al., 2019).
12 Not all tax systems determine an entity's tax residency by its place of incorporation. Some jurisdictions determine tax residency by the place of management, or a combination of both place of incorporation and place of management.
13 Oftentimes this is also the jurisdiction in which most of the firm's shareholders are located.
14 Our sample corresponds to all countries covered by the Interest and Royalty Directive (2003/49/EC) and the Parent-Subsidiary Directive (2003/123/EC) – i.e., all countries from the European Union and Switzerland.
15 Three countries (Lithuania, Latvia and Croatia) receive relatively large greenfield FDI flows (0.9% ±0.4%). However, given their small size and the fact that only a small fraction of their labor force is employed in foreign owned companies in the manufacturing sector, we do not consider them as countries that attract disproportionate numbers of manufacturing affiliates.
16 Arguably, with a strong presence of the Big Four, a high number of GUOs and high profit rates, Denmark would also be a candidate for this group. However, we decided

to exclude it for two reasons. First, the comparatively low value of equity assets held by companies in that country suggests that Denmark primarily harbors top holdings of rather small and inconsequential TNCs. Second, the low profit rates when compared with domestic companies suggest that the relatively high number of GUOs in Denmark has little to do with TNCs' tax planning strategies.

17 Assuming an employee cost of $100,000 US dollars across countries.

18 Estonia is worthy of special mention. It appears to have all the right conditions to be identified as a top holding jurisdiction – a small economy, lenient and efficient tax legislation, minimal taxation. It also harbors a large number of GUOs. However, the low scores of the country on all the other activity indicators suggest that the country may be attracting large amounts of top holdings of small and inconsequential TNCs (possibly related to personal finance and wealth management) but does not play a significant role as a preferred jurisdiction for top holdings of bigger TNCs.

References

Baaij MG, et al. (2015) Why do multinational corporations relocate core parts of their corporate headquarters abroad? *Long Range Planning* 48(1): 46–58.

Birkinshaw J, et al. (2006) Why do some multinational corporations relocate their headquarters overseas? *Strategic Management Journal* 27(7): 681–700.

Blinder AS (2006) Offshoring: The next industrial revolution? *Foreign Affairs* 85(2): 113–128.

Bondarouk T (2014) *Shared Services as a New Organizational Form*. Bingley: Emerald Group Publishing.

Braun B and Koddenbrock K (2022) The three phases of financial power: Leverage, infrastructure, and enforcement. In: Braun B and Koddenbrock K (eds) *Capital Claims: Power and Global Finance*. London: Routledge, pp. 1–30.

Breathnach P (2000) Globalisation, information technology and the emergence of niche transnational cities: The growth of the call centre sector in Dublin. *Geoforum; Journal of Physical, Human, and Regional Geosciences* 31(4): 477–485.

Bryan D, Rafferty M and Wigan D (2017) Capital unchained: Finance, intangible assets and the double life of capital in the offshore world. *Review of International Political Economy* 24(1): 56–86.

Cantwell J and Mudambi R (2000) The location of MNE R&D activity: The role of investment incentives. *MIR: Management International Review* 40(1): 127–148.

Cantwell J and Piscitello L (2002) The location of technological activities of MNCs in European regions: The role of spillovers and local competencies. *Journal of International Management* 8(1): 69–96.

Carlsson B (2006) Internationalization of innovation systems: A survey of the literature. *Research Policy* 35(1): 56–67.

Cerny PG (1990). *The Changing Architecture of Politics: Structure, Agency and the Future of the State*. SAGE.

Chen S, De Simone L, Hanlon M and Lester R (2019) The effect of innovation box regimes on income shifting and real activity. SSRN Scholarly Paper.

Coe NM, Dicken P and Hess M (2008) Global production networks: realizing the potential. *Journal of Economic Geography* 8(3): 271–295.

Dachs B, Stehrer R and Zahradnik G (2014) *The Internationalisation of Business R&D*. Cheltenham: Edward Elgar Publishing.

Damgaard J, Elkjaer T and Johannesen N (2019) *What Is Real and What Is Not in the Global FDI Network?* International Monetary Fund.

Desai MA (2009) The decentering of the global firm. *World Economy* 32(9): 1271–1290.

Dischinger M, Knoll B and Riedel N (2014) The role of headquarters in multinational profit shifting strategies. *International Tax and Public Finance* 21(2): 248–271.

Doh JP, Bunyaratavej K and Hahn ED (2009) Separable but not equal: The location determinants of discrete services offshoring activities. *Journal of International Business Studies* 40(6): 926–943.

Eicke R (2009) *Tax Planning with Holding Companies – Repatriation of US Profits from Europe: Concepts, Strategies, Structures*. Alphen aan den Rijn: Kluwer Law International.

Elkins Z, Guzman AT and Simmons BA (2006) Competing for capital: The diffusion of bilateral investment treaties, 1960–2000. *International Organization* 60(4): 811–846.

Ellram LM, Tate WL and Petersen KJ (2013) Offshoring and reshoring: An update on the manufacturing location decision. *Journal of Supply Chain.*

Evers L, Miller H and Spengel C (2015) Intellectual property box regimes: Effective tax rates and tax policy considerations. *International Tax and Public Finance* 22(3): 502–530.

Farole T (2011) *Special Economic Zones in Africa: Comparing Performance and Learning from Global Experience*. The World Bank (Directions in Development – General).

Florida R (1997) The globalization of R&D: Results of a survey of foreign-affiliated R&D laboratories in the USA. *Research Policy* 26(1): 85–103.

Fors G and Zejan M (2012) Overseas R&D by multinationals in foreign centers of excellence. IUI Working Paper. Available at: www.econstor.eu/handle/10419/94800

Garcia-Bernardo J and Takes FW (2017) The effects of data quality on the analysis of corporate board interlock networks. *Information Systems*. doi:10.1016/j.is.2017.10.005.

Garcia-Bernardo J, et al. (2017) Uncovering offshore financial centers: Conduits and sinks in the global corporate ownership network. *Scientific Reports* 7(1): 6246.

Gereffi G, Humphrey J and Sturgeon T (2005) The governance of global value chains. *Review of International Political Economy*.

Hines JR (1994) No place like home: Tax incentives and the location of R&D by American multinationals. *Tax Policy and the Economy* 8: 65–104.

Jensen NM (2008). *Nation-states and the Multinational Corporation: A Political Economy of Foreign Direct Investment*. Princeton, NJ: Princeton University Press.

Johannesen N, Tørsløv T and Wier L (2016) Are less developed countries more exposed to multinational tax avoidance? Method and evidence from micro-data. WIDER Working Paper.

Karkinsky T and Riedel N (2012) Corporate taxation and the choice of patent location within multinational firms. *Journal of International Economics* 88(1): 176–185.

Kleinbard ED (2013) Through a latte, darkly: Starbucks's stateless income planning. USC CLEO Research Paper No. C13–9; USC Law Legal Studies Paper No. 13–10). Tax Notes, pp. 1515–1535. Available at: https://ssrn.com/abstract=2264384

Lewin AY and Peeters C (2006) Offshoring work: Business hype or the onset of fundamental transformation? *Long Range Planning* 39(3): 221–239.

Lewin AY and Volberda HW (2011) Co-evolution of global sourcing: The need to understand the underlying mechanisms of firm-decisions to offshore. *International Business Review* 20(3): 241–251.

Maine JA and Nguyen X-T (2017) *The Intellectual Property Holding Company: Tax Use and Abuse from Victoria's Secret to Apple*. Cambridge: Cambridge University Press.

Malecki EJ (1987) The R&D location decision of the firm and "creative" regions – a survey. *Technovation* 6(3): 205–222.

McIvor R (2010) *Global Services Outsourcing*. Cambridge: Cambridge University Press.

OECD (2009) Foreign direct investment glossary. OECD benchmark definition of foreign direct investment 2008, pp. 227–243. doi: 10.1787/9789264045743-24-en.

Patel P and Pavitt K (1991) Large firms in the production of the world's technology: An important case of "non-globalisation". *Journal of International Business Studies* 22(1): 1–21.

Porter ME (1990) The competitive advantage of nations Harvard business review. *Harvard Business Review* 91.

Seabrooke L and Wigan D (2017) The governance of global wealth chains. *Review of International Political Economy* 24(1): 1–29.

Slangen AHL, Baaij M and Valboni R (2017) Disaggregating the corporate headquarters: Investor reactions to inversion announcements by US firms. *Journal of Management Studies* 54(8): 1241–1270.

Stopford JM, Strange S and Henley JS (1991) *Rival States, Rival Firms: Competition for World Market Shares*. Cambridge: Cambridge University Press.

Thomas K (2010) *Investment Incentives and the Global Competition for Capital*. Springer.

Vitali S, Glattfelder JB and Battiston S (2011) The network of global corporate control. *PLoS One* 6(10): e25995.

Voget J (2011) Relocation of headquarters and international taxation. *Journal of Public Economics* 95(9): 1067–1081.

Weichenrieder AJ, Mintz J and Others (2008) *What Determines the Use of Holding Companies and Ownership Chains*. Centre for Business Taxation Working Paper WP08/03. Oxford: Oxford University.

Weyzig F (2013) Tax treaty shopping: Structural determinants of Foreign Direct Investment routed through the Netherlands. *International Tax and Public Finance*.

Wilson MI (1995) The office farther back: Business services, productivity, and the offshore back office. In: Harker PT (ed.) *The Service Productivity and Quality Challenge*. Dordrecht: Springer, pp. 203–224.

Wójcik D (2013) Where governance fails: Advanced business services and the offshore world. *Progress in Human Geography* 37(3): 330–347.

12

CLAIMING THE WEALTH OF A NATION

Creditor-enforced privatizations in Greece

Benjamin Lemoine and Marie Piganiol

Introduction

This chapter examines the struggle over privatization and control of public resources in the aftermath of Greece's sovereign debt crisis, which was triggered by the financial crisis of 2009. Between 2010 and 2015, the International Monetary Fund (IMF), the Eurogroup and the European Central Bank (ECB) – then known as the "Troika" – granted Greece three bailout loans that would supposedly contain the crisis within the Eurozone. In return, they required the country to implement drastic adjustment programs starting with cuts in social spending, tax increases and large-scale privatizations. Public infrastructures, state-owned enterprises (SoEs), shipyards, public land, real estate, and islands as well as archeological heritage would need to be rapidly disposed of in order to generate 50 billion euros, an amount considered high enough to repay Greece's creditors.[1] EU institutions also required the creation of the Hellenic Republic Asset Development Fund (HRADF, more commonly known as TAIPED[2]), a technocratic organization that would conduct privatizations on behalf of international creditors and at a safe distance from the Greek government and domestic politics.

In 2015, Alexis Tsipras, leader of the radical left political party Syriza, came to power thanks to nationwide resentment towards the austerity measures international creditors had forced the country to adopt. But Tsipras' efforts to honor Syriza's commitments[3] would rapidly hit the wall of the debt repayment. EU creditors, foreign states, and private investors struggled to enforce their claims on Greek society, threatening the government to cut money supply – suspending, for instance, the provision of central bank money to the Greek domestic banking system – through the emergency liquidity assistance (ELA) mechanism. Popular members of Syriza left the government after Tspiras' decision, during 2015 summer, to negotiate adjustment programs with creditors, thereby discrediting the

DOI: 10.4324/9781003218487-15

referendum through which Greeks had massively voted against the Troika's austerity plan. A new government, called Syriza II, was formed a few weeks later with "pragmatic" leaders who aimed at regaining financial autonomy within such a highly constrained environment.

How did Syriza II reclaim sovereignty *vis-à-vis* the Troika's austerity program? What does financial autonomy mean in a country dependent on bailout loans? The Greek case offers a quasi-experimental setting to study the confrontation between various financial claims over public resources and their different modes of generation and uses. This is particularly true of the assets, companies and land privatizations, a battle Syriza II claims to have won – at least partially – amid many defeats. Victory initially seemed hard to achieve in this battlefield. Indeed, privatizations were part of the extremely politically intrusive conditionalities (Queralt, 2022) official creditors imposed on Greece: transformation and attempt at direct control of a large part of its public bureaucracy apparatus, i.e. statistical (Lemoine, 2018; Prévost, 2021), taxation[4] and privatization offices. Among the core EU countries, Germany, France and the Netherlands expressed their political will over Greece's economy, a "peripheral" country of the eurozone. To punish fiscal non-compliance and gimmickry regarding the Maastricht criteria,[5] but also Syriza's attempts to rebel against austerity, they made Greece pay. For European creditors, privatizations therefore embodied immediate financial interests but also political domination, a reaffirmation of neoliberal discipline, and a severe reminder of economic rules in the Eurozone. European creditors' institutions – an alliance of Member States and private finance – therefore made it a point of honor for Greece to carry out the privatizations asked for: a strict agenda and executive schemes of privatization were imposed as an essential condition for successive bailouts. The aim was short-term extraction: selling public assets quickly to repay Greece's creditors. Ultimately, Greece found its policy space severely constrained by EU official creditors, who acted as intermediaries and enforcers for their domestic private finance champions: German and French commercial banks, industries and investment companies. Historical literature has deciphered these consequences of the debtor-creditor international relationship through the idea of "a default-colonization nexus" that involved "the hypothecation of land in expectation of debt interruption" (Flandreau, 2016: 93–101; Cain and Hopkins, 2016).

However, the Syriza Greek government sought to maintain some control over privatization process and to avoid selling public assets at undervalued prices. This involved the progressive re-construction of a shareholding state, by prioritizing economic policy goals around privatization and by restructuring SoEs to achieve both financial profitability and social objectives.

To analyze Syriza's response to international creditors' claims, we use three sets of data: 25 interviews with European and Greek public officials, investors, and bankers all conducted in Greece in 2019, during the last year of Tsipras' term; a press review (from 2008 to 2020); and a quantitative database on privatizations since the 1990s, which we built based on TAIPED's archives.

We argue that privatizations that followed the financial crisis in Greece neither should be analyzed as an undisputed and direct foreign constraint and international pressure, nor as a sovereignty surrender or "dismissal" (Farah and Maucourant, 2022). Privatizations also represented an opportunity for some domestic technocrats whose interests where aligned with foreign creditors. This argument echoes the literature on post-socialist transitions which showed the role of local elites to explain both the success and the specificities of privatizations despite global pressure to de-collectivize (Bockman and Eyal, 2002; King and Szelényi, 2010; Stark and Bruszt, 1998). But, above all, the privatization operating mode raised a controversy relative to the best ways to organize the future Greek economy. On the one hand, EU supranational creditors aimed to enforce financial claims by intervening in the design of debtors' own administration, in the shadow of democratic bodies and away from social claims: TAIPED's independent agency was an organizational guarantee of foreign creditors' claims on present and future Greek public fiscal revenues. On the other hand, the Syriza II government reshaped the privatization process to serve national interests and reclaim financial sovereignty within a highly constrained environment. Tsipras' government favored bureaucratic solutions to defend Greek-driven organizations and public finance channels against creditors' attempts to interfere in domestic policies.

This paper highlights the entanglement of financial and political claim enforcement (Braun and Koddenbrock, 2022, this volume) by focusing on the conflicts fueled by the establishment of domestic bureaucracies tailor-made for the interests of European creditors. The shareholder state (Wang, 2015) approach to privatization, achieved arduously, makes it possible to reconcile financial interests with a certain vision, albeit financialized, of the conduct of social policies. The first part analyzes EU creditors' plans to enforce large-scale privatizations through independent organizations. European technocracy (the ECB and the European Commission, through the European Financial Stability Facility) created and temporarily maintained an institutional mode for coding capital (Pistor, this volume): foreign actors enforced financial claims, including by imposing major political conditionalities such as setting the public bureaucracy that suited their interests as financial creditors. The second part studies how the Greek government regained control over the privatization process and avoided selling assets at undervalued prices by restructuring SoEs according to EU standards.

The European creditors' claims: enforcing large-scale privatizations through independent organizations

The post-crisis period has widely been described in the media as the entry of Greece into the neoliberal era in which the state was forced to conduct unprecedented programs of large-scale privatizations. This is only partly true. Indeed, Greek governments started to privatize decades before the crisis, and privatizations were even more numerous in the mid-2000s, conducted by PASOK, the Greek social-democratic party (Souliotis, 2018; Souliotis and Kandylis, 2013; Souliotis et al., 2014; Souliotis and Afouxenidis, 2018). However, the crisis sparked a major turning point: since then, privatizations would no longer be conducted by Greek governments but would become a lever of reform used by international organizations to restructure the Greek economy. Indeed, the crisis transformed the power relations between the Greek state and EU institutions. While until 2011 governments abided quite voluntarily by EU standards and economic models, the crisis strengthened the power of EU and international creditors over the Greek state. From 2010 to 2015, negotiations between the Troika and successive Greek governments led to three bailout packages that required adjustment programs in return for financial assistance. One of the main conditions was the creation of TAIPED. This privatization agency was designed to be strictly independent from Greek public administration and government units, which the Troika considered to be corrupted, clientelist and consequently reluctant to pursue an efficient privatization program. The fund was designed in such a way that no political interference was possible. The account that received revenues from privatizations was an "escrow" account, isolated from the rest of the state budget and firmly earmarked for debt repayment.

TAIPED's governance structure would instead reflect the interests of international creditors, especially those of the International Monetary Fund, the European Central Bank and of the European Commission. TAIPED would gain ownership of state-owned goods and operate almost like a "bad bank". It would dispose of state-owned goods in order to raise, before 2015, the 50 billion euros required by the Troika to complete the bailout program. This was announced during a press conference in Athens on February 11, 2011. The idea came from Antonio Borges, a Portuguese economist-banker and director of the European Department of the IMF.[6] According to Borges, the Troika should not "overlook some innovative ideas" that could offer "enormous untapped potential". These innovative ideas included "the privatization of state assets and property" because "by some estimates, the value of the assets under Athens ownership was in the hundreds of billions of euros, enough to pay off much, if not all, of the government's debt" (Blustein, 2016). The figure of 50 billion euros marked a major leap forward in the pressure put on Greece with regard to conditionalities. In comparison, only 5 billion euros had been targeted in May 2010 during the first bailout program.

To achieve its mission, TAIPED recruited professionals from the private sector, particularly investment bankers, business consultants and corporate lawyers. Konstantinos Mitropoulos was appointed CEO of TAIPED; his career reflected the politics that the Troika planned to develop in Greece at the time. A Greek national, Mitropoulos graduated from the London School of Economics at the end of the 1970s. He spent his entire professional career in the private sector where he specialized as a consultant and then as a banker in privatizations. He began his career in the United Kingdom where he contributed to the privatizations led by Margaret Thatcher in the 1980s. His experience in the UK led him to work on privatizations in former socialist countries and beyond in the 1990s. As a banker, he opened SoEs to foreign investments in Bulgaria, Russia, Romania, Serbia, Turkey and Greece.

His transnational and banking experience differed from the state-centered and political background that characterized the senior civil servants and representatives who carried out privatizations in Greece before the crisis. TAIPED professonials were recruited to value state-owned assets just as any other asset manager would do in the private sector. Their wages and bonuses would depend on their capacity to privatize. Finally, each privatization would associate international and Greek bankers who would "understand" the domestic context and thus make state-owned assets as attractive as possible to financial investors.

TAIPED initiated two major changes in privatizations. The first was a diversification of saleable public goods. Between 2011 and 2019, TAIPED disposed of assets from all the economic sectors that had been affected by privatizations in the past: it sold shares and companies in banking, manufactures (a cigarette company), entertainment (lottery, betting licenses and radio spectrum bands), telecommunication, infrastructures, and urban and public services (the Greek railway company, regional and international airports, gas and electricity and the Port of Thessaloniki).[7] Taking advantage of the deregulation of urban and environmental planning allowed for the Olympic Games (Souliotis et al., 2014), TAIPED also started to sell state-owned land and real estate that had previously remained out of the scope of privatization. During the period, the privatization fund sold resorts and building plots in tourist areas, embassies abroad, the ministries' buildings in Athens as well as the entire neighborhood of Hellenikon located in the south of the city (Ibid.). The second consequence was a diversification of privatization channels. Sales outside the Athens stock exchange and public offers were in previous periods the main ways of privatizing state-owned goods – concession had only been used in the transaction of the Port of Piraeus. They were respectively used to privatize companies and manufacturing on the one hand, and infrastructure companies on the other hand. In addition to direct sales, public offers and concessions, TAIPED developed e-auction and licensed competitive processes. These two forms of transactions are common in the private sector. They are used to attract a wider scope of buyers and maximize the amount of money that can be made from state-owned assets.

The clarity of TAIPED's mission did not prevent disputes from occurring, including within its own ranks. After a few years, TAIPED was increasingly criticized by creditors, Greek officials and SoE managers. Creditors were quick to label TAIPED a failure in its capacity to secure bailout loans: in 2014, three years after the program began, only 530 million euros had been raised, a far cry from the 50 billion expected (Weeks, 2011). The program's relevance also caused divisions among creditors. In 2015, the International Monetary Fund admitted that the objectives of privatizations and debt-reimbursement set by the EU was detrimental to the Greek economy, thereby denouncing Germany's inflexible position on Greece's financial responsibilities (IMF, 2015). Until 2015, as the most valuable Greek assets were being sold off to foreign (and Greek) private investors and revenues channeled to the reimbursement of the national debt, Greek officials from Syriza condemned the Troika's interference in the Greek economy. Some of TAIPED's managers also started to doubt the legitimacy of their mission. Though fiercely liberal and a vehement believer in the economic virtues of privatization, a senior figure of TAIPED criticized during our interview[8] the earmarking of privatizations revenues and the specific channel as "a dedicated account for debt repayment in which all proceeds go". He believed that privatizations cannot be beneficial to the economy or the state if they are conducted with fiscal and short-term objectives. The design of privatization policies by the Troika broke with the structural and long-term agenda of classical promoters of privatization in Greece. "Privatization and public debt don't mingle well", he summarized. The assets had to be developed first, and were, according to him, "totally incapable of being used and monetized to repay debt". European priorities and conditionalities on privatization could be epitomized as "shifting from structural changes into financial desperation": "rather than improving the structure of the economy and getting it more efficient, it was 'How can you get some money into the coffers tomorrow morning?' [in order to repay the debt], which was very, very difficult".

The design of TAIPED revealed both the financial and the short-term priorities of the Troika. Selling state-owned property was intended to pay off the public debt and reassure creditors and capital markets. Therefore, the purpose of privatizations in Greece differed both from the privatizations that occurred in Western Europe since the 1980s and from the privatizations that took place during the market transition of post-socialist countries. In the Greek case, privatization was not solely justified on the grounds that the market and the private sector are more efficient than public monopoly – which is the justification for privatization in most Western Europe countries. It also differed from post-socialist privatization which fits in a broader transformation of property rights in the economy. TAIPED was criticized for its exclusive purpose, i.e. to generate income with which to repay the debt to official creditors.

The Greek alternative: following creditor standards while limiting foreign interference

These budgetary and short-term visions of privatization were far from being consensual, even among TAIPED officials. The distance between politics and the privatization projects became controversial with the coming to power of Syriza I, which campaigned in strong opposition to privatizations, especially those dictated by the Troika and official creditors. A member of the Greek Department of Economy and Development – governed by the minister Stergios Pitsiorlas, publicly known for his success in increasing foreign direct investment in Greece and his regular claims that Greece needs a "change in culture" in order to become "friendly to investors" (Hope, 2016) – explained that "the first major political difficulty was the fact that SYRIZA, as an opposition party, was against privatization".[9]

Initially Syriza wanted to go back and question the very principle of privatization, to freeze the projects in progress, to stop cooperating with the Troika and the EU institutions, and even to close TAIPED. Nadia Valavani, Greek Deputy

Minister of Finance in the Syriza I government (so-named after the government thus formed before the decisive referendum of the summer of 2015) explained that Alexis Tsipras was, at the time, in favor of what retrospectively appeared to be a buried alternative project of earmarking the revenues these state assets could generate, i.e funding social security and creating a public investment entity.

Such political bubbling during the early months of Syriza (before the turning point of the referendum) and the third EU memorandum, sparked financial panic in banking and financial circles. A senior French official who participated in the negotiations between the Troika and Greeks confirmed that the Syriza government was not "ex nihilo in favor of privatization. Simply, they are forced to find a way with Brussels, and it is a way between difficult things". At the end of 2015, a "superfund" aimed at supervising TAIPED, and accelerating its operations, was mentioned by the EU authorities in the third memorandum. But the specific design of this superfund – the way in which it would be governed (by the EU authorities exclusively or by giving way to Greek political power) and the precise definition of its objectives and missions – gave rise to tough negotiations. The EU's script for designing this fund, particularly on the German side, consisted in building a second independent agency, at arm's length from the Greek government, and dedicating 100% of its revenues to debt reimbursement (as TAIPED was designed to do). To perform this remote control of the Greek economy, the project considered locating the agency's offices in Luxembourg. The Syriza II government would stand up against this proposal.

The political credit of prime minister Alexis Tsipras and his administration was mobilized in order to obtain an acceptable version of this fund which, on the contrary, would be able to function as a sovereign and plural mechanism: the destination of its income would not be fixed by European creditors or solely focused on the short-term objective of debt repayment. The French socialist government of the time was helpful in this struggle, offering the expertise of the French Treasury – and in particular the *Agence des participations de l'État* (French State Investment Agency), the symbol of the French Shareholding State that manages public (or partially public) companies.[10] Above all, Greek senior officials would take the opportunity to create this superfund in order to criticize the very existence of TAIPED, as a vehicle deprived of a Greek specificity, whether politically or institutionally, and exclusively committed to financial purposes. Syriza leaders criticized privatizations carried out under the aegis of TAIPED, because they consisted in selling and renouncing the most economically profitable public assets, companies and "public goods" – such as the Port of Piraeus, Athens International Airport and some of the energy companies:

> There were a lot of assets, especially SoEs, and especially the stronger ones that were decided to be privatized either as part of previous programs, or as part of the current program, in the first stage. For me this was always the most difficult thing to swallow . . . why choose the path of giving the best assets to the private sector? And not creating bigger profits, because these are

> the assets that create bigger profits for both parties, even for debt repayment in the longer run. And you decide to have a one-off revenue even before you have a comprehensive debt deal. . . . I don't want to use expressions that might be a little strong, it's just how I felt. . . . So this was and still is my biggest regret about this whole thing. – *It was a fight you felt you lost against whom?* – Lost against basically Germany, and the European Stability Mechanism definitely . . . against all the institutions, I would say.[11]

For instance, an official from the Ministry of Finance responsible for economic policy for Syriza II, considered the hasty and and irreversible disposal of these strategic assets as "hard to swallow", since the decision had been made when pricing conditions were the least favorable (and therefore least "fair") for the government: at the height of the debt crisis.[12] Syriza opposition to TAIPED precisely consisted in challenging the sell of these Greece's economy strategic assets, which could have been used differently in the long run. This position was illustrative of the Syriza opposition to TAIPED, which was both technical and ideological. Not only were the most vital assets for Greece's economic sovereignty – and the ones capable of generating long-term revenues – not sold at fair value, but they were actually sold out. These disposals thus amplified the Greek economy's dependence on foreign investment without optimizing the value and return potential of these assets in both the short and long term.

The Greek authorities of Syriza II claim to have fought intensively to impose an economic (and not exclusively financial) agenda "for both sides" (EU and Greek) by generating long-term revenues for debt repayment and for Greek economic sustainability. The superfund, the Hellenic Corporation of Assets and Participations (HCAP), was thus created in 2016. For Greek civil servants, HCAP made possible a re-encoding in political and economic terms of the privatization operations that had previously been carried out. For the Greek administration involved in these negotiations, the superfund was an opportunity to build a system that kept at bay the sole financial objective of debt repayment. At the end of these negotiations, the Greek authorities ensured that some SoEs remained within HCAP, publicly subsidized and therefore fall outside of the TAIPED. They also ensured that this new institution was Greek-managed on a daily basis, in conjunction with the minister of finance, who was considered the shareholder and main decision-maker in drafting the "roadmap", i.e. the organization's strategic directions. Finally, the profits of HCAP were equally divided equally between debt repayment to official creditors and reinvestment in the Greek state and economy – "a big point of negotiation" and, in the end, "a victory" because HCAP was "something totally different from TAIPED", as an advisor to the Greek minister of finance, admitted in May 2019.[13]

This superfund was therefore an opportunity to allow the Greek administration to regain some room for sovereign action and to get out of the exceptional regime of public finance and government of the economy previously suffered in the context of the memoranda.

The shareholding state against asset-stripping

HCAP would be "Greek-owned and Greek-managed". The argument for the normalization of this kind of economic and corporate governance was openly raised on the Greek side: it was recalled that this mode of management corresponded to "what Germany and France are doing". HCAP operated as a critical institutional device, "an alternative" to privatization for these productive SOEs, according to an advisor in the Ministry of the Economy's cabinet:

> The idea of having a fund – I won't call it privatization fund, because that has been my sensibility since the beginning. We had a privatization fund in Greece that was imposed in the previous round of negotiations, not by our government, but the previous government, and that was TAIPED. So, it was politically known to us that the German government in particular had a special interest in privatizations, both of real estate and of state-owned enterprises, for two reasons. One, for the contribution to debt, I believe, and the second one is because they thought it logical that state-owned enterprises are not efficient enough.[14]

The first attempt was to organize an HCAP governance structure that could rebuild a delicate bridge between the Greek state apparatus and the European institutions – as opposed to the way the EU was governing TAIPED quasi-directly. Corporate governance standards, jointly set up with European institutions, became a tool for establishing such a reconnection – given that direct state control of companies was inconceivable because of pressure from European creditors. This resulted in a Supervisory Board dominated by EU agents and a Board of Directors managed exclusively by Greek officials:

> In this way we were able to bring the shareholder and the state closer to their property, but not close enough. We were trying to strike a balance between "not excluding foreigners", because we needed foreign expertise but, at the same time, there was a lot of sensibility and there still is a lot of sensibility, politically, on the issue, as the Greek people felt that this was a final giveaway of public property for reasons of debt retainment.[15]

According to Syriza II designers, HCAP would be set up as an organizational instrument able to ringfence the shares of the state in public enterprises and state-owned profitable companies. This imperative of protection was clearly opposed to the European template, since European institutions considered themselves the main creditors of the Greek "economy as a whole", and consequently in Greek public enterprises:

> [HCAP] is designed to provide security for European investors who have refinanced Greek debt. So that's what it's for. And it serves to verify that the

> value of Greek companies, under guarantee, is growing. So that's exactly what it is. It is about securing value and developing the business, both objectives, and all in a technical way.[16]

This conception went beyond the mere opposition between the Greek and non-Greek character. Rather, it referred to different forms of socialization: to the world of private enterprise and finance rather than to the public sphere. Thus, a Greek senior figure of TAIPED, who had previously worked in finance, stated that HCAP was a tool for distance learning, rather than a tool for rapprochement with the Greek government:

> I think HCAP is a very good landmark because it puts a distance between us and, let's say, the state. So, next there's a layer of technocrats, and in between, the structure of HCAP . . . I think the fact that I have a mandate, I have a contract, is different from what it was before. The government changed; the management changed. So, this continuity, this appointment of people who have been selected, and not just selected by whatever – I might say that all previous management was very good.[17]

This institutional divergence about the role of HCAP and its use for different purposes – a guarantee offered to private and foreign investors *versus* a tool of economic sovereignty – was also at play in the way the SOEs were considered "assets" or "liabilities". The nature, funding, and management mechanisms of the institution which would be held responsible for maintaining their value (and funding their activities, and which kind of activities) was also at the heart of the technical and political controversies.

SOEs' modes of existence: disentangled and "purely profitable" versus "socio-economic" entities

Two different political and normative versions of corporate governance and of the role of the state may be observed in discussions about the social and public policy roles of Greek SoEs. Voices from the Greek administration made clear that SoEs were entitled to provide services of general interest. According to them, these services should be financed by the revenues of their cost-effective and profitable core activity. This vision of SoEs was opposed by EU officials during negotiations on the Greek debt. They maintained that Greek SoEs should operate as any other firm and be *nothing but* profitable, without regard for the public good. In short, SoEs should maximize their own profits and should not be affected by services of general interest – for example, special tariffs for the most deprived or unemployed. In that vein, services that are not income-generating by nature had to be separated from the domain of the productive economy and be solely financed by the state budget.

HISTORICAL BACKGROUND: THE PROGRESSIVE SOES "DE-HYBRIDIZATION"

Manto Lampropoulou (2018) describes in her work how major SoEs were founded in Greece during the post-war era and after the Greek Civil War, giving the state power on "large investment projects in public networks, infrastructure and the utilities sector as part of the broader effort to achieve domestic reconstruction and stabilization". She emphasizes that the "key-feature of SoEs was their dual nature and the combination of commercial activities with a public mission, especially regarding public utilities. This duality was reflected in the mission of the enterprises, where social and economic goals coexisted". If SoEs were "primarily subjected to the rules of private economy", they "served the public interest" and "were used as policy tools for serving a variety of goals such as re-distribution, employment, inflation control, growth, industrial development and social programs". This pattern began to change in the mid-1990s, in view of the obligations that derived from the EU integration process, coupled with a broader reconsideration of the state's intervention in the economic sphere. In 1996, the law on the 'modernization of public enterprises' paved the way for a first round of transformations towards corporatization and privatization. Several SoEs were "affected by the EU-driven liberalization process", "transformed into joint stock companies (S.A.) and a gradual withdrawal of the state from their capital, through successive offerings of state-owned shares, occurred" (especially industrial sectors of telecoms and energy). "After the debt crisis hit the Greek economy, in 2010, and under the pressure of fiscal imbalances and mounting fiscal stress, the restructuring and privatization of SoEs became a priority policy area and was moved up the government agenda. Some enterprises were merged (transport), while others were divided (electricity) and almost all SoEs were restructured in order to delineate with corporate governance rules and improve their financial performance. In 2011, most of the major SoEs in the corporate and infrastructure sectors were transferred to the Hellenic Republic Asset Development Fund".[18]

For the EU authorities, HCAP is a critical vehicle for the "normalization" of SoEs and the Greek way of managing the economy. It is designed as a tool to reform SoEs in order to make them more profitable and efficient, with the aim of reshaping the role of the Greek state towards SoEs and public services in general. This "normalization" effort has three major (and contested) dimensions: (i) clarifying their corporate control by making HCAP prevail as shareholder over the Greek state; (ii) making SoEs fit for privatization; and consequently (iii) keeping SoEs' revenues away from any social obligation.

Normalizing SoEs first requires clarifying the structure of their corporate control. A major success for EU institutions was to confirm HCAP, the privatization superfund, as main shareholder of SoEs and consequently to marginalize the Greek state in its governance. In doing so they enabled HCAP to control the standardization of public companies and entitled it to act as the "guardian of the applicable rules and the general interest". The shareholder of HCAP remains is Supervisory Board and not the Greek state *per se*. During our interview, a member of HCAP Supervisory Board insists that things are under control, even more so than in any other EU state, such as France. Despite the efforts to bring about normalization, the "singularization" of Greece's mode of treatment re-emerges.

The second dimension of this normalization process consisted in making state-owned assets mature for privatizations. This core mission of HCAP was again highly contested by Syriza's governments. One of the reasons behind HCAP's creation was that TAIPED had not been able to make enough money to pay off the 50 billion euros required by the Troika. In order to increase revenue from privatizations, HCAP would then help TAIPED to prepare SoEs for privatization, meaning that they would need to restructure in order to become more attractive to investors. This implied that SoEs should not invest in long-term strategic developments but instead focus on restoring their profitability. Investments would only be legitimate if they clearly maximized the value of the good to stakeholders and investors. This objective was fiercely opposed by the Greek ministries of finance and of the economy. For them, SoE restructuring would only be acceptable if they the enterprises were dedicated to enhancing their socio-economic sustainability for the future and if they remained under state control.

The third and related dimension of this "normalization" process consisted in keeping SoEs' revenues away from any social obligation. In order to make Greek SoEs more efficient financially and economically, HCAP would prevent them from providing any social service that could impede their profitability. Greek officials from the ministry of finance tried to resist this definition of SoEs, which unbundled profitable activities from the non-profitable ones and reserved social policies exclusively for tax-financed budgetary policies. But they faced fierce opposition from the EU institutions. An early victory of the EU and HCAP was to require the Greek state to pay and compensate for SoEs' restructuring and, in particular, for downsizing measures and "voluntary exits". From this perspective, what the SoEs inherited from the state-centric economic system should be paid for by the state and not by their shareholders. The idea was to relieve these public companies from their social burdens in order to render them competitive, attractive and more valuable on the stock market, in accordance with the market fundamentals of the shareholder value. A senior figure of HCAP explained[19] that such high cost "has to come from the state":

> At the end of the day it's not an investment which has a return, it's an investment that needs to happen, to build something for the future and keep this company alive . . . We need to make sure that this cost is basically registered

> in the state budget. So, the state pays the cost to the companies. Because in the past, there was a distortion: usually, the government asked [SoEs] for all kinds of different services.

The underlying idea is that "new" SoEs cannot survive within the taken-for-granted context of financialized capitalism without consenting to social sacrifices (or transfer to the state budget) which are vital to maintain their competitiveness. Consequently, expenses that are not likely to increase the company market value should be socialized and transferred to the state.

Another issue concerned social tariffs in urban services. This issue was also raised for public services and transportation in Athens, and the attempt to implement a "left-oriented" policy for unemployed users of public transport and water ("cheaper water bills and transport tickets") in a highly constrained institutional environment. The issue of social tariffs on urban services for the precarious social groups hit by the crisis (in particular the unemployed) was a major sticking point between the Greek government on the one hand and TAIPED and HCAP officials on the other. For the government, social tariffs were more than just legitimate means to gain access to public services: they also aimed to compensate the wage cuts and tax increases that the Troika imposed on the Greeks in order to restore the country's finances. Syriza's senior officials maintained a "closed-loop" macro-economic and macro-social rationale and representation of reality, where SoE returns could serve social policy aims (helping the unemployed travel free of charge) that would benefit growth, increase demand, and, in turn, become a source of profit for both the public company and the state. However, TAIPED and HCAP officials were fiercely opposed to the idea of offering free access to Athens public transport or lowering water bills for people in need. They believed that this type of social arrangement would not only limit SoEs' profitability and their ability to provide efficient services; they also considered them to be illegitimate insofar as they encouraged clientelism and burdened the state's spending and consequently the taxpayers.

On the one hand, the EU institutions that sat on the HCAP board – but also TAIPED as a subsidiary of HCAP – and some of HCAP's directors saw HCAP as an institutional device that strove for the "maturation" of public assets, and as the natural path to privatization and financialization. This maturation consisted in unbundling and purifying public assets – separating profitable from unprofitable activities (resorting solely to state budget financing for their social commitments and obligations) before giving them to private and domestic or foreign investors. On the other hand, for Greek officials of Syriza II, HCAP was a device to regain sovereignty and political control over the economy, through public enterprise governance. They believed that the role played by EU institutions in HCAP was a temporary obstacle to direct and legitimate state control. They challenged the EU's vision of enterprise "maturation" that leads inescapably to privatization. For Greek civil servants, state governance of SOEs, allowed by HCAP, was not a "step" toward maturation and privatization but represented a sustainable equilibrium for companies. Rather, HCAP was considered a tool for keeping some "sanctuaries" of sovereignty and political intervention in the economy. It also helps to combine social and economic goals for SoEs.

The development of HCAP and the reshaping of the state's role towards its assets put privatizations in a new institutional and political environment. This framework impacts public services and spaces in general. The aforementioned disputes over tariffs and the legitimate investments that SoEs were now authorized to afford affected both access to urban services (such as public transport and water) and the way urban spaces were transformed to increase their attractiveness to investors. The consequences have been twofold. On the one hand, Syriza governments have resisted the complete commodification of urban services by acting on the state budget and by conducting legal battles in order to keep certain public goods out of the scope of privatizations. On the other hand, they have scarcely interfered in the financialization of state-owned land and real estate.

Conclusion

This chapter has analyzed a "left-oriented" government's room for maneuvre in a context highly constrained by European official creditors and private finance. It has shown how privatizations sparked disputes and various political reinterpretations in Greece. Official creditors required, by political and diplomatic means, that public asset disposals, fiscal revenues and SoEs should be governed at a distance from national politics and the Greek government. TAIPED and European institutions' version of the shareholding state fought to impose an ideological (and financially interested) vision of privatizations as a process of purification that would unbundle what could remain in the public asset and domain from the profitable enterprise: in other words, disentangling juicy and cost-effective economic characteristics from social purposes exclusively considered a burden. Such public-corporate governance schemes, like the precise design of a shareholding state, were controversial. The Greek ministry of Finance and some sections of HCAP opposed a linear and "developmentalist" view (disentangling social and economic characteristics) and tried, in 2019, to maintain a certain equilibrium and combine social and profitable roles for SoEs.

This chapter reminds us that the design of state institutions, their precise characteristics, matter in the enforcement of financial claims. Claims on the Greek economy and society (and the eventual control of fiscal revenues) raise a struggle over the formalization of technocratic organizations in charge of privatization, where the role and capacities of foreign creditors' are at the heart of the issues. In the case of Greece, for a significant period of time, financial and political elites of Eurozone-center countries established bureaucracies that allowed public asset forfeiture at the expense of the euro-peripheral zone. The Greek shareholder state approach to privatization, achieved arduously, made it possible to reconcile financial interests with a certain vision, albeit financialized, of the conduct of social policies and public services.

Notes

1 A huge amount compared to the Greek economy as it represents a third of the country's growth domestic product (GDP) and would produce a massive and unprecedented property transfer to the private sector if privatizations were to be completed.
2 HRADF was established in 2011 as an S.A. (*société anonyme*), aiming at preventing the Greek government from intervening in the privatization process.
3 The so-called Thessaloniki adopted by the Greek left-wing coalition in 2014. This anti-austerity program proposed a European "New Deal" set of policies promoting social justice, employment, direct democracy, and humanitarian responses to the refugee crisis.
4 An Autonomous Public Resources Authority (*Anexartiti Archi Dimosion Esodon*, AADE), which includes two representatives of the European Commission, replaced the Public Treasury for a time and took over some powers of the Ministry of Finance.
5 Which require countries to lower their public deficit under 3% of GDP and their debt under 60% of GDP.
6 Borges was recruited by Dominique Strauss-Kahn in late 2010 in order to "instill market savvy in the department (he had held a position at Goldman Sachs)". See Blustein (2016).
7 Source: Personal archive of TAIPED former high-ranking officer
8 Interview made in Athens. 07/05/2019.
9 Interview with a Member of the Greek Department of Economy and Development, 06/05/2019.
10 France still holds up sizable public sectors despite waves of privatizations. See Coutant (2014).
11 Interview with an important Member of the Greek Ministry of Finance, 09/05/2019.
12 Idem.
13 Interview with an advisor to the Greek minister of finance, 09/05/2019.
14 Idem
15 Interview with an important Member of the Greek Ministry of Finance, 09/05/2019.
16 Interview with a member of HCAP Supervisory Board, 08/04/2019.
17 Interview with a senior figure of TAIPED, 08/05/2019.
18 Quotes are extracted from Lampropoulou, M (2018, 491–526).
19 Interview on 06/05/2019

References

Blustein P (2016) *Laid Low: Inside the Crisis That Overwhelmed Europe and the IMF*. Montreal: McGill-Queen's Press.

Bockman J and Eyal G (2002) Eastern Europe as a laboratory for economic knowledge: The transnational roots of neoliberalism. *American Journal of Sociology* 108(2): 310–352.

Braun B and Koddenbrock K (2022) The three phases of financial power: Leverage, infrastructure, and enforcement. In: Braun B and Koddenbrock K (eds) *Capital Claims: The Political Economy of Global Finance*. London: Routledge.

Cain PJ and Hopkins AG (2016) *British Imperialism: 1688–2015*. 3rd ed. New York: Routledge.

Coutant H (2014) The state as a holding company? The rise of the agence des participations de l'état in the french industrial policy. Paper Presented at Annual Conference of the Society for the Advancement of Social-economics, July, Chicago, IL.

Farah F and Maucourant J (2022) L'ordre de la dette: les exemples grec et libanais, sur la défense de la richesse, partie 2. *Dette et Politique* 227–245.

Flandreau M (2016) *Anthropologists in the Stock Exchange: A Financial History of Victorian Science*. Chicago, IL: The University of Chicago Press.

IMF (2015) Greece. Preliminary draft debt sustainability analysis. *IMF Country Report* 15(165).
King LP and Szelényi I (2010) Post-communist economic systems. In: Smelser N and Swedberg R (eds) *The Handbook of Economic Sociology*. Princeton, NJ: Princeton University Press.
Lampropoulou M (2018) State-owned enterprises in Greece: The evolution of a paradigm 1996–2016. *Annals of Public and Cooperative Economics* 89(3): 491–526.
Lemoine B (2018) Démocratie des "faits" ou démocraite défaite? *Statistique et société* 6(2): 9–19.
Hope K (2016) Greek asset sell-offs begin to attract foreign investors. Long-awaited privatisations range from airports to utilities. *Financial Times*, December 19. https://www.ft.com/content/ed349728-b724-11e6-961e-a1acd97f622d
Prévost JG (2021) The battle over Greece's deficit statistics. *Journal of Modern Greek Studies* 39(2): 437–459.
Queralt D (2022) *Pawned States: State Building in the Era of International Finance*. Princeton, NJ: Princeton University Press.
Souliotis N (2018) The field of privatizations in Greece: History and current social structures. *International Workshop Public Real Estate Privatizations: Policies, Effects and Alternatives*, 28 June, Paris.
Souliotis N and Kandylis G (2013) Athens and the politics of the sovereign debt crisis. In: Fujita K (ed.) *Cities and Crisis: New Critical Urban Theory*. Thousand Oaks, CA: SAGE.
Souliotis N, Sayas J and Maloutas T (2014) Megaprojects, neoliberalization, and state capacities: Assessing the medium-term impact of the 2004 olympic games on Athenian urban policies. *Environment and Planning C: Government and Policy* 32(4): 731–745.
Souliotis N and Afouxenidis A (2018) EU economic governance and austerity: Exploring recent perspectives. *Sociology Compass* 12(5): 1–11.
Stark D and Bruszt L (1998) *Postsocialist Pathways: Transforming Politics and Property in East Central Europe*. Cambridge: Cambridge University Press.
Wang Y (2015) The rise of the 'shareholding state': Financialization of economic management in China. *Socio-Economic Review* 13(3): 603–625.
Weeks N (2011) Greece must speed up asset sales, win investment, minister says. *Bloomberg*, 20 May. https://www.bloomberg.com/news/articles/2011-05-23/greece-to-accelerate-asset-sales-as-bonds-drop#xj4y7vzkg

PART IV
Conclusion

13

THE RISE OF AUTONOMOUS FINANCIAL POWER

Katharina Pistor

Introduction

The introductory chapter to this book ends with a question, which in my view is the central question of our time: "The question is," write Benjamin Braun and Kai Koddenbrock (2022, this volume, Chapter 1), "whether, after half a century of expanding the creation, circulation, and enforcement of private financial claims, the capacity still exists to envision ways of planning and coordinating economic activity that is guided by the logic of social and environmental purpose, rather than by the logic of private profit."

A simple answer to this question would be that all social systems are human-made and could therefore be remade. It only takes a new vision. The development of such a new vision is well under way in the academy and among progressive policy makers, the Modern Monetary Theory (MMT) being perhaps the most ambitious of these radical re-envisioning projects (Kelton, 2020). These theories may not be flawless, but this is hardly the reason for why they are so widely resisted. They challenge the powers that be and offer an alternative configuration that increases the state's autonomous powers in relation to finance. What it would take to realize such a vision depends on the relative power of finance and states, which is the topic of this contribution. I will try to sketch out a theory of financial power that builds upon my own work within the legal theory of finance and the coding of capital, but that also incorporates the three powers of finance (leverage, infrastructural, and enforcement) as identified by Braun and Koddenbrock. This analysis leads me to answering the aforementioned question in the negative.

Toward autonomous power of finance

Theories of power have often focused on the state, but less so on economic or financial power. Exceptions prove the rule, but oftentimes even the exceptions

DOI: 10.4324/9781003218487-17

appear as an extension of the theories on state power. Morris Cohen, for example, who compared public sovereignty and private property rights, concluded the "captains of finance and industry" owe their own private power to the state delegating its power (Cohen, 1927). Legal realists writing in the 1930s have identified the judiciary as a critical conduit for transforming public into private power (Dagan, 2013). In this way even today, courts, but also legislatures and regulators, continue to play a prominent role. Power relations in the realm of contemporary global finance, however, transcend the power of single states. The power of private actors is not just delegated but assumed, and the relation between actors near the apex of the financial system and the monetary sovereigns at the top may be better described as mutual hostage-taking (akin to nuclear powers facing each other) than a well-organized hierarchy with clear lines of authority.

Braun and Koddenbrock introduce a new classification of financial power as leverage, infrastructural, and enforcement power. This system of classification has some affinity to Michael Mann's (1984) attempt to capture the state's *autonomous* power, which he divided into despotic and infrastructural powers. Despotic powers are exercised *over* society through charisma or by fiat, rather than the institutionalized coercive powers of the police force or the criminal justice apparatus in modern states. In contrast, infrastructural powers are institutionalized; they arise from and operate through institutions that are largely consensual and deeply penetrate society. They include the powers to tax, collect information, manage the economy, and provide subsistence in the form of "state employment, pensions, family allowances," but also the legal system (Mann, 1984: 209).

Braun and Koddenbrock use the term "infrastructural" in a narrower and more literal sense for finance. It "facilitates [the] creation and circulation" of financial claims and excludes the issuers and traders of financial claims. In short, it is the plumbing of the system. The examples of finance's infrastructural powers discussed in the book are index providers, central counterparties, and the messaging services for payment systems, all of them being private service providers. In contrast, public services, including the legal system and law enforcement, the money system, and the governance of foreign investment or privatization are grouped among finance's "enforcement powers." The third power is leverage, which is central to credit-based financial systems. The basic definition of leverage is the use of debt to finance income-generating projects. Leverage power fuels the private money supply, including the creation of new financial assets.

The role of banks as money creators is now well established. They do not need deposits to lend; they can create money "out of thin air" by promising a loan and balancing this liability with a claim to repayment against the debtor. In a similar vein, leverage serves as a means for boosting returns for investors in hedge funds or equity funds, as debt finance expands the resources to acquire assets the expected returns in which are used to repay the loan or as collateral for refinancing. The concept of leverage is central to Minsky's financial instability hypothesis, which implies the source of power of a highly levered entity: it can destabilize the entire financial system lest it is given access to liquidity (Minsky, 1986; see also Mehrling, 1999).

Conceptualizing financial power in this way is a major accomplishment. A comprehensive theory of financial power, however, arguably requires more: an account of the relative autonomy of finance in relation to state power, the well from which finance itself has sprung.

Michael Mann (1984: 188) developed a theory of *autonomous* state power, a power that stood "against the power of ideological movements, economic classes, and military elites." This (relative) autonomy distinguishes state power from just any relation of domination or extraction. In a similar vein, it is worth asking whether finance exerts autonomous power over others, and in particular, over the state. Answering this question in the positive will be critical for answering the aforementioned question and for resolving the puzzle Braun and Koddenbrock (2022, this volume, Chapter 1) use to motivate their analysis of "the power of financial actors to create and trade financial claims, to keep them alive, and to enforce them vis-à-vis debtors." For this we need an explanation for how finance keeps the powers of enforcement in its service and ensures that both infrastructural and leverage powers operate primarily to its benefit. In short, we need a theory not only of financial power but of the *autonomous* power of finance and primarily in relation to the state. The greater the autonomy of finance, the less likely that the "logic of social and environmental purpose" will take precedence over the power of finance.

In an attempt to develop such a theory, I will draw on the three powers that Braun and Koddenbrock have identified, including materials from some of the cases studies compiled in this volume (taking the liberty to tweak some of the interpretations to fit my purpose). Taking a cue from Thiemann (2022, this volume), I will attempt to combine them with the analytical framework I developed first in my paper on the Legal Theory of Finance (LTF) and later in the Code of Capital (Pistor, 2013, 2019).

Leverage power

The first power of finance is leverage power, the power to *create* claims, which the authors distinguish from the more commonly used concepts of capitalization and assetization. Closer inspection suggests that all three concepts have legal power as their common root.

Leverage is achieved by creating enforceable claims on an unknown future while capturing the gains and shifting to others (counterparties, the state) the risk associated with the transaction. Leveraging requires not just contract, property, and collateral law but organizational law and accounting rules. It requires enforceable commitments, but also the ability to transform future expectations into current cash flows by securing assets, separating asset pools from one another, and allocating control and cash-flow rights to different agents, and drawing lines between assets and liabilities. These claims and line-drawings must be respected by all, which requires recognition and backing by a state and its legal system.

The simplest example of leverage is the act of private money creation, which takes the form of the simultaneous creation of (future) assets and (current) liabilities by an entity that uses double book-keeping accounting rules and that has also partitioned its assets from those of its owners. Leverage in the shadow banking system similarly employs asset partitioning, usually by transferring assets against which claims are issued to a bankruptcy-proof trust or corporate entity. The legal institutions that do much of the work here are the same institutions that I call the "modules" of the code of capital (property, collateral, trust, corporate, bankruptcy, and contract law). They transform simple objects, claims, or ideas into capital assets by bestowing them with the legal attributes of priority, durability, convertibility, and universality (Pistor, 2019: Chapter 1).

Borrowing and lending may be thousands of years old (Graeber, 2011), but leverage is of more recent origin, and leverage on a global scale requires a complex set of legal arrangements that states can validate as binding. Hyman Minsky, whose Financial Instability Hypothesis is based on the recognition of leverage as critical financial practice in modern credit systems, saw this very clearly. This is why the reform package he developed in his magnum opus, "Stabilizing the Unstable Economy," includes legal reforms across a range of legal domains, including the reform of property, corporate, and antitrust law (Graeber, 2011).

A good example for leverage power as autonomous power can be found in Beck et al.'s (2022, this volume) account of the transformation of banking in the age of financialization, when banks assumed the role of broker-dealers that fund themselves in money markets and invest in capital markets – the essence of "shadow banking" (Mehrling et al., 2013). It is through this process that the banks "empower themselves" (Beck et al., 2022, this volume: XX). The offshore money markets discussed by Binder (2022, this volume) are another example for how financial intermediaries exercise power over states. Power, including monetary power, Binder suggests, is relational. There is no better place to uncover power relations than balance sheets, the *locus delicti* for leverage power. Offshore markets don't emerge spontaneously. They are the product of carefully crafted legal arrangements, including the delineation of offshore and onshore banking, and the use of foreign law to govern the debt of sovereign states, thereby diminishing their monetary sovereignty and enhancing the powers of creditors.

Whether states could use finance "for their own empowerment" instead of submitting themselves to the power of finance, the question that Sahil Jai Dutta (2022, this volume, Chapter 3) poses in his contribution, is a critical question. Given the relative autonomous power that finance has amassed relative to states, I am somewhat skeptical how realistic this option is at this moment. The reasons may lie not only in the difficulty that states face in asserting their autonomy vis-à-vis finance without risking a financial meltdown but also in the lack of political capacity to take on the complex policy challenges that a genuine shift toward MMT would require, as Sahr (2022, this volume) points out in his contribution. Greta Krippner (2011) may well be right that, if anything, the process of financialization that has given rise to the power(s) of finance has simultaneously eroded political capacity.

Infrastructural power

The second power of finance that Braun and Koddenbrock identify is *infrastructural power*, the power to trade claims. It refers to organizations and practices that facilitate the operation of the financial and money systems without the facilitators themselves holding or trading assets. Examples from the book include index providers, messaging systems for international bank transfers (SWIFT), and central counterparties (CCPs) for clearing and settling derivatives. Other facilitators include exchanges and trading platforms, rating agencies, as well as brokers (who do not trade on their own account).

Chapters 6–8 in the book all show finance's autonomous power at work. In their contribution "The new gatekeepers of financial claims," Fichtner, Heemskerk, and Petry (2022, this volume) describe index providers as gatekeepers for the global financial system. Their power presupposed (but arguably also enabled) "the shift from active to passive investing," where asset managers simply "replicate well-known benchmark indexes" instead of assessing the viability of financial products themselves. Index investing includes sovereign debt; qualifying for index membership is critical for accessing global lending markets. By determining their eligibility for membership, index providers wield enormous power *over states*, leading Fichtner et al. to compare them with the Bretton Woods Institutions – the International Monetary Fund and the World Bank – with the important distinction that index providers are private, not public agents.

The ability of gatekeepers to determine sovereign states' access to global lending markets signifies their autonomy in relation to them. Powerful sovereign states from the Global North sometimes rebel against this kind of private guardianship as France did with respect to rating agencies in the context of the European sovereign debt crisis. Rating agencies too would qualify as infrastructural power wielders, as they rate the creditworthiness of sovereign states even against their will. Even a country like France was ultimately unsuccessful in escaping the reach of their power as reflected in the fact that the European Central Bank still relies on the ratings of private rating agencies when assessing the risk of the assets against which it lends (Bindseil et al., 2017).

Payment systems – from the bills of exchange to inter-bank transfers – have long been held in private hands. Payment systems don't actually transfer physically the means of payment. Bills substituted for coins, and deposits or plastic for cash. Arguably, the most critical function of the payment system therefore is not transport but messaging, or records, of who owes whom how much and in what currency. The transnational messaging system known as SWIFT has its origins in the 1970s when a club of banks from the Global North founded an association in Belgium as recounted by Nölke (2022, this volume). The association operates outside and independent of states; it neutralizes their control even as it uses the nation state as a unit of account for allocating quotas for holding shares or board representation. This has not prevented the United States from trying to get access to SWIFT data in its anti-terrorism campaigns following the attacks on 9/11, or from lobbying to exclude organizations from SWIFT that violated US-imposed sanctions on Russia or Iran. While the United States has not been able to exert full control over the association, these examples suggest that states, not financial institutions, may have the last say.

More autonomous power is vested with the CCPs for derivative markets, which Thiemann analyzes in his contribution. These markets resembled a "spaghetti bowl," in the words of one observer (DeRosa, 2013), before regulatory reforms in the aftermath of the Great Financial Crisis mandated centralized clearing and settlement. In this setting, the CCP, not the counterparty, bears the risk of any member bank (or one of their clients) defaulting, and for this service they charge a fee. As Thiemann documents, this insurance business has been quite profitable for the CCPs, even as the ultimate risk of their failure remains with the state. The CCPs themselves are only thinly capitalized. Most of the assets that backstop the transaction come from the collateral that member banks must post, and from member banks' prefunded resources, with only a "a sliver of equity" of CCPs themselves.

Financial power in the case of CCPs operates like blackmail – a put on central banks or the government to be bailed out lest the entire system might collapse, which will be difficult to refuse (Singh, 2012). Like other systemically important entities, CCPs are taking hostage the states where they or their most important member banks are located. Within the framework suggested by Braun and Koddenbrock, this is infrastructural power, because the CCPs themselves neither trade nor invest. In Mann's framework, it might be more akin to despotic power, to power that is neither institutionalized nor consensual.

Enforcement powers

Enforcement power is quite literally about enforcing financial claims, about "different practices and strategies of keeping them alive and, eventually, of enforcement" (Braun and Koddenbrock, 2022, this volume: Chapter 1). Lacking, perhaps, is greater clarity about the actors that can seek or administer enforcement.

As Mertens and Metz (2022) show in this volume, states can intervene in asset markets and create conditions that make non-performing loans attractive for investors, even as they withhold similar support from the debtors of these assets. This is another way of "making claims," albeit not through leverage. As they discuss, enabling (able) debtors to buy their own loans at a discount would relieve them their debt burden. Instead, governments tend to privilege vulture funds and other investors who can profit from trading in distressed debt – with no relief for the ultimate debtor. In effect, governments create priority rights, ensure the convertibility of claims, and, in doing so, operate as market makers (Pistor, 2019). Importantly, governments have a choice. Siding with finance is not necessarily a manifestation of finance's autonomous power over states, although it may result from capture (cognitive or otherwise) or collusion.

The "great fragmentation," discussed by Reurink and Garcia-Bernardo (2022, this volume), displays some features of leverage power, but is also a good example for turning the state's enforcement powers against them. The authors show how to employ the corporate form and its asset-partitioning functions for *creating new assets* while shielding entities and their ultimate shareholders from liability. Foreign direct investment often is not what it seems. It is not a transfer of investment from country A to country B but "involves processes of legal restructuring and financial innovation that enable firms to strengthen their claims on *the future value* created through their globalized operational activities" (Reurink and Garcia-Bernardo, 2022, this volume, Chapter 11). Intermediate holding companies play a critical role in shopping for the legal arrangements that are most valuable in monetary terms (Pistor, 2020). The ability to pick and choose law from different states for the purpose of extracting profits for investors irrespective of whether this is consistent with the purposes for which these laws were made signifies a certain degree of autonomy. When this power is used to pick and choose foreign investment regimes and use them against states, this translates into autonomous enforcement power.

Similarly, when litigation is turned into an investable asset, financial criteria gain dominance over legal ones determining who will sue whom and on what grounds (Dafe and Williams, 2022, this volume). It is established not by the substantive legal basis of a claim or procedural standing rules but by the profitability of the claim to potential investors. Finance may not be able to dictate what suits will be litigated, but the lack of funding for cases that may have legal merits but are unlikely to produce substantial monetary rewards will shape the future development of case law.

Forcing Greece into privatizing critical state assets (the port of Piraeus and the airport) and employing market-based strategies in the management of state assets follows a similar financial logic, but the immediate power wielders in this case were the members of the Troika (the EU Commission, the ECB, and the IMF), not financial actors (Lemoine and Piganiol, 2022, this volume). Yet private creditor banks were the main beneficiaries. For Germany and France, rescuing "their" private banks, which were deeply exposed to Greek financial assets, took priority over the costs imposed on the people of Greece and the threat to monetary and political integration in Europe. Read in this way, the management of the Greek crisis, including the imposition on privatization mandates, displays features of hostage-taking by finance of sovereign states – not just, and perhaps not primarily, of Greece, but of the financial creditors' home states.

Summary

Money talks, and it has always done so. Wielding autonomous power over rivals, most importantly over sovereign states, however, requires more. In my reading, the chapters in this volume contain a lot of evidence for the rise of *autonomous* financial power. This power can be meaningfully explained with leverage, infrastructural, and enforcement powers, although it might require some tweaking of the framework introduced by Braun and Koddenbrock.

Autonomous finance through the lens of LTF/Code of Capital

In the previous section, I have drawn on LTF and the analytical framework informing "The Code of Capital." In what follows, I reflect on how these analytical frameworks might inform a theory of the *autonomous* powers of finance, including leverage, infrastructural, and enforcement powers.

Thiemann (2022, this volume) uses the example of CCPs to suggest that regulation is an important source of financial power, not just the coding of private assets or intermediaries by private lawyers. I don't disagree with this. The reason why I have focused mostly on private law and the coding of assets, transactions, and intermediaries by private lawyers is primarily twofold: First, private law is often excluded from the analysis of financial systems and questions about their governance. It is treated as background music, whereas regulation is foregrounded as the means by which states constrain the financial sector or, in the case of deregulation, let it loose. Instead, I have tried to draw attention to the fact that without the background music there would be no financial system to speak of. Second, private actors tend to lead rather than lag the evolution of finance. They employ legal arbitrage techniques to exploit gaps and ambiguities in the law for structuring new financial assets or intermediaries that are formally compliant with the law while escaping the costs associated with it. Private law serves as the toolkit for restructuring transactions that avoid regulatory constraints. Employing this toolkit does not require approval or interacting with a state agent. This does not mean that the relation between public and private actors, their relative autonomy vis-à-vis each other, or the power that they might wield over each other rests exclusively on private law.

The relation between states and finance is organized by different legal arrangements, including contracts, treaty law, regulation (including regulatory forbearance and deregulation). States may also explicitly delegate power to private actors to carry out state functions by way of "self-regulation." A good example is the major rating agencies, the most powerful among which are private agents that have been recognized as "National Recognized Statistical Rating Agencies" (NRSROs). This gives their ratings an authoritative sheen. Indeed, they came to be used as a reference point in financial regulation at least until the Great Financial Crisis. Other examples one might add here are accounting standards, which is often left to private organization, or the self-regulation of exchanges and other trading platforms, which operate only in the shadow of regulatory oversight.

Assuming that states are autonomous, the question is why states would opt for such power-sharing arrangements. This question is all the more pertinent in areas, such as finance, on which the state itself relies and depends. One conventional answer to this question is that, contrary to Michael Mann, states are in fact *not* autonomous. They are corrupt or have been captured by or collude with powerful interests. Regulation then is the outcome of a bargaining process between the state and powerful interest groups, which can be described in simple supply-and-demand terms (Stigler, 1971; Levi and North, 1982). While there might be instances in which this simple bargaining model makes sense, in my view it is too crude to explain the evolution of complex financial systems and the variance of arrangements that combine state and financial power within them. More to the point is an answer that can be found in the political economy literature, namely that capital commands power in the form of "exit" (Lindblom, 1977), which, of course, is one of the ways in which finance can exercise its relative autonomous power at least as long as institutions facilitate easy exit and entry.

The challenge then is to explain the rise of finance's autonomous power(s) without resorting to this simple model, to exclude for the purpose of the argument simple stories of capture, collusion, and corruption. After all, if this is all there is to explain, why not loot the state directly? Why go through the machinations of ever more complex financial assets, intermediaries, and regulatory arrangements?

Demonstrating the relative autonomy of private actors is easier for the bottom-up fashioning of private assets, transactions, and intermediaries in private law. The coding of capital (of which the fashioning of new financial assets is but one example) works, because attorneys can fashion these assets largely from *existing* law. Sometimes, they also lobby for legal change, but this is not the most important way in which they secure comparative advantages for their clients. Rather, the ability to combine and recombine old law into new assets and to take advantage of new coding opportunities when countries make law portable by prioritizing private autonomy (*sic*) over their own control over which law shall apply on their territory *is* the source of private wealth and private power. This works, because private law is malleable – in part, because it is impossible to write complete law, in part, because it is socially desirable that law can be adapted to socioeconomic change in a bottom-up fashion, and in part, because savvy lawyers have figured out how to push the limits of legal boundaries.

Admittedly, a weak point in this argument is that the products of these legal coding strategies can be challenged in court and might be struck down. This is where the autonomy of private actors ends, suggesting that states and their agents (in this case courts) have their final say. But a challenge requires somebody willing to take up the fight; if one can be found, there is still a chance that the challenged transaction will be upheld, and even if not, there is money to be made in the interim. Aggressive, often preemptive, coding strategies create relative spheres of autonomy that defy simple bargaining or principal–agency models. There is rarely direct bargaining between the two parties. Instead, the relations are configured in and mediated by the legal system.

These observations have led me to conclude that capitalism (including financial capitalism) is a hybrid system that is deeply imbricated with state power even as it operates relatively autonomous from it. This insight, I propose, can be transposed onto the public sphere, where it takes the form of implicitly or explicitly endorsing self-regulation or establishing the boundaries or regulations, including the exceptions and loopholes they contain. It is an alternative strategy for delineating in law the relative autonomous spheres of state and financial power.

To see this point, it might be helpful to move beyond the private–public law divide (which is contested for many reasons), and instead think of a continuum along which the relations of power can be configured in law – from empowering private actors to use law for governing their relations with each other on one end of this continuum and top-down controls of the scope of permissible action on the other. Somewhere toward the center is where self-regulation would be located, but also the implicit or explicit public insurance for private risk takers.

Relative autonomy confers power, but to answer the question posed by Braun and Koddenbrock, we need to go one step further and ask whether this amounts to autonomous power of finance over the state. This is where Mann's insight about the state's infrastructural power (as he defines it) might be helpful: Infrastructural power, he argues, penetrates society much more deeply than despotic power for two reasons. First, infrastructural power is institutionalized. It becomes part of the pattern of regularized actions and helps shape expectations. Second, the functions performed by infrastructural state power, including by communication, transport, the tax and legal systems, directly affect and help shape individual and social relations. The relative independence from any social constituency the state enjoys combined with the capacity to deeply penetrate social relations explains the strength of the state's infrastructural power.

Viewed in this way, the three powers identified in this book, the leverage, infrastructural, and enforcement powers of finance can be understood as the major channels through which finance penetrates society and the state itself. Leverage power transforms private legal power in a put on the state; infrastructural power insulates large-scale financial systems from state control even as it deepens the dependence on backstopping by the state; and enforcement power is reconfigured in the logic of finance even as state agents continue to implement it. The three powers may be located along the autonomy continuum discussed earlier, with leverage power furthest on the left where finance's autonomy is the greatest, finance's infrastructural power occupying the middle ground, and enforcement powers toward the right end where state control is at least nominally still strong.

The essential point is that financial power is derived from a set of legal relations that create relative autonomous spheres for finance, which can be used to exert powerful influence over states and over society. This is done by transforming the state's infrastructural powers, foremost among them its legal and monetary system, to fit the interests and needs of finance. At times, finance reverts to hostage-taking, which is a cruder form of power that operates outside the law. Still, the examples discussed by the case studies in this volume suggest that hostage-taking is only a means of last resort in relations that are deeply configured in law.

Conceptualizing the powers of finance as powers in relation to yet relatively autonomous from state power also helps illuminate LTF. This inductive theory of finance comprises of four building blocks: the legal construction of finance; the Law-and-Finance-Paradox (LFP); finance's hybridity; and its hierarchical structure. The relation between the three powers of finance and the first and third building blocks has already been discussed at length. They refine and illuminate the range of legal constructions and the shape of hybrid configurations. The LFP stands for the notion that law is critical to scale financial systems to size, but that law can also destroy financial systems when all legal claims are enforced irrespective of changes in circumstance. This outcome can be avoided by relaxing or suspending the law, which is by whoever (or whatever) holds the reigns over emergency powers, that determines its position at the apex of the hierarchically organized financial system. Finance's hierarchy becomes visible typically in times of crisis, and it is in crisis that the entity at the apex of the system is revealed or confirmed. It is also the moment in which the carefully delineated spheres of relative autonomy within finance and the state clash with each other and are reconfigured. As a general rule, the greater the mutual penetration of the respective spheres of influence, the greater the likelihood that the state will resort to despotic powers to rescue finance from the abyss. Paradoxically, doing so also signals its subordination to the interests of finance. This is because, as Mann has suggested, the despotic and the infrastructural powers of the state are inversely related. Strong despotic power typically means weak infrastructural power, and vice versa, but it is the infrastructural power that penetrates more deeply. The past two major crises, the Great Financial Crisis of 2008 and the Covid Crisis of 2020, have demonstrated the power of finance over the state. The logic of finance prevailed in the first crisis as demonstrated by the bailout, quantitative easing, and post-crisis reforms, which further affirmed its autonomy. This is the flip side of the state's infrastructural power, penetrating society (Mann, 1984, 1993). As Braun has shown, powerful private actors may also penetrate state power by commanding critical infrastructure – in this case, finance (Braun, 2020). And while the response to the Covid crisis had more society-regarding aspects, the response to the panic in repo markets and to the surge of inflation has revealed the grip of finance over both public and environmental concerns.

References

Beck M, Knafo S and Sgambatti S (2022) Leveraging financial claims: Transatlantic bank struggles and the power of US finance. In: Braun B and Koddenbrock K (eds) *Capital Claims: The Political Economy of Global Finance*. London: Routledge, pp. 33–49.

Binder A (2022) In good times and in bad: Offshore dollar markets and the international monetary power of borrowers. In: Braun B and Koddenbrock K (eds) *Capital Claims: The Political Economy of Global Finance*. London: Routledge, pp. 69–87.

Bindseil U, Corsi M, Sahel B and Visser A (2017) The ECB collateral framework explained. *ECB Occasional Papers* 189.

Braun B (2020) Central banking and the infrastructural power of finance: The case of ECB support for repo and securitization markets. *Socioeconomic Review* 18(2): 395–418.

Braun B and Koddenbrock K (2022) The three phases of financial power: Leverage, infrastructure, and enforcement. In: Braun B and Koddenbrock K (eds) *Capital Claims: The Political Economy of Global Finance*. London: Routledge, pp. 1–30.

Cohen MR (1927) Property and sovereignty. *Cornell Law Quarterly* 13(1): 8–30.

Dafe F and Phillips Williams Z (2022) The financialization of investor-state dispute settlement. In: Braun B and Koddenbrock K (eds) *Capital Claims: The Political Economy of Global Finance*. London: Routledge, pp. 189–204.

Dagan H (2013) Lawmaking for legal realists. *The Theory and Practice of Legislation* 1(1): 187–204.

DeRosa D (2013) Sponsored transactional patterns: Comments on Mehrling's "essential hybridity: A money view of FX". *Journal of Comparative Economics* 41(2).

Dutta S (2022) Countering financial claims: On the political economy of de-financialization. In: Braun B and Koddenbrock K (eds) *Capital Claims: The Political Economy of Global Finance*. London: Routledge, pp. 50–68.

Fichtner J, Heemskerk E and Petry J (2022) The new gatekeepers of financial claims: States, passive markets, and the growing power of index providers. In: Braun B and Koddenbrock K (eds) *Capital Claims: The Political Economy of Global Finance*. London: Routledge, pp. 107–128.

Graeber D (2011) *Debt: The First 5,000 Years*. Brooklyn, NY: Melvin House Publishing.

Kelton S (2020) *The Deficit Myth: Modern Monetary Theoary and the Birth of the Peoples' Economy*. New York, NY: Public Affairs.

Krippner GA (2011) *Capitalizing on Crisis*. Cambridge, MA: Harvard University Press.

Lemoine B and Piganiol M (2022) Claiming the wealth of a nation: Creditor-enforced privatization in Greece. In: Braun B and Koddenbrock K (eds) *Capital Claims: The Political Economy of Global Finance*. London: Routledge, pp. 232–247.

Levi M and North DC (1982) Toward a property-rights theory of exploitation. *Politics & Society* 11(3): 315–320.

Lindblom CE (1977) *Politics and Markets: The World's Political-Economic Systems*. New York: Basic Books.

Mann M (1984) The autonomous power of the state: Its origins, mechanisms and results. *European Journal of Sociology* 25: 185–213.

Mann M (1993) *The Sources of Social Power. Vol. II: The Rise of Classes and Nation-States, 1760–1914*. Cambridge: Cambridge University Press.

Mehrling P (1999) The vision of hyman minsky. *Journal of Economic Behavior and Organizations* 39: 129–158.

Mehrling P (2013) Essential hybridity: A money view of law and finance for foreign exchange. *Journal of Comparative Economics* 41(2): 355–363.

Mehrling P, Pozsar Z, Sweeney J and Neilson DH (2013) Bagehot was a shadow banker: Shadow banking, central banking, and the future of global finance.

Mertens D and Metz C (2022) Night of the living debt. Non-performing loans and the politics of making an asset class in Europe. In: Braun B and Koddenbrock K (eds) *Capital Claims: The Political Economy of Global Finance*. London: Routledge, pp. 169–188.

Minsky HP (1986) *Stabilizing an Unstable Economy*. New Haven, CT: Yale University Press.

Nölke A (2022) Geoeconomic infrastructures: Building Chinese-Russian alternatives to SWIFT. In: Braun B and Koddenbrock K (eds) *Capital Claims: The Political Economy of Global Finance*. London: Routledge, pp. 147–166.

Pistor K (2013) A legal theory of finance. *Journal of Comparative Economics* 41(2): 315–330.

Pistor K (2019) *The Code of Capital: How the Law Creates Wealth and Inequality*. Princeton, NJ: Princeton University Press.

Pistor K (2020) The value of law. *Theory and Society* 49: 165–186.

Reurink A and Garcia-Bernardo J (2022) Firm claims: Reinterpreting the global race for foreign direct investment. In: Braun B and Koddenbrock K (eds) *Capital Claims: The Political Economy of Global Finance*. London: Routledge, pp. 205–231.

Sahr A (2022) Claims to sovereignty. MMT as a challenge to money's technical imaginary. In: Braun B and Koddenbrock K (eds) *Capital Claims: The Political Economy of Global Finance*. London: Routledge, pp. 88–103.

Singh M (2012) Puts in the shadow. *IMF Working Paper* 12(229).
Stigler GJ (1971) The theory of economic regulation. *The Bell Journal of Economics and Management Science* 2(1): 3–21.
Thiemann M (2022) The benefits of network centrality: Central Counterparties, the enforceability of claims and the securing of extra-profits. In: Braun B and Koddenbrock K (eds) *Capital Claims: The Political Economy of Global Finance*. London: Routledge, p. XX.

INDEX

Note: Page numbers in *italics* indicate figures, **bold** indicate tables in the text, and references following "n" refer to endnotes.

For Product Safety Concerns and Information please contact our EU representative GPSR@taylorandfrancis.com Taylor & Francis Verlag GmbH, Kaufingerstraße 24, 80331 München, Germany